SIZE MATTERS

Books by Stephen S. Hall

Invisible Frontiers:
The Race to Synthesize a Human Gene

Mapping the Next Millennium:
The Discovery of New Geographies

A Commotion in the Blood:
Life, Death, and the Immune System

Merchants of Immortality:
Chasing the Dream of Human Life Extension

Size Matters: How Height Affects the
Health, Happiness, and Success of Boys —
and the Men They Become

SIZE MATTERS

How Height Affects the Health,

Happiness, and Success of Boys —

and the Men They Become

Stephen S. Hall

Houghton Mifflin Company BOSTON · NEW YORK 2006

For information about permission to reproduce selections from
this book, write to Permissions, Houghton Mifflin Company,
215 Park Avenue South, New York, New York 10003.

Visit our Web site: www.houghtonmifflinbooks.com.

Library of Congress Cataloging-in-Publication Data
Hall, Stephen S.
Size matters : how height affects the health, happiness, and
success of boys and the men they become / Stephen S. Hall.
p. cm.
Includes bibliographical references and index.
ISBN-13: 978-0-618-47040-2
ISBN-10: 0-618-47040-9
1. Stature, Short — Psychological aspects. 2. Stature, Short —
Social aspects. 3. Human growth. 4. Body image in men.
5. Body Image. 6. Puberty. I. Title.
QP84.H35 2006 612.6 — dc22 2006007304

Printed in the United States of America

Book design by Victoria Hartman

MP 10 9 8 7 6 5 4 3 2 1

Portions of several chapters have appeared, in
different form, in the *New York Times Magazine.*

For my nurturers past (Delores and Bob) and present (Sandro, Micaela, and Mindy), who still help me grow every single day

It matters greatly to the soul in what sort of body it is placed; for there are many conditions of body that sharpen the mind, and many that blunt it.

— CICERO, *The Tusculan Disputations*

In regard to bodily size or strength, we do not know whether man is descended from some small species, like the chimpanzee, or from one as powerful as the gorilla; and, therefore, we cannot say whether man has become larger and stronger, or smaller and weaker, than his ancestors. We should, however, bear in mind that an animal possessing great size, strength, and ferocity, and which, like the gorilla, could defend itself from all enemies, would not perhaps have become social; and this would most effectually have checked the acquirement of the higher mental qualities, such as sympathy and the love of his fellows. Hence it might have been an immense advantage to man to have sprung from some comparatively weak creature.

— CHARLES DARWIN, *The Descent of Man*

The period of growth and development occupies more than a quarter of the average person's lifetime; yet, surprisingly, one searches in vain for a detailed description of the bodily changes in form and function which occur during it.

— JAMES M. TANNER, *Growth at Adolescence*

CONTENTS

SIZE MATTERS

INTRODUCTION
"Squirt"

Anatomy is destiny.
— SIGMUND FREUD, *The Dissolution of the Oedipus Complex*

W HEN I WAS ELEVEN YEARS OLD, attending the sixth grade in a small mill town in Massachusetts, the boys would gather in the schoolyard before classes started to play games and work off energy, much as schoolchildren do today. The play sometimes got rough, especially when we engaged in a brutal Darwinian contest of survival sometimes known as British bulldog.

The rules, as best I can recollect, went like this: all but one of the boys lined up at one end of an outdoor basketball court, while the remaining boy stood in the middle of the court. At an agreed-upon signal, the mass of boys dashed toward the opposite end while the lone boy in the middle attempted to grasp, tackle, snag, impede, trip, dragoon, or otherwise wrestle to the ground one of the dozens of boys barreling across the court. Once a boy was tackled, he joined the growing group in the middle attempting to tackle the remaining participants. With each rush from end to end, more and more boys would get tackled and wind up in the middle. When there was no one left to tackle, that round of the game ended. And then it would start all over again — with the first boy tackled in the previous round standing alone in the middle.

The distilled, stylized aggression of this game resembled a minimalist football game in which there were only fullbacks and linebackers, all colliding and scrapping and plowing through the snow.

In retrospect, I realize that this brute-force exercise crystallized for me the parlous transition from boyhood to manhood. Like many games, it informally codified the cultural insistence on physical aggression (even violence) for boyhood "success." It ritualized, and elevated to mass entertainment, the serial ostracisms of the One, for each round of the game established the lowest-ranking member in the physical (but also, inevitably, social) pecking order. It thrived on the animating tension of isolation and exclusion, singling out one boy for ignominy (and thus inadvertently accentuating the loneliness many boys feel on the cusp of adolescence). And of course this daily rite of passage was built around a mindless set of rules, legislated by children and enforced in the absence of adults. It was also, I hasten to add, a great deal of fun. Boys *do* like to collide.

But the game always left me feeling chagrined for a completely different reason. The fundamental lesson I learned on the playground, rightly or wrongly, was that size matters.

Children are acutely aware of who among them is "bigger." In earliest childhood, this instinctual grasp of social hierarchy primarily involves age (that is, who's older), not size. But for most of childhood, and especially during puberty and adolescence, this consciousness evolves into self-consciousness, an excruciatingly diligent examination of differences in physical size, pubertal maturation, shape, strength, and appearance. I remember this elementary school gauntlet-of-the-fittest so vividly because in this particular school population, two boys were notably smaller than the rest, and consequently were always the first to be tackled. Indeed, they usually took turns trying to tackle each other when each new game started — a kind of inside game of humiliation and desperation that satisfied the demands of schoolboy aesthetics, which call for entertainment seasoned with cruelty.

One of the boys, Albert Destramps, was much smaller than all the other boys, with almost delicate, doll-like features. He endured the usual razzing, names such as shrimp and shortie, and I confess I probably lent my voice to the chorus of insults a time or two. His size, however, didn't seem to diminish his zest for participation or the stream of acid, often witty insults he habitually spewed.

To be tackled by Albert on this particular playing field was the height of preadolescent humiliation, and the desperation on the faces of those in danger of being brought down by this diminutive motor mouth remains etched in my memory still. The terrorized boys who found themselves even partially in his clutches had the look of farm animals striving to escape a burning barn, wide-eyed, thrashing, as if they were about to die — of embarrassment. An inability to tackle Albert, conversely, became an empty-handed trophy of failure. Thus are echelons of respect and fear, hierarchies of dominance, and psychological strategies of behavior incorporated into the deepest marrow of boyhood. It's a particularly intense form of emotional education, and each day's lesson was completed before the bell rang for the first class.

It became something of a ritual in this primal exercise that Albert, because he was such an easy target, would always be grabbed, tackled, and smothered at the start of each game (if he wasn't in the middle himself) by the next-smallest boy in the school. That boy was me.

Albert was the only kid I could pick on, the only kid over whom I could exercise even a nanosecond of physical mastery, and so, without regret and indeed almost with relief, that's what I did. I wasn't the only one to pick on him, of course, but I should have known better. Albert and I tormented each other down there on the lower rungs of the pecking order — and believe me, he gave as good as he got. But it was our shared destiny and bad fortune to be physically smaller than the rest of the boys at a time in male development when size becomes a prominent, even dominant, factor in status and self-esteem.

The fact that I so vividly remember the casual humiliations of those frigid Massachusetts mornings after more than four decades attests to the raw power of such childhood encounters. Many male friends to whom I've mentioned my interest in size, including the tall ones, have unburdened themselves of similar tales of size-related tribulations (if not traumas), which suggests that a child's experience of size disparity — and the sense of otherness it cultivates in the developing mind, the feeling of involuntary and unwanted citizenship in a despised land — is enduring, resilient, deep, almost universal. The playground, the lavatory, the cafeteria, the locker room, the hallways: to children during their formative years, and to boys in particular, these are fields of random cruelty, corridors of fear, chambers of dread. They are makeshift arenas of physical confrontation, where incidents we forever remember from our childhood and adolescent years become incorporated, like knots in tree bark, into the adults we will become. Wherever boys play games, as on the playing fields of nature, where predation and aggression have shaped animal behavior for tens of millions of years, sheer size makes a difference. You won't find that fact in many textbooks, but it may be the single most important lesson of unsupervised schoolboy existence.

The way those feelings of beleaguerment, insecurity, and behavioral adaptation live on in adult psychology has been insightfully captured by the cartoonist Garry Trudeau, the creator of *Doonesbury*. In a lovely 1996 essay called "My Inner Shrimp," Trudeau admits that "for the rest of my days, I shall be a recovering short person" with "the soul of a shrimp." Trudeau, unlike some of us, benefited from a delayed but explosive growth spurt that propelled his final height to over six feet. But it's the feelings he experienced at age fourteen, when he was the third-smallest kid in his high school class, that still perfuse his adult soul. Trudeau sometimes pondered going to a high school reunion to show off all those postpubertal inches. But the Little Man Inside nixed the idea.

"Adolescent hierarchies," he writes, "have a way of enduring; I'm sure I am still recalled as the Midget I myself have never really left behind."

"STATURE" IS ONE of those beautiful words that has a narrow meaning — in this case referring to physical height — but that easily expands to much larger, even metaphoric, dimensions when it refers to less quantifiable but more important human qualities that we admire, aspire to, and devote so much life energy to attaining. Turning the concept inward, "stature" also refers to how we view ourselves in the mirror as well as in that private chamber of self-identity where we *really* undress our hopes, fears, vanities, insecurities, and self-appraisals.

If Garrison Keillor's Lake Wobegon is that mythical place where "all the children are above average," I have lived most of my life way south of Wobegon. At any stage of physical development and growth, from infancy to adulthood, in any country on the planet — and we could be talking here about the Netherlands, where the average Dutch citizen is taller than the average height anywhere else on earth, or those parts of equatorial Africa where pygmies still gather and hunt — about half of us are, by definition, below average in height for our particular tribe. That's not to suggest that this half of the population is abnormal. But in a social context that focuses on physical appearance and celebrates physical performance, size is an aspect of our identity on which we are constantly measured throughout life, even though the quantity measured lies almost totally outside our control. In ways subtle and blunt, physical stature affects who we are and who we become: the way people treat us, the activities we pursue, the games we play, the spouses we choose, the respect we command, even the salaries we receive.

Although many men who were small as children or adolescents reach average or above-average height, the fear of remaining forever below average carves one of the deepest furrows in the otherwise hardscrabble surface of a man's emotional and psychological life. From a parent's point of view, size becomes one of the earliest areas in which we compare, as we all do, our own children against other children. They're all beautiful, of course, but we carry around in our heads our children's percentile positions on the growth chart just as proudly as we carry their photos in our wallets. Their height represents the signature of our genes scribbled, however briefly, on the unfurling scroll of human events. During adolescence, a child's deep emotional frustration about being short can yank parents down into the disturbing world of teenage anguish and pain and remind us of our own limitations as parents. Trudeau recalls the night he fell sobbing into his father's arms: "We both knew," he writes, "it was one problem he couldn't fix." The inability of parents to fix the "problem" of small stature, and the sense of betrayal that helplessness incurs in their offspring, can color, often darkly, the relations between parents and children.

Having lived this experiment, I know the feeling. Of all the childhood terms of endearment I endured — shrimp, runt, peewee, pip-squeak, punk, peanut, bug, mouse, gnat, midget, Mr. Peabody — I had a particular favorite: squirt. It might seem odd to embrace an insult, but I loved the short, explosive burst of energy the word captured. Though intended to diminish me, it was at the same time subversive, irrepressible, and relentless, perhaps even avenging. Nonetheless, all the nicknames were diminutives; on the phylogenetic ladder of adolescence, I was down there with mice and mascots. When I was a high school freshman, my height placed me in what would be the first percentile on today's standard growth chart. I didn't need a chart, however, to be reminded that 99 percent of my male peers were taller than I was. They reminded me every day, with teasing, taunts, and occasionally physical assault.

Since then I've inched upward to a fairly respectable smaller-than-average adult size. However, physical size was the most consuming emotional issue of my youth, especially during adolescence — more consuming than, but not unrelated to, peer acceptance, dating, bullying, classroom performance, sexual maturation, and almost anything else considered essential to adolescent self-image, not to say self-loathing. And I gather I'm not alone. I've been surprised at how widespread and intense this lingering obsession about developmental size is among perfectly normal, seemingly well-adjusted adults whenever the topic comes up. I think we never entirely outgrow the sensation of being small, of being different, of being physically vulnerable. The emotional impulses we learn, usually as a matter of day-to-day survival in the difficult, formative times of adolescence, are like the reptilian brain, deep inside, surrounded by more civilized tissue but never totally disconnected, just waiting for the right conditions — perhaps a sufficiently stressful situation — to emerge.

The human life cycle relentlessly reinforces the dominant role of physical size in our personal development. I have been in the delivery room when a ruler was first laid against the fat, writhing masses of my newborn children. I've been the last boy picked for sports games. I sent away for my Charles Atlas booklet when I was a scrawny twelve-year-old. As an adolescent with delayed puberty, I stood in front of the mirror searching — even praying — for the first visible hint of sexual maturity. I stood on tiptoes to kiss a high school date. And I grew increasingly impatient with and distrustful of my parents' repeated assurances that I would undergo a growth spurt — which, when it finally arrived, seemed too little and too late. I have spent a lifetime being asked by photographers to sit in the front row — except the photographer at my own wedding, who nonchalantly asked my wife to sit in a chair while I stood behind her, so that the disparity between my height and hers (about three inches) would not be so apparent.

At another level, though, size becomes a visual shorthand for *the* fundamental difference among us. With the possible exception of gender and skin color, our physical size is probably the first thing other people notice about us, especially if we vary significantly in any direction from the mean, whether short or tall, thick or thin. We are socialized to value cultural factors such as intelligence, creativity, empathy, and perseverance, but the society of children does not always embrace those values — especially when the adults are not looking. Kids are keenly aware of big and small, short and tall, strong and weak. Indeed, these categorizations are among the earliest organizing principles in how children see the world and their place in it. Before we even utter a word, other people think they know something about us. And, in a way, they are right, because size matters.

It matters from the moment we are born, for size at birth is of great importance. Babies whose birthweights are unusually low are at risk for a lifetime of inferior health. Indeed, provocative recent research suggests that low birthweight predicts serious adult health problems such as diabetes and cardiovascular disease. Size also matters to the parents of an infant, who — whether they admit it or not — thrill or fret, depending on which quartile of the growth chart their child inhabits. Size matters to the presocialized child, whose infantile impulses governing territoriality and aggression precede the civilizing influence of education. Children who are bigger than their peers quickly learn how to get their way. Physical aggression in humans actually peaks between ages two and three, according to one prominent researcher who has recently begun conducting experiments to prevent aggressive behavior, such as bullying, by intervening with pregnant women through counseling before the child is born.

Size matters in sports throughout childhood. As one of those Saturday-morning soccer dads, I've been struck by how physical size often — not always, but often — translates into physical superiority and athletic dominance, and how greater size can trump, or at least neutralize, greater athletic skill in a smaller child. Size matters especially during adolescence and even into adulthood, because it clearly has an impact on social perceptions, romantic interactions, workplace hierarchies, and our self-perception long after we've stopped growing. To hear some researchers tell it, adult stature may determine everything from our earning power to our happiness.

But *why* does size matter so much? The answer may be obvious, but it took a six-year-old child to make it clear to me.

DURING A SUMMER vacation in upstate New York a few years ago, I was sitting at the lunch table with my son, Alessandro. It was a hot, humid August afternoon, and as he munched on cheese and blueberries, he threw out an idle but astonishing observation: he said he hoped that he could continue to sleep in, as he had that morning, because that would mean he was growing taller. There is a kernel of truth in this misinformation: bodies tend to grow more at night, during sleep, and one's height can be as much as an inch taller at the moment of awakening than it will be by the end of the day. But I had told him, somewhat mischievously, that the more he slept, the more he would grow. In fact, I had joked the previous day that it seemed as if he was growing an inch or two every night. He had taken all this in and settled on a plan of action.

Parents — at least this parent — should know that even the most innocent throwaway line can become a bone that a child will gnaw on for hours, if not days. "Yeah," Sandro continued, "if I sleep in again tomorrow, I'll probably grow two more inches!" The motivation, it became clear, was to grow taller than his older sister.

"But what happens if you're taller than Micaela?" I asked him. "That doesn't mean you're going to be smarter or . . ."

"No, but it would be more *fun!*"

How so?

"You know, you could reach for more stuff?" he replied in that slightly sing-songy interrogative way children sometimes talk. "I could reach for the sky."

What struck me especially was the way this six-year-old groped to articulate the philosophical and psychological advantages of height. From one angle he saw height as a passport to a very practical level of achievement: reaching — presumably for the cookies and chips we deliberately place on the highest shelves of the pantry. But "reach" is a word that embraces both ambition and achievement; having greater height, at least in Sandro's eyes, meant being able to both aspire to more ("reach for") and attain more. And I couldn't ignore the remark about fun. To a growing child, being bigger is always more fun, because larger size suggests that all the discouragements and frustrations of early childhood will dissipate, that with parity in size will come the dissolution of the age and size hierarchies in which children are on the bottom rung.

The main point, however, is that at the level of emotional education, virtually every developing human being wants to be taller. You could even argue that the desire is an anchoring thread in the weave of human nature. Throughout early childhood, children are confronted with the "unfairness" of small size. Even if tall for their age, they are smaller than many of the other beings in their immediate world. They can't reach things. They can't make the rules. They can't dunk basketballs. They are thwarted in matters significant and trivial by people bigger than they are, from playmates a year or two older to "big kids" to parents. They associate their short stature, however temporary, with constraint, limitation, and frustration. They associate height with a solution to those problems, with dominance, with getting one's way — a desire not to be underestimated in children or in the imperfect adults they become. These raw emotional desires inevitably become tempered by myriad complicating issues of development and growth, but they are there early, they are powerful, and, I believe, they become part of almost everyone's subconscious psychological makeup during childhood. "It's a no-brainer," said David E. Sandberg, a researcher at the University of Buffalo who has studied the psychology of stature for many years. "Everyone wants to be taller. If you're five-ten, you want to be six-two. So when you ask a child 'Do you want to be taller?' they all say 'Yes!'" In the eyes of virtually all children, in other words, tallness is both a universal desire and a philosophical good.

My chat with Sandro unsettled me. I was saddened that my son seemed to have already incorporated into his vault of subconscious biases the lesson that bigger is, if not better, at least more fun and that greater size, however metaphoric or abstract his intent, would allow him greater self-actualization. This is subtle, shifting ground, of course, open to easy generalization. Every child wants to be "bigger." But I suspect that the fervent desire to grow turns effortlessly into a desire to be tall (or taller than average).

And that raises a key distinction to bear in mind when we think about size. Growth is a process; height is the product. Growth is biology; height is a measurement, a marker. Like all measurements, height can be distorted by social values that have nothing to do with science or health. The growth of most children is normal (though very different from one child to the next); when it is abnormal, it demands medical intervention. But height itself is never abnormal, unless small (or, rarely, tall) stature results from some underlying pathology, such as a failure to grow. So while medicine uses height to understand healthy growth, society — and, increasingly, some people in the medical profession — sees in it many of the same values that a six-year-old might: aspiration, self-actualization, happiness.

GIVEN THIS UNIVERSAL longing to be tall, and given the emotional distress that short stature can cause, it's surprising how relatively little attention we pay to the subject of growth. Not until I began to think in earnest about the issue of stature did I realize that I knew next to nothing about growth, which is, along with birth and death, among the most fundamental of shared human experiences. Size has an impact on every stage of our development, from the time we are in the womb to that agonizing instant when we realize that our bodies, shifting into reverse, have begun to shrink with age. Even subsets of size — penis size for boys, breast size for girls, brain size (increasingly, as we gain new tools to measure it) — become crude, misleading, yet culturally pervasive yardsticks by which we gauge our lot in society, our sense of self, our standards of identity.

Human growth is not the smooth, ascending line suggested by pencil marks etched higher and higher on a door frame. At the moment of birth, the rate of growth — known as growth velocity — will never be higher in all of one's lifetime, and even then the velocity is sharply decelerating. Growth speeds up and slows down; it is different for boys and girls; it is different among boys and among girls; it is even different among social classes, primarily because of variances in nutrition and access to medical care. How could such dramatic differences between siblings, peers, genders, and classes not have profound social and psychological repercussions?

You will notice that I'm talking primarily about boys. I do not mean to minimize the importance of size issues for girls, and in fact I often refer to the psychology related to their growth and development in this book. But I focus primarily on boys, because their growth and size represent phenomena that are significantly different, biologically and psychologically, from those in girls, and also because I am writing in part about, and from, my own personal experience. But girls play more than a walk-on role in this story. Just as females exert significant influence in determining male hierarchies in numerous animal species simply by choosing the male with whom they want to mate (sexual selection), girls confer dominance on certain boys in the volatile society of developing adolescents.

Even restricting the argument mainly to boys, the topic of size and stature quickly enlarges to embrace many developmental experiences, such as physical aggression, body image, and sexual identity. In the emotional inventory of male development, these experiences are big-ticket items. Although they are discussed all the time, they rarely are viewed through the lens of physical size.

Every time I mentioned this project to friends and acquaintances, especially men, I felt like a psychological acupuncturist: the slightest prick touched a nerve and immediately provoked a cataract of memories (mostly unpleasant), a gush of self-history both painful and instantly accessible. One friend, a writer of average height and far-above-average intelligence, immediately recalled how "huge" the issue of short stature had been during his adolescence. Another friend, a six-foot-four corporate consultant, suggested that context is critical; although he was above average in height even as a youth, he recalled how small he felt (and was made to feel) by his even taller brothers. Yet another friend, who writes about the arts, vividly described episodes of hazing and beatings at school when the topic of bullying came up. An immunologist I know — an excellent doctor and wonderfully levelheaded scientist — volunteered that he had pushed hard for one of his sons, who was short, to be treated with human growth hormone. "You know what it means to be short during adolescence," he told me ominously.

Perhaps the most important point was the *immediacy* of these memories. Although children, and the adults they become, dig deep wells to bury the memory of these experiences, they are easily tapped. Like radioactive waste with a very long emotional half-life, the unpleasant emotions associated with size persist for a very long time and can quickly surge to the surface. They are woven into our pasts, into our daily lives, into our families, our generational relationships, and our friendships. And the prickly issue of size is not limited to small stature, although that is the side of the divide with which I am most familiar. Friends who have always been taller than average frequently lament the psychological estrangement they felt because of their physical distinction. They too attracted unwanted attention because they deviated from the mean; they too were tormented for the uncontrollable sin of being biologically different. It is as if many of us slept in an emotional bed made by Procrustes, the bandit of Greek mythology who offered overnight hospitality to weary travelers and then, as they slept, either stretched out the bodies of those he deemed too short or chopped off the feet of those he considered too long. By Procrustean standards, any body that varied from the average faced a harsh reckoning.

At some level, variation in size, being tall or small, is merely a subcategory of being different, of being other, for which there has always been a social and psychological price to pay. In his memoir *Self-Consciousness,* John Updike perfectly captures our complex love-hate obsession with otherness. Although writing about his own bouts with psoriasis, he could as easily be describing small stature or any other visible physical shortcoming. The skin disease, he writes, "keeps you thinking. Strategies of concealment ramify, and self-examination is endless. You are forced to the mirror, again and again; psoriasis compels narcissism, if we can suppose a Narcissus who did not like what he saw." We can easily suppose a gnomish Narcissus, fascinated with, yet repelled by, his small size, his delayed development, his banjo-string muscles. "An overvaluation of the normal went with my ailment," Updike notes, "a certain idealization of everyone who was not, as I felt myself to be, a monster."

BUT THIS SELF-CONSCIOUSNESS is not merely a matter of what we see in the mirror. Size matters to all of us in some deep, fundamental way that connects the internal life of vulnerability and incompleteness to the external life of culture, history, morality, and human endeavor. Its essential nature underlies some of our most timeless and cherished myths: David and Goliath; Gulliver among the Lilliputians; Don Quixote and Sancho Panza; Mutt and Jeff; "the Stilt" and "Shoe" — Wilt Chamberlain and Willie Shoemaker, immortalized in the classic photograph by Annie Leibovitz; King Kong; Tom Thumb. As long as people have told stories about the world, made sense of the world, and made pictures of the world, we have framed our perceptions of the world, at least in part, in the wordless vocabulary of relative size.

The cultural obsession with height is omnipresent and, like Updike's psoriasis, may reveal society's underlying pathologies and anxieties. Not long ago, a gossip columnist in the *New York Daily News* reported that

Candace Bushnell, in her latest novel, *Lipstick Jungle*, had gleefully described a fictional Manhattan mogul as "small and uncannily rodent-like." The chattering classes were quick to venture guesses as to whom she meant. The same day, in the business section of the *New York Times*, a self-described "red-neck" entertainment lawyer boasted about his business acumen. The six-foot-one J. P. Williams said, "I'm into low costs and big profits, and I bet I make more money than the execs running the studios — none of whom are over six feet." In neither case was size central to the topic under discussion. Indeed, the casualness of both unremarkable anecdotes conveys, in cultural shorthand, a gratuitous human glee about the humiliating physical detail. If anything, these are the rare on-the-record utterances that reflect widely shared, if infrequently articulated, private sentiment.

The virtue of height, and the disparagement of short stature, is hardly a modern phenomenon. Everyone knows that Sir Isaac Newton attributed his genius as a scientist to having "stood on the shoulders of giants." It is less well known that Newton, in this seemingly humble statement, was taking a poke at a smaller scientific competitor. "The remark," as the science historian Walter Gratzer noted recently in *Nature*, "is generally interpreted as a dig at his detested rival, the diminutive Robert Hooke, rather than a mark of modesty, an attribute wholly alien to Newton's temperament." The favoritism accorded tall people colors the oddest corners of fiction. In the very first sentence introducing Harry "Rabbit" Angstrom to readers of *Rabbit, Run*, Updike mentions his height. Why? Because it says something about the arc of Harry's life, his character, his *entitlement*. "To be tall," writes the tall essayist Phillip Lopate, "is to look down on the world and meet its eyes on your terms." Even the king of Lilliput, as Jonathan Swift slyly reminds us, "is taller by almost the breadth of my Nail, than any of his Court, which alone is enough to strike an Awe into the Beholders." Size may be relative, but even in the land of the Lilliputians, it matters.

Lemuel Gulliver began his travels just as humankind began its systematic self-measurement. It would be nice to say that the thirst for pure knowledge drove this flurry of quantitative activity, but the reality is less flattering. The wide-scale measurement of human height began primarily as a way to recruit tall men to serve in eighteenth-century European infantries, and it is hard to ignore the martial sheen that tallness began to acquire in Western societies. The king of Prussia, who associated height with military prowess, created an elite corps of tall soldiers. To give classical legitimacy to this cultural celebration of size, the Prussian court reached back to Tacitus and Caesar, who frequently extolled strength and tallness as cultural virtues. By the nineteenth century, Francis Galton, the cousin of Charles Darwin, promoted the idea of measuring people, especially children, as a prelude to the selective breeding of desirable genetic traits, including height; he named that pursuit eugenics. Eugenics legislation enacted in the United States in the 1920s, which specifically targeted physical weaknesses, partially inspired the much more ruthless application of the philosophy in Nazi Germany. Perhaps it belabors a touchy point, but the Nazi justification of racial purity has been traced in part to a specific passage in Tacitus that also extols height as a particular physical — and moral — virtue of the ancient Germanic tribes. The intellectual roots of heightism, it seems, draw on a poisoned well.

The cultural fascination with variations in size has always been marbled with contempt, perhaps never more obviously than at the extremes: dwarfs and giants. Yet this contempt may be a perverse form of narcissism, an obsession with what the critic Leslie Fiedler called "the secret self." When we contemplate the extremes of size, of physical otherness, we aggravate nerves connected to our own vulnerability and fears. The morbid fascination with giants and dwarfs is another way of saying grace. As the sideshow impresario says at the beginning of Tod Browning's 1932 film, *Freaks*, "We didn't lie to you, folks. We told you we had living, breathing monstrosities. You laughed at them, shuddered at them. And yet, but for the accident of birth, *you* might be even as they are."

The seemingly modern impulse to objectify the body stretches back to ancient Greece and Egypt, where rulers kept dwarfs as objects of court fascination, and probably reached its sorry apex after the Renaissance. As Betty M. Adelson recounts in *The Lives of Dwarfs*, for centuries European monarchs "collected" dwarfs as if they were playthings. Peter the Great of Russia kept one hundred dwarfs at court, and the scaled-down apartments that Isabella d'Este, Marchioness of Mantua, constructed for her dwarf subjects at the turn of the sixteenth century are still a tourist attraction today. One of Diego Velázquez's most famous paintings, *Las Meninas*, depicts several dwarfs from the Spanish court. The original is in the Prado; reproductions hang in the hallways of many pediatric endocrinology clinics.

But the infatuation with dwarfs went beyond such royal collections. Several monarchs attempted to breed their dwarfs to create self-perpetuating colonies of little people. At the opposite end of the scale, King Frederick William of Prussia attempted to mate his special group of tall soldiers, the Grenadier Guards, with tall women to produce a class of giants. Such amateur experiments in eugenics, a clumsy harbinger of later attempts to create a master race, reduced human existence to a form of animal husbandry. The great eighteenth-century British surgeon John Hunter and his agents stalked a giant named Charles Byrne all over London in hopes of obtaining his body for scientific study after he died. As recently as 1906, the New York Zoological Society numbered among its recent "acquisitions" the famous African pygmy Ota Benga, who attracted streams of spectators to the Bronx Zoo. And at the 1933 World's Fair in Chicago, one of the most popular attractions was the Midget Village.

This cultural fascination with extremes of physical size, trespassing as it does upon human dignity, betrays social attitudes toward the extremely tall and the extremely small that probably play out, much less overtly, in daily life all the time. It would be nice to think that they were the product of earlier, less enlightened times, but then how to explain the brew of contempt and voyeurism that allowed the Fox Broadcasting Company to air a reality show in 2004 called *The Littlest Groom,* which chronicled the courtship of a pathetic dwarf named Glen?

There is a fascinating paradox in the social perception of size: although the contempt for extremes is a covert celebration of the average, we don't embrace average height, or any form of physical averageness, as a desirable value. We see the world through the eyes of a six-year-old: taller is better. The historical embrace of height as a cultural virtue survives, apparently, to the present day in the factors that guide our choice of America's most important military figure, the commander in chief. The tallest presidential candidate almost always wins; pip-squeaks need not apply for the Oval Office. That is merely the most obvious and topical of height-related cultural values. Indeed, tall stature has become so synonymous with success, wealth, leadership, and sexual desirability that a kind of "altocracy" — if I can coin a word — has emerged. Countless social science surveys have shown that the public uncritically ascribes positive traits to tall people — more intelligent, more likable, more dependable, and better leaders.

But as I hope to show, the social and psychological advantages of being tall are a little more complicated than they initially appear. A fascinating study published in 2004 by a group of American economists, for example, suggested that an adult male's income could indeed be predicted by his height — but *not* his height as an adult. Rather, it was his height as an adolescent, regardless of the height he ultimately attained as an adult, that appeared to be the key factor. "Inner shrimpdom" may have economic repercussions, too.

The notion of shortness as a psychological disadvantage — indeed, disability — runs deep and persistently through a huge scientific literature on human physical stature. For example, writing about growth hormone (GH) treatment in 1990, David B. Allen and Norman C. Fost noted, "If the goal is to alleviate the disability of extreme short stature, we should treat GH-responsive, short, healthy children only until they reach a height within the normal range." At the same time, there is an inescapable suggestion that such a "disability" can produce monstrous, world-altering behavior. Consider that noted amateur psychologist James Bond. In *Goldfinger,* one of Ian Fleming's most popular spy novels, Fleming writes, "Bond always mistrusted short men. They grew up from childhood with an inferiority complex. All their lives they would strive to be bigger than others who had teased them as a child. Napoleon had been short, and Hitler. It was the short men that created all the trouble in the world."

No wonder, then, that boys are self-conscious about their size; that growth can be normal, while stature can be seen as a sign of disease; and that people are willing to take extreme measures to increase their height. Fast-forward to the world of modern pharmaceuticals. In the summer of 2003, the U.S. Food and Drug Administration (FDA) approved the use of genetically engineered human growth hormone (hGH) for the treatment of normal, healthy children who happen to be unusually short, ranked in the first percentile of height for their age. Many bioethicists lamented this decision because it medicalized a condition in healthy children who just happened to be shorter than average. Roughly 4 million babies are born in the United States each year, about 125 million worldwide, and now 1 percent of them — roughly 40,000 each year in the United States, 1.25 million globally — by definition theoretically satisfy the newly relaxed criteria for using hGH because of this perceived psychological disability. (Nor is the obsession with height peculiar to Western cultures. A friend recently forwarded to me an article describing how thousands of men *and* women in China have opted for an expensive and arduous medical procedure to increase their height; called limb-lengthening, it involves severing the leg bones and then inducing the severed bone to grow longer. "Height consulting" businesses are thriving in Beijing, job applications in China often stipulate minimum height requirements, and, as the *Los Angeles Times* noted, "In this increasingly competitive society, height has emerged as one of the most visible criteria for upward mobility."

With this globalization of height awareness, many normal children may reasonably believe they have a disability because of the societal attitude toward small stature, and now that "disability" can legitimately be treated for many years with a powerful, expensive drug. To understand how radical this form of medical intervention is, consider an analogous situation. Imagine the FDA approving, for otherwise healthy and normal African Americans, a drug that would change their skin color to white, with the argument that it is easier to treat the disabling social "handicap" of skin color than to deal with underlying social attitudes that cause the "disability" in the first place. In effect, we have reached the point where we are treating the victims of social prejudice with pharmaceuticals.

If you pair this newfound technological ability with every child's plaintive cry of "I want to be bigger!" you begin to understand the enormous social pressures that are building up and nudging us toward wide-scale manipulation of physical size. The border between normal and abnormal, between acceptable human variation and unacceptable otherness, is becoming a battlefield peopled by doctors, surgeons, bioethicists, and drug companies. Contemplating the issue of size allows us to consider one of our oldest concerns in the context of our newest biological powers.

Fortunately, those myths about size can, in their own way, be medicinal. When David challenges Goliath (who is "over nine feet tall," according to the Bible), we are at first reading of a conflict between physical unequals. King Saul tells David: "You are not able to go out against this Philistine and fight him; you are only a boy, and he has been a fighting man from his youth." But then, the story of David and Goliath is not just another tale about fractious Middle Eastern politics, not just another lopsided boxing match. It is a metaphor about adversity and character, about underdogs against bullies, about taking on seemingly overwhelming physical challenges and managing to triumph, if not by sheer strength, then by skill and guile and divine assistance (it never hurts, of course, when God has your back). It is an attitude, a worldview, and an inspirational tale all in one, and you don't have to be small like David to identify with its message. The world, after all, is still peopled with Philistines.

THINKING ABOUT SIZE inevitably leads to thinking about growth, and that leads to what, for me, has been one of the major revelations of this book. In 1953, while James Watson and Francis Crick were toasting each other in the Eagle pub in Cambridge for having discovered "the secret of life" in the structure of DNA, a scientist named James Tanner was making monthly pilgrimages to Harpenden, a small village about an hour north of London, to measure the heights and weights of a group of children living in an orphanage. In the half century of molecular biology since Watson and Crick described the double helix, there have been spectacular discoveries, and scientific fame (as well as grant money and cultural attention) has attached to genes and what they do. By contrast, few areas of science seem more like a backwater, more a Victorian diversion, than the measurement of bodies and the study of human growth, in which the most sophisticated tool is a glorified ruler and the most significant data come in the same units of measure used by butchers and carpenters, namely inches and pounds. You don't need a microscope, much less a DNA gel, to produce data.

Among molecular biologists, there is a certain disdain for those poor fellows who try to do science dealing with real, messy, complicated human beings rather than microscopic bugs and genetically identical mice. But I'll argue here that growth scientists (and physical anthropologists), long before molecular biologists, understood that genes, though incredibly powerful, are nonetheless often hostage to environmental forces that regulate them. Since the completion of the Human Genome Project in 1999 — which has explained much, and yet much less than we may have been led to believe — the new buzzword in biological circles has been "epigenetics." That term refers to the factors that control when, where, and how genes are turned on and off. At a practical level, growth scientists have known about epigenetics all along. Indeed, they could not help but see the power of environment writ large upon genes as the bottom line of all their meticulous measurement. As far back as the beginning of the nineteenth century, a French public health official noted, correctly, that "physical stature is greater, and men grow faster, the wealthier is the country; in other words, misery produces short people, and delays the achievement of final height." That knowledge has made a huge difference in the health and welfare of children worldwide. Simple health practices that have improved gestational nutrition and perinatal medical care have arguably had a much broader impact on global well-being than anything that has yet come out of the genomics revolution. Tanner exemplifies the uncelebrated science that grasped the importance of nurture during key developmental periods and acted upon it.

Tanner's name crops up repeatedly in this narrative, for good reason. In addition to being a rigorous scientist of human biology and childhood health, his research, like that of all great scientists, has influenced and re-shaped entire fields of endeavor. His monthly trips to Harpenden yielded the first statistically sophisticated modern growth chart, now an indis-pensable document in the life history of all children. His charts also of-fered a more generous definition of normality in child development than subsequent growth charts used now in many parts of the world. His me-ticulous photographic record of the boys and girls of Harpenden, docu-menting the physical changes they went through during adolescence, made him the first scientist to visually and rigorously delineate the stages of pubertal development. The so-called Tanner stages are still widely used today, half a century after their initial publication. Recently it has become clear that certain genes trigger puberty and that these genes are to a certain extent under environmental control.

The Tanner stages reflect a philosophy about the study of human growth that in itself advertises another subtle but recurring theme of this book: much of the most valuable knowledge we have gleaned about the biology and psychology of human growth has resulted from longitudinal studies — measurements of the same group of people again and again over many years of development, whether of height or of aspects of child, adolescent, or adult psychology and behavior. As the famous British film documentary *Seven Up* and its many sequels show, the virtue of this sci-entific approach is that it can illustrate, with breathtaking clarity, changes that occur over time related to growth and maturation — changes that become clear only when you track specific individuals for years and years. One of many recent studies that will be discussed revealed that toddlers who were larger than average at age three were temperamentally more aggressive by age eleven and more likely to exhibit violent behavior as young adults. Such a conclusion would have been impossible to reach without a study that followed the same youngsters for two decades. Longitudinal studies, alas, are not easy. They require patience, a lot of money, long-term institutional commitments, and a scientific culture that values long-haul work. In addition, just as in *Seven Up*, such a study can suffer from attrition over time, as participants move, drop out, or decide they no longer want to be included. Such changes can dilute a study's statistical power. Nonetheless, these studies are especially crucial to understanding the biological, psychological, and emotional factors related to growth. Tanner's insistence on the critical importance of longitudinal studies has transformed our understanding of growth and the psychological implications of size.

The work of Tanner and many other great growth scientists of the past half century — Nancy Bayley of the Berkeley Growth Study, Alex Roche of the Fels Research Institute in Ohio, Robert Blizzard of the University of Virginia, and Andrea Prader of the University of Zurich, to name just a few — have shown how height provides an unexpectedly sharp lens through which we can view a larger biological (and, for that matter, social) phenomenon: the age-old debate about nature versus nurture. Preposterous as it may sound at first (as it did to me), the average height of a society, or of a particular group of people during a given historical era, can tell us a great deal about the environment in which they live. That environment, in turn, can tell us a great deal about the values of that society and the welfare of its citizens, according to a small but increasingly influential school of biologically attuned economic historians who were inspired — and whose work was legitimized — by Tanner.

How could mere height become a magnifying glass of socioeconomic values? Although an individual's height is determined by genetics more than environment, growth scientists have long known that the average height of a society as a whole, especially an economically developing society, reveals something altogether more interesting. It is a kind of mass statistical rendering of the nature-versus-nurture debate, in which nurture appears to play a far more dominant role than the current gene mania might lead one to believe. As Tanner recently put it, "If you are asking what determines the height of a particular individual, it's 90 percent genetics. Forget the environment. But if you're asking what determines the mean height of 100,000 individuals, forget the genetics, because that doesn't change. It's the environment. As the population as a whole gets taller, it's an environmental change." Research has shown that the average size of urban British children stagnated during the Industrial Revolution and that the average height of French males dipped in the early nineteenth century as a result of the many lives lost during the Napoleonic wars. After World War II, the average height of Japanese males shot up. Some researchers claim that the average height of native-born Americans has stagnated for nearly half a century. The reason for that is still very much up in the air, but some preliminary evidence suggests that it may reflect how inequitable a society we have become: our children's apparent inability to achieve full genetic growth potential may be telling us something very important about the quality of prenatal and postnatal health care in the United States. Similarly, the high birthweights of babies in Holland and Scandinavia may be a subtle advertisement for health care systems that not only promise but also deliver excellent perinatal care.

FINALLY, A PERSONAL note. I come to the subject of stature with two frames of reference — two biases, if you will. Having grown up on the lower slopes of the growth curve, I have a cerebral warehouse full of personal memories about the role of size in physical and emotional development. I can talk with firsthand knowledge about being a bully and, later, being bullied; about being a shrimp in the land of giants; about being a late maturer during puberty. Having made a living as someone who writes about science, however, I've tried to train myself to be wary of mere anecdote, to avoid jumping to emotionally or culturally pleasing conclusions, and to be open to every legitimate path that may lead to the truth, however much it may contradict my initial intuitions, however much it may turn common sense or conventional wisdom on its head. As a result, I've undertaken in these pages quite an eclectic journey through the landscape of size — consulting many scientists but also recalling many personal memories, quoting from the pages of *Nature* but also from the screenplay of *Revenge of the Nerds*. In some respects, I ended up in a different place than I expected when I began researching this book. But it has been science, not gut feelings, that has guided me along the way.

When I dipped into the field of animal behavior, I learned, not surprisingly, that physical size is closely associated with fighting ability, social dominance within a group, and mating success. However, I also learned that some of the traditional thinking about these issues is changing. One of the great "crossover" metaphors from the field of animal behavior to pop psychology has been the notion of the alpha male — the male in an animal society that dominates his peers and enjoys privileged mating access to females. But recent research suggests that dominance hierarchies are not as inflexible — as dominant — as we once thought. The advent of DNA testing, for example, has brought paternity tests to the world of animal societies, and it turns out that there's a surprising amount of subversive canoodling being perpetrated by lower-ranking animals. I'm not prepared to declare the death of the alpha male, but I hope to convince you that social dominance, and the role of physical size in maintaining that hierarchy, is not nearly as cut-and-dried as it once seemed.

When I looked into the evolutionary biology of aggression, I learned, not surprisingly, that physical size is a critical component in predicting which animal will win a fight, as was demonstrated in the pioneering mathematical models of game theory in the 1970s. However, it has become increasingly clear that a number of related behaviors — including deciding to get into a fight in the first place or to avoid an ill-fated fight with a bigger rival the second time around — depend crucially on neurobiology, and thus size-related behaviors are very much tied up with the biology of memory. Memory also helps people stay out of fights with particular individuals, but at a price: we never forget our childhood incidents of fighting or bullying. Other critical cognitive functions, such as assessing the attributes of a rival in terms of strength or gauging what is likely to be gained from a fight, involve different aspects of neurobiology. But if hermit crabs can size up a rival and calculate the relative benefits of combat before getting into a fight, surely evolution has built into the human brain the cognitive equipment to quickly appraise and compare relative strength and size. Such inborn abilities may affect not only the way we approach a possible physical confrontation but also the way we appraise other males at the gym, on the playing field, and perhaps even in the images deployed by contemporary advertising to manipulate us into buying a product.

When I wondered what natural selection had to say about physical size, I discovered that the fields of physical anthropology and evolutionary biology have recently been roiled by an argument about whether, from the viewpoint of Darwinian evolution, bigger is better. The fossil record provides considerable evidence that species tend to evolve toward larger and larger body size over time, up to certain well-known physiological limits. But natural selection is always a dialogue between genes and the environment, so when sudden changes occur in the environment — the sudden change of a comet striking the Earth 65 million years ago comes to mind — big (as in dinosaurs) may die out, while small (as in mammals) may survive and then evolve into walking, talking, adaptive creatures, capable of writing and reading and thinking about size. While reading Darwin's *The Descent of Man* one day, I was stunned to come across a paragraph in which he speculates that small size might have affected the course of human evolution, creating a selective pressure for a nonphysical sort of evolutionary fitness in the form of attributes such as intelligence, cooperation, and compassion. (The passage serves as one of the epigraphs for this book.) His statement strikes me as one of the most interesting (and overlooked) thoughts in the entire Darwinian oeuvre. It makes a lot of sense: if you can't get your way (evolutionarily speaking) through sheer physical dominance, you'd better develop some alternative skills if you want to survive and send your genes into the next generation.

Pursuing a more idiosyncratic avenue of curiosity, I wondered if I could find any scientific support for my intuitive notion, much in line with Trudeau's "inner shrimp" idea, that the experience of being short (or, for that matter, tall) in adolescence could mold adult psychology and behavior. Adolescence strongly shapes adult male psychology, and physical size and maturation strongly influence the experiences of adolescence. In the past ten years, evidence for the profound influence of developmental experiences related to size has accumulated in a number of disparate scientific areas. Some studies of childhood aggression, including bullying, have traced adult spousal abuse and, surprisingly, social leadership to childhood behaviors. Some studies of the biology and tempo of puberty conclude that children who mature earlier, which is commensurate to having an earlier growth spurt, are at heightened risk of indulging in self-destructive behaviors such as drinking, smoking, and using illegal drugs as adults. Studies of male body image disorders have shown that many serious psychopathologies in adults — including a sort of agoraphobia, or fear of leaving one's home, because of a perceived lack of muscle or strength — have their origins in adolescence. The evidence comes from far-flung precincts, but so far it suggests that adolescent experiences do shape the man and that many of those experiences have a deep connection to growth and physical size. Andrew Postlewaite, an economist at the University of Pennsylvania who headed a study showing that a man's wage-earning success is directly related to his height at age sixteen, said, "Clearly, something happens in high school that has important long-term effects."

BECAUSE OF FINDINGS like Postlewaite's, this book is also about memory. As we stop to ponder whom we've become and why, we're inevitably drawn back to formative experiences, developmental passages, and moments when personal history might have taken a different path. I've often wondered if my life would have been different had human growth hormone been more widely available when I was growing up normal but unusually short. Recent psychological studies suggest, however, that taking hGH makes remarkably little difference in quality of life (although years of daily injections would surely have made me more self-conscious about my "disability"). I often wonder whether my experiences as a short boy dealing with the problems of childhood society contributed in a positive but painful way to the empathy I try to marshal as an adult. I wonder if the social and sexual insecurities I experienced as a young adult had their roots in delayed pubertal timing, which also delayed my growth spurt. I even wonder, having read some of the more recent psychological literature, if I mistakenly used short stature as an undeserving focal point for all the complicated issues that contribute to adolescent insecurity and unhappiness. Size matters, but when it comes to psychological cause and effect, one size probably *doesn't* fit all.

Whether you consider short stature a disability, whether you consider social privilege a kind of birthright of tall people, the impact of human size on the psyche can be enormous. When asked by a *Playboy* interviewer in 1984 how being short affected his upbringing, the songwriter

Paul Simon summed it up this way: "I think it had the most significant single effect on my existence, aside from my brain. In fact, it's part of an inferior-superior syndrome. I think I have a superior brain and an inferior stature, if you really want to get brutal about it." Darwin's point exactly. In a world of cavemen, Paul Simon would never have become a major recording artist. But we don't live among cavemen anymore.

I'm trying not to overindulge the bias to which I've already confessed. Indeed, it's important to acknowledge from the outset an obvious danger: when making an argument, we tend to see the entire world through the narrow lens of that argument, raising expectations that cannot possibly be met, placing a burden on a hypothesis that it cannot possibly bear. Wary of seeing physical size (height in particular) as the single explanation of any or all adult male behaviors, I'm more tempted to offer it as a particularly rich, all-purpose metaphor for exploring the way being physically different during development can inform the adults we become.

Finally, we need to be wary of our own memories — not that they're necessarily false, but they are selective and often reflect a very self-serving version of our personal narratives. In the course of researching this book, I've talked to people who knew me as a child — my parents, of course, but also people I hadn't seen in thirty-five years or more: kids I bullied, kids who bullied me, the tall kid in high school, a few of my fellow shrimps. In part I wanted to hear about their experiences of size during childhood and adolescence and how those experiences affected the adults they became. But in part I wanted to hear their recollections of me. I recommend the exercise to everyone. It's a great way to scrape the mold off childhood mythology (especially one's own myths) and recalibrate one's memories. My mother, for example, recently reminded me that the baseball coach at my junior high school refused to let me try out for the team because I was too small and that I refused to pick up a ball and glove for months afterward. Until she mentioned the incident, I had no recollection of it. Yet I keenly remember the feelings attached to such externally imposed limitations.

And at the beginning of this introduction, I referred to the playground game that the sixth-grade boys would play before school started and described the rules "as best I can recollect." I did not recollect them entirely correctly. When I managed to track down my old nemesis and schoolmate Albert (we'll catch up with his story in the epilogue), he immediately remembered the game, and provided an additional detail I had forgotten. The boy in the middle did not randomly tackle one boy among the horde rushing by. He called out a name first. So the game was much more personal, primal, and potentially more humiliating than I had remembered. I may have gotten some of the details wrong, but the essential thing, the thing that really mattered, was size.

PART I

THE LITTLE ONES

1

"CHUNKY"

Gestation and Birth

> Man brings all that he has or can have into the world with him.
> Man is born like a garden ready planted and sown.
>
> —WILLIAM BLAKE, *Annotations to Reynolds's Discourse VI*

ON THE AFTERNOON of April 2, 1998, my wife, Mindy, and I embarked on one of those geographically modest but profound trips in which real-world biology impinges, with the suddenness of a baby's cry, on family life. While I was at work, she, pregnant with our second child, headed to Lenox Hill Hospital in New York City for a scheduled checkup. We soon learned that the hour of birth was at hand.

In fact, we had been expecting to hear this news for quite some time. For several weeks, Mindy had shown advanced signs of readiness, and during the weekly prenatal visits, both our doctor and the nurses predicted that she'd never make it to her April 2 due date. Meanwhile, every random cramp and rogue contraction, invariably occurring in the middle of the night, left us wide-eyed with logistical terror. Our obstetrician, Dr. Reginald Puckett, had warned us that given Mindy's ripeness, the birth could occur at any moment, adding that he was "a little nervous" about our ability to get from Brooklyn to the hospital in time.

To all these areas of parental obsession was added one of vain — okay, petty — concern: all things considered, I preferred not to have a child born on April Fools' Day. In retrospect, I realize this desire stemmed from memories of my own childhood and the heightened sensitivity that teasing can cause. Having been called every name under the sun, the insult often punctuated with a thump to the arm, I didn't want to visit even a coincidental hardship like that on my son.

By April 2, Dr. Puckett felt that the wisest course was to induce birth. And so, with the soothing strains of Satie's Gymnopédies as background music, we went into the birthing room. Despite all the recent propaganda about the value of male coaches, the fact is that in no other room, at no other time in their lives, do men fade more firmly into the background than during the minutes and hours when their mates are pushing a child into the world.

During those anxious moments, your mind focuses mostly on the child's immediate health and well-being. But lurking just beneath the surface of those medical worries is a concern that wavers between social curiosity and parental vanity: the baby's size. Big or small? Hefty or slight? Point guard or power forward? Peggy Fleming or Rosie O'Donnell? When the infant is laid on that nearby table, whether you realize it or not, a lifetime of measuring is about to begin.

But in fact the measuring, like growth itself, begins much earlier. And even before birth, I began to learn, a child's size may cast a morbid shadow all the way into adulthood — indeed, all the way to the grave.

IN 1938 TWO British scientists named Arthur Walton and John Hammond performed an unusual barnyard experiment that sheds light on the physical relationship between mothers and their fetuses. The mothers in this classic experiment happened to be mares.

The scientists had mated large Shire horses with petite Shetland ponies. When the mare was large (that is, Shire), the resulting foal at birth was also quite large, and when the mare was small, the resulting foal at birth was quite small. That is perhaps not surprising. But after several months, the two foals grew to the same size and continued to be the same into adulthood, their final size falling about midway between that of the two parents. In other words, two animals with very similar genetic endowments and almost identical postnatal growth potential seemed to tailor their prenatal size to the container, the womb, in which they were growing. The same phenomenon has been seen in other animals, including cattle, and illustrates how exquisitely sensitive is the relationship between the size of the developing fetus and the size of the mother. For better (as in this case) or worse, the growth and size of the fetus is attuned to its physical and biological surroundings, with implications for growth that extend months, and even years, after birth.

Any discussion of physical size must start with the process of growth, and growth begins essentially at the moment of fertilization. The advent of ultrasound technology, which began in earnest in the 1960s, has allowed the progression of this growth to be monitored and measured. By combining such measurements of live fetuses with an analysis of aborted fetuses, science has gained a view of the prodigious amount of "height" gained during the earliest stages of gestation. Humans on average go from about three centimeters (less that an inch and a half) at eight weeks to about fifty centimeters (about twenty inches) at birth. Since the average adult male in the United States is slightly less than seventy inches (five feet ten), a boy typically grows to nearly a third of his final height before he ever sees the light of day.

Although the means of monitoring early growth are high-tech, the curiosity driving such measurement is ancient and has not always been strictly medical in nature. The first systematic efforts to measure fetal size emerged in the late eighteenth century. Among the instruments used was an invention by a Frenchman named François Chaussier called the *mécomètre*, a forerunner of today's devices to measure newborns. Crime, alas, and not health, was the mother of this invention. Foremost among its purposes was to investigate the physical status of a fetus or newborn when there was a suspicion of criminal infanticide.

By the 1860s, doctors and scientists had accumulated enough data, largely based on measurements of aborted fetuses and stillborn babies, to create the first fetal growth charts. And in 1910, a German doctor named C. H. Stratz published the first convincing curves of fetal length and weight. These early, somewhat imprecise charts nonetheless offered the first hint about an aspect of growth that is now widely recognized: the rate at which length (or, if a fetus could stand, height) increases is highest at five months' gestation. Never at any point during the life cycle do we grow as rapidly as in the dark, watery confines of the womb about halfway through our prenatal journey from fertilization to first breath. Peak weight gain, as opposed to length, typically comes two and a half months later, much closer to the time of birth. So using crude but often ingenious instruments of measurement, doctors have understood the basic trajectory and benchmarks of fetal growth for more than a hundred years. Spectacular photographs by Lennart Nilsson and, more recently, computer-assisted images created by Alexander Tsiaras have allowed us even more intimate peeks behind the placental proscenium, revealing the drama of early human development in ever greater detail. And of course the sonogram has become so commonplace and its technology so advanced that parents now seek elective ultrasounds, formal echo-portraits of their gestating children, as inaugural entries in the family album.

Like much of postnatal development, this prenatal phase of growth has its own rhythm, its own division of labor and specialization, and its own pathologies. Indeed, one of the most provocative ideas in contemporary medicine involves the size of a baby at birth. The so-called Barker hypothesis argues that fetal events culminating in low birthweight may predispose an individual to serious adult diseases such as diabetes and high blood pressure. But even before there's a writhing, mewling mass to measure, size matters.

EXPERTS TEND TO time developmental growth from the date of the mother's last menstrual period. The "period of the embryo," as one growth expert put it, is considered to begin two weeks after fertilization, when the fertilized egg has successfully navigated the journey down through the fallopian tubes and implanted in the uterus, and to end eight weeks after fertilization. During this crucial interval, the single fertilized cell multiplies into about one hundred or so all-purpose, protean cells (these are the famous embryonic stem cells about which we've heard so much lately), which then branch off into specialized areas of physical development.

The earliest phase of this process of specialization, often called differentiation, creates a kind of three-dimensional grid that delineates front from back, head from toe, left from right. Upon the grid, the embryo begins to construct a heart, a brain, a skeleton, musculature, and other organ systems, each in the right place and in proper proportion. This general rough draft of human anatomy is controlled by a master set of instructions known as homeobox genes. Developmental biologist Sean Carroll, in his wonderful book *Endless Forms Most Beautiful*, refers to these as "tool kit genes" because evolution has repeatedly deployed them to sketch out the basic embryonic architecture of creatures as diverse as fruit flies, tadpoles, and, of course, us. In humans, the foundational work is, for the most part, finished by eight weeks — just in time for the very first ultrasound pictures. Even at this early stage of pregnancy, ultrasound can typically measure the distance from the back of the crown of the head to the rump. This measurement, like all the ones to follow, has one primary aim: to use size as a quick way to assess development and health. At eight weeks, that distance is typically about the length of a standard paper clip.

Then it's all building. In the human body, as the early researchers showed, the greatest velocity in height — that is, the highest rate at which longitudinal growth occurs — actually takes place about twenty weeks prior to a child's debut in the world at large. Most of this growth is due to the furious creation of new cells (in one such burst of development, 100,000 neurons, or brain cells, are created *each hour*), followed by the accumulation of proteins and other biochemical furniture in each of these cells as they swell in volume. By this time in the developmental history of your brain, you've got about as many neurons as you're destined ever to have; after six months' gestation, you've basically got all the muscle cells you'll ever have, too. What you do with them, of course, is another matter. As both a child and an adult, you "build" brainpower and muscles by expanding the cells you already have, not by creating new ones.

During the last ten weeks of gestation, the fetus devotes a great deal of energy to bundling up for the cold, cruel world outside the womb. One study has shown that from week 30 to week 40 — roughly the last two and a half months of pregnancy — the fetus accumulates 400 grams of the 430 grams of fat it possesses on average at birth. That's the difference between a pat of butter and nearly a pound of lard. This internal swaddling provides a large reservoir of energy for the first few postnatal days, when the growth rate actually takes a noticeable dip. Just as in the example of the Shire horse and the Shetland pony, the rate of growth of the human fetus typically slows as birth approaches — a natural mechanism in which the mammalian fetus senses the environment (in this case, its increasingly tight container, the uterus) and adjusts its growth accordingly.

Weight at birth is among the most crucial harbingers of future health. Infants weighing less than 2.5 kilograms (5 pounds 8 ounces) at birth are considered low-birthweight babies, and modern neonatal medicine has become very adept at rescuing the smallest of them. In 2004 doctors at Loyola University Medical Center in Chicago delivered a child that weighed only 8.6 ounces and nurtured it over three months to the point where she could go home. This is believed to be the smallest infant ever to survive.

But the health implications for such children can be significant. Numerous studies have indicated that low birthweight increases the likelihood of psychiatric and behavioral problems later in life, including depression, anxiety, and poor performance in school. Future health, however, also depends on the position that low-birthweight babies occupy on the fetal growth chart. Studies have shown that children who are preterm but normal in size for their stage of development can catch up and assume normal growth after birth. A number of studies in the 1960s and 1970s suggested that children born as early as twenty-eight weeks' gestation and weighing only 1 kilogram (2.2 pounds) could be nurtured for eight to ten weeks in a hospital incubator and achieve the normal weight of a full-term infant. Many enjoyed normal growth afterward. But a longitudinal study published in the *Journal of the American Medical Association* in 2005 gives a slightly more complex and grimmer picture. Researchers found that eight-year-old children who had been of extremely low birthweight (1 kilogram) were more prone to develop multiple health and functional problems, compared to normal-size infants. Among these problems were more dependent behavior; greater likelihood of asthma, cerebral palsy, and vision problems; and lower academic and motor skills.

If children are small after a full-term pregnancy — that is, small for gestational age (SGA) — the stakes suddenly become even higher. Studies have shown that these children, on average, swim upstream the rest of their lives. They tend to be smaller for their age, rarely catch up in size, and often fall short in mental ability compared to average children. Boys who are born unusually small after a full-term pregnancy may thus be destined to face many of the social, psychological, and cultural hurdles that can afflict boys of short stature. The die can be cast as early as the moment of birth.

Small size at birth may also, according to a theory advanced by British epidemiologists, increase a child's odds of developing serious chronic diseases such as heart disease and stroke as adults. The insight that led to this revolution in thinking about public health began with a map.

"I'LL GET THE MAP right now!" David Barker said as he bolted from his seat and rushed out of the room to fetch his epidemiological atlas. It was a Saturday morning, and we were sitting in the cozy den of a lovely 350-year-old farmhouse in rural East Dean, not far from Salisbury and Stonehenge in the south of England. Barker — white-haired, red-faced, and wearing a mustard-colored shirt and dark pants — was still shaking off the effects of an overnight flight from the United States. But there is no lag, jet or otherwise, in the energy with which he talks about the research that has animated the past twenty years of his scientific life.

Barker, a member of the Royal Society, the highest honor that England bestows on its scientists, returned to the room with a heavy black volume that had an equally heavy title: *Atlas of Mortality from Selected Diseases in England and Wales, 1968–1978.* This is a compendium of epidemiological maps showing the incidence of various diseases county by county. Barker opened it to page 11, which showed a seemingly unremarkable two-color map of England and Wales. In the mid-1980s, Barker and his colleague Clive Osmond kept staring at this map, trying to make sense of it. At the time, they headed the Environmental Epidemiology Unit of the Medical Research Council (the British equivalent of our National Institutes of Health), based at the University of Southampton, and the map posed a maddening puzzle.

It showed the geographic distribution of heart disease throughout England and Wales. A high incidence of disease appeared in shades of red and a low incidence in shades of green. Barker and Osmond were immediately struck by several paradoxes. The incidence of heart disease tends to increase with prosperity, but this map told exactly the opposite story. Men between the ages of thirty-five and seventy-four who lived in poorer sections of the two principalities, notably Wales and northern England, had higher rates of disease than those in the rest of the region. And London, seat of much of England and Wales's wealth, was deep green, indicating a very low incidence of disease. What clues lay in this pattern?

When Barker, Osmond, and their colleagues analyzed the diets and lifestyles in different locales, none of the usual smoking epidemiological guns appeared to play a role. There was no particular difference in the amount of dietary fat consumed, for example, or the number of cigarettes smoked. So Barker, on a hunch, began to wonder if early events in the men's lives could foreshadow the appearance, many decades later, of a chronic illness such as heart disease. He asked his staff to search for maternity ward records and infant welfare documents throughout England. Through this archival detective work — "epidemiological studies of a kind never undertaken before," he would say later — they uncovered the key to the puzzle in the pleasantly bucolic hills of Hertfordshire, north of London.

At the turn of the twentieth century, a fanatically precise nurse named Ethel Margaret Burnside had been "Chief Health Visitor and Lady Inspector of Midwives" in Hertfordshire. Bicycling from hamlet to hamlet, she had kept scrupulously detailed records on the size of newborns, their initial care (whether breast- or bottle-fed), and their health in follow-up visits. "Since 1911, the weight of every newborn baby had been measured," Barker explained, "and they'd been followed up till they were one year of age, when they'd been weighed again. And this was because of a national concern about the physique of British children, which was generated by concern about the physique of young men who wanted to join the British army to fight in the South African war. A lot of European countries became interested in children's welfare because of war and the raising of armies." In fact, Barker discovered that the county's chief medical officer at the time had offered an apocalyptic vision of the decline of the national physique. "This decay must betoken the doom of modern civilization as it did that of Rome and Greece," the bureaucrat wrote, "unless some new moral or physical factors arise to defeat it. It is of national importance that the life of every infant be vigorously conserved."

In 1986 Barker went to the records office in Hertfordshire seeking access to the birthweight data. At first he was rebuffed: the data were off-limits to researchers and would not be released for another fifty years. But "an amazing bit of good luck," Barker recalled, allowed him to overcome this bureaucratic obstacle. When the German air force began bombing London during World War II, he said, the British launched the largest evacuation of children in the history of warfare, relocating countless youngsters to the countryside. Among them was Barker himself. Along with his father, who had just returned from the war, and his pregnant mother, the five-year-old boy was sent to Much Hadham, a small village in Hertfordshire. In fact, Barker's sister was born there in 1943, and thus her birth was among the records presumably on file. "I said, 'Well, my family is in those records, and I'm afraid I don't follow the logic of this, because my mother wouldn't mind,' " Barker recalled. The senior archivist replied that some of the midwives had written pejorative things about the families. "But since you're a local," the official said, finally relenting, "you can have them." As it turns out, Barker's mother had refused to allow her baby to be weighed in 1943 and thus never received a visit from the county "health visitor." But thousands of other mothers had, and the information proved invaluable.

Barker's epidemiological team managed to track down more than fifteen thousand men and women who had been born in Hertfordshire prior to 1930. According to National Health Service records, about three thousand of them had already died, almost half from coronary heart disease. By comparing adult health with birth conditions, Barker, Osmond, and their colleagues detected a startling pattern: people who had weighed less than five pounds at birth were twice as likely to have suffered a fatal heart attack as those who had weighed ten or more pounds. Barker, Osmond, and their colleagues published these observations in 1989 in the *Lancet*. That was the birth of the Barker hypothesis, which could be boiled down to a very simple idea. "As a group," Barker has noted, "people who are small at birth or during infancy remain biologically different throughout their lives."

Low birthweight has long been a topic of intense medical scrutiny, because — adult medical conditions aside — it has always walked in grim lockstep with infant mortality. This has been known almost from the time that doctors started systematically weighing babies, a practice that goes back to the 1750s. A clinic run by J. G. Roederer in Göttingen, Germany, a beehive of activity when it came to measuring the size of newborns, generally is credited with initiating the practice, although it did not become widespread for another fifty years or so. Although the measurements were sporadic, they give us a glimpse of historical differences in birthweight. Some twenty thousand infants born in Paris between 1802 and 1815, for example, were dutifully weighed at the Maternité de Port-Royal hospital, and thus we know that the average weight of a French newborn two centuries ago was 6.25 pounds — roughly in the tenth percentile of modern growth charts for full-term babies. What was not understood until much later was that a mother's undernutrition during pregnancy and the infant's undernutrition shortly after birth could have devastating long-term effects.

The mother's nutritional status during pregnancy is critical, especially at the very beginning and very end of gestation. A reduced rate of fetal growth appears especially crucial in the last two to four weeks of development. According to growth experts, there can be a carryover effect from generation to generation, too: mothers who may not have achieved full growth potential themselves are more likely to produce smaller babies.

With the clues suggested by the Hertfordshire birthweight data, Barker and his colleagues did two things. First, they looked for, and found, similar correlations between reduced fetal growth and adult diseases among populations in Finland, the Netherlands, India, and the United States. At the same time, they began to explore biological events in the early embryo and fetus that could set in train medical events five or six decades later. One plausible possibility, they thought, lay in the unique circulatory plumbing of a nascent organism.

"The baby has three shunts," Barker explained to me, "three [circulatory switches] that allow it to shunt blood. The two organs that take the most blood are the brain and the liver. So the [developing] baby can shunt blood away from the liver so that more oxygenated blood gets to the brain. It's the brain that is the high-priority organ in fetal growth. Before birth, the baby has these really great mechanisms for protecting vital bits, which are all lost when it's born.

"So there are really two overarching biological thoughts in our work," Barker continued. "One is that the baby will prioritize the brain at the expense of other organs, and that involves the liver. Within the normal range of birthweight, there is a big variation in liver growth, and the liver is responsible for orchestrating the production of cholesterol and its breakdown. That's thought one. Thought two is that the baby's nutritional needs are served by the placenta, and the resistance in the blood vessels of the placenta mold the heart. Smaller babies have to pump blood through a higher-resistance network, and that shapes the heart for life." In other words, Barker believes that the size and the functional capacity of crucial organs are determined long before birth, and the shunting events he described respond with exquisite sensitivity to changes in the fetus's environment — changes that often involve the diet and habits of the pregnant mother. Fetal growth can be compromised by several classic socioeconomic insults. For instance, if the mother is a young teenager, her own still-developing body may make competing claims on resources that might otherwise go to the developing child. The same problem can occur if, through poverty or lifestyle, the mother is undernourished or doesn't receive a steady supply of vitamins and other essential nutrients.

The notion that organ size, overall physical size, and adult predisposition to disease is determined very early in fetal development is a controversial and sensitive issue, and Barker has recently begun pushing it in an even more provocative direction. He now argues that evidence from a variety of sources suggests that these trends begin to determine the size of organs, and therefore the fate of the organism, around the time of conception. If this view is correct, size begins to matter within hours of fertilization.

"We know now that the diet of a mother at the time of conception establishes the trajectory of growth that the fetus tries to sustain and that establishes its demand for nutrients," he said. Several lines of evidence support that view, he continued. For one, in vitro fertilization has shown that the chemical "brew" in which a fertilized egg is placed strongly influences the development of an early embryo. The egg is very sensitive to its biochemical and physical environment both before and after fertilization. A second clue comes from the world of animal husbandry. "In animals, it's been known for a long time — because they do it experimentally — that if you undernourish a female at or near the time of mating, you profoundly affect the growth of the [fetus]," Barker said. According to him, preliminary evidence is now emerging that undernourishment of the mother around the time of conception affects the way the nascent embryo divvies up its stem cells during the earliest days after fertilization. An organism's most primordial cells, which produce the entire material of gestation and growth, are allocated into two distinct classes just a few days after conception: one set of cells (embryonic stem cells) is destined to build the organism, while the other set (trophoblast cells) creates the nourishing placenta. Experiments with mice, rats, sheep, and cows all suggest that maternal nutrition during the earliest days after conception can, according to the embryologist Tom Fleming, "irreversibly" affect postnatal growth and physiology.

Fleming's group at the University of Southampton, for example, fed female rats a special low-protein diet for just four days after mating, which covers the period between fertilization and implantation of the embryo, before reverting to a regular diet. The biological impact of even that brief period of undernutrition was stunning. The developing embryos had fewer embryonic stem cells, fewer placental cells, and significant metabolic disturbances, including reduced insulin levels and elevated glucose levels, than embryos carried by rats fed a regular diet. As a result of this very transient period of maternal undernutrition, the resulting offspring had lower birthweight, a faster growth rate, a tendency to develop high blood pressure, and an abnormal ratio of organ size to body weight compared to the offspring of properly nourished rats.

"That's a very early event," Barker said, "and this is why it's all so serious. Imagine you're some dieting British girl and you've gotten pregnant by mistake, and the egg is working down the fallopian tube, having been fertilized, and these life-changing decisions are being made [by the embryo]. And they're being made in response to nutrition." Often this occurs before the mother is even aware that she is pregnant.

Important events toward the end of a pregnancy can also affect size, metabolism, possibly obesity, and certainly lifelong health. New evidence has emerged to suggest that poor or dire nutritional conditions during late fetal development educate, or "program," the fetus to expect similar deprivation upon birth. Once this metabolic thermostat is set shortly before birth, the newborn child is ill equipped to adapt to different conditions. According to this theory, a fetus that is programmed to expect skimpy nutrition becomes a child who is physiologically overwhelmed by abundant calories and fats and is therefore more prone to obesity and diabetes. In 2005 Barker and colleagues in Finland published an article in the *New England Journal of Medicine* that demonstrated the ramifications of prenatal and childhood growth even more. Detailed birth and growth records of males born in a Helsinki hospital between 1934 and 1944 allowed the researchers to show that low-birthweight babies who gain excessive weight between the ages of two and eleven are at particular risk of developing heart disease later in life. Moreover, some of the evidence suggests that the key to the adult onset of this illness derived from the way these children metabolized glucose.

Boys may bear a disproportionate share of the burden of these fetal effects. "The faster growing sex, the boy in humans, is more vulnerable," Barker writes in *The Best Start in Life*. "Generally in mammals if mothers are in poor condition, their male children are more severely affected . . .

Males are therefore more vulnerable in times of food scarcity. The advantage of large body size when males compete with each other to reproduce are offset by the greater risk of death when food is scarce."

At first there was considerable resistance to the Barker hypothesis. In some quarters, there still is. Barker told me that the late Oxford epidemiologist Sir Richard Doll walked out on one of Barker's lectures several years ago and that Doll's colleague Richard Peto has expressed considerable skepticism about the hypothesis as well. Barker's critics argue that the link between birthweight and later health is not nearly as statistically robust as has been suggested. But if it's an artifact, it's a very powerful and geographically widespread one. Numerous other scientific groups have duplicated aspects of the Barker hypothesis in Finland, India, Japan, and North America, and as a recent editorial in the *British Medical Journal* observed, "The importance of events before birth for lifetime health has been confirmed in many populations." And the Harvard Medical School professor Matthew W. Gillman, writing in the *New England Journal of Medicine,* said, "Mounting evidence . . . indicates that events occurring in the earliest stages of human development — even before birth — may influence the occurrence of diabetes, cardiovascular disease, asthmas, cancers, osteoporosis, and neuropsychiatric disorders."

In 1999, for example, Barker and a group of Finnish collaborators showed that low-birthweight infants who experienced "catch-up growth" following birth set themselves up for the later development of coronary heart disease. In 2000, the Barker team, working with a group at the Medical University of South Carolina, found a link between fetal undernutrition and the incidence of kidney failure later in life. In a 2005 study, Barker and British colleagues even suggested a link between an infant's growth and future earning power. Children who were smaller and grew slowly during their first year earned less as adults. As in all such epidemiological studies, these connections are simply correlations — that is, statisticians can detect the association of one event (low birthweight) with another (heart disease as an adult). Conclusions as to cause and effect remain hazy.

Despite the lingering controversy, the Barker hypothesis — now more commonly known as the fetal origins hypothesis — has broadened into a powerful idea that is influencing scientific thought about fundamental aspects of plant and animal behavior. In a recent essay in the journal *Nature,* Barker and fourteen coauthors — including the respected Newcastle aging expert Tom Kirkwood and the Cambridge ethologist Sir Patrick Bateson — ventured a provocative hypothesis suggesting that a mother's nutritional and metabolic status prior to birth offers a "forecast" of the environment the infant is likely to encounter and that the infant has the capacity to fix metabolic and genetic settings in anticipation of those conditions. It is as if organisms are programmed just before birth to adapt to — that is, take optimal advantage of — the conditions they expect to encounter. If the environment turns out to be different from the forecast, it can affect development and the susceptibility to disease. The British writer David Sharp has boiled down the evolutionary implications to modern argot: "For our hunter-gatherer ancestors there were advantages in having the unborn programmed physiologically for a nutritionally deprived environment, but such preparation works less well when babies grow up in a world with fast-food outlets on every corner."

Thus maternal gestational conditions may have profound public health implications. In many respects, small size is the least of them. In one Norwegian study, low-birthweight infants who were normal for their gestational age were able to catch up to normal growth curves, but babies who were small for their gestational age did not — suggesting that preterm birth per se is not necessarily an insurmountable hurdle. As James Tanner puts it in his classic book on growth, *Fetus into Man*, "Leaving the uterus early is not in itself harmful, whereas growing less than normally during a full uterine stay implies pathology of fetus, placenta or mother."

Low birthweight after a normal gestational stay is one of life's first size-related crises. As Tanner implies, the cause may be some chromosomal anomaly in the fetus (although most such anomalies result in spontaneous abortions very early in the pregnancy), a placental abnormality, or a nutritional problem in the mother. In addition to undernutrition, the mother may inflict on her fetus the sad lessons of alcohol consumption and smoking. I was raised with the injunction that smoking would stunt my growth; nobody mentioned that my mother's smoking may also have stunted it. Experts have calculated that a mother who smokes as few as ten cigarettes a day will rob her child of, on average, 180 grams of weight at birth and that this reduction in size will persist throughout childhood. Many children of low birthweight do not catch up with their peers, and a "considerable proportion," according to Tanner, fail to develop the same level of mental ability as normal children. The 2005 *Journal of the American Medical Association* article on extremely low birthweight grimly lends substance to this fear: 38 percent of low-birthweight babies had an IQ below eighty-five at age eight, nearly three times the rate of normal-size newborns (14 percent).

Clearly, prenatal care can have a dramatic impact on the height, and health, of a child. In recent times, Swedish babies have been the heaviest in the world: boys have averaged 3.65 kilograms (8 pounds) and girls 3.5 kilograms (7.7 pounds). Can these plump debuts be attributed to the prenatal care and social support networks typical in Scandinavia? Have the Dutch become the tallest people in Europe because of their extensive prenatal and perinatal health care system? David Barker believes that a culture that values good prenatal and postnatal care can prevent the kind of chronic disease predicted by the fetal origins hypothesis. He cites France as an example.

In 1871, following its defeat in the Franco-Prussian War, the French government made an institutional commitment to improve the stock of its military by paying heightened attention to the health of prospective mothers and the proper feeding of infants. This state-sponsored system, known as puericulture, promoted breastfeeding and may be among the principal reasons that France has one of the lowest rates of cardiovascular disease in the Western world despite a diet renowned for its abundance of butter and red meat. Some attribute this "French paradox" to the consumption of red wine. Barker believes that it stems from the long-standing French commitment to excellent prenatal care.

WITH NONE OF this research specifically in mind, my wife and I followed the modern syllabus of good nutrition as an antidote to low birthweight and SGA. Mindy attended all her prenatal visits, took her prenatal vitamins, and ate balanced meals. To the extent possible in a modern, two-worker family, we tried to minimize stress. Although it is not fully appreciated (or celebrated), one of modern medicine's monumental achievements is the knowledge that such modest behavior modification during the nine months of a pregnancy can so positively affect the outcome.

And out, ultimately, he did come. At exactly 11:20 P.M. on the evening of April 2, 1998, my son, Alessandro, made his debut. Like the birth of all children, his was an exhilarating exclamation point in a unique family narrative, but one that was superimposed on a very standard progression of biological development. After a relatively brief labor, Dr. Puckett eased

Alessandro out into the world. I noted in my journal, "He's a bruiser — eight pounds and eight ounces, broad-shouldered . . . thick-haired, wide-faced." The usual Apgar tests were performed to evaluate his physical condition, but the comment that stuck in my mind was the doctor's first assessment of our new family member: "Chunky," he said.

Chunky.

As I think back now on that deliriously happy moment, I realize that the very first characterization of my son — as is the case with most children — involved his size. That throwaway adjective "chunky" edged right up to the border of being pejorative, and it was uttered within seconds of his delivery, his hair still matted with blood, his eyes still puffy with the effort of squeezing through the birth canal, blinking into the glare of this strange new world, with its instantaneous judgments about appearance.

As he was hustled over to a nearby table to be cleaned off and swaddled in blankets, doctors laid the ruler to him for the very first time. In addition to his weight, we knew instantly that he measured 22 inches in length. His head measured 13¾ inches in diameter, larger even than his chest (13 inches). Thus began, for Sandro as for all children, a lifetime of measurement.

Thus began, too, a lifetime of parental obsession about where he fit on standard growth charts. Long before he was ever conscious of his size relative to others, Mindy and I busied ourselves with the import and implications of his height and weight at birth — and were thrilled with the fact that his early measurements placed him in the ninetieth percentile of growth, where he would stay for some time. Effortlessly, without thinking, we became obsessed with "percentility."

What I did not realize then is that the very notion of percentiles traces its intellectual roots to the man who is known as the father of eugenics and that the growth chart has become a social as well as a medical document — a visualization of our cultural definitions of normality and abnormality. I eventually also realized that although many of us have been conditioned to think that the adolescent spurt is the big bang of human growth, the reality is that, by a long shot, human beings are never growing faster than at the moment they enter the world.

2

"LONGITUDE" AND "PONDUS ABSOLUTUM"

A History of the Growth Chart

> Growth is the only evidence of life.
>
> —John Henry Newman, *Apologia Pro Vita Sua*

Jim Tanner pored over the growth charts of two children that were spread out on the table before him. Even at eighty-four years of age, he cast an authoritative eye over the documents, observing the annual dots marking height and weight, frowning at the paucity of information about the six-year-old boy, lingering over the meager data about the eight-year-old girl, but venturing a tentative — and, to her father, namely me, an unnerving — conclusion.

"We're already seeing that she is going into early adolescence," mused Tanner, peering over his glasses. "Eight and a half — hmmm. Well, probably, *probably*, it's the beginning. That would be slightly early, but for a takeoff for a girl nowadays? I mean, a bit early. But normal, absolutely." As for the boy, there were only three dots marking his growth trajectory, but that was enough for Tanner to hazard a guess. "If his tempo is somewhere near average," he said, "he will end up at about 182 centimeters." Just shy of six feet.

We were sitting in a one-hundred-year-old coach house in Devonshire, two hours southwest of London by train, and fifteen miles farther, by curving one-lane roads, from the train station in Taunton, the nearest big town. It may seem like a long way to go to ask a doctor to look at children's growth charts, especially when the doctor has been retired for twenty years. But this was no ordinary country doctor. As soon as I discovered his beautifully written and impeccably researched book *A History of the Study of Human Growth*, I knew that James Mourilyan Tanner was worthy of a pilgrimage.

The second half of the twentieth century produced a number of outstanding scientists devoted to the biology of human growth. But no one published as much about the subject, wrote as many seminal texts and scholarly histories, defined the onset of puberty so acutely, and pushed the study of height and physical size into so many surprising and provocative cultural corners as Tanner, whose work animates every chapter of this book, just as his career animated virtually every aspect of the biology, psychology, and sociology of growth.

Even in retirement, he remains one of the great experts on a subject about which everyone has firsthand experience yet few people seriously consider. On a more pragmatic level, it is to Tanner and his former colleagues at the University of London that millions of parents the world over owe a silent debt of gratitude, for the British researchers not only created a unique, statistically modern childhood growth chart but also did so in a way that embraced a much more forgiving and flexible definition of normality than many of the growth charts that preceded it — and, alas, many that have followed. The story of this growth chart begins, as all science does, with careful physical measurement. But it ends up making a cultural statement about what is normal and how we should view individuals, especially children, who live on that statistical boundary where normal difference slides into medical abnormality.

"I think the deep, fundamental point in all of this," Tanner said, lingering over the growth charts on the table, "is differences in the rate of maturation. A child who is small at a given age may be so simply because he is a slow maturer. If so, eventually he will complete his growth, and then he will no longer be small. But another child, who is equally small at that given age, may be so despite being of average maturity. And that child will end up as a small adult, unless something is done about it."

*   *   *

THE HANDSOME MAN waiting for me on the Taunton train platform was tall (just slightly below his onetime maximum height of six feet, he later allowed) with silver hair, high cheekbones, and eyes bright with wit. He also was unfailingly polite, bristling with energy and expertise. An effortless raconteur, Tanner filled me in on a long family history, which included a facetious aside about war profiteers (in the seventeenth century) and career military service, as he negotiated the narrow country lanes leading to his home, where he lives with his second wife, Gunilla.

Although he was a founding figure in the field of auxology (the technical name for the study of human growth), it quickly became clear that Tanner was something of an accidental auxologist. Born in 1920, the son of a career army officer, he grew up partly in Egypt and China before the family returned to England. He attended Marlborough, a private boys' school, where he excelled in athletics. In 1939 he was the British junior champion in the 110-meter hurdles. "I was on the Olympic training team," he said, "but we got knocked out by the war." While at Marlborough, he attended a lecture by D'Arcy Thompson, whose book *On Growth and Form* is one of the touchstone texts of growth science.

The first step in the direction of Tanner's eventual career as an expert in human growth began as an act of familial rebellion. Tanner was being groomed for a career in the military — his father wanted him to study mathematics and engineering in the army. But then his older brother, who had been "dragooned" into the navy, died during the frenzied retreat of the British Expeditionary Force at Dunkirk in 1940, and Tanner lost all interest in pursuing a career in the army. "I said I wouldn't do it," he recalled. "I couldn't do it, couldn't spend my life like that. I wanted to be a doctor."

He attended St. Mary's School of Medicine in London on something like an athletic scholarship, having agreed to train his fellow medical students in physical education in exchange for tuition. During the war, as London was pulverized by German bombs, the Rockefeller Foundation invited a handful of gifted British medical students to the United States to complete their studies. Tanner was among them, receiving his medical degree from the University of Pennsylvania and completing his internship at Johns Hopkins. He told a medical school interviewer that he hoped to conduct research in an area where "biology, psychology, and sociology meet." That turned out to be a perfect description of the way Tanner went about the study of human growth.

In 1946 Tanner took a job in the Department of Human Anatomy at Oxford, having completed his medical studies the previous year in London. At Oxford he quickly made the acquaintance of a future Nobel laureate, Sir Peter Medawar, in a rather audacious manner. He dropped a note to the notoriously arrogant Medawar, pointing out a mistake he had made about the biology of growth in one of his papers. It may have been one of the few times Medawar stood corrected, and they became fast friends.

Tanner's interest in athletics led to his initial foray into the subject of growth. He became fascinated with "somatotyping," assessing human body shape and size. In the late 1940s, he had begun to realize the importance of the shape of bodies (and their component parts) while investigating human cardiovascular physiology. Sir Wilfred Le Gros Clark, an Oxford professor, seized on this interest, requiring Tanner "to give a course, not only in differences in adult physique, but in how they came about during the growing period." That work actually nudged Tanner backward scientifically, from the final product of size to the process of growth that created it in the first place. Remarkably, there had been no formal biology of human growth at the time in England, no scientific discipline devoted to its study.

In 1948 E. R. Bransby, a nutritionist in Britain's Ministry of Health, needed a collaborator for a scientific study of childhood growth. The National Children's Home in Harpenden had been the site of a grim wartime study on childhood nutrition, occasioned by the realities of food rationing during the war. Bransby, the nutritionist who ran that project, realized that the data could be very important if someone continued a long-term study of the undernourished children and followed their growth. As Tanner himself later put it, "Few people in England were interested in human growth, however, and Bransby had to find somebody to run his study." Tanner, who had only recently begun to lecture on growth at Oxford, "was the obvious, indeed only, candidate." He agreed to take on the project, without pay. It is no exaggeration to say that the modern growth chart began to take shape in Harpenden, a small town about thirty miles north of London, and that the research Tanner conducted on pubertal development in those children still reverberates in virtually every clinic throughout the world where primary care medicine is practiced today.

Large, school-based studies of childhood growth had become all the rage in the United States, and Tanner began by making an extended tour of North America, visiting the sites of all the major American studies and consulting with the leading experts. He also began to familiarize himself with the fascinating history of human measurement stretching back to the eighteenth century. By the time Tanner completed this preliminary round of background research, he realized that the study of growth could hold up a fantastic mirror to the scientific, psychological, and sociological aspirations of a society.

The growth chart, a document 250 years in the making, reflects in sequence the Enlightenment's zeal for scientific measurement; the birth of modern statistics; the use of measurement to promote eugenics in the late nineteenth century; the culture wars between nature and nurture in the early twentieth century; the social definition of normal (or abnormal) height; and the increasing influence of commerce on the practice of medicine. In other words, the growth chart, while attempting to crystallize timeless truths about childhood development, has all too often been shaped by its times.

UPON THE BIRTH of his son in 1759, a French nobleman named Philibert Guéneau de Montbeillard did something that countless parents have been inspired to do with whatever implement lies at hand. He began to take regular measurements of his son's height.

In doing so, Montbeillard launched a long, multicentury journey on the path toward a more perfect growth chart. He was one of those adventuresome Enlightenment spirits who understood that bravery was not limited to battlefield valor and athletic heroism. In fact, decades before Edward Jenner, Montbeillard exposed his son, with "trembling hand," to variolation, a primitive but often successful form of vaccination against smallpox. It's a pity he couldn't have inoculated his son against the political contagions of the time as well. The young man ultimately lost his life to the guillotine, on orders from Robespierre.

Despite that tragic end, the young Montbeillard left a profound legacy to the field of human growth, for his well-documented growth curve is now recognized as the first scientific study of its kind. Every six months (with a few occasional gaps) from birth to adulthood, Montbeillard measured his son — first as pediatricians do today, while the child lay supine on a table, and later by making extremely careful vertical measurements as he was standing. The child was, in a sense, almost off the charts even as the chart was being invented. By recent standards, Montbeillard's son would rank above the ninety-seventh percentile in height. The reason that Montbeillard's experiment is viewed as having such historic significance by modern growth experts is his method: the frequent and sequential measurement of the same growing body.

What makes the data from this dilettante experiment so powerful is that it captured what modern growth experts recognize as the single most important aspect of growth: not the sheer vertical accumulation of height, whether plotted with scientific precision on graph paper or inscribed with pencil marks on a door frame, but rather the rate, or velocity, of growth. That can be gauged only by comparing frequent, accurate measurements of the same body as it grows over time — precisely what Montbeillard had the time, patience, and curiosity to do. These serial measurements of the same body over many years, when collected for a number of growing girls and boys, form a longitudinal study. Such studies are especially crucial to understanding normal variations in growth; therefore, they are, in a larger cultural sense, crucial to understanding what is normal and what is not.

Montbeillard's study of his son was first published in 1777, but, like many scientific studies, it was destined to become a lifeless column of numbers on an increasingly yellowed and brittle page, awaiting some trick of visualization to bring the measurements back to life. That moment did not come for 150 years.

In 1927 an expert in fetal anatomy at the University of Minnesota named Richard Scammon rediscovered Montbeillard's raw data, converted them to metric measurements, and plotted them as a graph of height versus age. Several years later, D'Arcy Thompson — who lectured at Tanner's school and whom the evolutionary biologist Stephen Jay Gould later described as "perhaps the greatest polymath of our century" — plotted the numbers as a growth velocity chart. This chart showed the periods of maximum growth during the life of Montbeillard's son, which happen to mirror the two most prominent growth peaks of every normal boy. One peak occurs during the first two years of life, when growth is most rapid, and the other occurs during the adolescent growth spurt (which for Montbeillard's son began around age fourteen). During his pubertal spurt, the young Montbeillard shot up 12.1 centimeters (about 5 inches) per year and 31 centimeters (more than a foot) during the entire spurt. This simple growth velocity chart has become an iconic image among scientists who study human growth.

On its own, Montbeillard's interest in his son's growth qualified as little more than parental idiosyncrasy. Within a century, however, the convergence of growth science, such as it was, and parental obsession, such as it was to become, propelled the research along. By 1876, for example, the British physician Percy Boulton issued the marching orders for generations of parents and their balking offspring when he wrote, "If parents would once a year have the children weighed and measured by a competent person, they would frequently gain information which would be of the utmost prospective value. They would detect at an early age irregularities of development which would act as danger signals to give warning of approaching mischief, for arrest of growth, whether in latitude or longitude, is one of the earliest appreciable signs of disease." The intent of measurement, therefore, was always to use growth as a harbinger of health. It has only been during our increasingly self-conscious times that height has become burdened with unusually heavy social and psychological baggage as well.

CHRISTIAN WIENER, WHO taught "descriptive geometry and graphical statics" at the Technical High School in Karlsruhe, Germany, matched Montbeillard in parental zeal, if not elegance. He seems to have greeted the birth of each of his four sons with a ruler. Beginning in 1856, he took it upon himself to measure each of them at least once a year, often much more frequently, sometimes twice a day, and in one instance up to the age of thirty-three. His youngest son was measured eighty-nine times.

The increasing attention to the size of children set the stage for a more scientific snapshot of the growth process. The aim, Tanner writes, was not to determine tallness or dominance or percentiles per se. "Always," he observes, "the question was the same: what is the probability that this particular child belongs to the motley army of normal children, of so many shapes and sizes; and what the probability that he belongs to another battalion altogether, the company of the sick?"

That sounds like a straightforward question, and yet it wasn't until the mid-eighteenth century that doctors felt any need at all to keep track of the height and weight of children. As was so often the case in early scientific revolutions, the guinea pigs for this effort were the poor, the disadvantaged, and the orphans. In the 1750s, Christian Friedrich Jampert began to measure children at the Friedrichshospital in Berlin, otherwise known as the Royal Orphanage, in what is credited as the first effort to compile a table of growth measurements of humans. The "children" ranged in age from one to twenty-five years, and a bit of folkloric whimsy informed the regimen by which they were measured. "I began the experiments in springtime," Jampert wrote, "soon after Easter of this year, when the tissues were neither constricted by cold nor yet made turgid by heat." He measured the children every day, "two hours before mealtime." Jampert recorded height as "Longitude" and weight as "Pondus absolutum." Published in 1754, this table was the first tentative growth chart for a group of children.

Jampert's study, though justifiably celebrated as pioneering, was also notable for other, less admirable reasons. It inadvertently advertised the dangers of amateur science. True, he was the first to discern from actual measurement a fundamental truth about human growth: that there is enormous variation from one individual to the next. As he put it, "The amount of growth varies greatly in different subjects." But he also committed the gravest of scientific sins, sullying this essential insight by throwing out some of the data that didn't fit his preconceived notions of normality. His table of measurements did not accurately portray the true range of variation because, as he admitted, "in those [measurements] left out, the deviation was greater."

In the same year of 1754, J. G. Roederer initiated an equally momentous medical practice: he started to record the weight and length of every newborn in the obstetrical clinic in Göttingen, Germany. Though technically not a growth chart since it was limited to babies, the information's avowed purpose was squarely aligned with the emerging aim of all growth charts: to look for anomalies of growth that might signal serious health problems. It is no accident that these first systematic attempts at widespread measurement occurred primarily in Germany. The mania for quantification that emerged in eighteenth-century Europe was particularly intense in German academic centers. Over the next 250 years, this mania would spawn massive childhood growth surveys, which began in Germany, England, and France, later spread to America in the late nineteenth and early twentieth centuries, and finally reached an apex of statistical sophistication in England in the post–World War II era.

TO CREATE A growth chart, data from a specific population have to be collected, and then those measurements need to be shaped, sanded, and, as the experts say, smoothed by statistical techniques. Although hundreds of researchers (and tens of thousands of children who stood straight and tall while being measured) worked to create the document that parents examine in the pediatrician's office today, several notable figures stand out.

One of them is Adolphe Quetelet, a Belgian prodigy with the mind of a mathematician and the soul of an artist. Born in 1796, Quetelet had great personal flair: he moved in the salon life of Paris; discussed the statistics of growth with his idol, Johann Wolfgang von Goethe; and is credited by some as being the person who invented the concept of crime statistics. Beyond all those considerable achievements, he flung himself into a rather quixotic mathematical mission: to determine the mean (average) measurement of human proportions, in the belief that those numbers represented an ideal of human beauty. (His notion of *l'homme moyen*, loosely translated as "the average man," had an enormous impact on cultural perceptions of body image at the time.) But his greatest contribution to the study of growth grew out of his realization that variation in the height of human beings seemed to follow, of all improbable things, the same rules as variation in the observations of stars made by astronomers.

During the 1820s, while visiting Paris, Quetelet became familiar with a revolution in mathematics advanced by Carl Friedrich Gauss and Pierre-Simon Laplace. These mathematicians helped launch the science of statistics and were responsible for what is popularly known as the bell curve. Gauss, a German, and Laplace, a French astronomer and mathematician, developed a mathematical law to account for errors in astronomical measurements. This law, initially known as the law of errors and now more commonly referred to as a Gaussian distribution, was based on the scientists' observation that in any series of astronomical measurements, the bulk of the numbers would crowd around the middle, but there would always be a few outlying measurements. This phenomenon could be depicted as a curve, which took the shape of an inverted U, or a bell. The deviation, or likelihood of error, increased as the measurements got farther from the peak of the bell, or the mean, and the reliability of those measurements diminished accordingly.

Quetelet tailored this mathematical law to the measure of man: he was the first to realize that the bell curve applied not just to the luminosity of heavenly bodies but also to the height and weight of mortal human bodies. In 1831, in the midst of his astronomical observations, he decided to conduct a survey of children's heights and realized that the variation in these heights at each age could be plotted in a curve that abided by the law of errors. Everything that informs current pediatric decisions and thinking about growth — what is normal, what is medically worrisome, what might justify the use of treatments such as human growth hormone — derives from this fantastically improbable insight.

Quetelet's growth survey was the first to be considered cross-sectional. Put simply, this means that in a population of children, he took all the five-year-olds, for example, averaged their measurements, and then plotted the mean height for age five on a chart. Next he measured all the six-year-olds, averaged their heights, and plotted that point on a chart. By averaging the heights of children at various ages and then plotting them all out, he created a growth chart based on the measurements of many children without having to follow each child for many years. This suggests one of the advantages of using cross-sectional data: Quetelet had his chart in one year, while it took Montbeillard eighteen years to compile his.

These distinctions profoundly influence what is considered a normal size at any stage of a child's growth. Cross-sectional studies tend to flatten the curves and constrain the range of "normality"; longitudinal studies tend to reflect more accurately the growth curves of real children. Fifty years after Quetelet published his first cross-sectional growth chart, the British surgeon Charles Roberts, a leading expert on growth, seized on this distinction, criticizing Quetelet's emphasis on "mere averages" and arguing that it was variation around the mean that was truly important in human growth. One of the examples Roberts used in making this argument is as relevant to children today as it was more than a century ago. If you took two "average" schoolboys in England and compared the difference in their average height between thirteen and a half and fourteen and a half years of age, he noted, it would be rather modest — about two inches. Yet that modest difference masked huge variations, as the difference between the tallest boy and the shortest boy in that age span was twenty inches — nearly two feet!

Some of these technical issues began to resolve by the late nineteenth century, and every modern parent who has fretted or exulted over a child's percentile on the growth chart has none other than Francis Galton, the father of eugenics, to thank. Not only did Galton invent the idea of percentiles as a way of organizing and presenting growth data on charts, but he also invented much of the equipment to conduct the measurements, including the stadiometer, the device used to measure height.

Galton flung himself into human measurement as only a bright and resourceful zealot could. He helped establish a society for anthropometrics — the formal measurement of human beings — as a section of the British Society for the Advancement of Science. In the 1870s, he doggedly sought to rouse enthusiasm for a height survey of British schoolboys, sending appeals to countless schools. Interestingly, only a handful, including Marlborough — Tanner's alma mater — expressed even mild interest. When that failed, he contrived to show up at the International Health Exhibition in London in 1884 with a thirty-six-foot-long Anthropometric Laboratory, where visitors could pay threepence to have their sitting and standing heights, along with many other bodily dimensions, measured. When the examination was finished, the person received a card with the results, and Galton gleefully pocketed a copy for his own research. By the time the fair closed, Galton possessed 150,000 physical measurements on 10,000 people. The analysis of this database led directly to the fundamental vocabulary of the growth chart.

For readers of this book, Galton's most enduring and influential contribution was a single word in the vocabulary of growth: "percentile." Using the measurements from the London exhibition, he was the first to recast the law of errors as a series of percentages on a chart. If a boy's height placed him in the ninetieth percentile, it was a statistical way of saying that he was smaller than 10 percent of all the boys who were the same age; similarly, a boy in the tenth percentile was smaller than 90 percent of his immediate peers. This is not, incidentally, the vocabulary that doctors, scientists, and drug regulators always adopt when talking to one another about height. Instead, they often speak of standard deviations, or SDs. Percentiles and standard deviations translate easily back and forth, but SDs are a difficult concept for many parents to grasp.

It would be fair to say that Galton's single-minded focus on anthropometrics pushed human measurement beyond mere science and into the realm of cultural signifier. He injected a creepy kind of nationalism into the childhood measuring campaigns then sweeping Europe and North America. In 1873, when Galton first asked the Anthropological Institute in Britain to sponsor a program of body measurements in British schools, he wrote: "We do not know whether the general physique of the nation remains year after year at the same level, or whether it is distinctly deteriorating or advancing in any respects. Still less are we able to ascertain how we stand in comparison with other nations, because the necessary statistical facts are, speaking generally, as deficient with them as with ourselves."

This formal concern with measurement and comparison nationalized an aspect of childhood identity that formerly was personal, and almost idiosyncratic. In terms of the science of growth, it marked a point of no return. Galton's passion for comparison soon extended to ethnicity and class. He advocated stratified sampling of children — that is, comparing different social classes by height. To modern ears, this may sound like eugenics at its worst, where genetic "deviation" would be identified and categorized according to ethnic and socioeconomic background. In fact, as we'll learn in several chapters on modern anthropometry, it has had exactly the opposite effect. Carefully conducted modern height surveys — in which a population, not an individual, is studied — reveal how significant a role nurture, or environment, plays in modifying the effect of nature, or genes.

Profound as its impact has been, the percentile is not as important as the original Montbeillard data. If a child's growth curve more or less fits the contours of these data — that is, if he or she continues to grow along the same general lines as that eighteenth-century example — the child is probably perfectly healthy. In Tanner's view, percentiles offer "a simple and clear statement of the chances of a given child belonging to the normal group," and in the nineteenth and early twentieth centuries the idea was adapted to large surveys undertaken in North America, notably in Boston by Henry Bowditch, in Iowa, and in California.

But there was still one missing element to make a growth chart truly meaningful. It would be discovered by a scientist who is almost never associated with the subject of growth but who forever changed our understanding of it. This scientist was, as one writer observed, "small in stature but formidably intense."

IN AUGUST 1888, the fateful intersection of human stature and human psychology began to unfold on a train traveling from New York to Ohio. One of the passengers was a wild-eyed, bearded physical anthropologist named Franz Boas, who was on his way to the annual meeting of the American Association for the Advancement of Science. Along the way, Boas struck up a conversation with the man sitting next to him on the train, one G. Stanley Hall.

The name may not resonate with modern readers, but it would have rung a bell in the late nineteenth century, for Hall was known as "the father of child study in America." Trained in Europe, he had set up the first psychology department at an American university, at Johns Hopkins, and was the first person to invite Sigmund Freud to lecture in the United States. "His vast domain was the unplumbed depths of the child psyche, in which he believed lay the 'soul of the race,' the secrets of growth," writes Ann Hulbert in her history of child-rearing advice. Hall had just taken a position as president and professor of psychology at the newly established Clark University in Worcester, Massachusetts. According to Tanner, Hall was "a firm champion of the view that psychology must be based on fundamental biological concepts and that the first thing in education was to understand the manner of growth of the body and the brain of the child."

Boas, for his part, typified the roaring and rigorous scientific mindset coming out of Europe. Trained by the great German pathologist Rudolf Virchow, he brought passion, precision, and social conscience to the study of cultures. He was particularly expert in languages, folklore, and cultural differences. Boas was working at the journal *Science*, but by the time the train pulled into Cleveland, Hall had raised the possibility of a job in the Division of Anthropology at Clark, which fell within the psychology department, and Boas quite accidentally stumbled into the field of human growth. His first paper on growth appeared in *Science* in 1892; his last, in 1941.

Shortly after arriving in Worcester, Boas began a major longitudinal study of childhood growth in local schools — believed to be the first in North America. Longitudinal studies were difficult, expensive, and prone to bureaucratic failure, for they required researchers to follow the same children year after year, from early childhood to the end of puberty. In Worcester, the problems were also political: local newspapers attacked Boas personally and questioned the need for schoolchildren to "have their anatomies felt of and the various portions of their bodies measured for no reason established in science." For the Worcester study, begun in May 1891, Boas took an ambitious battery of measurements: not just height and weight, but also sitting height, forearm length, hand breadth, and head length and breadth. Like many longitudinal studies, this one was ill-fated. A year after it commenced, Boas quit his professorship at Clark, in part to take a job heading anthropological exhibits for the World's Columbian Exposition of 1893 in Chicago. In this new position, he spearheaded the physical measurement of Native Americans and other ethnic groups, producing height data that continue to reverberate more than a century later (see chapter 14). Boas and his colleague Clark Wissler published some of the Worcester results as late as 1906, so despite leaving Clark University, he managed to keep a hand in this pioneering growth study.

Boas's great accomplishment was to grasp, probably in his initial study, the crucial importance of the "tempo of growth." "Though he couched it in obscure prose and almost impenetrable algebra," Tanner writes, Boas understood that pubertal growth acceleration happens at different times in different children, and that this variation in timing wreaks havoc with the normal way of plotting cross-sectional data on a growth chart. Early maturers skew the growth curve distributions toward a younger age. When these early maturers later slow down (again prematurely), they yank the curve in the opposite direction. Put more colloquially, the picture of normal growth that any growth chart hopes to capture is inevitably warped in two directions by what is known as sampling bias, just as a child's appearance can be distorted by a warped funhouse mirror. As early as 1897, Boas wrote that "young children grow more uniformly than older children. The increase in variability [of growth rate] is very great during the years of adolescence . . . this increase must be considered due to the effects of retardation and acceleration."

Factoring in each individual's tempo of growth is crucial because it defines, amid that thicket of percentiles and blizzard of dots, what falls inside and outside the normal range. "He found that the shorter children grew less than the taller in the years before adolescence," Tanner notes.

But during adolescence the shorter grew more; that is, they continued to grow at a time when the taller were stopping. He thus demonstrated for the first time the relative independence of final adult height and the speed with which it is reached. He overplayed his hand, perhaps, in concluding that "small children are throughout their period of growth retarded in development, and smallness at any given period as compared to the average must in most cases be interpreted as due to slowness of development."

Tanner adds, "But he felt himself to be championing the cause of the late developer, and he never lost interest in the subject, returning to it in his very last paper on growth, published in 1941."

If that were Boas's only contribution to the study of growth, it would nonetheless qualify as seminal. But he did much more. As head of physical anthropology for the Chicago exposition, Boas produced the first national standards for height and weight of North American children. He and F. W. Putnam, another major figure in early growth studies, developed a plan to plot definitively the growth and development of American children. By combining measurements from new and existing school studies in Oakland, Toronto, Boston, St. Louis, Milwaukee, and Worcester, the researchers achieved a sample size encompassing an astounding ninety thousand children between five and eighteen years of age. Published in 1898 in the *Report of the U.S. Commissioner of Education,* these standards for height represent the first attempt at a national growth chart for American children.

Boas then pushed the study of growth into uncharted cultural and socioeconomic waters. He investigated the tempo of growth among different nationalities and occupational classes, concluding that accelerated or retarded growth creates greater differences in the beginning of adolescence than in the last years of growth. Earlier than perhaps any other researcher in the field, Boas realized how straightforward measurement of the human body, despite its reasonable scientific intentions and its presumed scientific objectivity, could lead to considerable cultural mischief. By 1896, when Boas began joint affiliations with the American Museum of Natural History and Columbia University, his interests had evolved toward studying the influence of environment and heredity on body form. His study for the U.S. Immigration Commission, begun in 1908, was ostensibly intended to see if the recent influx of immigrants had created a diminution of the physique of the American population, but it turned into a study of enormous scientific and cultural impact. Boas and his group measured nearly eighteen thousand immigrants and their American-born children — not just height and weight, but head length, head breadth, and other inferential markers of brain size, otherwise known as the cephalic index. All were from New York, and about a third were twenty-five years of age or older, but the majority were children. The original results were published in 1912 as "Changes in Bodily Form of Descendants of Immigrants."

Coming so soon after Galton, the title alone unleashed a rumble of sociological thunder that would reverberate all through a century of racism, eugenics, and, by extension, genetic determinism. If immigrant body forms changed from generation to generation, as Boas claimed, it was not simply, or even predominantly, a preordained story written by genes, but rather one in which the environment was coauthor, with significant input and influence. Tanner emphasizes how a study of physical size could strike at the heart of cultural prejudice. "Boas's findings, that stature was a little greater in children growing up in America and that head length and breadth were a few millimeters more, would scarcely be regarded as surprising nowadays," Tanner writes. "But anthropologists of the time had astonishing belief in the fixity of what they called human types or races, and when Boas showed that even the central tabernacle of the doctrine — the cephalic index — was built on sand they chorused their displeasure and disbelief."

Nearly one hundred years ago, Boas saw, in seemingly mundane human measurements such as height and weight, compelling evidence that the environment has a much louder voice in the physical size of humans than the eugenicists would have it. The tremendous arc of this insight will become apparent as we continue to recount the story of growth. Recent studies have confirmed, to a surprising, if not shocking, degree, how much environment shapes the size we become, the hormones we make, the personalities we adopt, and the behaviors that typify our adult existence — how much it empowers, or undermines, our genetic potential.

At age seventy-two, after a long hiatus, Boas returned to the issue of human growth in 1930. He was particularly intent on studying the relationship between adult height and the growth spurt. To explore this question, he used height data collected at a number of prestigious schools, including the Horace Mann School, Ethical Culture Schools, and City College of New York. In the papers that emerged, Boas demonstrated that, on average, boys who experienced an early adolescent growth spurt "were already taller by age eleven, but not necessarily taller when adult stature was achieved." In 1935 he added that "each individual has by heredity a certain tempo of development that may be modified by outer conditions." The internal metronome that sets this tempo remains a mystery to this day, but its biological rhythm very much determines the psychological tune we whistle during adolescence and probably well into adulthood.

Two other American scientists had stumbled upon the central importance of tempo of growth, and Tanner paid both a visit during his North American tour. The first was Frank Shuttleworth, a researcher at Harvard who had compiled an early longitudinal study of growth that for many years was the standard reference in textbooks. The other was Nancy Bayley, a visionary psychologist at the University of California. In 1928 Bayley had been recruited to head the landmark Berkeley Growth Study, a small but influential longitudinal study that reflected her interest in mental and psychological maturation. With Boas, she was one of the earliest scientists to suspect that variations in tempo of growth affected emotional and mental development, and that growth during adolescence in particular had profound social and psychological ramifications.

One of the biggest surprises to Tanner was that the work of Boas, Shuttleworth, and Bayley seemed to have been ignored by a new generation of growth experts in the United States. Yet everything he had learned in his research confirmed the primacy of growth velocity and the value of longitudinal study. As he later put it, the rate of growth "reflects what is happening *now*; size, or, as we might call it, distance traveled, reflects too much the events of the past."

By the time he returned to England, Tanner had a very good idea of the kind of growth science he wanted to do. It would pay keen attention to variations in growth tempo and it would be based on longitudinal data. But it would aspire to something more. In creating "growth standards," Tanner and his colleagues sought nothing less than to guide the optimal growth of children. This chart was intended to suggest the best possible trajectory of human growth and could be applied to individual children. ("Reference" charts, such as the current Centers for Disease Control–developed growth charts in the United States, by contrast, simply offer comparisons to how other children of the same age and gender are growing. They show growth patterns for groups of children, but are not intended for individuals.) The resulting chart would set the first major postwar growth standards using modern statistical techniques.

IN THE AUTUMN of 1948, after moving back to London, Tanner tackled the Harpenden Growth Study in earnest. He started by taking on an assistant, nine years his senior, named Reginald H. Whitehouse. "Innocent of any academic training," as Tanner put it, Whitehouse possessed a qualification perhaps even more useful when it came to keeping dozens of squirming, recalcitrant children under control: he'd been in the army and had served in the Royal Army Medical Corps. Although Tanner received no pay for his Harpenden work, he insisted that Whitehouse receive a salary. "I knew how important this guy was going to be in my life for a while," he told me. As a legendary "hyphenate," Tanner-Whitehouse generated seminal growth studies for decades.

The famously productive collaboration continued until Whitehouse's retirement in 1976. The two men ran the Harpenden Growth Study together, first out of a basement office at St. Thomas's Hospital Medical School and then from the newly formed Institute of Child Health at the University of London. Even then, Tanner pursued a remarkably broad attack on the study of growth. While conducting the Harpenden study, he organized a biochemical group to pursue the biology of what is now known as insulin-like growth factor-1; a group of statisticians developed new ways to handle longitudinal growth measurements; a clinical arm at the Hospital of Sick Children studied illnesses related to growth; and there was even an ethology team, studying maternal and child behavior in a colony of macaques maintained on the roof of the Institute of Child Health. "He dealt with childhood growth from the level of molecules to the final product," recalled Noel Cameron, who trained under Tanner during the 1970s.

At Harpenden, Tanner and Whitehouse measured height; sitting height; hip, shoulder, elbow, and knee width; circumference of upper arms, calves, and thighs; foot length; weight; and four skinfolds. The measuring team took measurements every six months (increased to every three months during puberty). They followed many of the children until their growth ceased. All the participants were orphans, either at birth or because of family breakups, and came primarily from working-class or lower-middle-class backgrounds. "Every measurement on every child on every occasion was done by Whitehouse, a robust man," Tanner noted. A picture of Whitehouse in Tanner's *History of the Study of Human Growth* shows a bespectacled, sharp-nosed, dark-haired man with long sideburns who, even in profile, bristles with the peremptory no-nonsense bearing of a military officer. Whitehouse designed a whole new armamentarium of precise measuring instruments, including the Harpenden anthropometer with a digital readout, the Tanner/Whitehouse skinfold caliper, and the Harpenden stadiometer to measure height. (They are still manufactured and sold today by the Welsh company Holtain.) X-rays of arms, calves, and thighs also were taken, for growth experts such as Nancy Bayley had shown that the maturation of the skeleton (or bone age) offered a far more precise metric of developmental stage than a child's age.

All this attention to the mechanics of physical measurement may seem trivial, but it is not. Tanner correctly suspected in the 1940s — and it has been reiterated in studies that have come out as recently as 2004 — that it is exceedingly difficult to measure a growing human body accurately. This seemingly simple procedure is prone to great error. Pediatricians, who do most of the measuring, rarely receive specialized training in how to do it well, and the standard equipment in most doctors' offices often looks like war surplus. The errors that occur when doctors attempt to assess the rate of growth are particularly insidious because this assessment requires at least two measurements and therefore introduces two margins of error. The inability to measure height correctly can have significant clinical consequences. A study by Linda Voss of the Wessex Growth Study in England documented the ease with which errors in pediatric measurements can occur, and researchers at Children's Hospital of Philadelphia recently suggested that inaccurate measurements were the norm, not the exception, in most family practices. To this day, half a century later, the Harpenden measurements are considered a model of their kind.

Ultimately, some 450 boys and 260 girls lined up to be measured (85 boys and 48 girls were followed for ten years). Later, Tanner and his colleagues at the Institute of Child Health incorporated data from several other longitudinal growth studies in Europe to create an unusual "tempo-conditional" growth chart, first published in 1966. Unlike the cross-sectional charts currently in use in the United States, the British charts featured three separate sets of growth trajectories, each with its own percentiles, to show early, average, and late maturation in both boys and girls. Tanner showed me one of these charts when I visited him in Devonshire, and it was remarkable. One set of curves, in red, showed early maturation, with its own array of percentiles, for boys. The same chart had a second set of curves, in black, showing "on-time" maturation. And there was also a third set, in green, showing late maturation. Each set of growth curves had its one hundred percentiles, and although the main percentile lines (twenty-fifth, fiftieth, seventy-fifth, and so on) were very close together at age two, when rate of maturation is less of an issue, the lines began to separate around the time of puberty. "There are more ways of being normal than are shown here," Tanner said, nodding at the American-style charts I had brought.

The difference is not terribly significant for the vast majority of children, who are measured by their family doctors and who fall within the normal range. But in cases of extreme shortness, especially around the time of adolescence, cross-sectional charts can give a misleading impression of an individual's growth. "He's absolutely right about the limitations of cross-sectional charts," said Alan D. Rogol, a growth expert in Charlottesville, Virginia. "You mush things together when you make a growth curve for a population." This may sound like a technical quibble, but speaking not as a science writer but as a onetime shrimp, I would argue that it is much more than that. Even if it were an illusion and had no bearing on my particular growth trajectory, I would have found great psychological comfort in looking at one of those charts when I was an adolescent. The fact that even late maturers came back to the normal range in such a graphic and unambiguous fashion wouldn't have changed the misery I felt at the moment, but it would have suggested that the moment wouldn't last forever. I discovered that some prominent American growth doctors still use the Tanner curves, even though they're reduced to using photocopies now. "Those charts are *wonderful*," said Leslie Plotnick of Johns Hopkins School of Medicine.

During the period when most baby boomers grew up, from the 1940s through the 1960s, there was no official national growth chart. Much of the United States and the world used a chart developed at Harvard in the 1930s, which was based on a population of children raised in Boston. Only in the 1970s did the U.S. government prepare national reference charts, which were based on growth studies done by the Fels Longitudinal Study in Ohio (birth to age two) and on a cross-sectional survey organized by the National Center for Health Statistics. That chart was issued by the federal Centers for Disease Control (CDC) in 1977.

Tanner has made the point many times that most growth charts created before the 1960s failed to incorporate Boas's insight about tempo of growth, with all its scientific, medical, and even psychological implications for normality. The inclusion of tempo only became formalized with the British charts beginning in 1966 and was later adapted for international use. It should be added that growth charts are not cast in stone. They are like dialects — local, evolving, understandable only within a given population, and difficult to translate outside the confines of that population. They must be updated periodically, especially since there has been what growth experts call a "secular trend" — a trend toward greater average height — in most Western and industrial societies over the past century.

The growth chart has, of course, undergone much revision and updating since the 1960s — but not always, in Tanner's opinion, for the better. He has been particularly critical of the cross-sectional data on which the first national growth chart in the United States, issued in 1977, was based. Other scientists have agreed with his assessment. Although the World Health Organization (WHO) adopted the American chart for international use, there was considerable grumbling in the scientific community. Mercedes de Onis, who now heads WHO's growth department, coauthored several papers in the 1990s criticizing the cross-sectional chart for several methodological shortcomings, including the fact that they were based on homogeneous socioeconomic populations. Some of these problems were addressed when the U.S. Centers for Disease Control issued an updated set of charts in 2000, but these also are based on cross-sectional data and have been criticized by the international community for, among other things, not taking the mother's nutritional strategy (breast-feeding versus bottle-feeding in the early months and years of a child's life) into account. The larger point, according to Noel Cameron, now a growth expert at the University of Loughborough in England, is that "cross-sectional charts should be used for *groups* of children, not individual children. Most people don't understand that this is not how an individual grows."

THE GROWTH CHART is also a cultural document, and one of recent vintage. Since the first modern British charts came out only in the 1960s, and the first U.S. national charts appeared only in 1977, it's really been little more than a generation of parents who have been drawn into the vortex of its scientific version of normality. But we linger on its implications, instantly sensitive to the way it positions our children amid the great mass of humanity.

Although the growth chart may seem like an innocuous, even indecipherable piece of paper to many parents, the way its data are collected, presented, and interpreted can have huge implications for families. A cross-sectional chart, like the one currently used in the United States, is less forgiving of normal variation than a Tanner-style chart, which makes clear that glaring discrepancies in size during adolescence largely resolve by the time growth is completed. Moreover, if early growth is as important as the Barker hypothesis suggests, current charts based on formula-fed infants may provide a misleading picture of healthy growth. Finally, the merciless one-size-fits-all nature of cross-sectional charts can instill a lasting fear of deviation, in both children and parents, about a temporary biological situation. Attaching a number to parental anxieties about a child's size may make height more of an issue than it might otherwise be.

Tanner saw this firsthand in the 1980s. He was a member of the British committee responsible for choosing a small number of children in Britain who would qualify for treatment with hGH, which at the time was in exceedingly short supply because it could only be harvested from human cadavers. When several patients in the United States and Britain died in 1985 from a rare infectious brain disease spread by the hormone, therapy was immediately suspended. But not all families agreed with the decision to suspend treatment. "Some parents, amazingly, said, 'We'll take the risk,'" Tanner told me. "And I said, 'Yeah? For an inch, two inches?' And the parents said, 'Yeah.' We didn't accede, of course, but that's in the context of how terribly important they thought height was."

Other growth experts acknowledge the cultural message embedded in the cross-sectional charts' narrower curves. David Sandberg, a psychologist at the University of Buffalo who has studied the psychology of short stature, told me, "It [the cross-sectional chart] certainly affects in a fundamental way how we think about growth. Without using longitudinal charts, it gives the impression that so many kids are doing poorly . . . So many of the kids that concern is expressed over are in all likelihood just these normal late maturers."

David B. Allen, a pediatric endocrinologist at the University of Wisconsin, almost pined for the Tanner-style charts. "I think it would be helpful in pediatricians' offices and things like that if we used those kinds of growth curves," he said, "the kind that had the early developer and the late developer, and getting the lines on there. You don't get any sense of this dimension [the time axis] on the growth curve right now, in terms of what's the time that's required for normal children to finish their growth, and it makes it look like everybody's going through puberty at exactly the same time. So it's misleading."

If anyone still believes that the growth chart is a scientifically neutral table of numbers — independent of social or cultural, or even commercial, pressures — consider this recent development. In the fall of 2004, Allen mentioned in passing that Eli Lilly and Company had created its own version of a growth chart that it had begun distributing to doctors. It looks like the standard CDC growth chart. In fact, it *is* the standard CDC growth chart, the one revised in 2000 and available to any citizen over the Internet. There is just one subtle difference: the lowest line on the Lilly chart marks the 1.2 percentile of growth (on most charts, the outer lines of the bell curve show the ninety-fifth and fifth percentiles, or the ninety-seventh and third percentiles). The 1.2 percentile, marked by a bright red line, happens to be the cutoff point that the U.S. Food and Drug Administration approved in 2003 for the use of growth hormone in children who are unusually short but otherwise medically normal. The new percentile line is there, Allen explained, "so that it's easy to tell when a child is in the area that would qualify them for growth hormone therapy."

There is nothing inaccurate about the new chart; it just increases the likelihood that parents and children will fret over a child's location down there among the lowest percentiles. Doctors might not be fooled, of course, but everyone understands that parental anxiety — and a child's misery — drives the use of growth hormone as much as medical judgment. In that sense, the chart itself may sometimes be causing stress and ultimately "disease."

3

A BRIEF INTERRUPTION
FOR A BICYCLE ACCIDENT

The Growth of Bones
and the Creation of Height

> Full fathom five thy father lies;
> Of his bones are coral made;
> Those are pearls that were his eyes:
> Nothing of him that doth fade,
> But doth suffer a sea-change
> Into something rich and strange.
>
> —WILLIAM SHAKESPEARE, *The Tempest*

SEVERAL YEARS AGO, during our annual block party in Brooklyn, my daughter took advantage of the barricades blocking traffic at both ends of our street to zoom up and down the middle of the road on her bike. At one point, while making a turn, she descended into a kind of death spiral of diminishing velocity.

I didn't actually see her fall, but I heard that uniquely warbled cry that tells every parent his or her child has suffered an injury neither superficial nor exaggerated. She was holding her right arm, and we rushed off to a nearby emergency room. The doctor took one look at the x-ray of Micaela's right wrist and muttered the dreaded "Well, what do you know!" Not one but two bones were broken, right where the long bones of the forearm — the ulna and the radius — meet the wrist.

Two days later, we found ourselves in the office of Dr. David Scher, a pediatric orthopedist and surgeon, at the New York University Hospital for Joint Diseases and NYU School of Medicine in Manhattan. (He now practices at the Hospital for Special Surgery uptown.) The fracture was confirmed, and Micaela's arm was put in a fluorescent green cast.

The NYU doctors had taken another set of x-rays, and Dr. Scher slapped them up on the screen and pointed out the fractures with his pen. "The growth plate doesn't seem to be affected," he said in passing. I nodded as if I knew what he was talking about. I knew that growth plates were important but didn't exactly know why.

Later, I went back to talk to Dr. Scher. I realized that what he had pointed out so hastily with his pen is one of the most magical and underappreciated parts of human anatomy. Growth plates are the launching pads of a growing body. They sit, barely as thick as a percale sheet, primarily at the ends of the long bones and are the factories of height.

"MICAELA'S FRACTURE WAS near the growth plate, but not at it," Dr. Scher explained on the morning I interviewed him. We were looking at x-rays of a broken wrist. "That dark part there is the growth plate," he said. "It appears as a gap."

All bone begins as cartilage, which is invisible on an x-ray. This kind of cartilage is related to that tough, rubbery material we sometimes encounter as the inedible portion of a chicken leg. In humans, the early fetus lays down a rough draft of the skeleton, including major limbs, as cartilage; this rubbery body plan is typically in place by about eight weeks after fertilization. Then, during later fetal development, the center of this cartilage breaks down and is replaced by bone. The bone forms the skeleton with which a baby is born. Many of a fetus's bones retain cartilage-like flexibility, for which many mothers are grateful — that flexibility facilitates the passage of the fetus through the birth canal and out into the world.

Shortly before birth, a separate bone-generating mechanism begins to take over, preparing to convert cartilage into actual bone once the fetus enters the real world. These sites are called "secondary centers of ossification," and they appear as hard caps covering the ends of the "long bones," including bones that don't seem so long, such as vertebrae and the bones in our fingers and toes. The principal long bones — the ones that are the real foundries of childhood growth and adult height — are the upper arm bone, or humerus; the two forearm bones, the ulna and radius; the thigh bone, or femur; and the two bones of the lower leg, the fibula and tibia.

But not all long bones are created equal when it comes to generating size and height. Certain growth plates, Dr. Scher explained, are more active than others. As a result, the places where the largest amount of growth occurs are fairly limited and well known to doctors: the shoulder end of the humerus, the wrist ends of the ulna and radius (the ones that Micaela broke), the knee end of the femur, and the knee end of the tibia. Beginning at age ten, a child adds 10 millimeters (about ⅜ inch) of height per year on average, just at the growth plate where the femur meets the knee; another 6 millimeters (¼ inch) is added each year at the growth plate where the tibia meets the knee. At the other ends of those bones, growth occurs at a slower pace, in increments of about ⅛ inch per year. (During adolescence, however, a significant part of longitudinal growth occurs in the spinal vertebrae.) Like adjusting the legs of a handmade table, it requires a great deal of biological coordination and sophistication to get all the limbs the same size, and in fact Nature is not always a master carpenter. Dr. Scher pointed out that an estimated 75 percent of all people have uneven long bones, where one arm or leg is up to 5 millimeters shorter or longer than the other. Despite that difference — 5 millimeters is about the thickness of a stack of three twenty-five-cent pieces — doctors usually don't detect any ill effects. Problems occur when the difference between limbs exceeds 2 centimeters.

Studying the long bones may help us understand where height is manufactured, but it doesn't help us understand how. For that we need to explore some very special and unusual cells.

CONSIDER THE GROWTH plate where the femur touches the knee. This junction produces the single greatest increase in height in the human body in the course of a lifetime. The cap of the femur forms part of the knee joint, but just above it is the growth plate. If you made a horizontal slice through the bone, you would see the growth plate: a very thin — "millimeters at most," said Dr. Scher — disk. It's very hard to convey the growth plate's feel and consistency. Even Dr. Scher, who frequently performs surgery at or near the growth plate, struggled to characterize this part of anatomy. "It's firm, but not as hard as bone," he said. "It feels like cartilage, but it's a different kind from the cartilage at joints — maybe like a very hard sorbet." Almost immediately, however, he disowned that analogy, which suggested a friable substance that might crumble under pressure. "It's not as brittle as bone," he continued. "It's softer than wood, not as hard or brittle as plastic. Sort of like . . . caulking."

This little disk of tissue is the site of neat rows of highly ordered and incredibly dynamic cells that, like a molecular parade, march upward from the cap toward the main shaft of the femur. As these cells migrate upward, they go through a series of dazzling biophysical transformations — morphological somersaults, you might say — and biologically reinvent themselves as bone. The march takes about three weeks from growth plate to hard bone.

The process goes like this. The brain issues a "go" signal in the form of growth hormone that tells these bone-related adult stem cells to get busy. Once hormonally turned on, each stem cell in the growth plate spews out a neat column of sixty to one hundred daughter cells. These clones — stacked flat like coins, side by side, row by row, in a three-dimensional array — march from the end of the bone upward, toward the shaft.

At the prompting of a second hormonal signal known as insulin-like growth factor-1 (IGF-1), the daughter cells turn into proliferative cells. As the name implies, they multiply rapidly while still on the march. About halfway to their destination, these proliferative cells undergo a second dramatic change. Each of them expands to about four times the size it was at the beginning of the march. Then the cells begin to send molecular signals that attract minerals such as calcium to their immediate environment. Put simply, these cells literally entomb themselves in the hard mineral of bone, at once dying and adding, by the width of one cell, to the ever-growing length of the femur. Finally, another class of cells known as osteoblasts arrives to cement and solidify the material that has formed outside the proliferative cells. Ergo, bone.

The process of thousands and thousands of cells traversing the distance from the growth plate to the edge of growing bone sounded to me like the process of building a coral reef, and the analogy seemed surprisingly apt. "I don't know how coral reefs form," Dr. Scher remarked, "but coral is made of hydroxyapatite, which is the same substance as bone. In fact, we use coral as a substitute for bone sometimes."

One of the most interesting aspects of this process has nothing to do with hormones or stem cells. Instead, it has to do with physical tension and stress. Putting weight on bones encourages activity at the growth plates. Research scientists have seen this effect on adult stem cells grown in the laboratory. When subjected to physical forces, these cells differentiate, or begin to specialize. In the context of growing bodies, this suggests that exercise is as important as nutrition in encouraging bone growth. Increased physical activity during adolescence is, as one medical paper recently put it, "necessary to maximize skeletal mass."

This type of bone growth occurs steadily throughout childhood, but there is a large release of growth hormone and IGF-1 during puberty, which feeds the obvious growth spurt of adolescence. Children who fail to make enough growth hormone or IGF-1, or whose cells don't seem to receive the signal the hormone carries, often suffer from short stature. The window for growth — and thus for the pharmacological remedy for growth hormone deficiency — is limited. As growth slows toward the end of puberty, the growth plate gets thinner and thinner, until finally the bone shaft breaks through the "caulking" to meet the cap and the growth plate disappears entirely. In more technical parlance, the growth plate, or physis, is said to have fused, or closed. This fusion is caused in part by the sex hormones, which is why growth usually comes to a halt during puberty.

Not all animals follow this growth pattern. Rodents and the ancient fish known as teleosts continue to grow until they die. And the ends of bones in elephants never fuse. As a result, elephants also continue to grow throughout their lives. This continued growth seems to affect their reproductive success and social dominance: the dominant males in elephant groups are always the oldest, in part because they haven't stopped growing.

No such luck for human adolescents. "Boys tend to close the growth plate around the knee at age sixteen," Dr. Scher said, "and girls do it at around fourteen." Once the bones fuse, even gallons of growth hormone will add not a micron of height.

THERE IS PRELIMINARY evidence that American youngsters aren't growing bone as well as they used to. According to a 2003 article in the *Journal of the American Medical Association*, researchers at the Mayo Clinic reported that the incidence of distal forearm fractures — exactly the kind my daughter incurred — shot up significantly in the course of just one generation among children in the Rochester, Minnesota, area. Forearm fractures in boys rose 32 percent from 1969 to 2001, according to the report. Forearm fractures in girls jumped even more dramatically, by 56 percent, during the same period. The largest increases occurred in children in the early stages of puberty.

"It's been known for decades that during the growth spurt, fractures go up, especially these distal fractures," said Sundeep Khosla, lead author of the study. The most vulnerable ages for potential bone fractures are eight to eleven for girls and eleven to fourteen for boys, he said, reflecting the time when they are entering puberty. The larger question is, of course, why the increase in broken bones?

Pediatric orthopedists have ventured several hypotheses. One is that children's intake of dietary calcium, primarily from milk, has declined in recent years, making the bones more vulnerable to fracture. (Insufficient calcium intake during childhood is yet another example of how environmental factors such as nutrition during development can set up adult medical conditions. Such undernutrition can increase the likelihood of osteoporosis later in life.) "The thinking is that during the growth spurt, with its rapid growth, in order to meet the calcium needs for longitudinal growth, there may be a decrease in bone mass," Khosla explained. Another explanation may be as simple as elementary physics. With the increasing incidence of childhood obesity, Khosla said, "when kids fall, there's more weight falling on the bone." Yet another possible explanation is that not only are more children participating in competitive sports, but the nature of that participation has changed, with more game playing and less conditioning. The result is that the number of sports-related fractures is on the rise.

Six weeks after Micaela's bicycle accident, when she went back to Dr. Scher to have her cast removed, he insisted on taking another x-ray to make sure the bones had healed. That is another miracle of childhood growth: broken bones usually mend very rapidly. I wouldn't wish a fracture on any child, but as I gazed at the ghostly image of Micaela's wrist on the x-ray, with that occult sliver of tissue known as the growth plate, I was grateful to have glimpsed, by accident, one of the most remarkable parts of our anatomy.

PART II

"MY, HOW YOU'VE GROWN..."

4

THE INVENTION OF CHILDHOOD
Growth from Ages Two to Ten

Although a prolonged period of juvenile helplessness and
dependence would, by itself, be disadvantageous to a species
because it endangers the young and handicaps their parents,
it is a help to man because the slow development provides
time for learning and training, which are far more extensive
and important in man than in any other animal.

— THEODOSIUS DOBZHANSKY, *Mankind Evolving*

GOOD MORNING, munchkins!"
It is morning at the elementary school that my children attend, and
they are greeted with this all-purpose diminutive at the gate by our beleaguered but much-appreciated playground monitor.

The scene could probably play out on any schoolyard, in any country,
at that hour of the day. If you are a parent, you know that milling, yell-
ing, scooting, darting, laughing uproar of children enjoying their last
few minutes of unfettered motion before the bell rings. The older girls
generally stand in small clots apart from the older boys, precociously
diffident and oozing disdain. The boys, typically rowdy and exuberant,
occasionally bowl over smaller children while chasing down a spaldeen
hurled against the wall. Even at this early age, the various segregations
are fairly standard: by gender, by socioeconomic background, by age, and
by grade. At the appointed hour, the teachers come down to fetch their
students, and the chaos of the playground alchemically changes into or-

derly lines — short in front, tall in back — that disappear not quite noise-lessly into the school building.

Since I drop my children off at school almost every morning, I've be-come a quiet but fascinated observer of the roiling before-school tumult of the courtyard, in part because it invariably triggers memories of my own school days and in part because I can see social and psychological dynamics in the interactions about which I had not a clue decades ago. When my son and his first-grade classmates play their wild version of tag, I am especially attentive to the relative size of the participants — not so much because of the athletic ability physical size confers to the players, but because of the seemingly benign identifiers that get slapped on children as part of the game. As this daily horseplay unfolds, cries such as "Get the Little Kid!" may not be permanently damaging slurs, but they are a kind of social shorthand for the child's physical stature, and they may mark his childhood as indelibly as a grass stain marks his pants.

In some respects, the youngest children in this heterogeneous group strike me as relatively size-blind. You don't typically hear nicknames or diminutives among these first graders. They usually refer to one another by name. But on this particular morning, the younger brother of one of the students joins the game. As a smaller child, and also as an outsider, he is quickly tagged metaphorically as well as physically: "Get the Little Kid!" Not surprisingly, this smaller boy struggles to catch up with the other players, and he is also introduced to the casual cruelty of older chil-dren on the fields of play. The bigger boys allow him a momentary, illusory proximity during the chase, then dash off, trailing squalls of laughter and taunts. Far from being humiliated, the Little Kid appears to enjoy the attention, and the interaction is so harmless, so mirthful and normal, that it transpires below the radar of adult attention. And per-haps that is the point: in a world where parents, educators, and child-hood development specialists have become increasingly (and rightly) vigilant about overt physical aggression and outright bullying in play-ground confrontations, this minor labeling seems like innocent, good-spirited fun by comparison. But even in the seemingly innocuous act of naming someone according to his or her physical attributes, whether Shortie or Fatso or String Bean or the Little Kid, children create a kind of physics of identity. It is there, it is palpable, it has mass, and either you become weighted down by it or you push back against it. Either way, it is shaping your sense of who you are.

How aware are young children of their own size compared to that of their classmates? It obviously depends on age, on the child, and on the situation. My sense is that younger children are aware of it, but not overly fixated. When my son was six, he knew his relative height compared to his classmates' because at the beginning of the school year, all the students were asked to line up according to size, front to back. As the tallest, he took pride of place at the back of the line. When children pose for class photographs, they are usually sorted and arranged by size. When they play games at recess, they are internally aware of big guys and little kids. So there are common rituals — indeed, daily rituals, when you consider the amount of time children spend in school — that reinforce an emerging social hierarchy and shape, in subtle ways, a child's physical confidence. In older children, especially older boys approaching middle school, this awareness begins to intensify. One parent of a fourth-grader at our school told me that her ten-year-old son talked obsessively at home about the relative strength of classmates. When I sat in on a fifth-grade reading group discussing Jerry Spinelli's novel *Wringer,* a book about peer pressure, the conversation veered into the ways labels get applied to children. Size emerged as one of the most dominant preoccupations — not just for boys but also for girls. To my ears, it sounded like at least as prevalent a concern as ethnic and gender labels.

But those are just anecdotal impressions. The reality, at least for elementary school children, is that disparities in size are generally modest. On any growth curve, the range of variation from shortest to tallest is much narrower earlier in life than later on, in childhood and adolescence. Which is not to say that the kids are totally size-blind. In terms of aggressive behavior, children learn very early that size has its privileges. If you believe the research of Richard Tremblay, a Canadian psychologist whom we'll meet in chapter 5, the big begin to lord it over the small as soon as children begin to mix socially, in the earliest years of preschool. And, like other social animals, they learn this in the course of precisely the kind of play that transpires in a typical schoolyard.

"If you look at a group of rhesus monkeys, for example, the young ones are aggressing each other all the time," Tremblay told me. "Part of it is play-fighting, and it's true in humans also. You learn how to control your physical aggression a lot through play-fighting, because in the play-fighting you understand how strong the other one is. And you understand also that if you're hurting the other one, he will react, and he will hurt you . . . A bigger child in the play-fighting will easily dominate a smaller child, so size is important. And there is one study that indicates that if you're physically bigger, it's harder to learn to control your physical aggression, because you're winning all the time. So there is reinforcement in that behavior."

These early events, more and more research suggests, set the tone for later behavior. According to psychologist Adrian Raine of the University of Southern California, there is a critical period between ages three and eleven when a child's physical size advantage is incorporated into basic behavioral psychology. A longitudinal study found that three-year-olds who were larger than average were temperamentally more aggressive by age eleven. They were also more likely to exhibit violent behavior as adults. So children learn very early on that height confers distinct social advantages.

The elementary school grades — give or take a couple of years — offer a fairly neat, self-contained period encompassing the early-childhood growth processes. The span from preschool through fifth grade roughly corresponds with the span in age from two to ten years. That may sound like an awfully big interval, but those ages form distinct parentheses in the physical development of a child. Around age two, physicians and growth experts typically shift to a different method of growth measurement, no longer laying a writhing mass of baby fat and attitude supine on a table. Now they are able to measure a somewhat more tractable child while he or she is standing. (In some growth charts, you can even discern a little fault line in the growth curves at age two or three, a subtle disjunction that reflects this hiccup in data between horizontal and vertical measurement.) At the other end, age ten is roughly the time when girls begin their adolescent growth spurt. That is a transforming event not only for girls but also for boys, who lag so many months behind and are forced to watch the process from afar for so long.

Most of all, the years of childhood are a period of steady, unspectacular, harmonic growth. Infants and toddlers can bounce around on the growth chart during the first two or three years of life, but after that children tend to settle down into a steady trajectory of growth, along a particular channel on the chart, until puberty, gaining on average slightly less than two inches in height each year. Just because the changes are gradual, however, doesn't mean that they're not momentous.

Indeed, the gradual changes may disguise one of evolution's greatest inventions. Those munchkins dashing around the playground don't appreciate it, but they are in the midst of enjoying one of the most powerful biological advantages that natural selection has ever conferred upon an animal species. Humans, unlike virtually all other animals, enjoy an unusually protracted childhood. As a life-cycle event, puberty seems delayed by design, and "childhood" lasts almost twice as long as for many other, nonhuman primates. Why? To answer that question, we need first to understand exactly what kind of growth occurs during childhood.

GROWTH IN CHILDREN is most obviously (and superficially) about elongation. The visual evidence of that dramatic process can be summed up in two very good twentieth-century visualizations based on one very old set of data.

As mentioned in chapter 2, the French nobleman Montbeillard measured his son every year after his birth in 1759. These "data," such as they were, appeared in a 1777 supplement to Buffon's *Histoire naturelle,* one of the most famous compendiums of scientific knowledge in the eighteenth century. Early growth experts knew of the "experiment," but then the numbers gathered dust for nearly a century, until Richard Scammon at the University of Minnesota rediscovered the table that listed Montbeillard's measurements. Scammon created a graph based on that archetypal growth chart that was published in *The Measurement of Man,* a book he coauthored in 1930. The picture that emerged from those eighteenth-century numbers makes for a perfectly serviceable twenty-first-century Everyman picture of a child's growth trajectory. If the numbers are plotted as cumulative height versus age in years, as in a standard growth chart, the resulting graph looks like the side of a mountain; there is a very steep rise in "length" (that is, height) over the first two years, a more gradual but steady climb until around age fourteen (earlier for girls), a short two-year steepening during the adolescent growth spurt, and then a leveling off that corresponds to mature height.

Another venerable giant (literally and figuratively) in the field of growth completed this picture. D'Arcy Thompson — "over six feet tall, with the build and carriage of a Viking," in Peter Medawar's memorable phrase — was among the first scientists to understand that the *rate* of growth is perhaps the most important single factor to consider in the process. Thompson also used Montbeillard's numbers, but in a different and equally revealing way: he calculated the boy's rate, or velocity, of growth between measurements and plotted out the numbers. The resulting picture looks very different from Scammon's — more like an underwater ravine than a mountain. This is because growth velocity, never higher than at the moment of birth, declines steeply to age two, after which it declines more gradually to age twelve and then shoots up again briefly, peaking at age fourteen.

In a very rough sense, this general shape of a normal child's growth is as true of children today as it was of the child of an eighteenth-century European nobleman. But there are always minor fluctuations and variations in growth among children. Indeed, variation is the norm. As the Berkeley growth expert Nancy Bayley once put it, "The more one goes over these cases, the more evident it becomes that the pattern of growth in each child is unique."

Many children experience a minor burst, known as the mid-childhood growth spurt, between the ages of six and eight. Compared to the first two years of life, and the three years of pubertal growth, this little blip is quite modest, barely discernible to the untrained eye on a growth or velocity chart. There are seasonal variations in growth, too. Studies have consistently shown that children grow faster in spring and summer than in autumn and winter. Sometimes the difference can be considerable. One British study found that in children between the ages of seven and ten, the rate of springtime growth can be as much as three times faster than the rate during the slowest part of winter.

If we think of growth purely in terms of height, however, we miss the incredibly symphonic interplay of its different aspects during the course of childhood — an interplay that, once again, was most vividly rendered in a graph created by Richard Scammon. Using both research on the size of internal organs, which had been published in the medical literature, and his own measurements of lymphatic tissue from children who had died in accidents, Scammon realized that different parts of the body — the neurological system, the immune system, and so on — grow at distinctly different rates during childhood. In this race to maturity, the brain and the size of the head are the sprinters; they grow very rapidly, achieving 80 percent of their adult size by age four. The painter Raphael is credited by growth experts such as James Tanner with having noticed this anatomical oddity and accurately depicting it in Renaissance paintings. Raphael's infants and cherubim uniquely capture the correct scale of early-childhood head and eye size.

The growth of lymphoid tissue — basically, the immune system — is not far behind that of the neural tissue. The immune system has its own little growth spurt from birth that continues throughout preadolescence. In fact, by age twelve a child's body typically generates 200 percent of its lymphoid tissue, or twice as much capacity as he or she will need as an adult. The thymus — so named because its pyramidal shape reminded the ancients of a thyme leaf — is a small nub of tissue located directly behind the breastbone that serves as a kind of classroom for immunological cells. Here, white blood cells known as T (for thymus) lymphocytes learn to discern between the molecular "uniform" of one's own cells and the molecular outfits worn by outsiders. By the time puberty begins, however, school is out; the thymus begins to shrivel, and the organ does not appear to play a role in adult immunology.

The skeleton, muscles, and internal organs, by contrast, grow at a somewhat slower and more deliberate pace, essentially following the curves of a typical growth chart. Reproductive tissues are the laggards; they grow hardly at all from birth to puberty and then enlarge dramatically. When Scammon plotted these varying growth rates against a child's age, the resulting graph presented a remarkable picture of syncopated growth that clearly represents a great deal of internal, invisible coordination. So rather than one overall growth curve, there are several overlapping, nonsynchronous curves going on in a child simultaneously, all presumably obeying some unknown choreographer. Put simply, growth invests most of its energy and resources in brainpower and immunological defense at first, giving the organism a better chance to survive and learn before it is ready to reproduce. As we'll see, the learning part is particularly crucial.

Anthropologists have been especially keen to add another growth curve to the picture: dentition. In fact, Barry Bogin, a biological anthropologist at the University of Michigan, argues that the eruption of molars at around age six represents a singular event in human evolution. It allows children to begin eating an adult diet, making them less dependent on their parents for survival. Bogin divides the period of growth between infancy and puberty into two distinct phases. As he describes in

The Growth of Humanity, childhood begins with the end of weaning (around age three) and lasts for about four years, marked by a dependence on parents for food and protection. This postweaning period of helplessness and dependence is biologically unique, he argues, because in most other social mammals, including nonhuman primates, offspring go directly from weaning to independence — though with many primates, offspring nurse much longer, on the order of four or five years. Once the brain and teeth have completed their initial development by age six or seven, Bogin argues, humans enter a juvenile stage that lasts until puberty. The offspring, while not sexually mature, no longer are utterly dependent on their parents for food and survival. These may seem like subtle distinctions, but they assume enormous evolutionary significance when we compare the life history of humans to that of other mammals.

Inevitably, there have been attempts to discern loftier aspects of human development along with physical growth. During the heyday of eugenics, Francis Galton virtually fetishized the measurement of head size, believing that the so-called cephalic index was a powerful indication of intellectual prowess. That impulse found its way into very large, school-based size surveys in the United States at the turn of the century. William T. Porter measured the head sizes of some thirty-five thousand schoolchildren in the St. Louis area in 1895, arguing that these measurements — and height in general — reflected the dimensions of mental capacity. But physical anthropologists, Franz Boas being foremost among them, dashed those hopes, and for decades the idea of correlating physical growth with mental maturation became a sensitive area of research. Growth scientists stepped gingerly when they revisited the idea after World War II.

Using longitudinal data from the pioneering Berkeley Growth Study, Nancy Bayley and her colleagues at the University of California were among the first to attempt to chart, in a rigorous scientific fashion, the intellectual and emotional growth of children in parallel with their physical changes. When she described some of the initial results at a meeting of the American Psychological Association in 1954, however, her charts and graphs bore several sobering messages. One was that intellectual and emotional maturation did not track as easily as inches and pounds. The instruments of measurement were vague, limited, and contingent. Second, the children who were intensely studied in Berkeley displayed unique, almost defiantly idiosyncratic patterns of development. In other words, they were utterly normal yet infinitely variable. And, less obvious then than now, the measurements of "intelligence" were very much limited by the science that created the instruments. Bayley's pioneering effort to assess psychological maturation was ahead of its time, but the motivation behind it was timeless and something any parent could identify with. "We want to be able to predict, to know *how*, and how early we can tell what a child will turn out to be like," Bayley said. That burning curiosity to track physical growth longitudinally while documenting behavioral and mental maturation was effectively abandoned in the 1960s. Only recently have researchers rekindled it in studies that connect pubertal timing with social, psychological, and intellectual performance.

Many growth-related medical problems become apparent during early childhood. Growth failure can be due to hormonal problems (such as growth-hormone or, more commonly, thyroid deficiency), kidney and liver diseases, gastrointestinal disorders (such as celiac disease or inflammatory bowel disease), a chromosomal disorder in girls known as Turner's syndrome, poor nutrition, or simply psychological stress. The availability of limitless amounts of genetically engineered human growth hormone has transformed the treatment of many of these growth-related disorders, but there is a cruel irony in the use of this drug. Size — specifically, short stature — becomes an issue of intense psychological urgency for boys and their parents around the time of puberty (that is, around age twelve). But by that time, according to many growth experts, intervention with growth hormone treatment is only of limited value. Indeed, some endocrinologists refuse to treat children with growth hormone at that age. The flip side is that at earlier ages, boys of small stature may not be nearly so psychologically conscious of their size and its consequences. And the final irony is that most of those short-stature boys, once they finish their growth spurt (however delayed), will find themselves smack in the land of normal.

I WANT TO return to that schoolyard scene for just a moment. The fourth-grade girls, among them my daughter, are still standing apart, ignoring the rambunctious boys around them, who continue to hurl their spaldeens against the brick wall and travel in little retaliatory packs, punishing other boys who have failed to catch the ball without muffing it. The girls stand in the midst of this maelstrom, calmly talking about books and clothes and (if a few overheard conversations at birthday parties are any indication) how immature they find most of the males in their peer group. They, by contrast, appear focused, self-possessed, more mature. In fact, they are peering at their male classmates across one of the deepest divides of early-childhood growth: gender.

In the race to puberty, boys are behind girls literally out of the box. Girls gain their lead in growth halfway through the fetal period. Their skeletal development in utero is about three weeks ahead of that of boys. By the time of a normal, full-term birth, they are about four to six weeks ahead of boys in their development and continuing to pull away. This trend continues through much of early childhood.

Development, it should be added, is not the same thing as size. At the moment of birth, boys, on average, are slightly larger and grow slightly faster than girls, but only for a short while. By seven months, boys and girls have the same growth velocity, and then girls start to pick up the tempo, maturing faster until about age four. Their teeth emerge earlier — their canine teeth erupt almost a year earlier, on average, than those of boys, and their first molars appear about two months earlier. By twenty-one months of age, girls, on average, reach the halfway point on their journey to adult height. That doesn't happen in boys until twenty-four months, so they are already three months behind.

Why do girls mature earlier than boys? The differences in the timing of tooth maturation, bone formation, and the development of other parts of the anatomy "must represent the small change of evolutionary advantage through some better cooperative arrangements for survival and for the rearing of young," Tanner speculates, "but it is hard now to guess what they might have been. The earlier maturing of females is a characteristic shared by many mammals and nearly all primates so far examined." Although it mischievously overstates the science to suggest that boys are born to be immature, the biology argues strongly that they are slower to mature, on average, than girls.

If, as often happens, boys become larger than girls during later childhood, the size difference is slight and is quickly obliterated when girls rev into their adolescent growth spurt, which happens months if not years before most boys do. The "typical" girl in the United States begins her adolescent growth spurt at about age ten and reaches peak velocity — the highest rate of growth — about eighteen months later. Boys are typically two years behind. The figures vary from country to country and change over time.

When the growth curves of girls and boys are shown on the same chart, there is a fateful intersection — as much sociological and psychological as biological — where the two lines cross and girls are, on average, taller than boys. This temporary height superiority lasts for only a couple of years but clearly has important psychological implications for boys. "Catch-up growth" is traditionally a medical term, referring to the way an undernourished, ill, or otherwise sluggishly growing child can make up the deficit with rapid growth. But there is also a psychological dimension for boys, because throughout much of childhood, and especially during preadolescence, they are struggling to catch up with girls.

The delayed pubertal growth spurt of boys has a bit of a silver lining, however. It allows males to build a higher launch pad for their growth spurt when it finally comes. In recent years, the average height difference between men and women has been thirteen centimeters, or about five inches. Most of that difference, on the order of eight to ten centimeters, is achieved before the growth spurt. And when girls reach a certain developmental threshold — probably in the amount of circulating sex hormones they have, which occurs about eighteen months after they reach their peak rate of adolescent growth — the growth show is over for them. As mentioned in the previous chapter, the sex hormones seal the growth plates, and adult height is essentially reached at this time. The two-year lag is the price boys pay for an extra couple of years of prepubertal growth. That growth is the reason men, on average, end up taller than women.

WE TAKE THESE developments so much for granted that we rarely step back and appreciate the singularity and wonder of human childhood. The vast majority of other animals do not enjoy the luxury of a prolonged growth process. Mice, to cite but one example, go from weaning to reproductive maturity in three weeks. In many animal species, according to endocrinologist William F. Crowley Jr., there simply is no "childhood" and no puberty at all. And although the general shape of human growth curves is shared by apes and monkeys, Mother Nature has bestowed on humans a much more extended childhood. Chimpanzees, for example, nurse longer, have their adolescent growth spurt on average around age five, and are able to reproduce (at least in captivity) by age nine.

Clearly, the relative delay in human adolescence allows the development of a more sophisticated brain and perhaps a larger body, but it has been grist for speculation among auxologists and evolutionary biologists for decades. "The prolongation of the time between weaning and puberty appears to be an evolutionary step taken by the primates, reaching its most pronounced development in Man," Tanner writes in *Fetus into Man*. "The increased time necessary for the maturing of the primate brain has been sandwiched into this period. At least some of the evolutionary reasons are not hard to find. It is probably advantageous for learning, especially learning cooperation in group and family social life, to take place while the individual remains relatively docile and before he comes into sexual competition with older individuals."

Barry Bogin recalls reading Tanner's thoughts on human evolution in the 1970s and thinking, "There must be more to it than that!" In the past thirty years, he has synthesized a great deal of research from growth scientists, anthropologists, and biologists to propose a "life history" model of human evolution, which argues that a protracted childhood and adolescence has allowed humans to cultivate language skills that lead very directly to our cultural success as a species.

The "dilemma" of human development begins with a long-recognized paradox. As early human ancestors became hunter-gatherers, survival was enhanced by bipedal movement for more efficient locomotion. But this came at a price: bipedalism selects for a narrower pelvis, and that in turn makes childbearing more difficult and dangerous. How could human females deliver a big-brained child through a narrow pelvis? Evolution's answer was to defer much of the brain's enormous growth until after birth. Bogin cites research suggesting that humans devote much more metabolic effort during infancy and childhood to the brain than do other primates. In newborn humans, for example, 87 percent of the resting metabolic rate is devoted to the brain, whereas in chimpanzees it is 44 percent. At age five, the human brain still sucks up 45 percent of metabolic energy, while in chimps it sinks to 20 percent.

But childhood is about more than brain building. To succeed, according to Darwin's ultimate scoreboard, animals must reproduce and send hardy offspring into the future, and childhood confers an advantage to humans in this respect. The early cessation of maternal nursing and the cultivation of familial and social networks of childcare have allowed human females to reproduce every couple of years. By contrast, chimpanzee females do not wean their offspring until they are four or five years old, thus postponing the next cycle of reproduction. At the same time, humans put off childbearing until relatively late. This sounds like a disadvantage, but a recent theory argues that it is not.

Bogin and linguist John Locke of Lehman College in New York recently published a fascinating paper arguing that the extended childhood and delayed adolescence of humans allows us to develop the language skills to select better mates, develop social cooperation, and intellectually mature before reproduction. A prolonged childhood, in this view, gives us an advantage in terms of building up human capital — language, social intelligence, and the creation of social networks — that increases the odds of survival for our offspring.

Childhood itself appears to be a relatively recent invention. Bogin suggests that it grew out of the hominid ancestor *Homo habilis*, about 2.6 million years ago. Some research suggests that it might even be more recent. In 2004 researchers at the Max Planck Institute for Evolutionary Anthropology in Leipzig, Germany, did some clever experiments suggesting that childhood may have emerged as a prominent feature of human biology in the past 500,000 to 1 million years — in evolutionary time scales, quite recently. They ventured this conclusion after subjecting the 1.8 million-year-old fossil of a *Homo erectus* infant's skull to a CT scan to calculate its brain volume. In so doing, they realized that the child's brain size resembled that of modern apes but was smaller than that of modern humans. This may sound contrary to expectation at first, but what it suggests is that the well-established larger volume of human versus other primate brains is the evolutionary product not of gestation, but of growth after birth. This finding lends experimental evidence in support of the growing notion that childhood is a major factor in distinguishing humans from all other creatures. An extended childhood allows the brain not simply to grow, but to develop formidable neural patterns of connection forged by experience. It demands prolonged childcare by parents, with all the socializing implications of such relationships. It allows learning, especially the learning of language, with all its cultural implications. As the science writer Sharon Begley recently suggested, "It took childhood to produce truly modern humans."

Put another, cruder way, an extended childhood gives us a better chance to learn how to act civilized before the sex hormones kick in. But, as we'll find in the next several chapters, all that learning does not inevitably produce more civilized behavior. We learn — very early — that aggression has its rewards. We learn that children with a larger body size get their way more often. We learn to assess the physical strength of our peers, both through play and through increasingly sophisticated cognitive analysis based on visual examination and social memory. And, alas, very early on, we learn how to bully.

5

THE BULLY INSIDE ME
The Consequences of Being a Bully

> It should be noted that the games of children are not games,
> and must be considered as their most serious actions.
>
> — MICHEL DE MONTAIGNE, "Essays"

I CAN STILL PICTURE the contemptuous curl to his lip, his diffident manner, his name, the place, the time. Sixth grade, morning recess. It was late in September, cool but not chilly. I remember the sky being mostly blue, with high, gauzy clouds. The sixth-grade boys had gathered on the asphalt playground behind the school. As boys are wont to do, we were running around playing a game called Whoever Gets It, Gets It, in which a ball was flung in the air and whoever caught it attempted to evade a swarm of tacklers. The girls stood along the edge of the playground. They may have been jumping rope; they may have been talking. I can't say I troubled myself to notice. I was too busy rabble-rousing.

It was the fall of 1962, in a small town in western Pennsylvania. I was ten years old, soon to turn eleven. There was a fair amount of tugging and scrapping and grabbing at the ball as the game continued, and I got tangled up with another boy. At first our tussle was just about the ball.

Then I noticed who the other boy was. His name was Jimmy. And in a mindless, split-second escalation of animosities, we stopped fighting over the ball and started fighting each other.

We ended up grappling with each other, wrestling and rolling and twisting, struggling for the advantage. At one point, his shoe failed to gain a purchase on the asphalt, and his feet began to slide. I gained enough leverage to flip him to the ground, hard. He ended up ripping his pants, just over the knee. His chest heaving, he staggered away. Suddenly, the bell announced the end of recess. No adult witnessed or broke up the altercation. It probably began and ended within thirty seconds.

Even as we filed back into the classroom, two thoughts competed for primacy in my hyperventilating brain. First, I was intensely proud. I had won the fight, such as it was. Second, I was ashamed, because I knew my aggressive behavior had been emboldened by a campaign of intimidation and social exclusion that had gone on for weeks. Perhaps that is why, when classmates whispered "Way to go" or patted me on the back, I had mixed feelings.

As I've described the incident up to this point, I've made it seem like a confrontation that grew out of the heat of the moment. But like many episodes of school antagonism, this one had a history. We had been teasing and taunting and ignoring Jimmy since the beginning of the school year. Was it smallness that made Jimmy different? Not entirely. He was certainly smaller than most of the other boys, but not much smaller (if at all) than I was. Was it his name? His last name was Finkelstein, and I wonder now, with the perspective of decades, if our animosity betrayed a kind of mindless, group anti-Semitism that came easily to small blue-collar communities like ours. Was it his age or his intelligence? Well, in that regard he *was* different, and that's why he was despised by all the other sixth-grade boys. Jimmy had just been moved up a grade — he was a year younger (and thus a little smaller) and obviously clever. He also possessed a somewhat abrasive, unyielding attitude that suggested he didn't understand his proper place in the very rigid pecking order of sixth-grade boys. All of these factors contributed to Jimmy's "difference," and from the first day of school, he was marked for subtle insult, social shunning, and, finally, on that morning in the playground, physical assault.

As a parent — indeed, as the parent of a child who has been moved up a grade in certain subjects — I'm now horrified by the cruel and estranging violence that can be visited upon a child whose greatest social sin may be academic excellence. As a onetime, short-lived bully, however, I also recognize the avenging dynamic of groupthink when it comes to picking victims, and the relentless, targeted campaigns of casual belligerence, both emotional and physical, that gain momentum in a school setting. I also think that the incident teaches us a lesson about bullying — one that has been borne out in recent research, and one that becomes an essential component of life on either extreme of the growth chart: size per se, especially small size, does not beget bullying so much as difference in general does. Smaller children *do* get bullied more often than larger children, but physical size is merely one flavor of variation. And a child's experience of bullying, as perpetrator or victim, can feel like a life-altering event.

At a distance of more than forty years, I'm surprised by the degree of detail I can recall. I think it's partly because of the remorse I felt at the time. Soon after the playground altercation, I had to be hospitalized for a week with an infection. As I lay in the hospital bed one day, watching the 1962 World Series on TV, my mother came in with a pile of get-well cards that my classmates had sent. I distinctly remember the one from Jimmy, because its clipped tone was conspicuously grudging, its handwriting hasty with insincerity. I was later told that he had initially refused to write a card at all; our teacher, Mrs. Fattman, had made him do it. He hated me, and I couldn't blame him. From his point of view, I was the frontman for an oppressive mob. (Jim Finkelstein didn't remember the fight when I tracked him down in Georgia, where he is a successful lawyer and ran in the Democratic primary for the U.S. Senate in 2004, but he vividly remembered being an outcast in sixth grade. "There was absolutely no question that I was miserable," he said. "I went from being an average kid to being what was [considered] small, and it probably changed my whole life. Kids need to be with a group they can be with, physically and socially.")

My scuffle with Jimmy suggests to me that anyone is capable of bullying, as protagonist or as part of the supporting cast, under the right circumstances. The obvious aspect of physical confrontation aside, bullying gains its power most of all as a form of psychological warfare between individuals of uneven power. Physical size is a component in those asymmetric power relationships, as studies have repeatedly shown, but so is social rank, appearance, behavior, and even general health. And such incidents, invariably brief, can have a lasting impact. My career as a bully lasted about fifteen minutes, but I'm going to use it as an excuse to talk about the role of size in creating bullies and physical aggressors. Since the psychology of victimhood is so different, and my career as a victim of bullying so much longer and distinguished, I'll address those issues in a later chapter that discusses puberty.

PIETER BRUEGEL'S 1560 painting *Kinderspiele* ("Children's Games") is a time capsule that captures the long history of physical aggression among children. Amid the traditional child's play of rolling hoops and leapfrog and tug of war, several gangs of peasant youth can be seen engaged in an equally traditional but less innocent form of child's play. In one corner, half a dozen ruffians have grabbed a boy by the hands and feet and are dragging the lad, who looks singularly alarmed, across a board. Nearby, two boys are walloping a third with their fists while another youth lies on the ground, looking stunned and rubbing his aching head. The Bruegel painting makes clear that nearly half a millennium ago, boys would be boys, capable of taunting, teasing, and physically ganging up on others. The victims peopling this scene also wear timeless expressions: of dread, anxiety, and hurt.

Bullying is far older than Bruegel, but our heightened sensitivity to it is recent, largely the result of highly publicized, media-driven accounts of some horrifying modern episodes. A certain macabre thread runs through many recent press accounts of bullying. When a sixteen-year-old Canadian schoolboy was found dead in June 2001 in Stony Plain, Alberta, news reports were quick to point out that Gilles Moreau was "regularly picked-on" and "had difficulty fitting in." According to a classmate quoted by the Canadian Broadcasting Company (CBC), "People used to throw him in garbage cans and leave him for over two hours and he used to do nothing. He used to still consider them friends and I don't think he deserved what he got." The boy's mother, according to the CBC account, "said her son was singled out because he was small and wore glasses. He also had a learning disability."

In cases where bullying is associated, or may be associated, with death, either suicide or homicide, huge amounts of attention focus on the incidents — a cultural sensitivity that has been heightened by the rash of school shootings in recent years. The most obvious is the Columbine High School massacre in Littleton, Colorado, in 1999, in which bullying was said to be a contributing factor in the mindsets of the perpetrators. Before that, syndicated columnist Bob Greene held the media flashlight on the story of an eighth-grade honor student in Burlington, Iowa, named Curtis Taylor, who had endured years of physical and verbal abuse, finally got worn down by the treatment, and shot himself to death in 1993. And before that, a pioneering group of psychologists in a different part of the world investigated the suicides of three boys, ages ten to fourteen, in northern Norway in 1982. Provoked by bullying, these suicides touched off a regional round of soul-searching about the problem. The Norwegian incident led to the first systematic nationwide study of bullying and the birth of bullying as a legitimate area of academic and social inquiry.

The dean of modern bullying studies is Dan Olweus, a Swedish psychologist based at the University of Bergen in Norway. It is no accident that a detail from Bruegel's *Kinderspiele* appears on the cover of Olweus's book *Bullying at School*. Although the problem has been around and documented at least since the mid-sixteenth century, only in the 1970s, and only in Scandinavia, did the study of bullying rise to the level of academic respectability and social urgency. Olweus's first paper on the subject appeared in 1973. Barely a decade later, the 1982 tragedy in Norway catapulted Olweus — and the study of bullying — into international prominence.

Olweus defines bullying as follows: "A student is being bullied or victimized when he or she is exposed, repeatedly and over time, to negative actions on the part of one or more other students." He goes on to define "negative action" as "when someone intentionally inflicts, or attempts to inflict, injury or discomfort upon another — basically what is implied in the definition of aggressive behavior." Inflicting discomfort is a baggy definition that obviously gathers a lot of behavior in its capacious reach. Being brutally honest with someone, for example, often inflicts discomfort. But the spirit of Olweus's definition is clear, and its breadth has the virtue of including nonphysical forms of verbal aggression that many children recognize from firsthand experience as no less painful. With this working definition, Olweus and his colleagues launched a massive school survey in Norway and Sweden in the 1980s to discover how prevalent the phenomenon was. They discovered not only that bullying was very widespread, but also that it began early in childhood and was rooted in school environments.

The Scandinavian researchers found that about 15 percent of elementary and middle school children reported occasional or frequent involvement in bullying either as aggressors or victims. More than 9 percent — almost one in ten children — were the victims of bullying. Olweus's team reported that bullying was worse in elementary school children than in children in grades seven to nine, and that bullies tended to be older than their victims. As he later put it, "It is the younger and weaker students who reported being most exposed." Boys were more often exposed to bullying than girls, and bullying among boys tended to be more physical than among girls. Although it seems unremarkable now, the Scandinavian researchers also turned some of the conventional wisdom about the geography of bullying on its head. Whereas it had long been argued that most bullying occurred during trips to and from school, their results showed that "the school is without doubt where most of the bullying occurs" — to which I add an anecdotal "Amen."

With Olweus's work, research on bullying took off in Europe and Australia; less so in the United States. Such research has been a respected staple of childhood development in Norway, Finland, England, Scotland, Ireland, and Canada for decades, and consequently those societies were the first to move on to the next phase of the campaign: designing programs to reduce the amount of bullying in schools.

Despite certain limitations in methodology, the literature on bullying converges on several salient truths. The first is the notion of an imbalance of power between the tormentor and the tormented. This imbalance is often physical. Linda D. Voss and Jean Mulligan, researchers at the Wessex Growth Study in England, published a paper in 2000 showing that "short boys were more than twice as likely as control boys to be victims and much more likely than control boys to say that bullying upset them." This finding is particularly significant because Voss and her colleagues have published multiple studies arguing that children of short stature do not, in general, suffer unusual psychological disability.

An imbalance of power need not be physical. With heightened adult scrutiny of physical intimidation in recent years, experts have come to recognize another, subtler form of psychological violence that can rise to the level of bullying. They have found that the imbalance also can be social (the popular kid versus the outcast, or the established kid versus the newcomer, as I was with Jimmy) or numerical. Despite the cliché of the lone, belligerent bully towering over the cowering sissy, many studies have shown that bullies often act in groups. The classic word for bullying in Norwegian (and Danish) is "mobbing," and early research in Scandinavia made clear that bullying is often a group activity. Olweus refers to the supporting cast as "passive bullies" or "henchmen." In other words, bullying is a much more complex social phenomenon than simply big versus small.

Bullying comes in distinct gender flavors as well. Boys tend to be overt in their physical and verbal abuse, while girls tend to be more indirect and psychological, shunning particular children or spreading unflattering gossip about them. The age of computers, e-mail, and instant messaging has provided greater technical means for spreading mischief, with the added cover of digital anonymity. Experts now include "cyber bullying" as part of the package.

Whether bullying takes the physical form of shoving and bumping or the psychological form of exclusion and verbal humiliation, it is the inherent imbalance of power that makes the behavior so insidious. Feeling outnumbered or outmuscled contributes to the sense of helplessness that invariably accompanies an unpleasant situation that is repeated on a daily or weekly basis and about which you feel you can do nothing. Thinking back on the circumstances surrounding my scuffle with Jimmy and viewing them through the filter of recent research, I realize that what made my behavior bullying was not so much the playground fight as the power imbalance that had been unfolding since the beginning of the school year: the difference in age, the fact that Jimmy was new to the school, and the regrettable fact that, for weeks prior to the fight, I had participated in what had been organized, persistent shunning of the new kid by most of the other boys in the class. The fight itself was almost an afterthought — albeit an afterthought that has lived on for decades. That's part of the power of bullying.

Another emerging truth is that a bully's apprenticeship most often begins when the child is still in diapers. Bullying has been observed in children as young as two years of age, and Olweus reported in 1993 that 17.5 percent of second-grade boys said they had been bullied. Beyond elementary school, the percentage of boys who admitted to bullying others, he found, tended to peak during middle school (roughly grades five to nine) and diminish during high school. By ninth grade, according to the same Olweus study, only 6.4 percent of boys and 3 percent of girls reported being bullied. Although bullying may decrease during adolescence, the stakes may be much higher in terms of the potential for dreadful humiliation — but more about that later.

HOW IS A bully created? Or, restated in a slightly narrower way, how does a child become a physical aggressor, and what role does size play in that transformation? The answer, at least according to a scientist who has done exemplary research in this area for many years, is that size matters, but physical aggression is not learned. It is present from the earliest moments of conscious behavior in virtually every child. Most children simply unlearn physical aggression as part of normal socialization. The children who fail to become socialized at a very early age are the ones who tend to enter a developmental trajectory that often (though not inevitably) passes through stages of bullying, delinquency, antisocial behavior, violence, and crime. No one has identified and illustrated these trajectories better than a Canadian researcher named Richard E. Tremblay.

Those who think that bullying is a latter-day obsession of touchy-feely parents probably skipped philosophy and classics courses in college, because the early education of children has been, as Tremblay points out in his essay "The Origins of Youth Violence," the subject of extensive philosophic musing. It stretches from Rousseau, Hobbes, and Erasmus all the way back to Plato. Tremblay suggests that the study of childhood aggression has not qualitatively moved much beyond the insights offered by Saint Augustine in the fifth century A.D. "Thus it is not the infant's will that is harmless," Augustine wrote of infant aggression in his *Confessions*, "but the weakness of infant limbs . . . These things are easily put up with; not because they are of little or no account, but because they will disappear with increase in age. This you can prove from the fact that the same things cannot be borne with patience when detected in an older person." Indeed, for the past thirty years, Tremblay has assembled a huge amount of scientific data (through longitudinal research) in support of Saint Augustine's observations. Augustine, says Tremblay, "may have written the most sensible page on the development of aggression . . . 1,600 years ago!"

The indirect influence of James Tanner's work on growth reaches even into the field of childhood aggression. Tremblay received his doctorate in the 1970s at the University of London, where his group often interacted with Tanner's eclectic team of growth scientists at the Institute of Child Health. Tremblay came away from those encounters convinced of the power of longitudinal research to chart behavioral changes tied to human development. While Olweus focused on bullying, with both its physical and verbal aspects, Tremblay deliberately narrowed his focus to physical aggression. Over the past three decades, his group at the University of Montreal has studied youth violence. If his results are to be believed — and he has undertaken some of the best-controlled, longest-running longitudinal studies in the field of childhood development — physical aggression (and, by extension, certain forms of bullying) begins in infancy, begins at home, and, in a metaphoric sense, may even begin in the womb.

It took quite a while for Tremblay to realize that aggression emerges so early. From the late 1960s to the mid-1970s, he worked with prison populations and criminal offenders in mental hospitals, trying to reduce the incidence of aggression in these populations through psychological counseling. "I started to work with adults, and realized that we were not having the impact that we were hoping to have," he told me. "So then I worked with juvenile delinquents, and this led me to realize that a deep, deep treatment was not having the impact we were expecting, so that led me to work with kindergarten children." That was in the early 1980s, at which point Tremblay, by then based at the University of Montreal, began longitudinal studies of young children in a lower-class French Canadian neighborhood in Montreal. "This led us to realize that physical aggression was not what we were thinking," Tremblay said. "It wasn't that children were learning to physically aggress." It was the exact opposite.

"All the longitudinal studies that I've looked at in the past five or six years are all coming to the conclusion that the peak of physical aggression is in early childhood and decreases with age," Tremblay said. "The peak is at around two to three years of age. So now we've been following children from birth and hoping to follow them up until adulthood, to be able to really get the picture right." Thirty years after attempting to treat physical aggression in prison inmates and other adults, he has concluded that the best time to intervene is during infancy. "Physical aggression is there early, by the end of the first year of life," he said. "And it increases rapidly between twelve months and thirty-six months, and then starts going down."

If this suggests that toddlers are protodelinquents in diapers, that's exactly what Tremblay's data show. "Let me just come back to the bullying part," he continued. "The people who study bullying, using this sort of global concept, have been focusing on schoolchildren, either elementary-school or adolescents, or adults. But it's very clear that the bullying is starting as soon as the physical aggression — so by the end of the first year of life. We've been filming children, very young children, and the amount of bullying that's going on is *tremendous!* Between twelve and forty-eight months of age, the bullying is there. It's not organized in the same way that it is later on, when psychologically it becomes much more complex. But an eighteen-month-old boy who wants a toy that another one has will bully to get it. He won't start talking to the other child, try-ing to convince him. He will not use psychological bullying. He will just go in there. And the threatening part of bullying is there *very* early."

After age two or three, according to Tremblay's research, physical ag-gression diminishes, but indirect forms of aggression — particularly ver-bal aggression — increase. And there is a gender component to this, too. "We see that girls are using indirect aggression much more than boys, and that they start earlier, so there's a big sex difference," he told me. "Girls use less physical aggression than boys." This suggests that there may even be a developmental component to the generally nonphysical form of aggression preferred by girls.

"Fortunately, because of their size, physical aggression from two-year-olds does not constitute a major threat to the public," Tremblay has wryly noted. But, as research by Tremblay and others suggests, it does represent a threat to the future of the bullying child. If children do not learn to control these socially disruptive behaviors by the time they enter school, they have already embarked on a trajectory that will have a profound im-pact on their lives, as well as on the lives of others. This includes not only the children they may bully in school but also the adolescent violence they may wreak, the spouses they may later abuse, the offspring they may similarly abuse, and the crimes against society they may ultimately com-mit.

A very large study published in 1984, based on a survey of more than sixteen thousand Canadian children from age four to age eleven, showed that four-year-old boys and girls displayed the highest levels of physical aggression, while the eleven-year-olds showed the lowest. This is not to say that aggressive behavior entirely disappeared. To the contrary, "indi-rect aggression" — defined as "behavior aimed at hurting someone with-out the use of physical aggression" — increased with age in both boys and girls, and in girls more than in boys. Tremblay suggests that "the process of socialization may involve learning to use indirect means of aggression rather than physical aggression."

This raises an interesting question. If, as Tremblay argues, the frequency of physical aggression is at its highest at the end of the second year after birth, at what age does it begin? The notion of "onset" is tricky, but the results of recent work, based on another longitudinal study, of children in Quebec, by the Montreal group, make clear that physical aggression begins very early. By age seventeen months, about 90 percent of a large group of infants were, in the view of their own mothers, physically aggressive toward others at least some of the time.

What does any of this have to do with growth and size? First, we often forget — and Tremblay's work sharply reminds us — that the first two years of growth in any child are physiologically tumultuous and psychologically convulsive. In the first twenty-four months after birth, babies essentially grow to half of their ultimate mature height and nearly triple their weight. From a state of near-total physical helplessness at birth, when they are unable even to raise their heads or roll over, they increasingly acquire physical mastery of their environments — grasping objects at around six months, crawling at around nine months, walking at around twelve months, running and climbing stairs by twenty-four months.

To these exploding physical capabilities are added dramatically increased cognitive recognition of the self and others. Of primary importance in this environmental education is social activity. As Tremblay puts it, "The frequency and complexity of interactions between babies and other persons in their environments increase at least as rapidly as their physical growth." More and more, these interactions involve negotiations with others, especially over the possession of objects. With only rudimentary tools of communication and self-discipline, these interactions often lead to conflict, and conflict very often leads to physical aggression. Thus, Tremblay believes, the social learning that occurs in toddlers, at precisely the moment when they are faced with the need for communication skills and self-control, is crucial to the long-term trajectory they will travel in terms of physical aggression. As he writes, "Learning to wait for something you want (delay of gratification) and learning to use language to convince others to satisfy your needs may be the most important protective factors against chronic physical aggression." In other words, the elementary school bully probably enters kindergarten with a temperamental inclination toward physical aggression because he or she has not been socialized by then.

Very early on, physical size seems to contribute to that temperament. In a fascinating large-scale study of children growing up in the island nation of Mauritius, researchers focused on a large group of three-year-olds beginning in 1972. The researchers — led by psychologist Adrian Raine of the University of Southern California and crime expert David P. Farrington of Cambridge University — measured three particular aspects of the children's physical and psychological development: body size, novelty-seeking behavior, and fearlessness. (In terms of body size, the researchers used a measure of "bulk" rather than the more conventional body mass index (BMI), with the argument that BMI is a better marker for obesity than large size per se.) Eight years later, the researchers went back and assessed physical aggression in the same youngsters when they were eleven years old. They found that greater body size at age three, as well as greater fearlessness and greater sensation seeking, predicted greater aggression at age eleven. In a 1998 paper, they wrote that "children with increased height and body size early in life may, through instrumental learning processes, learn that use of aggression can be an effective strategy in winning social conflicts. Such children would be more likely to have aggression reinforced, in contrast to smaller children, who do not have the physical capacity to successfully execute physical coercion." In an innovative follow-up to this longitudinal study, Raine and colleagues showed that a surprisingly simple program of intervention — enriched nutrition, physical exercise, and education — with children ages three to five resulted in a lower incidence, relative to a control group, of antisocial behavior at age seventeen and less criminal behavior at age twenty-three. Among other things, the Mauritius longitudinal study is notable because the children were largely Indian or African Creoles. Many other studies of childhood aggression, arriving at similar conclusions, have been done in Western populations.

In this endless chicken-and-egg hunt for the origins of aggressive behavior, Tremblay and his collaborators began yet another research project in 1996, this time focusing on babies as young as five months of age. They looked for factors that might be associated with the emergence of physical aggression by age three and a half years. Because the study was longitudinal, researchers followed the development of specific children over time. Mothers were the primary source of information, rating their own infants on frequency of hitting, biting, kicking, fighting, and bullying. The good news is that the vast majority of children in the study were generally tractable: about 58 percent had a trajectory of modest aggression, and another 28 percent displayed little or no physical aggression. But approximately 14 percent of the infants followed a path of high physical aggression from the earliest months of life. (The overall numbers were considerable for a study of this kind, with some 572 families participating.) When Tremblay's group analyzed the factors that predicted, at or before birth, a child's likelihood to be among the most physically aggressive children, a number of familial factors popped out. The more aggressive children tended to have younger siblings and to have mothers who exhibited "high levels of antisocial behavior before the end of high school," who began to have children early, who tended to come from low-income families, and who smoked during pregnancy.

By the time a child was five months old, several other factors emerged as important predictors of a trajectory toward high physical aggression. Among these factors were family dysfunction and what researchers called "coercive parenting behavior" by the mother. Overall, the most aggressive children seemed to have mothers who displayed high levels of antisocial behavior and bore children early. The study claimed to show, for the first time, that "the intergenerational transmission of antisocial behavior probably starts as early as infancy with high levels of physical aggression." Only a longitudinal study of this sort could begin to tease out the way nurture, alongside genes, shapes aggressive behavior in the future. And even then, the analysis of the impact of environment was nuanced: poverty was a significant predictor of aggression but single parenthood was not. It hardly comes as a surprise that family dysfunction and "coercive" parenting would predict high levels of physical aggression in children. The surprise, if the Tremblay results hold up, is that these factors in the first year of a child's life exert such a powerful and lasting influence.

If bullies are made in infancy, of course, it is not entirely preposterous to ask if they are made, in part, even before birth. In other words, is there something going on between a mother and a child in utero that sets up a proclivity for bullying after birth — a proclivity that is triggered, for example, by being larger than other children? Tremblay told me that he has a clinical trial currently under way in Quebec to test the idea that psychological counseling of pregnant mothers and their families prior to a child's birth may diminish the likelihood that the child will become physically aggressive. This represents nothing less than a radical psychosocial vaccination against bullying before a child is even born.

AS SOMEONE WHO both bullied and was bullied, someone who knows firsthand and marrow-deep how profound an influence this kind of behavior has on childhood and adolescent development, I am dumbfounded that no solid national data on the prevalence of bullying in the United States existed prior to 2001. That is when researchers at the National Institutes of Health, led by epidemiologist Tonja Nansel, published a report in the *Journal of the American Medical Association* (*JAMA*). This much-discussed and important study occurred, if not as an afterthought, at least as an appendage to a much larger study, which was conceived, organized, coordinated, and executed by European researchers.

The American researchers gathered their data in 1996 as part of a continuing survey of adolescent health run by the World Health Organization (WHO), according to Mary Overpeck, an epidemiological statistician then at the federal Health Resources and Services Administration in Bethesda, Maryland, who was one of the senior authors of the *JAMA* paper. WHO had been coordinating these international health studies since 1984, and, as Overpeck recalled, the Europeans, inspired by Dan Olweus's early work, had already been measuring the incidence of bullying. The American study, funded by the National Institute of Child Health and Human Development (NICHHD), used a questionnaire mandated by European researchers who had been tracking the incidence of bullying for many years. "When we went into the international studies, the questions [about bullying] were already there," Overpeck explained. "We were kind of tagging along with them."

The American findings, however belated, helped establish how widespread and significant the behavior is. Some 15,686 students in grades six through ten at public, private, and Catholic schools throughout the country participated in the study, and although questionnaires have their limitations, the numbers were substantial. Overpeck, who has studied childhood health issues for decades, said the late-1990s survey "was the first time where we had enough numbers. We've got kids' perceptions, which is about as good as anything, because it reflects their behaviors and their fears. Both teachers and parents don't really know what's going on." And according to this study, there's a lot going on. The main result is that nearly a third of the children (29.9 percent) reported "moderate or frequent involvement in bullying." About 13 percent identified themselves as bullies, 10.6 percent as victims of bullying, and 6.3 percent as both bullies and victims.

These percentages translate into staggering numbers of incidents of childhood aggression. Extrapolated to the entire U.S. school population, these results would indicate that about 3.7 million young people from grades six to ten (roughly ages eleven to fifteen) perpetrate moderate or frequent bullying and approximately 3.2 million are victims of a similar degree of aggression. "Males both bullied others and were bullied more often than females," Nansel and her colleagues wrote. "Bullying occurred most frequently in sixth through eighth grade . . . Males reported being bullied by being hit, slapped, or pushed more frequently than did females. Females more frequently reported being bullied through rumors or sexual comments." In the midst of all this pushing, shoving, whispering, and innuendo, the researchers also managed to identify a surprising code of behavioral honor that cropped up in the data. They concluded that racism did not appear to be a factor in bullying, noting that black youngsters reported significantly less bullying than children from other ethnic groups. "It may be more socially acceptable," the authors wrote, "for a youth to taunt peers about their appearance than to make derogatory racial statements."

Since the bullying data represented a small slice of a much larger survey of health behaviors in students, the researchers also were able to draw more general conclusions about the psychological health of bullies and their victims. They found that bullies tended to have a larger constellation of behavioral problems — more likely to drink and smoke, more likely to struggle academically — yet they didn't completely conform to the thuggish, antisocial stereotype. Bullies, for example, "reported greater ease of making friends," the authors noted. This observation indirectly complements one of Tremblay's more interesting findings: that the transition from physical aggression at a young age to indirect (or verbal) aggression at an older age is often associated with the emergence of social leadership.

And the victims? Children who were bullied, according to the researchers, "demonstrated poorer social and emotional adjustment, reporting greater difficulty making friends, poorer relationships with classmates, and greater loneliness." In a larger sense, they didn't fit in. Children who both bullied and were bullied had their own set of problems: poor social and emotional adjustment, social isolation, poor academic performance, and more problem behaviors.

As someone who experienced both the triumph of being a bully and the agony of being a victim of bullying, I was naturally surprised to see this dual existence described in the *JAMA* paper as "an especially high risk group." Olweus had previously characterized this subset of bullied children as "provocative victims" — kids who are so temperamentally aggressive that they effortlessly pick fights, even with kids they should by all means avoid fighting. Many of us probably remember children from our school days who were almost constitutionally abrasive, who could barely walk down a hallway or last through a gym class without starting a fight. Even then, those kids struck me as misfits, adolescent kegs of emotional volatility and social clumsiness.

The NIH study touched a surprisingly raw national nerve. As Mary Overpeck recalled, "We were in the field [collecting data] before Columbine happened. When Columbine happened, and there was the suggestion that bullying was a factor, I think that put it on the national scene here. Since Columbine, there've been a number of shootings, and it comes through time and time again that bullying is indeed a factor." In fact, a recent report by the U.S. Secret Service, analyzing the profile of attackers in thirty-seven school shooting incidents, concluded that bullying frequently contributed to the outbreak of violence, adding, "In a number of cases, attackers described the experiences of being bullied in terms that approached torment. Attackers told of behaviors that, if they occurred in the workplace, would meet the legal definition of harassment."

When the *JAMA* paper finally came out in 2001, two years after Columbine, the intense public reaction stunned the researchers. "The e-mails never stopped," Overpeck said. "The phone calls never stopped. The press calls never stopped. People would get in touch with us and say, 'No one understood what I went through.' This was primarily from males. I even had postdocs who were six feet tall who came in and said, 'You don't know what I went through.' "

Reading the *JAMA* paper now and thinking about early adolescence, I find myself recalling a slightly different dynamic among kids who both bullied and were bullied. In small groups of children, certainly of boys, there is usually a clear-cut pecking order, and it's not hard to imagine situations where middle-ranking boys in this hierarchy can be both bullies and bullied. In fact, it reminds me of a situation that occurred in a group of neighborhood boys with whom I hung out at age fourteen.

David was, for lack of a better term, the dominant male. He was bigger, stronger, tougher, and (this is important in terms of physical intimidation) more volatile than anyone else. John was next, and I was the lowest in rank. There were times when Dave would say something insulting to John — a relatively benign but nonetheless persistent pattern of needling and belittlement that might qualify as indirect bullying by some modern definitions. If I had the misfortune to laugh at what Dave said, John would immediately turn on me. I can still hear him say, "What are *you* laughing at?" This would be followed by a punch to my upper arm. He who is belittled instantly turns to the next-littler victim. I suspect this chain reaction style of retaliation happens quite often in small, stable groups of friends, and I can further confirm that the trickle-down effect reaches into the family. Out of my frustration, for example, I physically tormented my younger brother. Within families, boyhood aggression is often a pyramid scheme.

It's easy to dismiss this as the kind of adolescent horseplay that has characterized boyhood from time immemorial, as harmless and evanescent as a puerile joke. I would argue otherwise. First of all, the punches hurt. Second, and much more important, to avoid them I changed my behavior, out of fear of retaliation. And with the power of hindsight, I realize now that I diminished myself by constricting my behavior: I suppressed laughing in those situations; I kept my own verbal repartee on a tight leash; I minded my place in the hierarchy. Both Dave and John were much bigger than I was. They didn't beat me up, but then they didn't have to. They settled for a more modest, but nonetheless symbolic, form of intimidation, and I behaved accordingly.

The obvious question a reader might ask at this point is, so why did you subject yourself to this pattern of intimidation and belittlement? The answer — obvious to any adolescent, mystifying to many parents — is that being treated badly was the price of belonging to the group in the first place. Especially during adolescence, belonging to a group — *any* group — is much more desirable than being an outcast. What children don't realize until much later is that the price of belonging is much higher for boys (or girls) on the lower end of whatever hierarchical social group they belong to and that, unlike baboons and other social animals, their future success (reproductive or otherwise) will ultimately not depend on physical domination.

WHAT IS THE ultimate fate of the bully? Captain of industry? Cultural hero? World-class diplomat? I'm being a little facetious with those suggestions but offer them with the thought that bullying behavior by adults, however indirect, has effortlessly infiltrated our social conversation about politics and commerce. Those who master the transition from physical to verbal aggression (or simply discover that verbal aggression is a fine way to dominate rivals) seem to enjoy considerable success in adult endeavors. Physical size is often (though not always) a silent partner to this aggressiveness, and diminutive size, for some bewildering reason, invites contempt decades after we've all retired from the playground.

Michael Eisner, who headed Disney for many years, reached far down into the name-calling vernacular of the playground when he famously dismissed his colleague Jeffrey Katzenberg as a "little midget." When Arnold Schwarzenegger, legendary bodybuilder and later governor of California, libeled his political opponents as "girlie men," he revealed the same petulance and willful desire to get his way as one of Tremblay's toddlers. And John Bolton, the U.S. ambassador to the United Nations, has left a long trail of bullying and intimidating behavior toward former colleagues at the State Department. I'm not suggesting they would literally beat up a rival, but I wonder if the emotional satisfaction of intimidating others (which, as in the case of my childhood friend Dave, often gains its power from both physical superiority and unpredictable outbursts) has convinced them that verbal bullying confers psychological, political, and business advantages. Anyone who has seen the 1977 documentary *Pumping Iron* may have a hard time separating Schwarzenegger's physical superiority from the creepy delight he clearly feels in being verbally aggressive and psychologically manipulative. In the film, his cruel and relentless reps of verbal zingers, aimed at bodybuilding rivals such as Lou Ferrigno, are a textbook example of what Olweus would consider "inflicting discomfort," and it's hard to imagine that those satisfying lessons of youth do not set the stage for adult comportment. Studies of bullying behavior in the workplace by Harvey A. Hornstein of Teachers College at Columbia University have found that "managers bullied subordinates for the sheer pleasure of exercising power." Hornstein told the *New York*

Times, "It was a kind of low-grade sadism, that was the most common reason. They'd start on one person, and then move on to someone else."

People who successfully adapt bullying tactics to adult life may be the exception. As Richard Tremblay's research has shown, boys who fail to curb their impulses for physical aggression usually become socially isolated, shunned, and rejected by mainstream society. One of the finest and most vivid literary accounts of this social estrangement can be found in Jonathan Eig's first-person story in the *Wall Street Journal* about the bully who traumatized his youth.

Eig managed to track down the family of Douglas Milteer, a boy who had bullied him during elementary school in Monsey, New York, a suburb of New York City. Several decades after the fact, Eig went back and interviewed Milteer's mother, brothers, and friends, reconstructing a riveting portrait of a young man whose life, in details large and small, seemed to embody many recent findings on the connection between the home environment and physical aggression. Milteer, Eig reported, came from a rugged and broken family. His older brothers frequently beat him up, their mother would hit or whip the children with a belt, and the parents ultimately separated when Douglas was in the fifth grade. In that terrible, trickle-down effect of physical abuse and psychological terror, he took out his frustrations on classmates, including Eig, and later on girlfriends. As an adult, Milteer enjoyed success as a contractor in Beverly Hills but continued to have domestic problems. His marriage lasted only one month, he had difficulty forming lasting relationships with other women, and he was homeless when he ultimately died of AIDS in 1997. "We had no control at home," Douglas's brother Scott told Eig, "so we had to have control everywhere else. We controlled the bus. We controlled the bus stop. We controlled the baseball diamond. At gym, we controlled the red ball."

I asked Eig if he thought size had anything to do with his travails with Douglas. "I always assumed that it was because I was a little guy," he told me. "I was definitely among the three or four shortest kids in my class. But when I went back and looked at pictures, he wasn't that much bigger than me. A little bigger, but definitely stronger, and stockier." One of Douglas's brothers told Eig that "if kids stood up to them, even once, they left them alone."

6

RUNTS, SNEAKS, AND DOMINATORS
Size, Aggression, and Animal Behavior

"Nature, red in tooth and claw" remains the dominant image
of the animal world. Animals just fight, and that is it? It is not
that simple.

— Frans de Waal

It is an unspoken rule of science journalism that when we
write about animal behavior, we do so not because chimpanzees or hermit crabs are intrinsically interesting to newspaper readers, but because
these stories are, at some level, about us. When the research we write
about is particularly striking, it might even remind us of the ultimate developmental passage of human biology: high school. Such was the case
with a Stanford University study in 2004 about a sudden tragedy that be-
fell a large, close-knit social group — in this case, a troop of olive baboons living in the savanna of East Africa. As the story unfolded over
more than a decade, researchers discovered, almost by chance, how "an
accident of history," as primatologist Frans de Waal put it, "wiped out all
the male bullies" in the group, with startling consequences.

In 1982 a number of male baboons belonging to a group known as
Forest Troop had developed the habit of moseying over at dawn to an
open garbage pit near a tourist lodge in the Masai Mara Reserve of Kenya

and foraging for food. The troop slept in trees about a half mile from the lodge, but not all the males from the troop participated in these daily food raids — while the more social males stayed home for the morning grooming rituals, the scrappiest and most aggressive adults headed off to the dump. Indeed, the primatologists who studied Forest Troop later speculated that aggressiveness could be viewed as "a prerequisite" for such foraging, because the baboons had to compete with similarly belligerent males from a rival group, the Garbage Dump Troop, for table scraps and leftover food. Then tragedy struck. Contaminated meat from the dump triggered an outbreak of tuberculosis that decimated nearly all the Garbage Dump Troop and every male from Forest Troop that participated in the food raids. Thus the hammer of mortality did not fall randomly: it struck the most aggressive males in Forest Troop during their last road trip, and the mass death dramatically changed the social dynamics of the group, not least because females suddenly outnumbered males two to one.

Robert M. Sapolsky, a neurobiologist and primate researcher at Stanford University, had been studying Forest Troop since 1978 and was among the first to report the fatal epidemic in 1985. In fact, Sapolsky was so emotionally devastated by the epidemic that he felt compelled to shift his research attention to another group of baboons some thirty miles away. "I was very attached to that troop, and the death of half my males was sufficiently upsetting that I wouldn't even go near that corner of the park for years afterward," he admitted later. But around 1993, he decided to pay a visit — in part to show his new wife, Lisa J. Share, "the troop of my youth" — and even casual observation of Forest Troop revealed some striking departures from normal baboon behavior. Sapolsky and Share, his research collaborator, were privileged to witness this momentous change. "By 1986," they later wrote, "troop behavior had changed markedly, because only less aggressive males had survived." Although these surviving males still maintained social rank by asserting their dominance, physical encounters (known in the trade as dominance interactions) increased among males of close ranks. Put more colloquially, the male baboons started picking on animals their own size, and the high-ranking males were found to be more tolerant of low-ranking males. This subtle shift in "bullying" behavior, if you will, along with other social changes in the troop after the epidemic, apparently translated into major health consequences within baboon society — measurably lower amounts of a key stress hormone. Sapolsky has studied stress for decades, and prior to the tuberculosis outbreak, he had found that low-ranking male baboons lived in what amounted to "a chronic state of stress." Their physical encounters with the more dominant males were so unpredictable, so one-sided, and so unpleasant that the harassed baboons hunkered down into a pathological physiological state.

The change in social structure extended to relations between the sexes, too. The male baboons that survived the epidemic — the less aggressive group — minded their social manners better with the females, participating in grooming and other "affiliative" behaviors. In other words, the sudden subtraction of the most aggressive guys — "the biggest, nastiest, most despotic males," as writer Natalie Angier put it — from a troop of baboons led to a more egalitarian, less misogynist, and more tolerant society, where the new "alpha males" (a term, incidentally, found more commonly these days in the popular media and in pop psychology than in the scientific literature) mostly picked on peers their own size and didn't terrorize the less dominant males.

Since male dominance in primate society is linked to fighting ability — and if you make the further leap, fighting ability is often associated with relative physical size and strength — you can see how wiping out the most physically aggressive males in that society would create a more peaceful community. And that is what Sapolsky and Share reported in the April 2004 issue of the journal *Public Library of Science — Biology*. Although the societal transformation began in 1983, the changes were maintained at least through 2004, by which time an entirely new generation of high-ranking males — which, as in all baboon society, were born outside the group and joined Forest Troop as immigrant adolescents — had assumed dominant positions in the troop. Once instilled, the new tolerance seemed to be passed down not genetically but culturally. It became a tradition.

Whenever I read accounts of animal behavior like this, I find myself giving in — and it *is* an indulgence, a yielding to anthropomorphic mischief — to an exercise I'll call comparative adolescence, extrapolating from the animal case study to an analogous human setting. Almost invariably, that setting is high school. As it turns out, I wasn't alone in thinking about old school days while digesting this latest news from baboon society. "Me, too," Sapolsky confessed in an e-mail message, adding that he went to a "humane high school, but junior high was hell."

Such fictions probably have little merit beyond playful acts of imagination. There is, after all, only so much even the best human observers can understand about animal society and behavior, and that is especially true concerning primates, whose behavior can vary markedly from species to species and even within the same species from one locale to the next. Nonetheless, we study animals, especially primates, because they can tell us about the dynamics of evolution and, if we're lucky and persistent, perhaps something about the evolutionary forces that have shaped human behavior. And a lot of animal behavior emerges from the volatile convergence of social dominance, aggression (in males), fighting ability, and body size.

It would be reckless to read too much into the antics of a bunch of apes, but it would be equally foolish to ignore what they might tell us about human impulses. And, as it turns out, relative size is a very big deal — to nonhuman primates, of course, but also to spiders and crickets, fish and hermit crabs, even to the earliest, shrewlike mammals that prowled the earth 100 million years ago and the baby dinosaurs they occasionally dined upon. In every genus and family of animal life on the planet, there are giants and squirts, and the way they come to terms with one another is part drama, part farce, and all about living long enough — and sometimes sneakily enough — to send offspring into the next generation.

At the same time — and this is perhaps the more surprising recent development — size may matter a little less than we previously thought. To understand what ethologists think today about animals and aggression, we have to go back to the early history of the field — back to World War III.

LORD OF THE FLIES, the stark, black-and-white 1963 film directed by Peter Brook and based on William Golding's novel, is in many respects the ultimate boys' movie. There is not a single female character, there is not a single adult for all but the last minute or so, and there are, as the film progresses, fewer and fewer civilizing influences to constrain the boys' behavior. Although the circumstances are a little murky, a large group of British schoolboys ends up on an isolated island. We are made to understand that a war, possibly nuclear in nature, has required their evacuation from England, but the plane carrying them has crashed near a tropical island (in reality, Puerto Rico and the nearby island of Vieques, where the film was made).

The film was very much of its time, and that time was rife with the message, from the world of ethology, that aggression is an animal instinct just barely beneath the surface of civilized behavior and that there is an internal urge, in humans as in animals, to attack. As a metaphor for the breakdown of civilization and as a cautionary tale about the chaos that rushes in to fill the absence of rules and order, *Lord of the Flies* is both transparently schematic and hauntingly effective. Its exploration of the instinctual aggression and warlike nature of humans — especially of boys — has an unsubtle quality probably more apparent to our eyes than to the population at mid-century, brutalized by the recent atrocities of World War II and traumatized by the specter of even more hideous devastation in the nuclear age. But it was precisely the fear of nuclear annihilation that colored not only the film but also the science of human and animal behavior as it unfolded in the cold war years.

In the movie, the young castaways initially elect a boy named Ralph — well-spoken, older, perhaps a tad taller than the rest — as their leader. But his rival, Jack, who possesses the only knife, organizes a smaller group of boys to be the hunters. They chase down wild pigs on the island, and soon enough their hunting chant — "Kill the pig! Slit its throat! Bash it in!" — is redirected at their human rivals. Their first victim is a small boy named Simon, whose mortal sin is reason: he is killed as he attempts to deflate the runaway belief that the island is inhabited by a beast-spirit that needs to be appeased. Next is the intellectual boy, Piggy (the only one to possess spectacles). Ralph, his dominance now threatened and his social isolation increasing, is next to be chased. He is about to be killed when, fleeing the others, he falls on the beach, at the feet of the British sailors who have arrived to rescue them. By this time, the boys under Jack's leadership have completely regressed — shedding their clothes, brandishing spears, shouting bellicose chants, wearing fearsome war paint, persecuting and then executing enemies, and making pagan offerings to the island spirit as a way of bargaining down their superstitious anxieties.

As a grim fiction about how much civilization can erode in ninety minutes, the movie is a tour de force. What is equally amazing, at this distance in time, is how pervasive, burdensome, and wearying was the connection between nuclear anxieties, the science of aggression, and cultural fears about where human behavior might lead us. Konrad Lorenz, whose animal research led him to the conclusion that all animals (including man) have an instinctual need for aggression as part of their biological makeup, might as well as have been an unnamed collaborator on the screenplay.

Lorenz was the dominant scientist explaining the behavior of aggression during that era. He was among a pioneering generation of ethologists who were cultural crossover artists, carrying the emerging messages about animal behavior to the general public. A key focus of study was aggression, and it is not an accident that this literature was repackaged for general consumption in the anxious years following World War II and during the height of the cold war. In Lorenz's *On Aggression* (1966), in Desmond Morris's *The Naked Ape* (1967), and in the writings of the Oxford zoologist Niko Tinbergen, the particulars of animal behavior may be in the foreground, but nuclear annihilation — and the role that human aggression might play in it — clearly looms in the background, sometimes explicitly so. Tinbergen, who shared a Nobel Prize with Lorenz and Karl von Frisch in 1973 for their pioneering research on animal behavior, said as much in a 1968 essay. While expressing an almost urgent need for greater research on aggression and behavior, he lamented, "But research takes a long time, and we must remember that there are experts who forecast worldwide famine ten to twenty years from now; and that we have enough weapons to wipe out all human life on earth." It was almost as if there were a fuse burning on animal research, that understanding animal behavior could be a form of global salvation.

The ethologists were happy to oblige. They have always been fascinated with the essential "to-do list" of living organisms: feeding, nesting, mating, and fighting. None of those activities is determined solely by size, but relative size can have a significant impact on an animal's success in all of them, from defending a territory (especially a nesting site) to muscling a rival suitor out of the way. "There is a huge literature on how size influences behavior during contests and particularly how it influences the outcome," says Robert Elwood, a researcher at Queen's University Belfast. "Basically, the larger animal usually wins."

As many of these examples suggest, size and courtship are deeply intertwined in animal behavior. Dominant males enjoy privileged access to females across a number of species, and size is certainly a contributing factor in their dominance. That in turn brings us to a related behavioral factor in mating that is a seemingly permanent feature of life not only in the African savanna but also on the asphalt playgrounds of schools throughout the world: aggression. Yet just as *Lord of the Flies* was black-and-white, so too were some of the cultural lessons drawn from the earlier research on aggression and behavior. When researchers gained more experience observing animals in the wild, it became clear that aggression was part of a much more complex system of dominance, mating success, and, surprisingly, memory.

IN 1961 THE evolutionary biologist R. D. Alexander of the University of Michigan performed a groundbreaking experiment with crickets illustrating that even insect psychology, or some rudimentary invertebrate version of it, could be shaped by physical confrontations. Alexander created a model of a cricket, a kind of insect Terminator, for the purposes of the experiment. It was slightly bigger and much stronger than a natural cricket, and virtually invincible during insect combat. He used his man-made robot to beat up on real crickets. While it probably overstates matters to call Alexander's model a "cricket bully," its antics definitely affected the subsequent behavior of the vanquished rivals. Alexander discovered that the crickets that lost fights with the robot were more likely to lose subsequent fights against real crickets. This behavior, in the view of some evolutionary biologists, is the product of a rudimentary form of memory. Crickets don't seem to recognize individual foes, much less man-made impersonators. But they *do* remember defeat and act accordingly the next time. A similar phenomenon, sometimes called the loser effect, has been reported in many species, including mammals.

"Crickets have a general memory of what happened in past fights," writes the biologist Richard Dawkins, perhaps the finest modern explicator of Darwinian natural selection, in his book *The Selfish Gene*. Dawkins renders explicit the connection between memory and behavior, aggressive and otherwise. "A cricket that has recently won a large number of fights becomes more hawkish," he writes. "A cricket that has recently had a losing streak becomes more dovish . . . Each cricket can be thought of as constantly updating his own estimate of his fighting ability, relative to that of an average individual in his population. If animals such as crickets, who work with a general memory of past fights, are kept together in a closed group for a time, a kind of dominance hierarchy is likely to develop." In other words, physical encounters — plus memory of the outcome of those encounters — shape future behavior. Does the example in crickets extend to other creatures?

Dominance hierarchies are a critical feature of many animal groups. Indeed, another term for the phenomenon is pecking order, in homage to hens and the way they establish a hierarchy when the population is in flux and new members are introduced. Dominance hierarchies are almost always established by physical superiority, by fighting ability, or by the threat of physical action. In the case of the henhouse, when new chickens arrive on the scene, a great deal of fighting ensues. Once it is clear which individuals dominate and which do not, a hierarchical order is established and, not coincidentally, the overall amount of fighting diminishes. Whether cricket or monkey or chicken, the idea is, as Dawkins writes, that "individuals lower in the order tend to give in to individuals higher in the order." As it turns out, the same sort of henhouse kerfuffle can happen among humans, at least in certain circumstances; Richard Tremblay has noted that among prison inmates, a similar pattern of fighting breaks out when new inmates join the population, and that the fighting subsides once the dominance hierarchy is recalibrated.

Animals assert dominance for a number of reasons: they are defending a territory, seeking a mate, or trying to establish and maintain power within a group. Once we move beyond crickets and other invertebrates, with their relatively primitive neural systems, however, we add a more complex psychobiological component to dominance hierarchies that is especially relevant to humans. Dominance and social rank depend critically on a fairly sophisticated form of memory — not only the memory of getting thrashed in a fight but also the memory of the individual who thrashed you. In a purely mnemonic sense, dominance hierarchies are personal. This makes evolutionary sense, of course, because remembering a rival who could beat up or even kill you and avoiding future physical clashes probably improves your chances of surviving and having offspring — to a point. Since many of these hierarchies determine access to mating partners, an animal may still be so far back in the mating queue that it won't have an opportunity to spread its genes, even if it avoids a fight.

In the context of human behavior, there's an even more important point: this complex form of memory shapes future behavior. The prodigious increase in brain size that most primates (especially humans) enjoy over other animals has in part been ascribed to the need for an enormous amount of cognitive horsepower to sort out these complex social relationships and to remember the implications. As Dawkins puts it, "If you are a monkey, a monkey who has beaten you in the past is likely to beat you in the future. The best strategy for an individual is to be relatively dovish towards an individual who has previously beaten him." Dovish and hawkish — past physical confrontations not only condition future behavior, but they also begin to shape what sounds like a personal philosophy or worldview.

This hardly comes as a surprise, yet the intensity of these agonistic memories in humans is a thing to behold, if personal experience is any indication. I am in the sixth decade of life as I write these lines, yet I can vividly recall virtually every physical confrontation of my youth — hitting another child, and being hit with a block (actually, a long two-by-four) in nursery school; a fight in the snow in a church parking lot in Pennsylvania when I was eight; the playground altercation at school when I was in sixth grade; and physical humiliations too numerous to mention here (although I look forward to recounting nearly all of them in due time) during my adolescence. In the aftermath of such intense confrontations — with heart racing, with those hyperventilating sobs that fall somewhere between respiration and shock — we are probably more like crickets or mice or baboons than we'd care to admit.

In pondering the role of memory in shaping behavior, I wanted to hear what Joseph LeDoux had to say about it. LeDoux is a neurobiologist at New York University, an expert on the biology of fear, and an author of several excellent books, among them *The Emotional Brain*. His research has teased out the way the brain processes signals of fear and danger, using an ancient and instant neural pathway involving a small structure in the middle of the brain known as the amygdala. "My research suggests that the brain uses the simplest possible cues to activate the fear system," LeDoux said over lunch. "The amygdala can be activated by angry faces or fearful faces." He mentioned that recent research by Sumantra Chattarji's group in India demonstrated how the fear circuitry in rats became enhanced with chronic stress, and he also noted a recent paper by Paul Whalen and colleagues at the University of Wisconsin. Using human volunteers and MRI machines, they showed that the fear circuitry could be activated by as discrete a cue as seeing the whites of another person's eyes. "Let's say that there's a dominant male that's beaten up on you in the past," LeDoux continued. "One component might be the eyes, and maybe that's important in initial learning. But maybe later, other cues that are unique to the person, like smell, would trigger the memory. As you become more familiar and more afraid of this individual, the stimulus becomes more complex."

Although "social memory" of this sort is indeed enormously complex, it is clear from modern neurobiology that evolution has built our brains to register threat and remember danger. And when someone like LeDoux mentions in passing his recollection of being whipped with a telephone cord by another student on his first day of kindergarten, it's equally clear that these memories stay with us for a very long time. Neurobiology alone, it seems, argues that bullying and aggressive behavior can leave an enduring residue in the brain and that physical conflict — or the threat of it — influences our behavior. So where does size enter into this very serious game of physical conflict? First we'll talk about the rules of the game; then we'll talk about size — which is exactly how the pioneering evolutionary biologists went about it.

BEGINNING IN THE early 1970s, evolutionary biologists became fascinated with concocting imaginary, but realistic, scenarios in which different behaviors could be pitted against one another to see which strategy of aggression was most successful. It became a particularly fascinating Darwinian branch of game theory, and one of the most interesting explorations of this was done by the great Oxford evolutionary biologist John Maynard Smith. In 1973 Maynard Smith and G. R. Price created a boys-only mathematical war game of sorts, an imaginary contest among males in which five rival strategies for social aggression were pitted against one another. These were not one-shot, winner-take-all confrontations, but rather a series of repeated encounters over time, of the sort that defines any social community. This repetition allowed for memory — and retaliation — to come into play. The game aimed at the heart of animal existence. As Maynard Smith and Price wrote in *Nature*, "In a typical combat between two male animals of the same species, the winner gains mates, dominance rights, desirable territory, or other advantages that will tend toward transmitting its genes to future generations at higher frequencies than the loser's genes."

Dawkins has an excellent, lucid account of the game in *The Selfish Gene*. The original participants were called Hawk, Mouse, Retaliator,

Bully, and Prober-Retaliator, and each had a specific behavior. Hawks invariably attacked and kept fighting unless seriously injured; Mice (dubbed Doves in Dawkins's retelling) might threaten but invariably retreated from a fight; Retaliators initially acted like Mice/Doves, refraining from fighting, but would attack if they were attacked; Bullies pretended to be Hawks, but if attacked they would run away; and Prober-Retaliators acted like Retaliators, except that occasionally they went on the offensive and attacked for no particular reason. The aim of the game was to run these scenarios hundreds of times until the virtual combatants reached a kind of equilibrium in terms of the behavior in a population — what Maynard Smith called an "evolutionarily stable situation." In this particular scenario, only the Retaliators could not be bettered over time and thus achieved stability. All of the others ended up getting trumped sooner or later.

When these mathematical models were first described, they revolutionized scientific thinking about animal behaviors such as aggression, because they allowed competing strategies to play out over time, arriving at conclusions that, as Dawkins points out, were "not far from what actually happens in most wild animals." But the limitations also became increasingly apparent, and one was particularly problematic, an oversimplification that any freshman gym student could have pointed out. The working assumption was that the participants were essentially identical in attributes, capabilities, and so on — were "symmetric," as scientists put it, in what they brought to the fight. "This means," Dawkins writes, "we have assumed that the contestants are identical in all respects except their fighting strategy. Hawks and doves are assumed to be equally strong, to be equally well-endowed with weapons and with armour, and to have an equal amount to gain from winning." But, as Dawkins concedes, this is "not very realistic." Indeed, one of the natural world's most fundamental asymmetries is, of course, physical size.

Recognizing these real-world shortcomings, Maynard Smith and his colleague G. A. Parker went back and restaged their computerized wrestle-a-thon with some built-in asymmetries. One of these, not surprisingly, was physical size. Here is Dawkins's crisp summation of Maynard Smith and Parker's subsequent findings, which were described in several papers in the 1970s: "Large size is not necessarily always the most important quality needed to win fights, but it is probably one of them. If the larger of two fighters always wins, and if each individual knows for certain whether he is larger or smaller than his opponent, only one strategy makes any sense: 'If your opponent is larger than you, run away. Pick fights with people smaller than you.' " But then he adds, reasonably, "Things are a bit more complicated if the importance of size is less certain."

In chapter 15, we'll more thoroughly explore evolution's take on the size of an organism — if, over the course of millions of years, natural selection likes its species big and brawny or small and sneaky. It goes without saying that, whether in computer simulations or in real life, size does not necessarily equal fighting ability, and fighting ability does not necessarily offer the best option for conflict resolution. That muscle-bound version of Darwinian fitness has gone out of fashion for a very good reason. It is too simplistic, and it doesn't capture the complexities — one is tempted to say perplexities — of animal behavior, including ours. But embedded in these game theory results are two profound evolutionary ideas related to size. One is that if animals make decisions about engaging in a fight based on relative size, evolution has probably built into all of us the cognitive machinery to assess and understand differences in size; these are clearly fundamental survival skills. The other idea is that if, as Dawkins suggests, an animal is aware that an opponent is larger than it is, then there must be a self-awareness — one is tempted to say a self-consciousness — about one's own size.

Behavioral scientists have become increasingly conscious of these subtle complexities in the past few years. Applying DNA fingerprinting to animal paternity, observing primates in the wild more carefully, and devising more complex experiments that get beyond the Goliath effect, ethologists have become much more sophisticated at probing the role of physical size in shaping animal behavior. Whether in a guppy-size fish called the medaka or a fifty-pound baboon, smaller animals within a species constantly concoct new strategies, and even develop what might be called subversive attitudes, to help them overcome size disadvantages. Indeed, words with a distinctly different human resonance from "hawkish" and "dovish" have begun to pop up in recent scientific papers. For example, baboon watchers refer to sneaky forms of courtship, and fish watchers speak of persistence.

THE HERMIT CRAB is a fussy squatter that lives in abandoned shells — fussy because it won't set up housekeeping in just any old empty shell.

The European hermit crab greatly prefers a periwinkle shell, of just the right size. In a devilishly clever and manipulative set of experiments that plays on those preferences, Robert Elwood and his colleagues at Queen's University Belfast reinvented themselves as fight promoters, setting up a series of bouts between different-size hermit crabs over the ownership of these shells.

In a typical eviction battle, a larger crab will attack the smaller crab, grabbing its shell, shaking it, rapping it against another object, and even reaching in to extract the homeowner. Elwood and his team attempted nothing less than to see if the outcome of these fights was affected by manipulating the motivation of the two fighters. They divided all the crabs by size, one group larger and one group smaller. All the smaller crabs were set up in periwinkle shells that offered a perfect fit for the larger crabs. The larger crabs, meanwhile, were divided into two groups with distinctly different motivations: about half started out with shells that were too small for them but would be cozily appropriate for the smaller crabs: the other half were given shells that fit them rather well but would be uncomfortably roomy for their smaller opponents. Then the researchers turned the crabby antagonists loose.

As expected, the larger crabs seemed to understand that they had the physical advantage. As Elwood and his colleagues noted, "Relative size is assessed before a fight . . . [and] virtually all fights are initiated by the larger crab." Contrary to game theory, however, the researchers discovered that relative size didn't provide as much motivation to fight as did an uncomfortable abode. When larger crabs had the additional motivation of an ill-fitting shell, they were more determined to win the battle. The attacking crabs whose shells were too small achieved evictions of their foes 90 percent of the time; the attackers whose shells were more commodious achieved an eviction rate of 76 percent.

To cite another example, in the golden orb-weaving spider (*Nephila clavipes*), it has long been known that although females in general are much larger than males (which is true of many invertebrates), larger males have an advantage over smaller males when it comes to mating. But when researchers at Tulane University looked at other factors related to mating, they found an advantage of smaller size in one important area: the effort to *locate* females. "Field observations as well as capture and release experiments demonstrated that smaller males travel further distances in shorter periods of time," noted Christopher Linn and Terry

E. Christenson. "Furthermore, smaller males are more likely to find their way to female webs than larger males." It is only when several males congregate on the female's doorstep that larger size becomes an advantage; the larger males almost always claim a closer position to the female. In baboons, this habit of sexual hovering is called mate guarding. In spiders, as in baboons, proximity to a fecund female increases the odds of reproductive success.

Here's yet another example. Researchers recently discovered a surprising wrinkle in mate selection in a fish called the convict cichlid (*Cichlasoma nigrofasciatum*). Both males and females of this species increase their chances of reproductive success when they select larger mates. But at least in laboratory experiments, some cichlids don't always mate according to Darwin's playbook. In these experiments, males sought out larger females for mating, as expected, but females often preferred smaller males. Even though a larger mate presumably offers a better-protected nesting site, with all the reproductive advantages that confers, females did not choose the biggest possible mates. "It may be that females prefer males who are compatible with their own size and reproductive state, not simply large," wrote Simon Beeching, Amanda B. Hopp, and Ginger L. Ruffner. "It appears that males and females are using different strategies in the evolutionarily significant process of mate choice."

Primatologists have observed a similarly intriguing situation in several species, including mandrills, large nomadic baboons that live in large hordes in the Central African forests. Research by Kate Abernethy and her colleagues at the International Center for Medical Research in Gabon has shown that the courtship strategy of male mandrills depends on their size. In field observations, one set of male mandrills was very large and very aggressive; another set in the same group was relatively smaller, about the same size as females or juveniles. This difference in size basically dictated a difference in mating strategy. "The large males are seen to mate very openly, whereas the smaller ones are seen to mate surreptitiously," explained Bill Sellers, a primatologist at the University of Loughborough in England, who has described the research in lectures. "It remains to be seen which strategy is the most successful in the long run since it's only with the advent of DNA fingerprinting that we can be certain about paternity." In recognition of this dogged determination to procreate, whatever an animal's size and whatever the obstacles, a new term has begun to appear in descriptions of primate behavior: sneak copulation.

Testing animals' paternity has proven to be an excellent way to figure out who's canoodling with whom, in the lab or out in the wild. A recent experiment in genetic modification in fish even suggests that engineering large size could have a deleterious effect on the survival of the normal, or wild-type, species. Researchers at Purdue University inserted the growth hormone gene from salmon into a different species of fish, the Japanese medaka, which is relatively tiny, weighing a mere 300 milligrams. The genetically engineered fish grew to a size that was 83 percent larger, on average, than Mother Nature's version. Then came the fascinating part. Richard D. Howard and his colleagues set up a laboratory situation where the larger male medakas were allowed to compete with normal-size males for females. The genetically engineered giants in most instances outmuscled the competition; they nipped the smaller males and chased them away whenever the smaller males ventured too close to the amorous couple. But did the small fry give up? Not at all. The smaller males developed several clever strategies to overcome this size disadvantage. In some instances, they attempted to knock the larger fish away from the females during mating. In other instances, they adopted a ménage à trois strategy, joining a coupling already in progress and thus creating the possibility that their sperm would outrace that of their rivals (this is where the paternity tests came in). Alas, many of these desperate tactics came to naught, but not all. The genetically engineered giant medakas won these courtship battles about 75 percent of the time.

But the expected triumphalism of larger size came, at least in this experiment, with a hidden evolutionary cost — the ultimate cost, really, if survival of the species is the name of the game. It turned out that the offspring of the genetically engineered larger fish were less hardy than the offspring of normal-size medakas. Using the data from their experiments, Howard and his colleagues created a mathematical model to predict what would happen if the genetically engineered giants invaded a native population. The model showed that the larger fish would erase the normal medaka population within fifty generations — essentially drive them into extinction. In the short term, the larger fish were successful. But in the huge gulps of time at which evolution operates, they too were doomed to become extinct. The compromised hardiness of the genetically engineered giants might reduce their prospects for survivability, too.

SIZE ALONE DOESN'T dictate baboon mating patterns either. Susan C. Alberts of Duke University, Heather E. Watts of Michigan State University, and the veteran primatologist Jeanne Altmann of Princeton University have been studying a troop of baboons living at the base of Mount Kilimanjaro in Kenya for many years. In 2003 they published a paper on the mating habits of the baboons that turned the idea of dominance rank on its head. It involves the notion of sexual queues.

Baboon watchers have long assumed that a male's place in a troop's dominance rank essentially equals a place in line for access to females in heat, with the top-ranking male first in line and everyone else waiting his turn — in order, and perhaps in vain. Alberts and colleagues analyzed years of observations of their well-known group in the Amboseli basin and came to a somewhat surprising conclusion. Baboon sexual behavior may appear to be an exercise in waiting in line, but upon closer observation it ends up looking a little like Peyton Place. As Alberts put it, "Dominance rank is a queuing system, but like any queuing system, it's vulnerable to cheating."

Alberts and her colleagues found that mating success accrued not only to the most dominant, aggressive males, but also to a furtive set of "queue-jumpers" — an almost subversive subculture of less dominant males who contrived or connived to cut in line and therefore succeeded in mating when traditional dominance hierarchy would argue that they should have been elbowed out of the way. The research suggests that the canonical dominance of the big, bad, top-ranked baboon may be a little exaggerated. If the troop is large, if there is a big age gap between the top-ranked prime male and his older competitors, and if the older guys stick together and gang up against the top dog, the hierarchy breaks down. And if dominance hierarchies break down, there's only so much that size can contribute to the equation.

To be sure, this doesn't mean that dominance hierarchies as a concept are in total collapse or that females can be choosy about their mates. In baboon society, the dominant male typically guards a female in heat, and given the size disparity between the two, the male effectively monopolizes reproductive access. "Male baboons are twice the size of females,"

Alberts told me, "and if the male is guarding the female, it doesn't matter what she wants. She can't do anything about it." Nonetheless, the researchers observed occasions where young males ganged up to distract or attack the ranking male, causing a breach in the queue. Based on more recent, preliminary data using genetic analysis of parents and offspring to establish paternity, Alberts said, "Subordinate adult males never mate-guard, but they fathered 1 percent of the offspring. That suggests some sneaking is going on."

Research like this, which documents in the field the ways a hierarchical system can break down, points out the limitations of the original game theory models of behavior, where everything transpires in a computer. "I think it's been understood that [game theory is] a very stripped-down system," Alberts told me. "It gave us more understanding about dynamics than about animal behavior in the real world."

Robert Sapolsky, whose observations of Forest Troop also led to a more flexible interpretation of dominance hierarchies, agreed that recent field studies have begun to change thinking among primatologists. "There are two major trends in the literature today — 'female choice' and 'alternative male strategies,'" Sapolsky said. "The old model was that all males cared about was male-male competition, and the outcome of it completely determined who got to mate with whom. In other words, males can only think of one thing and females have no control over anything relating to mating. Both turn out to be wrong, and increasingly, it's recognized that an alternative male strategy is to actually be friends with a female, who then has covert means to mate with him, rather than with whoever is the winner of explicit male-male fighting."

Albert concurs. "We see evidence all over the place of males finding ways other than size for selection [by females]," she told me. "Natural selection is wily, and males in many social systems experience selection for bigger size. But there will be other selective pressures that will act in concert with — or, in some cases, in opposition to — large size at the same time." Joan Roughgarden, an evolutionary biologist at Stanford University, details a huge inventory of these alternative courtship strategies — song, color, display behavior, and so on — in her book *Evolution's Rainbow*.

Ever since the publication of Darwin's *The Origin of Species* in 1859, there has been a long-standing cultural temptation to inject Darwinian natural selection, clumsily, into human social dynamics. In the nineteenth century, this mischief took the form of evolutionary "fitness" and ended up in, as Stephen Jay Gould so memorably put it, "the mismeasure of man" and the pseudoscientific legitimization of eugenics. In our time, studies of animal behavior — and, more specifically, of dominance hierarchies — have led to appealing but perhaps overly simplistic interpretations of human behavior once again. As people like Alberts and Sapolsky never tire of pointing out, baboons are brutes, and their social rules are generally brutish. The more a society is civilized, the less physical attributes such as size necessarily determine hierarchies and dominance. As the paternity testing of everything from fish to baboons suggests, there's always a way to subvert even a brutish system. And it's useful to recall that a key asymmetry in the original game theory research was not just physical size but weaponry. The making of tools in general, and of weaponry in particular, is increasingly a function of advanced intelligence rather than physical superiority. (The use of these weapons, of course, is another matter.)

There is a cautionary lesson here as well about popular culture and its embrace of complicated, nuanced concepts such as the "alpha male." Anyone who thinks of the alpha male as the biggest, strongest, most aggressive brute who dominates all the other males and wins all the females should read a paper by Yukio Takahata and colleagues about the mating and reproductive success of the male Japanese macaque. An earlier paper by a different research team suggested that the alpha male of a particular troop enjoyed the usual mating success; when Takahata and his team undertook a longitudinal survey of the same troop, however, they discovered that the alpha male almost batted zero. During one mating season, the alpha male made 160 courtship attempts and was rejected by females 159 times. In analyzing this behavior, the researchers concluded that females "do not choose males as mating partners on the basis of rank alone" and that they often choose middle- to low-ranking males. "Simply put," the authors concluded, "male and female strategies do not always coincide, and in such cases, it is normally the female that prevails."

So alpha status isn't all it's cracked up to be. The term itself, Alberts told me, is "sort of old-fashioned," and many contemporary primatologists prefer not to use it. "I don't like it," she said, "because it implies a special role in a group that isn't there. There's nothing special about the dominant male, except that he can beat everybody else up for a while. But that is often an ephemeral stage in his life."

Finally, even dominance is a hugely complicated social phenomenon. As Frans de Waal painstakingly documents in *Chimpanzee Politics*, his longitudinal study of a primate population in captivity, dominance in a socially sophisticated animal community is much more complicated, and unfolds over a much longer time, than your typical henhouse dustups that settle a pecking order. As he wrote in *Science* not long ago, "High-ranking individuals are not necessarily the strongest, but the ones that can mobilize the most support."

PART III

THE SPURT

7

"TO GROW HAIRY"
Puberty, or the *Schuss*

> The imagination of a boy is healthy, and the mature imagina-
> tion of a man is healthy; but there is a space of life between,
> in which the soul is in a ferment, the character undecided,
> the way of life uncertain, the ambition thick-sighted: thence
> proceeds mawkishness.
>
> —JOHN KEATS, *Endymion*

> I would there were no age between sixteen and three-and-
> twenty, or that youth would sleep out the rest; for there
> is nothing in the between but getting wenches with child,
> wronging the ancientry, stealing, fighting.
>
> —WILLIAM SHAKESPEARE, *The Winter's Tale*

FOR TWENTY-SEVEN YEARS, until his death in 1750, Johann
Sebastian Bach led three male choirs in Leipzig. Most of the singers were
teenagers, and almost all of them were musical prodigies who boarded at
the legendary Thomasschule. Given the times, German school officials
kept excellent records on each of these students, including his date of
birth, academic performance, and family history. More than two centuries later, an enterprising medical historian had the idea of poring over
these records in an attempt to document, retrospectively, an adolescent
trait that is very pertinent to the male choir business.

One of the classic physiological changes of puberty — indeed, one of
the most gratingly obvious — is when a boy's voice cracks, or deepens. In
the late 1960s, S. F. Daw, a researcher at Worcester College in Oxford,
England, had the idea of trying to correlate the change in voice — and
thus the timing of puberty in eighteenth-century boys — with the part

each of Bach's schoolboy choristers sang. Music historians believe that boys whose voices had not yet broken sang soprano, the highest vocal part for male adolescents in those days. Boys in the midst of changing sang alto, and boys in whom the change was complete sang tenor and bass.

As good as the record keeping was, it was not flawless. Only once was the name of a particular chorister paired with the part he sang, and therefore the results, which Daw published in 1970 in the journal *Human Biology*, could only approximate the onset of puberty. They suggested that the average age of a boy whose voice was changing was about sixteen and a half to seventeen years — about three years later than the comparative age for a modern European boy.

Many of the changing physical features of puberty, such as height and shape and sexual maturation, are obvious, but less obvious aspects of growth are also happening throughout the adolescent body. Voices break, for example, because of a growth spurt in the larynx, or voice box. This growth stretches out the size of the vocal cords and, like loosening the strings on a guitar, lowers the voice.

The cracking of the voice proved useless as a marker for puberty because it happens relatively late in the process. In my case, it happened very late, in a way that had an important impact on my social interactions. But that is one of the fascinating aspects about this stage of physical growth: the timing of puberty and the growth spurt can have a huge impact on whom we hang out with, how we feel about ourselves, the chronology (and speedometer) of our life experiences, and ultimately the behaviors we carry, for better or worse, into adulthood. This stage changes the way we look, the way we talk, and the way we think, including how we think about ourselves. At a moment of heightened and excruciatingly attentive self-consciousness, we suddenly have much more uncontrollable anatomical chaos to be self-conscious about. We change from unformed, infertile children into conspicuously enlarged sexual beings, with all the psychological thrill and physical uncertainty that accompany that transformation. And for boys in particular, puberty is a kind of rehearsal. "Because their adolescent growth spurt occurs late in sexual development," growth expert Barry Bogin has noted, "young males can practice behaving like adults before they are actually perceived as adults."

The word "puberty" derives from the Latin *pubescere*, "to grow hairy," in acknowledgment of one of its most conspicuous adornments. The entire cycle of change unfolds on average over a period of three years; the rub is that the starting gun for these enormous changes goes off at different times for different children. For some, puberty starts early, and for others, it starts insufferably late. The timing has significant — and, scientists increasingly believe, lifelong — ramifications for the psychological makeup and well-being of adults, affecting everything from emotional attitudes such as self-esteem to unhealthy adult behaviors such as substance abuse. Although those three years of growth can seem like an eternity for a teenager literally growing out of his or her skin, the Germans have a lovely word for it — "*Schuss.*" It is the perfect onomatopoetic term for a change so startlingly transformative that it is like a rocket blasting off. That is exactly how adolescent growth feels.

If the German word for the adolescent growth spurt is rather antiquated, so too are some of the popular mythologies that have grown along with it. We often speak of teenagers "drowning" in hormones; actually, they don't. Rather, the brain gently and discreetly pulses these powerful chemicals into young bodies, most commonly at night. During other parts of the day, the puberty-initiating hormones are barely detectable in the blood. We speak of unbridled growth; it is not. Pubertal growth is actually fitful, a series of small spurts punctuated by seasonal leaps and lags. Even in adolescence, growth is greater during the summer, slower during the winter. We often say that this growth is "in the genes," but children actually require environmental cues, including adequate nutrition, for all that growth to take place, or even to begin. As primatologists Jeanne Altmann and Susan Alberts noted in a recent paper, even adolescent baboons observed in the wild display stunted pubertal growth when they don't receive sufficient nutrition. The entire hormonal cascade typical of puberty can be shut down when a female primate misses a single meal.

Scientists have been studying puberty in humans for decades — with x-rays to gauge skeletal maturity, orchidometers to measure the volume of growing testicles, and photographs of the Tanner stages of pubertal growth (the table assembled by James Tanner in the 1950s to classify the progressive development of pubic hair, penis, and breasts). But there is still a central mystery about the pubertal process and the growth spurt it triggers. Children are suspended in childhood until the brain registers some unknown combination of environmental cues and then unleashes a cerebral signal — thus puberty really begins in the head. All the tumultuous shudders of physical change in the groin, bones, and armpits begin with a biochemical rustle deep in the brain. At some point in development, a small nub of neural tissue known as the hypothalamus, weighing but four grams, begins to emit a barely perceptible chemical whisper. This slight hormonal pulse sets off an enormous physiological din.

This process remains "one of the great mysteries in human biology," according to endocrinologists. But we've come a long way from the cracking voices of Bach's choristers in Leipzig. In a scientific story that has unfolded in Boston, France, and the Middle East, some of the mystery surrounding the onset of puberty has begun to dissipate. That has happened because of a few unfortunate "children" who simply couldn't reach puberty, even though they were in some cases married and in their twenties. They typically realized that something was medically amiss when they went to fertility specialists complaining about an inability to conceive children. That is ultimately how scientists, treating an extended family of Bedouins in the 1980s, ended up finding the "Harry Potter gene" in 2004. That discovery marked the climax of a scientific odyssey spanning a quarter century.

IN THE 1970S, two furiously competing scientists, Roger Guillemin and Andrew Schally, raced to discover the hormone that controlled sexual development in humans. When the dust settled, both had a hand on the prize: a molecule known as gonadotropin-releasing hormone, usually abbreviated GnRH. The two men's discovery was immortalized by a Nobel Prize in 1977, and their legendary antipathy — "the longest, closest, and most bitterly fought race in modern biology" — was immortalized in Nicholas Wade's fine book *The Nobel Duel.*

The discovery of GnRH essentially reshaped the working biochemical definition of puberty that had prevailed until the 1970s and 1980s. "In endocrinology, everyone thought the pituitary was the master gland," recalled William F. Crowley Jr., who began practicing endocrinology just after the Schally and Guillemin discoveries. "It turns out that the pituitary, like all of us, works for someone else. The real boss is the hypothalamus."

The new, molecular version of puberty goes like this: The hypothalamus releases little squirts of GnRH at the beginning of puberty. This chemical message travels just two or three millimeters — the length of a hyphen — but conveys enormous news to the pituitary gland, a tiny oblong sac that hangs down from the hypothalamus. Even when the boss whispers, the orders get followed. Once the pituitary receives word from the hypothalamus, the symphony of puberty begins very quietly and — from an external observer's perspective — almost invisibly, with a small pulsed secretion of two pituitary hormones into the bloodstream. They are follicle stimulating hormone (FSH) and luteinizing hormone (LH). The pituitary typically begins this tiny hormonal secretion a year before the first external signs of pubertal change are apparent. These hormones act on the sexual organs of boys (testicles) and girls (ovaries), causing them gradually to increase in size. As these organs grow larger, they release other increasingly potent sex-specific hormones — estradiol in girls and testosterone in boys.

It isn't as if these two hormones, which kick-start sexual development, have been in hiding throughout a child's life and wait until adolescence to make their debut. To the contrary, like many adolescents, they've been sleeping in late, in a kind of molecular hibernation since early infancy. Researchers have long known that LH and FSH are present in fairly substantial amounts during fetal development and in young babies during the first half year of life. "Three-month-old boys have as much testosterone as you and I," Crowley said. "And then, around six months, it shuts down." Boys then enter "a mysterious period of dormancy during childhood," Crowley and his colleagues have written, until being aroused again at the beginning of puberty.

In the early 1980s, many doctors believed that the discovery of GnRH would lead to better diagnosis of several rare disorders of sexual maturation, which can take the form of very early development (central precocious puberty) or, conversely, no puberty at all. Crowley, then a young doctor at Massachusetts General Hospital (he now heads the Reproductive Endocrine Unit there), thought the hormone could be used as a human therapy, and he had an astonishing case with which to make the point. It was that of a two-year-old girl who had already entered puberty, with rapid growth, vaginal bleeding, and breast and pubic hair development typical of a girl nearly halfway through sexual maturation.

Ernst Knobil, a researcher at the University of Pittsburgh, conducted experiments in animals suggesting a possible treatment for this extreme condition. Knobil showed that giving GnRH to a primate in pulses initiated puberty, but giving the same hormone continuously, without the pulses, shut it down. In other words, puberty depended not only on the hormone, but on the pulsatile way the body delivered it. So Crowley's team treated the girl with constant, low doses of a synthetic agonist, or stimulant, of GnRH. Such constant stimulation actually fatigues and overwhelms the pituitary, which stops sending hormone messages to the sexual organs. After two months of treatment, the girl's development normalized, and she went back to being a toddler. Crowley and colleagues published the results in 1981 and reported similar results in five girls, including the two-year-old, in the *New England Journal of Medicine* later that same year.

Next Crowley tackled the opposite situation — inducing puberty in men who otherwise couldn't achieve it. These rare medical cases — six patients, all male, ranging in age from eighteen to forty-four — were, biologically speaking, trapped in childhood. Experimentally, Crowley and Andrew R. Hoffman began to treat these patients with the recently discovered GnRH. But to be effective, the drug, they discovered, had to be given in pulses, just like the hypothalamus releases it. To simulate this pulsatile rhythm, the Mass General team fashioned a customized, portable infusion pump that gave a dose of hormone every two hours. These pulses induced all the clinical and biochemical changes of normal puberty within three months, and the patients achieved normal sexual development. In addition, every patient rapidly experienced several of the more annoying features of puberty — outbreaks of acne and, as the researchers delicately described it in another *New England Journal of Medicine* report, "early-morning and spontaneous daytime erections."

By then, researchers had a keen interest in identifying the genes that controlled puberty and sexual development, but they would have to wait more than a decade for the genetic tools — and good fortune — that would allow them to make real progress. The tools came as a by-product of the Human Genome Project, and researchers' luck began to change in the late 1990s. A colleague in Crowley's lab named Yousef Bo-Abbas was preparing to return to his native Kuwait, and Crowley asked him to take on an unusual assignment. "I told him to go home and find me a good Bedouin family," Crowley recalled. "And he did. He took the enterprising step of going on TV with one of these IV pumps and asked if anyone knew families that were suffering from infertility. Remarkably, Bo-Abbas found some." They turned out to be members of a large Saudi Arabian family. Doctors in the Middle East quickly ascertained that there had been three marriages between first cousins in this extended family and that the children produced by these unions were at great risk of never achieving puberty. Four of eight children of one couple, including three boys, failed to achieve puberty (the technical terms is idiopathic hypogonadotropic hypogonadism, meaning the chemical that triggers puberty is essentially undetectable); one girl among four offspring of the second pair of cousins had the disorder; and one son among five siblings in a third family had the same problem. In other words, six of seventeen children in these three families failed to achieve puberty. To a geneticist looking for a gene related to puberty, this increased the number of needles while dramatically diminishing the size of the haystack.

Even then, it took an elaborate genetic analysis of the Saudi family members for Crowley, Stephanie Seminara, and their colleagues to pinpoint the problem. The initiation of puberty — at least in this instance — required the activity of a gene occupying a small segment on human chromosome 19. The gene contains the instructions for a protein, GPR54, which was known to be a receptor — a kind of biochemical satellite dish sitting on the surface of certain cells in the hypothalamus. (A team of researchers in France zeroed in on this genetic target at about the same time.) In 2003 Crowley's group at Massachusetts General Hospital and Harvard Medical School, along with colleagues in England and Kuwait, suggested how this gene might kick off the process of puberty. Using the DNA of the original Saudi patients as well as other, European patients, the biologists figured out that GPR54 appeared to be defective in these men. A tiny flaw in a single bead in the string of amino acids that make the protein was enough to warp the antenna, obliterating its ability to receive signals. By coincidence, a biotech company in England working with Crowley's group had isolated and systematically examined dozens of unknown genes belonging to this family of receptors, naming each uncharacterized gene after a famous orphan. Thus it turned out that the company had independently identified GPR54 and dubbed it Harry Potter, after the famous orphan of children's literature. Crowley's response? "I told them they gave it the wrong name," he said. "They should have named it the Peter Pan gene, because these kids never grow up."

What molecular message did the brain fail to receive when this receptor wobbled like a wind-torn satellite dish? In 2005 Crowley, along with researchers at the University of Pittsburgh and the Oregon National Primate Research Center, provided the beginning of an answer. They intimated that puberty begins with a genetic kiss. Specifically, they reported that another brain protein, with the suggestive name kisspeptin, "kisses" the GPR54 receptor and flips the switch on puberty.

Kisspeptin had been known for quite a while by another name, metastin, and for another purpose, as an anticancer agent. In 1996 cancer scientists had independently discovered it as a substance that appeared to thwart the spread, or metastasis, of certain malignancies. Little did anyone suspect that the gene KiSS-1 might also be a universal key in the ignition of puberty. What triggers KiSS-1? No one knows — yet. But its discovery has brought biologists closer to understanding the molecular origins of puberty's big bang. "Their finding is already very important," said Sergio Ojeda of the Oregon National Primate Research Center, who has shown that KiSS-1 triggers puberty in nonhuman primates as well. "But I believe it will be the tip of the iceberg in terms of finding a *network* of genes in the brain that will control the initiation of puberty."

As in other areas of growth biology, the ultimate answer — at least in part — appears to come from the environment. Cheryl L. Sisk and Douglas L. Foster pointed out in a recent review article that to trigger puberty, "the individual must perceive whether it has grown sufficiently (through metabolic cues), what its relationship is to other individuals (through social cues), and whether conditions are optimal to begin the reproductive process (through environmental cues)." Those are a lot of cues, a lot of signals, coming from the outside world, and it probably requires a lot of neural circuitry to integrate all those inputs into a single coherent message.

Crowley noted in an interview that a great deal of sensory information from the environment is funneled into the hypothalamus. "The hypothalamus," he said, "is a junction box, where signals from the outside — smells, taste, weight, how much you've exercised — come in as electrical signals from the environment and are changed into a biochemical signal." It is very likely that the combination of these cues adds up to a partial trigger for puberty, especially since it's already known that puberty can be postponed or aborted by negative environmental signals. "We see that in adult women who starve themselves in anorexia nervosa, and we see that when athletes exercise too much," Crowley said. "You turn on reproduction when the time is right and turn it off when you are in danger." There is research suggesting that girls who live in stressful home environments experience an early onset of puberty. And as noted previously, animal studies have shown that malnutrition can delay or impede sexual maturation.

As far as we know, among all the creatures on this planet, humans alone have evolved a very specially delayed onset of puberty, with tight biological control over the microscopic spigots of the cells that release the timekeeping hormones. "Whatever it is," James Tanner writes in *Fetus into Man*, "it has played a large part in human evolution; as we go from monkeys to apes to man the interval between birth and puberty has progressively lengthened, providing for a longer and longer period of learning before reproductive life begins. During the turned-off period some sort of timer, some tally of the degree of maturation, continues to tick away. Puberty is not something which appears suddenly out of a clear blue sky; it is the culmination of a long train of timed events."

Tanner wrote those words in 1980, but not even the recent genetic discoveries undermine his main point: the activities of genes such as GPR54 and KiSS-1 seem to be the first notes that signal the start of puberty, but they may also be the concluding notes of a quieter, less obvious biological overture that has gone on for months or years, and about which we know, at least for the moment, virtually nothing.

IN 1948, WHEN James Tanner agreed to inherit the wartime study of malnutrition in orphans in Harpenden, England, little did he suspect that on the monthly trips with his colleague Reginald Whitehouse they would end up documenting as never before an archetypal passage in every human life: adolescence. More than half a century later, their atlas of pubertal change still guides virtually every pediatrician in the world.

By the time Tanner and Whitehouse completed the Harpenden study in 1971, they had slapped their calipers on virtually every measurable aspect of pubertal change. Tanner used the study to pursue a special interest in adolescence. (His first academic book, *Growth at Adolescence*, was published in 1955 and is still considered a classic.) He placed each child at Harpenden on a turntable during the monthly measuring sessions and rotated the table while taking photographs, from ten meters away, of front, side, and back. These photographs, the eyes blanked out on otherwise naked bodies to protect identity, have appeared in countless medical textbooks and growth studies because, like time-lapse pictures of human sexuality flowering, they document the development of pubic hair, armpit hair, penis length, breast formation, facial maturation, and other changes that transform a child's body into that of a sexually mature person. They are globally known as the Tanner stages of adolescent development, although Tanner insists he had nothing to do with calling them that and attributes the pioneering work to researchers in Germany and the United States. ("All I did was tidy it up, make it practical, and produce it," he told me.) Tanner and Whitehouse even made a brief, ill-fated foray into the physiological changes of puberty when they took urine samples from the children. This effort was soon abandoned, Tanner noted, "bottle-sharing and beer-substitution being excessive."

In 1962 Tanner published the five-point scale for rating the development of puberty-related characteristics, such as pubic hair, genitalia, and breasts. The message here, once again, was variation. "One of the results of this work," Tanner wrote, "was to show that children differ even in the speed with which they complete each particular developmental sequence, for example of breasts, as well as in the age at which each sequence starts." The Tanner stages still influence everything from the work of pediatric endocrinologists (who assess pubertal development in children), to drug companies (whose applications to the U.S. Food and Drug Administration for growth hormone use depend on clearly defined pubertal staging), to recent studies in the social sciences that link adult psychology and behavior to the timing of pubertal maturation.

In boys, the first outward sign of the physiological upheavals of puberty occurs when the testicles begin to enlarge. This occurs at roughly eleven years of age, at least in boys in North America. (These changes begin about four months later on average in European boys.) As we get into the sensitive chronology of pubertal development, including when it begins and whether or not it is starting earlier now than in the past, readers should bear in mind that all the ages mentioned in this chapter are averages, that the averages vary from country to country by anywhere from one to six months, and that there is a huge amount of individual variation by gender, ethnicity, geography, and genetics in terms of when puberty begins, both on the early and the late side. As one of countless examples, the testicles can begin to enlarge as early as nine and a half and as late as thirteen and a half years of age. Delayed puberty is more common in boys than in girls; precocious puberty, by contrast, is more common in girls than in boys.

Whenever puberty occurs in boys, early or late, one of the first announcements that change is underway is not only the increasing size, but the altered appearance, of the testicles. As they begin to enlarge, the skin of the scrota, the wrinkly sacs in which the testicles rest, changes in color and texture. These are fairly subtle changes, but they are somewhat advanced heralds of much greater changes to come. For example, the first scrub brush of pubic hair typically doesn't appear until about six months after the first observable enlargement of the testicles; the first inklings of change in penile size won't appear for another year; and the similarly dramatic takeoff in overall size due to the growth spurt is about twelve months away, with the peak of the spurt still two years off. Once the testicles begin to slowly ramp up the production of sex hormones, however, these life-transforming changes are well in train. The child is leaving childhood for good.

Tanner and Whitehouse were chroniclers, cartographers, and photographers of this momentous transformation. With a battery of instruments, they charted every aspect of pubertal change — from the topography of emerging breasts in girls to the first appearance of whiskers in boys — with almost military precision. They observed exactly when axillary hair — the tufts of hair that grow under the armpits — began to appear (well into the growth spurt, after age thirteen). They created a time-lapse map charting the appearance of hair on the face of adolescent boys: the first wisp crops up at the corners of the upper lip, then marches inward across the entire upper lip, then spreads to the upper cheeks and that little central divot below the lower lip, and then finally fills in the sides and recesses of the chin. They defined the physical changes, not only in height but also in shape, that occur with the growth spurt, as well as the differences in the timing and characteristics of these changes between girls and boys. By 1970 they had produced a kind of syncopated, orchestral map of puberty for both boys and girls.

Once the testes begin to enlarge, multiple changes are set in motion. Shortly after age twelve, pubic hair first begins to show in boys. Around twelve and a half, the penis begins to enlarge, and other, less obvious reproductive changes also take place. Both the prostate gland, which adds lubricating secretions to sperm as it is ejaculated, and the seminal vesicles, the pipes that carry the seminal fluid to the penis, begin to grow in concert with the penis. The first hint that this replumbed reproductive network is up and running often announces itself, rudely, as a wet dream, or nocturnal emission. This typically begins to happen about one year after the penis has enjoyed its little growth spurt and occurs, as Tanner wittily put it in one of his books, "often during sleep and accompanied by appropriate dreaming." But Tanner also made a point that is often overlooked: although the machinery of reproduction technically functions, it doesn't function particularly well at first. Boys produce fewer and less hardy sperm at the beginning of puberty, rendering them not as fertile as they ultimately will be. An analogous situation pertains in adolescent girls, who may not produce a mature egg until months or years after they begin menstruating.

The growth of the penis is not only an intense physical change but also (it goes without saying) is part of a psychological and indeed cultural obsession that is older than the codpiece jokes in Shakespeare and as recent as the latest Calvin Klein advertising campaign. For the record, researchers affiliated with the Institute for Sex Research reported in 1979, in a follow-up to Alfred Kinsey's famous survey of male sexual practices, that the average Caucasian penis measured 3.86 inches long and 3.16 inches around in a flaccid state; the average African American penis measured 4.34 inches long and 3.78 inches around. All of those measurements carried what might be considered a psychological as well as a statistical margin of error: they were based on self-reporting.

Some of the most important changes in male puberty are far less visually apparent. As we have learned from the work of psychologist Richard Tremblay, one of these changes, the increased secretion of testosterone, clearly affects male behavior — although, as his research also shows, a boy's environment influences the amount of testosterone he makes in the first place. Perhaps the subtlest yet most profound changes occur in the brain, where an adolescent growth spurt can be detected with modern technology. This growth spurt is, paradoxically, measured by the *subtraction* of neural tissue.

In 1992 a research team headed by Judith Rapaport at the National Institute of Mental Health began a longitudinal study of more than one thousand children, in which researchers tracked neural development using MRI images. They have reported that regions of the brain associated with language systems grow noticeably prior to puberty, that there is a "second wave of neural development" during the teenage years, and that the brain simultaneously shrinks, or loses tissue, during this period. "The number of nerve cells is not changing," Jay N. Giedd, a member of the team, told me, "but they are growing more connections." In several recent publications, Giedd and his colleagues have reported that the volume of gray matter in the frontal cortices — the part of the brain associated with higher cognitive function — peaks in girls at age 11 and in boys at age 12; volume of the temporal lobes, however, doesn't peak until age 16.2 in boys and 16.7 in girls, and several parts of the brain do not reach adult size until the mid-twenties. Do these changes affect behavior? Giedd has noted that the dorsal lateral prefrontal cortex, "important for controlling impulses, is among the latest brain regions to mature without reaching adult dimensions until the early twenties."

"My best working hypothesis," Giedd said in an interview, "is that in children, there are more twigs, more roots, and the nerve connections are bushier, and then after puberty, the advance is by pruning. So even though the bush is skinnier, the quality is better. I guess the best analogy is to Michelangelo and a block of marble, where the quality improves as you take things away. That's what experience teaches — what to keep and what to throw away."

Thus it may be better to think of this neural growth spurt during adolescence not so much as the creation of new brain mass, but rather as the sculpting and grooming of what was already there. Much of this "growth" comes in the form of new connections between existing neurons. One of the biggest questions in neuroscience today is whether puberty "seals off" brain growth the way sex hormones seal the ends of bones. One hypothesis is that as the amount of testosterone generally increases in boys (and as estradiol increases in girls), wiring patterns in the brain, sculpted by a childhood's worth of highly personal and individual experiences — nurture, nutrition, fights, abandonment, flute practice, all sorts of large and small endeavors and behaviors — become more or less permanently fixed. It is as if a neuropsychological circuitry is tentatively mapped out by the experiences of childhood and adolescence, and then the reproductive hormones typical of puberty solder that circuitry in a much more permanent fashion. Not rigidly and irrevocably — otherwise, education would be useless once the ends of our bones fused — but tentatively. Thus a basic architecture, contributing to a basic probability of neurocognitive tendencies, may well be fixed by the end of adolescence.

This process remains unclear in humans. But researchers have discovered that in birds, for example, an animal's flexibility in learning the song system can be extended when testosterone is removed from immature males. Cheryl Sisk, a psychologist at Michigan State University, suspects that there is a neural equivalent to the way puberty seals bone growth. "I'm betting there is, based on our behavioral data," she said, "but we don't yet have empirical evidence for permanent structural changes induced by steroids during puberty."

If this hypothesis is proven, this change would be among the most invisible that occur during puberty, and also among the most profound in terms of adult behavior. So while it's clearly not true that puberty is all in your head, that's where it starts, as best we know, and some of its most lasting effects may be cemented into place there.

THE MAIN PHYSICAL changes of puberty don't require a microscope or a brain scan or even a striptease to see. Hormonal changes produce the growth spurt, which leaves its mark, in body and mind, as height. Boys (I'll talk briefly about girls in a moment) tend to be slightly taller on average than girls prior to the adolescent growth spurt, but they become considerably taller afterward. This is a remarkable period of physical transformation, and the word "schuss" captures it perfectly.

The adolescent growth spurt typically lasts about three years. It reaches its peak about eighteen months after it starts — in boys, at roughly age fourteen (that is, it peaks about two and a half years after the testicles first begin to enlarge). The rate of growth is stunning. Although it is not even close to the explosive growth rate at the time of birth, it is certainly the fastest growth of which humans are fully conscious (not to say self-conscious). During the first year of the spurt, a boy will grow on average about 7 centimeters, or about 2¾ inches. In the next year, at the peak of the spurt, he'll grow about 9 centimeters, or 3½ inches. And in the last year, he'll grow another 7 centimeters, or 2¾ inches. In other words, a typical boy will shoot up about 9 inches in three years, and many boys grow even more than that.

The main drivers of physical growth are, not surprisingly, hormones, and the pituitary gland is once again the central spigot. Like a drenched, pea-size sponge, the pituitary fairly drips with growth hormone, which is a thousand times more prevalent than any other pituitary hormone. Growth hormone is released in short-acting pulses that last roughly ten to twenty minutes each and is then cleared from the body. When doctors have examined the blood of robustly growing adolescents, they have found that there are many times during a twenty-four-hour-period when growth hormone is virtually undetectable. At the beginning of puberty, the amount of growth hormone is at about the same level as it is in a young adult, and it climbs dramatically in concert with the growth spurt, then subsides again to the young-adult level. As pediatric endocrinologist Ron G. Rosenfeld has noted, "It has been said, without too great a stretch of the imagination, that a rock will grow if one gives it enough growth hormone."

Growth hormone acts most conspicuously as a biochemical elixir for bones, but it's not a solo act. In the case of longitudinal bone growth — the kind that produces height — physical change is the result of a duet between two complementary hormones. The first, growth hormone, is the holistic driver, if you will. Once released by the pituitary gland, it diffuses through the body and acts on molecular receptors in a broad range of tissues — not just at the ends of bones but also in the internal organs, in the larynx, in the bony brow of the forehead (where the skull thickens), in the lower jaw (which grows prominently forward), and elsewhere. Triggered by pulses of growth hormone, the liver begins to churn out a complementary hormone. It was originally called somatomedin C, but now it is more commonly known as insulin-like growth factor-1 (IGF-1). A growing body needs both of these hormones to trigger the transformation of cartilage into bone. In a lovely example of the body's self-governing growth controls, the surge of signals from the hypothalamus triggers the release of pituitary hormones. These include growth hormone, but also FSH and LH, which provoke the maturation of the testicles, which in turn begin manufacturing testosterone. And it is the sex hormones — testosterone, its levels building up during puberty and diffusing throughout the maturing male body, and (surprisingly) estradiol — that ultimately seal the ends of bones and turn off major growth.

Which part of a teenager's body schusses the most? One of the most counterintuitive aspects of adolescent growth is that more of the pubertal spurt occurs in the trunk — that is, from the neck to the waist — than in the legs. Experts in growth — as early as Franz Boas at the turn of the century — have rigorously measured the "sitting height" of children, from the pelvis up, including the head. This is a way of distinguishing leg growth from growth of the rest of the body. Tanner and Whitehouse discovered that over the course of the adolescent growth spurt, the trunk grows faster than the legs. Put another way, leg growth peaks first, followed by chest and shoulder growth. Tanner translated this biological oddity into a quotidian idiom that any parent can understand: "Thus a boy stops growing out of his trousers (at least in length) a year before he stops growing out of his jackets."

During puberty, boys grow more in the shoulders and muscles than girls, who grow more in the hips. This kind of sex-specific physical difference, common throughout the animal kingdom, is called sexual dimorphism, and it has very clear physiological explanations in human biology. In boys, cartilage cells in the shoulders have receptors — that is, molecular docks — for testosterone and other androgens, the male sex hormones that gradually increase in amount around the time of adolescence. In girls, cartilage cells in the hip joints have estrogen receptors, resulting in the pelvic growth typical of the female growth spurt. Since cartilage is the raw material for bone growth and skeletal maturity, these differences on a molecular level result in physical differences as boys and girls mature. Thus boys undergo dramatic changes in their trunks, as well as dramatic increases in physical strength.

IF THERE WAS a bombshell that came out of the Harpenden study, it was something that had been suspected since the time of Aristotle but had never really been pinned down. Any growth chart that shows boys and girls together will reveal it, and it is a physical fact with enormous psychological repercussions: girls enter puberty earlier than boys, mature sooner than boys, and finish their major growth before boys. "After birth," Aristotle noted, "everything is perfected more quickly in females than in males."

Tanner and his associates defined five stages of pubertal development for girls, chronicling genital development, breast formation, and other physical changes. Unlike boys, however, girls have a clear demarcation of reproductive maturity: the initiation of ovulation, which leads to the first menstrual period, or menarche. Because there is a huge amount of variation in girls as well as boys in terms of tempo, these changes can begin as early as age eight or as late as age fourteen while still falling in the normal range.

The larger point is that most girls are well into their final maturation before many boys begin. It is not a silent or invisible trend. It is as apparent as the physical changes in the adolescent girls' breasts and hips, the onset of menstruation, and the generally more mature, adult bearing of the girls. Boys as a group, and slowly maturing boys in particular, face one of the most profound lessons of puberty: this developmental lag affects psychology and temperament, the self-image you nurture and the persona you project, the company you keep, the range of experience you sample, and the very comfort and confidence you feel about your body and yourself. Tom Stoppard, the British playwright and screenwriter, once joked, "Maturity is a high price to pay for growing up." According to growth scientists, however, those payments are spread out over a long time, and there's a very good evolutionary reason for that stiff price tag.

"Adolescence became part of human life history," Barry Bogin writes, "because it conferred significant reproductive advantages to our species, in part by allowing the adolescent to learn and practice adult economic, social and sexual behaviors before reproducing." Bogin and linguist John Locke have suggested that the extended childhood and adolescence of humans parallels more-mature vocal physiology and increasingly sophisticated use of language, which promotes social interaction and enhances sexual selection. Frans de Waal has suggested that "small talk" is the human equivalent of grooming among primates. And to use an often cited analogy of evolutionary biologists about the ways males make themselves attractive to prospective mates, idle chatter or witty repartee may be the peacock feathers of humans.

IN THE UNIVERSE of changes associated with puberty, the time when a boy's voice cracks may seem relatively insignificant. But it is the source of one of adolescence's most enduringly contemptuous putdowns, "pipsqueak," and can be concealed only by silence — a behavioral adaptation that is not always positive. I had more in common with Bach's choristers — in age of change, not talent — than other boys of my era, and this fact had a significant impact on the social worlds I inhabited as an adolescent. I attended a junior high school in Michigan that had a very ambitious choral program, and the music director there cultivated a core group of singers in small, specialized ensembles. My voice was one of the highest, and I was invited to participate in an eight-person, all-male choral group that performed a classic barbershop repertoire. Decked out in red-and-white-striped bibs, black bow ties, and boaters, we gave concerts everywhere from the Detroit Yacht Club to Michigan State University.

I mention this for several reasons. One is that, if you lined us up, with the high-pitched first tenors on the left and the low-pitched basses all the way on the right, we looked like a picture of the Tanner stages of puberty set to music. The first tenors tended to be small, boyish, and biologically juvenile. As the voices got deeper, the bodies got increasingly larger. And it wasn't just that the basses on average were bigger — they were huskier, hairier, and more muscular. Heck, they shaved. They even had blunt, monosyllabic names to go with their hulking stature: Gar and Dolph. This is not just a picture of singers in ridiculous getups; it is a portrait of adolescent social status and anxiety. At least that's the image I'm left with.

But if you look at the picture a different way, you begin to appreciate a different aspect of pubertal maturation: the way it shapes the company you keep. I realize now, in a way I never appreciated before, that the squeaky voice that came with delayed maturation bought me a ticket to the world of choral music. Through this quirk of nature, I learned to read music, to *appreciate* music — not just the early Stones and Hendrix, which I listened to at home, but Bartók, Ives, masters of the German lieder, and composers of religious music. I sang some of those songs to my children when they were infants, from eighteenth-century sacral music to "Coney Island Babe." A love of music can be, as epidemiologists like to say, vertically transmitted.

Buoyed by such fabulous music, swept along in the luscious cataract of human sound that is choral singing, I found my voice. As I gained confidence as a performer, I learned the discipline and courage that goes into small-ensemble performing. It wasn't exactly the same as athletic bravery, and it was nothing like being the quarterback of the football team, but it took a potential adolescent liability and gave it some redemptive value. Indeed, my fluttering tenor voice resided high enough in the register that I was recruited to sing in adult church choirs, which expanded the circle of acquaintances for a boy in junior high school and exposed me to some of the greatest music ever composed — including, of course, hymns penned by Johann Sebastian Bach and doubtless sung by his adolescent choristers.

The pretty divorcée with the husky alto voice in the church choir took a liking to me, and when girls your own age don't give you a second look, this kind of attention takes on a special significance. She was no Mrs. Robinson, but she did give me a pet snake (Freud would have a field day with that), which, moreover, turned out to be classically neurotic. It refused to eat, recoiled from tiny mice — its usual prey — and eventually died of starvation.

And yet my voice was still high-pitched, excitable, and warbling — even when I wasn't singing. That was more of a social liability, and it may have led to a growing, generalized reticence during my middle school and high school years. Because of an obscure aspect of cartilage growth in the larynx, I was, in every sense of the word, a pip-squeak. Where once I had been close enough in stature to my peers to at least taste the triumphalism of bullying (however shallow and short-lived), I now found myself clinging to the lowest part of the growth curve. I wasn't big, I wasn't hairy, and I was falling farther and farther down that pitiless dominance hierarchy of adolescent boys, until I became the target of taunts, teasing, and worse. If it is indeed part of our evolutionary heritage to be aware of size, adolescence is a particularly perilous crossing, because our inborn attentiveness to size converges with the insecure self-consciousness that teenagers have turned into performance art. At the same time, we are becoming aware that the world has very strong feelings about whether it is better to be big or small. That is why bullying in middle school and high school can be particularly traumatic.

8

BELITTLED
The Consequences of Being Bullied

> Many children do not grow properly despite good food, because coming home from school they still feel the pain of rough blows and anticipate their renewal with anxiety and fear, so that they are never happy or light-hearted.
>
> —HIPPOLYT GUARINONI, 1610

IF, AS EXPERTS INCREASINGLY agree, bullying arises out of an imbalance of power, one of the greatest imbalances of all is in the power of attendant memory. An episode of random humiliation may matter so little to the perpetrator that he will barely remember it by the end of the day, while the victim will likely husband his memory of the episode, in all its belittling detail, for decades. It's long been my hunch that around the time boys enter puberty and on through adolescence, these episodes (and the memories they create) have a particularly corrosive and personality-shaping power, precisely because physical or even verbal humiliation at the time of sexual awakening cuts very close to the bone.

In my own personal pantheon of humiliation, the place of honor goes to an episode that occurred on an unseasonably warm day in the fall of 1965. I was a freshman in high school, a new kid in town, and it was the beginning of the school year — in other words, prime hunting season for bullies. I felt a little like the deer in that famous Gary Larson *Far Side* cartoon: it has a huge bull's-eye on its chest, and a fellow animal commiserates, "Bummer of a birthmark, Hal." By almost any psychological or physical yardstick, I was overqualified for the role of victim: not just new to the school (a large, factory-size high school in the western suburbs of Chicago), but also small of stature (four feet nine, according to school records I recently consulted), squeaky of voice, bespectacled, insecure, and nerdy. As it turns out, the incident conformed to many of the recent research findings about the nature of bullying — where it takes place, who does it, and at what developmental stage. In this case, it was in a gym class — where practitioners of bullying always enjoy a home-field advantage — full of thirteen- and fourteen-year-old boys.

The afternoon was sunny and warm, although it had rained heavily the night before. Huge puddles of water dotted the athletic fields where the freshman gym class met. When you deprive everyone of their usual wardrobe and force them to wear a standard white gym outfit, the sheer uniformity of the garb tends to accentuate the physical differences between boys, and the differences are never as clear and unforgiving as among thirteen- and fourteen-year-old boys. Some of the boys were tall, some short; some were as thin as saplings, a few corpulent (not as many, probably, as there would be today). Limbs were scrawny, poking out of white T-shirts and gym shorts; whiskers were wispy, if present at all; Adam's apples were sticking out as sharply as elbow joints; and acne was omnipresent.

Although my height placed me in roughly the first percentile of modern growth charts for age and gender (the first U.S. national charts wouldn't come out for another decade or so), I was not one of those boys terrorized by gym class. In fact, I loved it. Despite my small size, I was a good athlete, faster and more coordinated than a lot of the larger boys. At eighty-two and a half pounds, I obviously didn't bring much mass to the physics of competition, but between speed and quickness, a talent for suddenly changing direction, and an abject terror of getting hit hard, I had always been elusive, even in physical games such as football. And, truth to tell, I got a kick out of faking out the early maturers in games of skill.

Early in the school year, I gravitated toward another small classmate of mine in gym class, a tough-looking and tough-minded boy named Scott Novotny. He also was a good athlete, and we ended up on the same flag football team in gym class — a team that regularly used to defeat bigger (and slower) opponents. Maybe our success contributed to the Wishbone Incident.

Gym class always began with calisthenics — halfhearted sit-ups, trembling semi-pushups, lolling Gumby-like jumping jacks. As we went through the motions of these exercises on the wet grass, the phys ed instructors walked up and down the rows, flat clipboards perched on rotund guts, addressing the students by last name and ridiculing this boy's quivering biceps, that boy's scrawny butt as it arched like the Rialto Bridge at the height of a pushup. At the conclusion of calisthenics, we were sent off to run around the perimeter of several football fields at the rear of the school. Then we spent the rest of the period playing whatever game was part of that week's "curriculum."

On this day, for no reason that I could discern, two boys waited in ambush for me at the far turn of the football fields. One of them was named Ken. He was a broad-shouldered, square-faced kid with a kind of hooded, malevolent squint. During my first few weeks at school, he had been the welcome wagon from hell, dumping my books or "accidentally" bumping into me in the hallway. Nothing dramatic, just the kind of persistent physical hazing that has you looking over your shoulder all day. I can't remember the other boy. Anyway, as I was running my lap, trailing toward the rear of the pack, they came toward me suddenly and knocked me down. Then each of them grabbed one of my legs, and, yanking them a bit apart like a wishbone, the boys dragged me along the ground and through a very large puddle. It might as well have been Lake Michigan. There I was, on my back, bumping along the ground, squishing through the mud, staring up at the sky while my butt made a blunt prow through water and weeds. A bunch of unattractive sensations vied for ascendancy in my mind: shock, helplessness, embarrassment, shame, abandonment. Physical pain was the least of it. Perhaps the greatest part of the humiliation I later felt was the sense of ease and impunity with which the assault was committed. Their physical mastery over the situation — and me — was so complete that I have no memory of crying out, shouting, or cursing. I know that no one came to my aid, and I seem to remember that Ken, after letting go of my leg, proud and smirking, wiped the grass and mud off his hands before finishing his lap. The whole thing seemed so casual, so simultaneously cruel and indifferent, that it was as if they'd done nothing more emotionally taxing than drag a bag of leaves to the curb for garbage pickup.

The psychological shock of this kind of assault almost always exceeds the physical pain. I wasn't hurt, but that was little consolation. Coated with water and mud, sluggish with the insult, wondering why it had happened, I straggled back to where all the other students were waiting. My bedraggled appearance inspired comment, of course, but provoked nothing like outrage. One of the gym teachers remarked that my gym uniform had better be clean by the next class or I'd get marked down for it. If he was concerned at all about what had happened, his lame joke suggested that it was just a matter of boys being boys.

On that lonely run back to the group I felt not just humiliation and helplessness but also a larger sense of social isolation. After such an experience, those feelings of social isolation don't disappear right away. You put on a brave face, participate in the class as if nothing unusual has happened, take your shower along with everyone else (watching the mud and grass clippings wash down the drain), and take those muddy clothes home to be washed. If your mother asks what happened to your clothes, you just say you fell playing football and leave the room before she has time to ask a follow-up question. (When I wrote about this incident in 1999, it was the first time my parents had ever heard about it.)

But you can't wash away the residue of physical assault. And this, from my perspective, is the truly insufferable part of bullying, especially when it happens during adolescence. If you are smaller than the men-children who have their growth spurts early, there's not much you can do about it except change your behavior. You try to steer clear of boys like Ken, even though there's no way you can avoid all contact. You become more attentive to potential ambush; you avoid certain places at certain times of day. You try not to attract too much attention, which can extend to classroom participation and academic performance. You do all these things to avoid a repeat of the assault, but they end up becoming an integral part of the way you act. In adapting your behavior to avoid a reprise, you begin to curtail who you are. Bullying not only physically belittles you; it can diminish you psychologically and stunt your emotional growth. This is especially true in situations where there are repeated episodes, with neither warning nor apparent incitement, and where adults — such as my gym teacher — show no inclination to intervene.

Although I put it off for a long time, I finally worked up the nerve to contact Ken. When he returned my call and left a message on my machine, my heart actually began to race at the sound of his voice. He still lived in the western suburbs of Chicago, where he worked as a manufacturer's representative, and he sounded genuinely chagrined when I explained why I was calling. "Oh, Jesus!" he said after I described the incident in gym class. "I apologize for that." Not that it actually stuck out in his memory. "I got into a lot of fights," he admitted, "but I don't remember that. I mean, I don't deny it, because I was such an asshole in those days. It took me quite a while to grow out of it, if I even have." It was an unexpected, if anecdotal, confirmation of how many of us feel that our behavior during adolescence persists long after we leave school behind. We ended up having a very pleasant conversation, during which he reminded me that he had weighed only 120 pounds in his freshman year and always considered himself a small guy, not a bully. But the conversation also made clear that he had been gotten into his share of boyhood scraps. He recalled getting suspended for a fight in the cafeteria, and he also recalled getting into several fights while defending a "mentally challenged" friend whom other kids were picking on. "I didn't like to fight," he said, "but it was just something you did. I think a lot of it back then was about earning your stripes. If kids picked on you and you stood up to them, they would leave you alone."

Adolescent bullying feels distinctly different from grade school bullying to me. For one thing, there is less physical aggression among adolescents; my anecdote notwithstanding, numerous studies have shown that physical abuse tends to diminish after middle school. And yet indirect aggression — verbal abuse, taunts, and teases — becomes not only more pronounced but also more complex. The insults are cleverer and more pointed, the timing is meant to be more humiliating, and the cruelty plays to a larger, and in some ways less empathetic, audience. The victims may be more vulnerable, too. It's been my perception (and, no doubt, my bias) that boys are especially susceptible to the effects of bullying in their adolescent years because of the added insecurities inherent in pubertal maturation and sexual development. Physical aggression is not just a matter of large and small; it is also a matter of manhood, strength versus weakness, and ultimately attractiveness to the opposite sex. Indirect aggression, perhaps even worse, achieves a kind of psychological humiliation in public among your peers at a time when the adolescent personality — appearing to be enigmatic, detached, cool, emotionally in control, sexually adept, and mature — is perched on a fulcrum of self-esteem so fragile it's like an I-beam balanced on an egg.

According to recent statistics, well over 3 million schoolchildren in the United States alone deal with bullying of one degree or another. If the victims of bullying respond the same way I did, that's a lot of involuntary behavior modification, a lot of personalities getting sanded down to the minimum, a lot of wings unnaturally tucked in.

And although the psychological literature on short stature is divided in many ways, it's not split on this issue: smallness definitely places an adolescent boy at risk for bullying. Time and again, studies have suggested that shorter kids get picked on. Linda Voss of the Wessex Growth Study in England stated it clearly and succinctly in a much-cited 2000 paper, which looked at thirteen-to-fifteen-year-olds below the third percentile in height versus a control group of taller peers. "Short boys," she wrote, "were more than twice as likely as control boys to be victims." In terms of adolescent bullying, small physical size is indeed a "bummer of a birthmark."

IN CHAPTER 5, I wrote about the psychology of the bully, especially during early childhood and the elementary school years. In this chapter, I want to talk about the victims of bullying, especially during the middle school and high school years. The intersection of biology and aggression has always fascinated scientists; when the intersection occurs in the neighborhood of puberty, the interest falls somewhere between philosophic and prophetic. A lot of research on childhood aggression has either reinforced the notion of man's inherent and inherited predisposition toward aggression, first brought to popular attention by Konrad Lorenz in the 1960s, or sought to challenge it. For every study suggesting that the adolescent rise in testosterone levels leads inevitably to greater strength and more aggressive behavior, there is another to suggest that children learn to aggress from the influence of bad social environments, whether family or peer groups. "It is an interesting paradox," Richard Tremblay observed in 2000, "that the more humans become 'civilized,' the more they appear to be preoccupied with violence."

Among the scientific experts who study physical aggression in adolescents, few have thought longer or harder about it than Tremblay, whose work we first met in the earlier chapter on prepubertal bullying. Tremblay's work has increasingly focused on the very earliest periods of infancy and childhood, but in 1998, benefiting from data generated by one of his longitudinal studies, he published a fascinating account of the interaction of testosterone, aggression, social dominance, and physical size in early adolescent boys between the ages of eleven and thirteen.

Beginning in the 1980s, Tremblay and his colleagues at the University of Montreal and in France studied the development of antisocial behavior in a large group of males that they followed from the boys' kindergarten years on. The boys, numbering more than a thousand at the start of the study, came from a somewhat narrow demographic slice of Canadian society: they were all from low-socioeconomic areas of Montreal, exhibited low educational status, and had French-speaking parents. In the mid-1990s, Tremblay decided to concentrate on a subset of these boys for a more focused study. They were evaluated by their teachers, their peers, and themselves in terms of social behavior; they were tested for testosterone levels in their saliva on an annual basis for three years; and they were measured at ages twelve and thirteen for height, weight, wrist and head circumference, and other physical features.

What did the Canadian researchers find? First off, they at least partially disentangled the physical from the behavioral when it comes to aggression. They found that early adolescents with a large body mass were more likely to be physically aggressive or socially dominant than boys with smaller body mass. Yet early adolescents who were socially dominant tended not to be physically aggressive and tended to have higher testosterone levels than those who were physically aggressive. Interestingly, puberty really hadn't taken off for most of the eleven-year-old boys; almost 90 percent of them had no detectable levels of testosterone in their saliva.

Let me repeat that finding in a slightly different way, because it contradicts a very common cultural assumption about testosterone and behavior. By the time the boys reached age twelve, physical aggression was associated not with high levels of testosterone, but with low levels of the hormone. Higher levels of testosterone were, however, associated with social dominance, which Tremblay distinguishes from pure physical dominance and likens to a more socialized and socially acceptable form of aggression. Furthermore, height per se did not seem to influence a particular behavior, but size — in the form of body mass — did. As Tremblay and his colleagues wrote, "Boys with a larger body mass at twelve years of age reported themselves to be more physically aggressive and to be more delinquent than boys with smaller body mass." Distinguishing between height and body mass may seem obvious, but in fact this distinction has only recently been a feature of social science research, and the implications are clear: thinking in terms of short and tall may not tell you nearly as much as thinking in terms of big and small. Indeed, many tall men with whom I've spoken point out the obvious: the tall skinny child may be as much a target of bullying as the small skinny child. Anyone who has spent five minutes on a playground can intuit the importance of body mass in the way physical interactions unfold.

This careful Canadian study, itself part of a larger and equally careful longitudinal survey, does not lend itself to snappy, concise interpretation — not least because the results conflict in part with some other studies looking at testosterone and antisocial behavior. But the data allowed Tremblay and his colleagues to venture several provocative hypotheses. Their results suggest that testosterone levels at the beginning of puberty predict social dominance a year later. But they take that notion much further. Here is the money passage from their 1998 paper (I've omitted the parenthetical citations from their text):

> We suggest that the testosterone-dominance link, if it exists, should be present from infancy onwards. Competition for objects and physical aggression appear to be more frequent during the first thirty-six months after birth than at any other time in life. Dominance hierarchies are clearly present during the preschool years. If perinatal testosterone exposure [that is, detectable amounts of the sex hormone around the time of birth, which is a well-established biological fact] has an impact on sexual and social behavior through its impact on the organization of the brain, why would it not have an impact on early expression of dominant behavior? And why would early dominance experience not have an impact on dominance during the early adolescent years and adulthood?

Put crudely, they are suggesting that the infant is father to the bully.

Tremblay and his colleagues go on to draw some very fine distinctions about how their previous questions might be answered:

> Children probably learn early on from their environment who and how to successfully dominate. The better socialized will learn to use language and prosocial behavior instead of physical aggression, the less well socialized will continue to use physical aggression. Depending on the social context they encounter, their behavioral style will lead to successful or unsuccessful dominant status. Physical aggression can lead to dominance in a camp for

disruptive children, in a delinquent gang, or in a prison. In these samples testosterone, aggression, and dominance should be correlated. However, in the average classroom, or the average workplace, physical aggression does not lead to social dominance. In these samples we should observe a correlation between testosterone level and social dominance, but not with physical aggression.

This is excellent, even thrilling, science, not because of what the researchers conclude (they wisely refrain from providing a simple take-home lesson), but because they suggest that behavior, and even biology, depends very much on a shifting environmental situation, just as Sapolsky's baboon study showed (see chapter 6). This should be Darwin 101 to anyone who understands natural selection, yet in our gene-besotted age, we are often too quick to place all our conjectural chips on the genes and not on the environment in which they operate. Tremblay's research suggests that physical aggression is rewarded with social dominance only in certain environments (gangs, prisons, camps for delinquents), and *only there* do testosterone levels rise. The same physically aggressive behavior in the "wrong" environment leads not to social dominance, but to social isolation, and testosterone levels plummet in response. Thus, testosterone does not produce the aggressive behavior; rather, behavior produces or suppresses testosterone, depending on the social situation. "If you are socially dominant, and this means that other people recognize you as a leader, it will have an impact on your testosterone level, compared to someone, for example, who is physically aggressive, who can physically dominate others, but is rejected by others," Tremblay said. "That person will be socially rejected, and being socially rejected reduces your testosterone level."

If this interpretation holds up, it also suggests that bullying — at least the more physically abusive form of bullying — is most likely to occur at the boundaries where a better-socialized population comes in contact with a more poorly socialized population. This typically does not occur within small groups of like-minded peers — any socially homogeneous gathering of people with homogeneous interests, such as chess clubs, choruses, swim teams, or stamp collectors. Rather, these boundaries inevitably crisscross the larger social structures in which adolescents of disparate backgrounds are flung together — not school per se, because even classes can indirectly segregate children by different socioeconomic strata or academic achievement, but in all those familiar and dreadful places where adolescent subcultures collide, where diversity is an inevitable by-product of large numbers of people converging geographically: gym class, the locker room, the cafeteria, the hallways, the bathrooms. (It is no accident that in the 2003 film *Elephant*, which chronicles a Columbine-like shooting, director Gus Van Sant set much of the action in precisely those peripheral, undersupervised locations.) Unfortunately, if school grounds represent a collection of these boundaries, the adults who monitor the cafeteria and hallways — the educational equivalent of border police — are rarely well-trained, well-paid, and esteemed in school communities.

There is one area of aggression that Tremblay and his colleagues do shed much light on: the verbal aspects of aggression — the taunting, the teasing, the daily or weekly campaigns of hazing. This is called indirect aggression, and some of the impetus to examine it came out of research on female nonhuman primates by Sarah Blaffer Hrdy in the early 1980s. Soon after Hrdy's work, researchers in Finland reported that early-adolescent girls (ages eleven and twelve) committed more indirect aggression than boys the same age. In recent times, e-bullying has become a particularly prevalent form of indirect aggression. Electronic mail and instant messaging have allowed humiliating gossip to be broadcast in a way never before possible, and schools have been forced to adopt antibullying policies that extend to the digital realm. Interestingly, the anonymity and verbal nature of e-bullying reduces the role of physical size in determining perpetrators and victims.

Recent research looking at these issues in a national context emerged in 2004. Mary Overpeck, formerly an epidemiological statistician at the federal Health Resources and Services Administration in Bethesda, Maryland, specializes in childhood behavior and aggression. She headed a group of researchers that looked at the relationship between bullying and pubertal maturation. Like Tremblay, they found that height was not associated with bullying. Pubertal status, however, leapt out as a factor. The distinction here is subtle but important: being big wasn't enough by itself, but being big combined with pubertal maturation was related to aggression. "Body size isn't it," Overpeck told me, summing up the data. "Maturation is." In fairness, body size and height are often products of pubertal maturation, and this connection may be more apparent in terms of the victims of bullying. Although Overpeck was still analyzing the data when we spoke, she said, "I think the victims themselves are probably smaller, shorter, or thinner."

SINCE MY DAYS in school, bullying has become big business — in educational circles, of course, but also among lawyers who have begun filing lawsuits on behalf of the bullied, among reporters (and writers) who love to describe it, and among academics who mount huge studies of schoolchildren to detect its underlying causes and effects. Schools compete to have the most enlightened antibullying programs, and bullying studies are a staple of the academic literature. There is even a *Journal of Interpersonal Violence*. Whenever school violence erupts, recognizable rosters of experts begin showing up immediately on TV.

As horrendous as the more notorious outbreaks of violence unquestionably are, Columbine and Red Lake are rare and unusually extreme examples of a much more pervasive, rather more modest, yet insidious pattern of everyday life for elementary and middle school students. An essential component of the bullying dynamic was powerfully exposed by a recent court decision involving a long-running episode of bullying at a public school in New York City that veered out of control just as the boys reached the cusp of adolescence.

In the spring of 2004, a jury in Queens, New York, awarded $195,000 in damages to a student named Joey Bari, who had been verbally harassed, bullied, and ultimately injured by a fellow fifth-grade student in a campaign of intimidation that had been going on for years. The financial settlement predictably attracted the attention of local journalists, but it is the prosaic details of the case — not just the bullying but also the institutional indifference to the bullying — that make it more emblematic of the problem than cases like Columbine. The episode, according to court testimony and press accounts, began not with physical scuffles, but with name-calling. It started in the third grade with a single epithet: Frecklejuice.

What made Joey Bari a bullying victim? As a sports handicapper might say, you pick 'em. He was the new kid in his class at Public School 98 in Douglaston, Queens. He was very small for his age. He had a lot of freckles. He wore his hair slicked back with gel, in homage to Elvis Presley. He wore preppy clothes. His mother, recently divorced and single, reportedly complained regularly to school officials about the situation. If you dip into the scientific literature on bullying, you'll run across many of these factors — size, physical appearance, outsider status, even the overprotective mom — as statistically significant traits associated with the victims of bullying. And yet, looking at the problem through our idiosyncratic lenses, we're always tempted to ascribe the cause to one factor. Amid this constellation of possibilities, it is foolish to try to identify a single leading cause. (Those who subscribe to the myth that all of Napoleon's problematic behavior stemmed from his physical size, for example, are reminded that his childhood nickname — *Paille-au-Nez,* or "Straw-nose" — had nothing to do with his height.)

In the end, perhaps the reason the bullying occurred isn't important. The bully — his identity was protected in court records because he was a minor — repeatedly harassed Joey with taunts of "Frecklejuice" and threatened physical violence. In fifth grade, he made good on those threats, kneeing Joey in the stomach on one occasion, knocking him down on the playground on another (which resulted in Joey's breaking one wrist and spraining the other). A variation on this kind of behavior probably occurs in every schoolyard in every school district in the land. But the potential for physical harm increases around adolescence because of growing disparities in size, and the potential for psychological harm probably increases, too, because of the heightened emotional vulnerabilities of puberty.

A more interesting question is not what caused the Queens episode to start, but what allowed it to continue. That in essence is what the court case was about. On numerous occasions, after Joey complained at home about incidents with the bully, his mother went to the school and sought help from the principal. She asked, for example, that the two boys not be placed in the same class. At each meeting, the principal reportedly assured her that he would look into it and then reportedly did nothing. The decision of a New York State Supreme Court jury, in making its award of damages some eight years after the bullying campaign began, may be seen as a rebuke not to the bully but to the school, for failing to intervene when the problem became obvious.

Adult intervention is perhaps the most important variable in bullying behavior. Like my sixth-grade fight with Jimmy, and like the Wishbone Incident, these episodes begin and end within seconds; adults are rarely aware that they have occurred. Wendy M. Craig and Debra J. Pepler, two prominent Canadian researchers, have quantified exactly these factors during what they have called "naturalistic observations" of bullying on school playgrounds and in classrooms. Using a remote-controlled video camera focused on a playground, for example, they recorded incidents of physical aggression. In the course of documenting hundreds of these incidents, Craig and Pepler found that episodes of playground bullying "occurred regularly" (once every seven minutes in their observations), lasted on average thirty-eight seconds, and almost always escaped the attention of adult supervisors, who in any event rarely intervened. Adults stepped in only 4 percent of the time, while peers intervened only 11 percent of the time. When the researchers placed their cameras indoors, they observed about two episodes of bullying in the classroom per hour, mostly indirect and mostly targeting boys. The teachers intervened in only one in five of those episodes and, as the authors noted, were often "not aware of the covert activity." According to Pepler and Craig, "Adults intervened in relatively few episodes and were judged to be unaware of the vast majority of episodes."

This, I think, is the crucial issue in bullying. Schools can talk all they want about schoolwide socialization policies and zero tolerance of bullying, but these policies have to be backed up by adult monitoring and intervention, and that requires people, time, and money. I can think back on numerous episodes of bullying from my own upbringing when adults were either not present, not observing, or, worst of all, present *and* observing but indifferent. When you are the victim of bullying, adult indifference can be particularly devastating.

As soon as social scientists began studying bullying in a systematic way, the lack of adult intervention emerged as a central problem. Dan Olweus reported in his early work that 60 percent of secondary school victims of bullying (and about 40 percent of elementary school victims) felt that teachers had "almost never" or only "once in a while" tried to put a stop to bullying. And, according to his research, both bullies and their victims realized this. In other words, everyone understands adult indifference as one of the rules of the game.

Some people suggest that society is overreacting to a normal and generally harmless phase of childhood development. But that's true only if you choose to ignore the mounting evidence that bullying carries significant health costs to perpetrator and victim alike. Joey Bari's experience accords very well with the recent scientific literature on bullying and aggression, right down to the psychosomatic symptoms, such as stomachaches, that he began to suffer. A recent study of Dutch school-children that appeared in the *Journal of Pediatrics*, for example, found that children who were bullied reported a much higher rate of psychosomatic complaints and illnesses, including headaches, abdominal pain, anxiety, sleep problems, and depression. Pepler, Craig, and their colleagues have recently suggested that elementary school children who are chronically victimized by peers may be at heightened risk of developing severe psychological distress akin to posttraumatic stress disorder. The stress may be particularly acute, they speculate, around the time of the emerging sexuality and sexual identity that mark puberty, when adolescent bullies may target "vulnerabilities associated with sexuality."

Some of the parallels to animal research on stress are striking. In recent experiments, for example, researchers reported that mice exposed to persistent physical intimidation by larger, more aggressive adversaries showed "long-term neuronal changes" in the brain circuitry related to several prominent mood disorders, including social aversion and depression. One of the leading factors contributing to a state of chronic pathological stress in baboons in the wild, as Robert Sapolsky and Lisa Share have reported, is the spontaneous, unpredictable, and unprovoked nature of attacks by dominant males. That sounds like high school. It's not just that you've been shoved or punched or verbally abused; it's that it can happen again at any time, without a moment's warning, for no apparent reason, and with no evident remedy. In that sense, even periods of relative calm are misleading, and even intervals of peace are stressful. The victim, alas, has been conditioned to expect the next blow, and these fearful expectations may reflect nothing less than long-term changes in the brain.

ANTIBULLYING PROGRAMS HAVE now become big business. You can order booklets from the Olweus Bullying Prevention Program or consult government-sponsored Web sites such as Stop Bullying Now!, an especially informative site maintained by the Health Resources and Services Administration. The amount of advice is Himalayan in terms of mass and gravity. It's beyond the purview of this book to assess the many antibullying programs and philosophies currently available. The main point is that solutions to bullying in the school setting need to be community-wide. School populations need to be taught that bullying is unacceptable, and when an incident of bullying occurs, it should be the school community — not the victim — that identifies the perpetrator. It's the difference between one person "tattling" and a community saying no. This cultural change is especially important given the research, from Sapolsky's baboons to Tremblay's aggressive adolescents, suggesting that physical aggression (and, by analogy, bullying) is strongly influenced, and can even be moderated, by the social context in which it occurs.

Some parents — and, for that matter, some cultural critics — feel that the emphasis on bullying has gotten out of hand. And when you riffle through the behavioral guidelines for the New York City public school system, where the descriptions of "Level 5 infractions" include "using extreme force" on students or school personnel and "possessing or using a firearm," you realize that calling someone shortie or fatso doesn't rise to the same level of violence or transgression. And there are also legitimate questions about the research.

Almost all of the data on bullying has been based on what are called self-report questionnaires, in which children — often young children — are asked to assess and report their personal experiences. These surveys are for the most part thoughtfully conceived, professionally executed, and far more sophisticated than earlier attempts, and the research community deserves credit for trying to use this admittedly soft instrument to pry out hard answers from a notoriously reticent population. But questionnaires are, in the words of one critic, "notoriously unreliable," and surveys require a certain degree of self-awareness and perception that not all students possess. Some respondents may be reluctant to confirm their emotional and physical humiliations, even in an anonymous setting; others may be only too willing to provide deliberately misleading answers as a form of mischief. I've seen evidence of both behaviors, and although researchers try to design questionnaires and recruit enough children to statistically smooth out these potential wrinkles in data collection, surveys simply are not as clean, clinical, and objective as the kind of experimental questions one can ask, and answer, in a test tube. On the other hand, the Pepler and Craig studies, in particular, are important because the cameras in the schoolyard and the classroom have largely corroborated what children say about bullying in questionnaires.

You can also make the case that lumping physical assault and teasing under the same umbrella of bullying muddies the issue. One possible reason that Pepler and Craig found no evidence of posttraumatic stress disorder in older schoolchildren is that the children have learned to cope with teasing and taunting, which is certainly a useful lifelong skill. But I find the cultural critique of bullying research unconvincing, disheartening, and, in some cases, ideologically motivated. As writer Ann Hulbert recently noted, "The antibullying crusade is practically begging for a backlash, and conservatives have been among the first to oblige." There is the persistent suggestion that, serious bullying aside, much of the physical and verbal aggression that marks male development is relatively innocuous, boys-will-be-boys behavior — that it is, in syndicated columnist John Leo's words, "taking a lot of harmless and minor things ordinary children do and turning them into examples of bullying." Even Hulbert, in a poke at Olweus's research and the international adoption of antibullying measures developed in Norway and Sweden, has invoked the image of "Scandinavian wusses" and puts the phrase "culture of cruelty" in quotation marks, as if it were a sociological invention rather than an everyday reality of childhood and adolescence. To the contrary, it seems to be a unique feature of primate life: Frans de Waal points out that apes, like humans, possess the "imagination" to be cruel to others.

Rather than deride those who are attempting to address a pervasive problem of childhood, apparent in virtually every culture in which it's been examined, it seems wiser to figure out better, more effective ways for that temptation for cruelty to be socialized out of children. Every child is a potential ally in this effort, because every child is part of the problem, even if his or her only sin is to silently watch the humiliation of others. This observation of bullying has begun to emerge in the research. Craig, Pepler, and colleagues recently reported that bullying often plays to a large audience. By their calculations, peers are present during 88 percent of bullying episodes, but these children intervene only 19 percent of the time.

I am still haunted today by an episode that occurred at the junior high school I attended in Michigan, when I was thirteen. It happened one afternoon while students were arriving for choir class in the large music room. The target was a boy named David, who sat in the first row. He wasn't small; indeed, he was larger than average, with thick fleshy lips, a ruddy complexion, and blond hair. But he did have some sort of physical disability, the exact nature of which I can't recall, and walked with a kind of herky-jerky stagger. He may even have had braces on his legs. This detail should have targeted him for empathy, not ridicule, but it actually heightened the odds of his becoming a victim. (One study has reported that children with physical disabilities are more likely to be picked on than children without disabilities.) It didn't help that he spoke in a high, lispy voice. He was, in other words, guilty of that most venal of adolescent sins: he looked and acted different, through no fault of his own. A perfect victim.

Choir was a very large class. Students typically milled about for several minutes before sitting down, amid a hubbub of voices. When David wasn't looking, someone placed several shiny tacks on his seat. As I picture the scene in my mind's eye — the piano in the front of the room, clefs and signatures on the blackboards, the shuffling of sheet music as we prepared to rehearse our songs — virtually everyone in the room, dozens of kids, were aware of the humiliation that was about to take place. I know I was. Indeed, that is probably the most debilitating psychological aspect of bullying to its victims. Long after the immediate physical pain subsides, the emotional pain of realizing that so many others witnessed and in some cases knew in advance of an act of public humiliation, without a single one intervening in your behalf, is a devastating blow to adolescent self-confidence.

Mr. Poland, our choir teacher, had not yet made an appearance in the room when David readied himself to sit down. All eyes were riveted on the chair. Down he went, and then up he predictably rocketed, with a series of high-pitched, wounded shrieks I will never forget. The shock on his face, the fury and the twisting reaction to pain and the sense of communal betrayal, were enormous, animal-like. In a roomful of thirty or forty adolescents, there were stifled giggles, suppressed laughs, and, I'd like to think, a few conflicted young minds whose avid voyeurism competed with empathetic horror. But not one single child from a suburban community of enlightenment and privilege tried to prevent the humiliation, and not one single child disclosed the identity of the perpetrators, as far as I recall. We were all complicit, to a greater or lesser degree, in the culture of cruelty. Was this just the rough-and-tumble of childhood, as some would have it? Or was it demeaning in a particularly sadistic way — targeting the weak, humiliating the disabled, demonizing the odd? What other name is there for such behavior than cruelty, and what word other than "culture" captures the silence with which three or four dozen people could witness such an event?

Bullying is not just about the bully and the bullied. It is about the audience, too, about the culture of silence that is itself a form of maladaptive behavior that diminishes us all. In a moral sense that can never be captured by a tape measure, accepting behavior that physically or psychologically demeans another child makes all of us a little bit smaller.

9

THE PRUSSIAN CURSE
Heightism, or the Birth of the "Altocracy"

The most beautiful girl or woman in the world would be a matter of indifference to me, but (tall) soldiers — they are my weakness. He who sends them to me can lead me wherever he will.

— FREDERICK WILLIAM, king of Prussia

IN 2006, SOME forty years after the fact, I can still tick off the exact height of the starting five players on my high school's varsity basketball team. The center was six feet nine, the forwards were six feet eight and six feet seven, and the guards were six feet five and six feet two. That would be a little short, though still respectable, for a National Basketball Association team these days, but these were sixteen- and seventeen-year-olds back in the mid-1960s. Nothing would have pleased me more than to be a hotshot on the hardwood back then, but I was a five-foot aus-lander in a land of giants.

One day in gym class, I took part in a pickup scrimmage with one of the varsity players, the six-foot-eight Owen Brown. The one lay-up I attempted probably showed up on radar at O'Hare after Owen swatted it away. Like many adolescent boys, I got my first lessons in the liabilities of small size in the gym. But that blocked shot was merely a narrow, circumscribed form of rejection hinting at a much broader social reality. If adolescence is a time of heightened self-consciousness (about size, appearance, and just about everything else), it is also a time of burgeoning awareness about how one fits into the larger world. Put another way, you suddenly become aware of the various lenses society uses when it looks at you. When the lens is size, the world clearly prefers tall to small, and not just on the basketball court. My hunch is that precisely around the time of puberty, short teenage boys become intensely aware that there are distinct social advantages to being tall, and clear social liabilities to being small, in ways they haven't noticed before.

Part of this unhappy reckoning is purely biological. When you look at the standard growth chart, you see that the curves widen fairly dramatically around age ten or so, a graphic indication that the gap between tallest and shortest becomes much greater. If you look at the Tanner-style charts, the size disparity becomes even more apparent, because the early maturers have a whole set of curves to themselves. But it is more than a matter of feet and inches. It is a matter of social attitudes. Puberty, of course, is the time of sexual maturation and just about the time boys start paying attention to girls. It is hard not to notice that height (and early maturation) has its privileges in the adolescent mating game.

Looking back, I think that my adolescence ushered in an intuitive awareness that fortune seemingly smiled not only on the basketball players but also on a larger subculture of taller kids — the student council officers, the thespians, the guys in the lettermen's club, the cool kids. (They weren't all tall, of course, but that's what happens when you view things through a distorted lens.) And although at some level I realized that culture followed fortune's lead, it wasn't until recently that I began to wrestle, less intuitively and more quantitatively, with the way culture seemed to smile upon those lucky enough to be lofty, too. Indeed, researchers in 2004 reached the startling conclusion that one's height during the teenage years appears to be a crucial factor in the accrual of what economists call human capital. That human capital pays enormous financial and social interest in part because our culture so clearly embraces tallness. When I started to look into the history of cultural attitudes toward height, I discovered that this embrace goes back a long time and is deeply interwoven with human history, moral values, militarism, psychology, and even evolution. The more I learned, the more I began to think of this cultural preference for height as the Prussian curse.

*   *   *

ABOUT THREE HUNDRED years ago, in January 1712, a small, sickly infant named Friedrich entered the world with fanfare in Berlin. Small, sickly children were, of course, of no particular distinction in eighteenth- or nineteenth-century Europe. Indeed, their sad lot was immortalized by James Compton Burnett in the unsentimental title of his book *Delicate, Backward, Puny and Stunted Children,* which chronicles the use of home- opathy in the treatment of small stature or delayed growth. The birth of this particular child, however, was greeted with cannon fire and cathedral bells, because he was the grandson of the king of Prussia, destined to en- dure the kind of social and political scrutiny reserved for heirs apparent. The boy's father, Frederick William of Prussia, would, within a year or so, ascend to the Hohenzollern throne, at which point this small toddler would assume the title of crown prince. Throughout nearly a quarter century of rule, one of the major themes of the reign of Frederick Wil- liam was his troubled and antagonistic relationship with his delicate, backward, and puny son.

Young Friedrich had the misfortune to be born at an utterly mad cul- tural moment when it came to the issue of height and physical stature. Frederick William himself stood barely five feet five in height, but he would soon become famous (and infamous) throughout Europe for his obsession with human height. Long before Francis Galton used his ruler to prod science toward eugenics, long before the "secular trend" that pushed average human heights ever higher during the past century, and long before human growth hormone therapy and other pharmaceuticals made the addition of inches in height a medical and cosmetic possibility, this hairy fireplug of a monarch began to reconfigure the cultural equa- tion between physical height and social stature, linking height to military might, cultural desirability, and a nationalistic strain of moral strength in a way that had not been seen, or championed, in civilized society since the time of the Roman Empire.

The modern obsession with tallness — its perceived association with strength, physical superiority, and moral virtue — has many roots, but rarely have the political and familial implications of the topic so dramati- cally converged as in the relationship between young Friedrich, crown prince of Prussia, and his stubby, coarse, vividly Germanic father. Ac- cording to historians, Frederick William was a mercurial, boorish man who embraced physical culture and military trappings. (One biographer describes him as "a short, fat, and very rude Hohenzollern monarch, who would soon become an outrage of a man.") After fighting in the War of the Spanish Succession, Frederick William found self-definition and nationalistic ardor in the army. His closest friends and advisers were military men, his dress mirrored military fashion, and he cultivated a military ethos of strict discipline, incessant drilling, and avid recruitment of prime human specimens for his army. In 1713, when Frederick William became king, the Prussian army numbered 38,000. By the time the king died in 1740, its ranks had more than doubled, to 83,000 men.

It was not just the size of this army but also the size of its soldiers that became the talk of Europe. Frederick William displayed, as his biographer Robert Ergang put it, "an almost pathological love for tall soldiers." He collected them like stamps and deposited the tallest of them in a privileged regiment known variously as the Grenadier Guards or Potsdam Giants. None reportedly measured less than six feet, and the drill leader, a man named Hohmann, was said to have been more than seven feet tall. Although the term "grenadier" technically refers to a soldier who hurls grenades, a practice that fell out of specialized use well before the eighteenth century, there were nonetheless plausible military reasons for recruiting talent at the upper reaches of the growth chart. Taller soldiers have longer strides and thus could cover much more ground during the tactical ambulations of eighteenth-century conflicts. In close fighting, they also enjoyed an advantage when it came to bayonet thrusting, and they could more easily reload the long-barreled muskets then in use.

In the grip of "gigantomania," Frederick William sent agents throughout Europe in search of unusually tall young men. Even before the publication of *Gulliver's Travels* in 1726, the Prussian army was busily assembling an elite corps of Brobdingnagian soldiers within its ranks. One Swedish mercenary imported to the guards in 1728 reportedly measured eight and a half feet tall. In some instances, these giants were conscripted in the normal fashion. In other cases, European monarchs presented as gifts to Frederick William their tallest national youths; Peter the Great of Russia regularly made "donations" of tall, strapping young Russians to the Prussian military. Others of these towering soldiers were obtained through outright purchase, essentially bought and sold as military chattel. As James Tanner once noted, Frederick William's giants represented "the tallest men ever assembled until the birth of professional basketball."

Perhaps more to the point, gigantomania attached economic value to height in a way civilized society had never seen before. Tanner writes in his history of human growth that the Prussians procured tall bodies for the Grenadier Guards "with transfer fees that modern football clubs could scarcely rival." This is probably among the earliest instances in which greater human height translated into greater market value, a distant echo of today's many studies that correlate greater height with higher salary. The crown prince, that small and sickly lad, once plunked down six thousand talers — an amount that would purchase about twenty good riding horses at eighteenth-century prices — to buy a six-foot-four giant in England as a gift for his father. Frederick William may even have pioneered a form of occupational bias, for height became the crucial factor in judging the merits and advancement of his soldiers. "Thus an officer of small stature, though a man of extraordinary ability, had little chance of being promoted," a biographer of the king noted.

Late in life, Frederick William confessed that the Grenadier Guards were his "one and only vice," and he often joined their rollicking weekly bouts of food and drink. In an account of the Prussian court, Nancy Mitford captures the daffiness of Frederick William's "oddest whimsy" — his "collection of giants for his Potsdam Grenadiers."

> They were an obsession; he would spend any money, even risk going to war with his neighbours, to have tall men (often nearer seven than six feet in height, and generally idiotic) kidnapped, smuggled out of their native lands and brought to him. Finally, he acquired over two thousand of them. His agents were everywhere. Kirkman, an Irish giant, was kidnapped in the streets of London, an operation which cost £1,000. A tall Austrian diplomat was seized when getting into a cab in Hanover; he soon extricated himself from the situation, which remained a dinner-table topic for the rest of his life. The biggest of the giants was a Prussian — no ordinary man could reach the top of his head. When the Grenadiers marched beside the King's carriage they held hands over it. The kidnapping became so expensive that Frederick William tried breeding giants. Every tall man in his dominions was forced to marry a giantess. But that method proved slow and unreliable — too often the children of such marriages were a normal size. So he went on with the kidnapping while letting his fellow rulers know that the most acceptable present to him would be a giant.

Historians who have studied the archives of Frederick William's reign have noted how the incessant recruitment or kidnapping of tall, hapless men often triggered diplomatic tensions with neighboring duchies and countries. At one point or another, England, Holland, and Austria all expressed diplomatic exasperation at the practice. The Potsdam Giants even rose to the level of political currency when they became a bargaining chip in the backroom maneuvering that typified European politics in those days. According to historian Robert Asprey, in 1726 the Holy Roman Emperor's envoy to Berlin, in the midst of delicate treaty negotiations, wrote to Vienna pleading for "tall men for four of Frederick William's favorite generals and colonels."

Mitford notes that Frederick William took his infatuation to the level of applied genetics, attempting to breed giants within his kingdom by mating his gigantic soldiers with tall women. This early and ill-fated foray into state-sponsored eugenics did not escape the notice or comment of Charles Darwin. Writing in *The Descent of Man* more than a century later, he noted that humans, unlike livestock, had never been specifically bred to select for certain characteristics. He continued, "Nor have certain male and female individuals been intentionally picked out and matched, except in the well-known case of the Prussian grenadiers; and in this case man obeyed, as might have been expected, the law of methodical selection; for it is asserted that many tall men were reared in the villages inhabited by the grenadiers and their tall wives."

To the end of his days, Frederick William adored his Potsdam Giants. As the king struggled with failing health in the months before his death in 1740, one of the few sights to hearten him was a parade of hundreds of the giant soldiers marching through his room.

FROM THE MODERN perspective, there is some debate whether a soldier's tall stature actually translated into military superiority. One historian, Edith Simon, has dismissed the guards as "an expensive luxury of dubious military value." But there is little disagreement that the Prussian creation of an elite unit of unusually tall soldiers influenced military thinking throughout the world. The fame achieved by the Grenadier Guards — and the fear they inspired — provoked a kind of infantry arms race, measured in feet and inches, that ultimately shaped the armies of Europe, the history of anthropometry (the systematic measurement of the human body), and the way height would be viewed as a cultural asset, with clear-cut economic value. Other European monarchs, both friends and foes of Prussia, felt obliged to pay attention to height when they recruited soldiers. Wolfgang von Goethe, working for the Duke of Sachsen-

Weimar, once found himself employed at canvassing the countryside for tall young conscripts, although he seems to have had a dubious view of the practice. A drawing by Goethe dating from 1779 — a copy is reproduced in Tanner's *A History of the Study of Human Growth* — shows a scene where a young recruit's height is being measured against the wall of a military recruiting station with a fairly sophisticated stadiometer. (Goethe slyly created a phony regimental shield on the wall in the background. The design on the shield appears to resemble the stadiometer but is actually a gallows, which, as Tanner puts it, seems "to reflect Goethe's feelings about military life.")

The scene captured in Goethe's sketch was replicated, with less subversive humor, all over Europe. Indeed, the birth of anthropometry grew directly out of the military obsession with the size of recruits. Norwegian military height records date from 1741 (the year after Frederick William died). Similar records of the Royal Marines in Britain date from 1755. Young men drafted into military service were routinely measured, not simply to satisfy minimum height requirements but also as a means of identifying deserters. Long before photographs and fingerprints, height served as one of the essential markers of social identity. Deserters quickly took advantage of an idiosyncrasy of human biology to subvert this form of identification. Since a person gains about an inch in height after a night's sleep (only to have that gain erased by the ambulatory stresses of daily activities), soldiers who had fled their companies took to lying in bed during the day as a way to increase their height and avoid capture. In a very concrete sense, height not only became an integral part of human identity by the middle of the eighteenth century; it fed a very pragmatic form of self-consciousness.

Measuring young men to assess their suitability as soldiers ultimately extended to sailors, and as infantry-heavy wars roiled Europe over the next two centuries, these military-driven surveys became a part of national culture and identity — and, alas, a tragic index of the loss of young, albeit tall, lives. Growth experts in France noted that the average stature of French males took a noticeable dip in the early nineteenth century, a decrease they attributed — without conclusive proof — to the enormous loss of life during the Napoleonic wars.

Later in the nineteenth century, Francis Galton seized on this nationalistic obsession with physical size to promote his own interest in breeding superior human beings. With rhetoric that adverted to the creepy nationalistic sentiments that began to attach to tallness, he argued for national growth surveys so that British children and adults could be physically compared to those of other nations. In the 1880s, he created his famous Anthropometric Laboratory in London, where he began to assemble a database on height and size that he hoped would later form the basis of eugenics programs. David Barker (of the Barker hypothesis) told me that in England at the beginning of the twentieth century, the lack of adequate-size military recruits around the time of the Boer War spurred calls for yet more national growth surveys to determine why British youths were so small and why so few males physically qualified for military service. There was even an Inter-Departmental Committee on Physical Deterioration in the United Kingdom.

One can reasonably look back to the early eighteenth century, therefore, and to King Frederick William I as the beginning of what might be called the "altocracy." Primates, human and otherwise, have been sizing one another up for millions of years, and also paying a physical price for a hasty or mistaken assessment, so comparative height and size have always been an intrinsic part of the social order in both animals and humans. But the mania for tall soldiers in eighteenth-century Prussia seems to have institutionalized the desirability of height for the first time in a large, postmedieval society. Enormous market value became attached to height, thanks to the outrageous amounts paid by Frederick William's recruiting agents for tall young men. Tallness also assumed a formal psychological value. After all, part of the raison d'être for having gigantic soldiers was to inspire fear in enemy troops.

SO IT IS not a huge exaggeration to suggest that the modern cultural value attached to height was military in origin, autocratic in worldview, and Germanic in accent. But the Prussians themselves credited classical sources for this sentiment. In the annals of the Roman Empire, for example, tallness is associated not only with strength but also with a kind of moral virtue, which is a subtext that runs long and deep through the history of the altocracy. The author to whom this moral equation is most frequently attributed is the Roman historian Tacitus.

In *The Germania,* his account of the founding tribes of Germany, Tacitus speaks with unambiguous admiration for the valor, fighting ability, and moral rectitude of numerous Germanic tribes — a kind of moral varnish slathered upon their physical traits. In this very brief history, the great Roman historian on several occasions explicitly exalts the stature of the ancient Germans. In one chapter, he remarks that "their physical characteristics, in so far as one can generalize about such a large population, are always the same: fierce-looking blue eyes, reddish hair, and big frames — which, however, can exert their strength only by means of violent effort." In another, he writes, "In every home the children go naked and dirty, and develop that strength of limb and tall stature which excite our admiration." Of the Suebi, the generic name for a number of tribes that accounted for roughly half of the early Germanic peoples, he directs particular attention to the elaborate coiffures of knotted, erect hair atop warriors' heads. "These are no love-locks to entice women to accept their advances," Tacitus notes. "Their elaborate coiffure is intended to give them greater height, so as to look more terrifying to their foes when they are about to go into battle."

Tallness, aggression, intimidation, domination — throughout *The Germania,* these moral and cultural strands are braided together to form one overwhelming impression: height is associated with military ferocity and domination; height induces fear in adversaries. For those familiar with the classical roots of the doctrine of racial purity exploited by the Nazis in the twentieth century, it is chilling to realize that Tacitus's very first mention of height in *The Germania* is prefaced by the following line: "For myself, I accept the view that the peoples of Germany have never contaminated themselves by intermarriage with foreigners but remain of pure blood, distinct and unlike any other nation." As translator Harold Mattingly has observed, Tacitus "can never have dreamed of the terrible abuses which would grow out of his simple statement." However much or little one cares to ascribe twentieth-century attitudes (including genocidal ones) to classical sources, the fact remains that Tacitus's remark about "pure blood" forms an ideological couplet with the idea that tallness and strength are tribal virtues.

As Tanner points out in a lovely scholarly dissection of the classical Latin, Tacitus and Julius Caesar, who also sang the virtues of the ancient Germans, were not merely making a point about physical size. Their train of thought bore considerable moral freight and was explicitly linked to pubertal behavior. In his book on the Gallic War, for example, Caesar writes of the Germans, "Those who preserve their chastity longest are most highly commended by their friends; for they think that continence makes young men taller, stronger, and more muscular. To have had intercourse with a woman before the age of twenty is considered perfectly scandalous." Tacitus echoes this line of thought in *The Germania:* "The young men are slow to mate, and thus they reach manhood with vigor unimpaired. The girls, too, are not hurried into marriage. As old and full-grown as the men, they match their mates in age and strength, and the children inherit the robustness of their parents."

Tanner provides the context: "Written in A.D. 98, Tacitus' book was strongly moralistic in tone and contrasted the pure, strength-giving life of those free and rural people with the enervating luxury of Rome, where children did *not* reproduce the robustness of their parents, in his view. In Rome sexual promiscuity was considered smart but amongst the Germans there were no corrupting spectacles nor exciting banquets, and chastity was well-nigh universal." Hence two of the most influential and enduring voices from classical times proposed that tallness was a biological reward for moral virtue in general and sexual abstinence in particular. That message, transparently and fatally flawed in the era of modern biology, nonetheless survived the Middle Ages, the Renaissance, and the Enlightenment, and even received a degree of approbation from Charles Darwin.

Perhaps it's human nature to conflate physical height with moral fiber, as if the sinews of character attach naturally to the longer bones that beget greater size, for throughout medieval and Renaissance literature, feet and inches similarly influenced society's view of moral value. A Renaissance scholar named Levinus Lemnius, who initially studied medicine and then entered the priesthood, hailed "comely tallnesse and length of personage" in his 1561 book *De habitu et constitutione corporis,* attributing such comeliness to "the abundance of heat and moisture, where the spirit is thoroughly and fully perfused."

As Tanner's history makes clear, prior to Frederick William, humankind had for centuries repeated — and, from a cultural view, amplified — the message that tallness confers moral strength and social domination. By the eighteenth century, Tacitus had been rediscovered and embraced, and height became an exalted commodity for both soldiers and civil society. The Prussians even employed a kind of unofficial court philosopher, Johann Augustin Stoller, to anoint Frederick William's strapping collection of militaristic youth with a glistening sheen of moral superiority. Trained as a doctor, Stoller treated members of the German nobility, but his notoriety resides mostly in a 1729 book titled *A Medical Historical*

Investigation of Human Growth in Length, which glowingly refers to Frederick William's army in its appropriately long subtitle and implicitly sought to curry favor with the king with its exhortations about height. "Nobility of soul," Stoller wrote, "accompanies tallness of body." To the extent that Stoller's equation still persists in contemporary perceptions of height — as psychological, sociological, and economic studies often suggest — it gives little comfort to realize that such sentiments were originally drafted by Prussians, who dipped their pen into the ink of an ancient historian whose views legitimized the most inhumane instincts of twentieth-century totalitarians.

ALMOST A CENTURY after Frederick William ascended to the Prussian throne, scientists of the Enlightenment infused even more moral fervor into the idea of human size. And if tallness reflected moral virtue, shortness came to be seen as some form of depravity. Some of the most enduring psychological clichés about height date to this period.

The emergence of short stature as a moral liability can be traced back at least to the early nineteenth century. In an influential 1816 article on growth in one of the leading medical encyclopedias of the day, the French doctor and pharmacist Julien-Joseph Virey linked the origin of short stature to behavioral lassitude, an opinion widely shared in the nineteenth century. "Nowadays we are soft and effeminate," he wrote in *Dictionnaire des sciences médicales.* "The age of puberty is advanced because of a precocious awareness, because of the pernicious solitary pleasures which bring on prematurely the sexual organs and exhaust youth. Thus turning the greater part of nutrition towards the excretion of sperm stops growth, and people stay short in stature. The promiscuity in towns and amongst the rich makes them feeble." Soft, effeminate, feeble, promiscuous — this was the "scientific" vocabulary employed by scholars and leading medical experts in an effort to cast shortness as an expression of character.

Fortunately, for every "scientist" who tailors biology to morality, there is usually a real scientist who derives social conclusions from sound biological observation. Scarcely a decade after Virey's priggish speculations, another Frenchman, Louis-René Villermé, offered a vastly different — and, as it turns out, incredibly prescient — interpretation of the way environment affects stature. Villermé survives as one of the most thoughtful and incisive intellects about human growth, and in 1829 he floated an idea that ultimately animated a good deal of twentieth-century historical research and indirectly led to a Nobel Prize in economics. "Human height," he wrote, "becomes greater and growth takes place more rapidly, other things being equal, in proportion as the country is richer, comfort more general, hours, clothes, and nourishment better and labour, fatigue and privation during infancy and youth less; in other words, the circumstances which accompany poverty delay the age at which a complete stature is reached and stunt adult height."

In 1979, approximately a century and a half after Villermé ventured that daring thought, James Tanner and Phyllis Eveleth published a book called *Worldwide Variation in Human Growth.* The book provides page after page of data supporting the notion that average height within a given population at a given time — Norwegians during the Nazi occupation, the Japanese after World War II, even Kalahari bushmen living in South Africa in the 1950s — sheds light on the environmental conditions (including socioeconomic factors) of that time. The growth expert Alan D. Rogol restated Villermé's principle to me in much more colloquial fashion: "You tell me the average mid-arm circumference of children growing up in a developing country, and I'll tell you the gross national product of the country they live in."

Viewed that way, height may indeed be a surrogate measure of social values, though not necessarily the kind of moral values that Virey, Tacitus, and Caeser had in mind. If we understand a moral society to be egalitarian toward all its citizens — and to be one that abhors socioeconomic deprivation, especially among young children during their most vulnerable periods of growth — morality is indeed connected to stature, for the average height of a population turns out to be an exceptionally good reflection of the quality of life in that particular population at that particular time. It reflects, growth experts point out, nothing less than the care a society bestows on its children — not just the children of privilege, but *all* children.

VILLERMÉ NOTWITHSTANDING, THE idiosyncratic altocracy of eighteenth-century Prussia added to the challenges of being a small and puny crown prince. Just as society began to embrace tallness as an economic virtue, short stature began to bear the taint of a cultural negative.

Numerous histories of eighteenth-century Prussia make it abundantly clear that the issues that divided King Frederick William I and his son were not simply a matter of feet and inches. Despite an early predilection for music, art, philosophy, and "soft silk robes, touching the floor like women's dresses," the crown prince was raised in an atmosphere of Spartan surroundings and military rigor. So tempestuous was the relationship with his father that in 1729 the young Friedrich conspired to escape to England with two colleagues in the Prussian army. The plot was uncovered at the last minute, and the crown prince was imprisoned, disinherited, and threatened with execution by his father, who forced him to witness the beheading of coconspirator Hans Hermann von Katte, one of his closest friends (and, some historians have suggested, his lover).

No story of a small, puny childhood is complete without the redeeming event of the adolescent growth spurt, however delayed or modest. In the dedication to his book, Johann Augustin Stoller acknowledges this remarkable transformation in the well-lathered, obsequious prose of a court toady, noting that the future king, "in former years known to be delicate has been cured by nothing else but a speedy growth in length. God grant him still further to grow, and, without check to his health, to bloom royally to the joy of his Most Serene Parents and the whole land." The crown prince had a somewhat different view of an upbringing marked by parental disappointment and corporal punishment. "Impressions received in childhood," he later wrote, "cannot be erased from the soul."

In 1740, upon the death of Frederick William, the crown prince ascended to the throne of Prussia. His modest boyhood stature seems not to have affected his accomplishments as a monarch. Indeed, the moral of this story is that size often does *not* matter. Friedrich soon led the military conquest of Silesia, created a financially modern bureaucracy, and found time to cultivate a celebrated friendship with Voltaire — military, political, and cultural achievements that legitimized his ultimate fame as Frederick the Great. Among his first acts as king was disbanding the Grenadier Guards.

If Frederick the Great no longer shared his father's obsession with tallness, he nonetheless seems to have absorbed a geopolitical lesson about the metaphoric import of size. As he wrote in 1783, shortly before his military adventures began to reconfigure Europe, the "fundamental principle" of great monarchies was anticipating the strategy of enemies and outwitting them. "It is a question," Frederick wrote, "of their ostensible glory; in a word, they *must* increase in size."

The eighteenth-century Prussian infatuation with tall soldiers helped to stimulate an era of militarism in Europe that led, in a surprisingly clear and direct line, to one of the great twentieth-century cultural clichés about short stature: the Napoleon complex. Even as Frederick the Great was dismantling the Potsdam Giants, armies all over Europe were recruiting and measuring young men like mad, increasing the size of their standing armies in the Prussian tradition, plucking the tallest and strongest, and, sometimes, bending long-established minimum height standards for military service to increase the number of soldiers. In search of glory and greater size, one European military leader in particular pushed such recruitment to new heights: Napoleon Bonaparte.

This is hardly the place to assess Napoleon's military campaigns (or, for that matter, his personal stature, although it is hotly debated on Internet Web sites). But it is worth pointing out that "in order to make his conscription net gather its necessary load of doomed men," as Vernon Kellogg recounted in a fascinating 1913 article in the *Atlantic Monthly*, Napoleon twice took the controversial step of reducing the minimum height standards for French army recruits. In 1799 he changed the minimum height of conscripts, established by Louis XIV in 1701 at 1,624 millimeters (162.4 cm, or about 5 feet 4 inches), to 1,598 millimeters (an inch less). In 1804 he lowered it another two inches, which made the overall reduction about three inches less than the standard that had been in place for nearly a century. This policy change left a devastating mark on French society, no less abrupt and savage than if one had taken a machete to the bloom of French youth. Because war-related mortality disproportionately claimed men above the height minimum, reverse eugenics inflicted shorter stature on children born during the war years. The average height of Frenchmen notably dipped in the generation that reached maturity about two decades after the Napoleonic wars. In his dream of European domination, Napoleon sent hundreds of thousands of soldiers to their deaths.

And it was precisely this behavior — this mindless "bellicosity," as historian Paul Johnson calls it, in the face of overwhelming odds — that created the mythology of Napoleon and led to his most enduring legacy, at least to the world of psychology. In 1908, not quite a century after the Battle of Waterloo, the American psychotherapist Alfred Adler cited Napoleon as a classic example of the way individuals with an inferiority complex compensate for their shortcomings. Ultimately, the idea of the

Napoleon complex — a phrase inspired and legitimized but not actually coined by Adler — has come to characterize the behavior of men who feel inferior because of their short stature. To complete the circle, the historian Peter Gay points out that Freud's famous "Anatomy is destiny" dictum, published in 1924, was inspired by a similar remark by Napoleon. The idea of the Napoleon complex has come to encompass the broader notion of a small male overcompensating for his stature with wildly aggressive and reckless ambitions, and it has had as firm and white-knuckled a grip on cultural perceptions as any idea the altocracy has come up with in its centuries-long celebration of height. The thread of bias against people of short stature runs from Adler to Napoleon to those giant soldiers parading through the moribund Frederick William's bedroom.

ADOLESCENTS, EVEN STUDIOUS ones, don't usually bother reading Tacitus and Napoleonic history. I certainly didn't. Until recently, I was unaware of the rich cultural roots of the altocracy. But at a subconscious and self-conscious level, I was steeped in its lessons. For all his bombast, King Frederick William I of Prussia was onto something.

The mere fact of being tall begets social respect. The reaction may be reflexive and unearned, but it seems to be a consistent feature in a broad number of cultures. And puberty, because of its link to sexual maturity and more independent social behavior, is when boys really become aware of it. John Kenneth Galbraith once opined that the favoritism enjoyed by tall people was "one of the most blatant and forgiven prejudices in our society." Still, this kind of anecdotal impression qualified mostly as folklore for much of the past few centuries. But when sociologists and psychologists began to train their somewhat fuzzier measuring instruments — usually questionnaires, not rulers — on the social and psychological ramifications of size, they began to quantify what Leslie F. Martel and Henry B. Biller have called the "inherent disadvantages in being much smaller and shorter than one's peers."

In their 1987 book, *Stature and Stigma*, Martel and Biller, of the University of Rhode Island, provide a swift but thorough survey of social science research on the social and psychological implications of height. As far back as the 1950s, it was reported (perhaps superfluously) that in a survey of men, those who were the most satisfied with their height were six foot two, while those who were the least satisfied were "unusually short." As one early researcher into the subject wrote in 1973, "All other things being equal, the large man is viewed as more manly. We know that tall men tend to get better paying jobs than short ones, presumably because they make a more forceful impression." Although the research was a bit skimpy on details and interpretation, early psychological and sociological studies indicated that height was typically associated with a broad range of positive characteristics, including likability, sensation-seeking, and self-direction. In addition, tall people were less prone to depression and more attractive to the opposite sex.

But the earlier literature on height and social (or economic) success is not entirely satisfying. Like much social science research, it relies on college students for much of its data. One of the earlier studies looking at height and income, a favorite topic of social science research, came out in 1971. According to a survey of University of Pittsburgh graduates, those who measured six feet two or taller received starting salaries that were 12.4 percent higher than those who were under six feet. In one of the classics of the social science literature, headhunters faced with a hypothetical hiring, when forced to choose between equally qualified candidates, chose the taller candidate three out of four times. But that last "study," cited by Martel and Biller among many others, appeared as a one-paragraph item on the front page of the *Wall Street Journal* in 1969. (I have been unable to track down the actual research in a peer-reviewed journal.) And another height-related study, by William Graziano and colleagues in 1978, is frequently cited with the suggestion that it supports the notion that females find taller men more attractive. The actual findings were quite the opposite. Women shown pictures of short, medium, and tall men found medium-size men "significantly more socially desirable than either short or tall men," while men shown the same pictures "rated short men more positively than they did tall men."

Despite the mixed messages conveyed by the early studies, greater height does seem to translate into workplace advantage. Malcolm Gladwell polled about half of all Fortune 500 companies for his recent book *Blink* and reports that the average height of male CEOs was slightly less than six feet. As he notes, although only about 14.5 percent of males in the United States are six feet or taller, 58 percent of the CEOs polled met that criterion.

Economists have increasingly looked at the correlation between height (usually adult males' height) and salary. The findings have generally been minor variations on the same theme: added height translates into added earnings. This has become such a reliable subject of popular interest that at least once a year (or so it seems), a story goes out over the wire services reporting on the latest study linking height with income. As a recent example, researchers at the University of Florida and the University of North Carolina reported that each additional inch above average translated into an extra $789 in annual income.

Readers should regard some of these findings with a grain of salt. Retrospective studies — the kind that look at data collected after the fact — rarely have the statistical, and therefore explanatory, power of prospective studies, in which researchers define the type of data they want to collect and design the study accordingly. By those standards, a lot of the evidence suggesting a cultural and economic bias against short stature still exists as a correlation, not a matter of cause and effect. As one recent, and fairly sophisticated, study put it, researchers have not been able to "open the black box between height and workplace success." On a gut level, the link between height and income may appear to be true (especially if you're part of the undercompensated minority), but as Carl Sagan famously said about truth and anatomy, "I try not to think with my gut." Furthermore, the results of these height and income studies can easily be confounded by socioeconomic upbringing, educational background, family history, and other factors much less easily quantified by yardsticks and dollar signs. Researchers obviously try to control for these factors, but they often have to do so in indirect ways. Even the Barker hypothesis — the idea that birthweight predicts some aspects of adult health — raises the possibility that very early developmental events or environmental factors, not size per se, may affect adult incomes. In a retrospective epidemiological survey of Finnish men born decades earlier, David Barker and colleagues in Finland compared adult income to birthweight records. In 2005 the researchers reported that men of lower birthweight had smaller incomes than a control group of men who were average-size babies. All of these findings may be reasonable, but they may not tell us as much about cause and effect as we might think.

One recent study merits attention, however, for going well beyond the obvious and arguably reaching the most startling conclusion of all. In 2004 three economists published yet another study comparing height and earning ability. This was an especially enterprising bit of economic research based on several well-known, large-scale longitudinal studies.

The three authors — Nicola Persico and Andrew Postlewaite at the University of Pennsylvania and Dan Silverman at the University of Michigan — investigated what they called the "height premium" as it affected a man's wages. They used data from two long-running longitudinal studies (Britain's National Child Development Survey and the United States' National Longitudinal Survey of Youth) that have gathered an enormous amount of information — everything from height and weight to profession and earnings — about men who have been followed from early childhood to mid-adulthood. Their results in effect trace the roots of the altocracy's smug attitude to its place of origin, and the location is fairly shocking.

First, the team confirmed earlier studies by showing that height was indeed associated with greater earning power — among the British, each additional inch of height equaled a 2.2 percent increase in wages, while among Americans, each additional inch of height equaled a comparable 1.8 percent increase in wages. Those differences may sound slight, but when they are superimposed on the growth chart, they translate into substantial disparities in earning power. The tallest 25 percent of male workers, for example, earned a median wage 13 percent greater than the shortest 25 percent. And here is the first surprise: the impact of size on wages, according to the authors, was comparable to disparities associated with more traditional forms of discrimination, including gender bias and racial bias.

A second and bigger surprise arose when the researchers tried to tease out the reasons for this finding. They naturally wondered what accounted for the wage disparity. Was it an employer's bias in favor of tall adults? A prejudice against short adults? Those are deeply entrenched cultural beliefs, but the data ruled out both possibilities. Did it have anything to do with socioeconomic background? Again, the rich database allowed them to conclude that it did not. But one factor popped out after all the number crunching: an individual's height during adolescence predicted higher or lower income. As the authors put it, "Height at age sixteen uniquely influences future wages." In other words, instead of focusing on the link between *adult* height and earning power, as so many surveys had previously done, the economists were able to use more comprehensive data from the longitudinal studies to compare adolescent height and adult earning power. Their analysis essentially shows that Garry Trudeau's "inner shrimp" is destined to carry a lighter wallet.

The obvious question is why, and that is much more difficult to determine. According to Dan Silverman, "There's something going on" in the adolescent years between ages eleven and sixteen, when the effect kicks in. "What it is, we can't tell exactly. We can be confident of what it's not. It's not bias. It's not health, or disadvantages from parents. A lot of the usual suspects don't explain the correlation." The authors speculate that the difference might be attributed to "human capital," and it seems related to social activity during adolescence (and perhaps even earlier). As they put it, "In the U.S. data, those who were relatively short when young were less likely to participate in social activities associated with the accumulation of productive skills and attributes. About half of the wage differential can be accounted for by variation in participation in school-sponsored non-academic activities (such as athletics and clubs), and a smaller fraction of it can be explained by greater levels of schooling." According to this interpretation, these social factors — participation in sports and afterschool clubs — enrich human capital, allowing an adolescent to develop social skills that presumably contribute to greater wage potential as an adult. Tall adolescents apparently develop these skills, but "those who were relatively short when young are less likely to participate in social activities that facilitate the accumulation of human capital like self-esteem and social adaptability."

Being curious economists, Persico, Postlewaite, and Silverman decided to do some further number crunching in a rather scary province: the economics of cosmetic enhancement. Having determined the height premium for a tall teenager, they went on to calculate the economic return that a monetary investment in adolescent height would fetch. How, you might ask, does one "invest" in adolescent height? You increase it, of course, by paying for treatment with a height-augmenting drug such as human growth hormone (hGH). According to the researchers' cost-benefit analysis, growth hormone therapy represents an "indirect investment" in the accrual of human capital, and in at least certain circumstances, this investment is worthwhile. Men who expect to have average annual earnings of more than $100,000, they conclude, "have a monetary incentive to undertake the hGH treatment." That is true only if the treatment adds significant inches, however, which, as we'll soon see, is very much open to debate. But just to reinforce the notion that exploiting male insecurity about size, of all sorts, has always been good business, the results of this study have appeared as a prominent part of the sales pitch for a growth-promoting substance called Growth Booster Plus. The results also appear on a Web site called altPenis.com, a compendium of information about penis size.

The paper by Persico, Postlewaite, and Silverman is one of the most interesting pieces of research in the entire literature on stature. It provides a peculiarly modern perspective on the economic value of sheer tallness first established by Frederick William back in the eighteenth century. True, this is only one study, but it attaches real wage-earning power to height, and, perhaps most surprisingly, it suggests that the roots of the altocracy may lie in adolescence.

Height during adolescence may not, however, be the sole contributing factor to human capital. Another crucial factor is the timing of pubertal maturation. Whether a boy (or a girl, for that matter) reaches puberty early or late can have an enormous impact on adult psychological behavior. There were hints of such profound implications in the scientific literature half a century ago, but it took much more recent longitudinal research to suggest just how profound those effects might be.

PART IV

TIMING

TIMING *IS* EVERYTHING
Early and Late Pubertal Maturation

> You see, to tall men I'm a midget, and to short men I'm a giant;
> to the skinny ones I'm a fat man, and to the fat ones I'm a thin
> man. That way I can hold four jobs at once. As you can see,
> though, I'm neither tall nor short nor fat nor thin. In fact, I'm
> quite ordinary, but there are so many ordinary men that no one
> asks their opinion about anything.
>
> —NORTON JUSTER, *The Phantom Tollbooth*

I WAS ALWAYS SMALL," the man was saying. "When I started college, I looked like I was twelve years old."

"Alan" looked quite a bit older — but not a great deal taller — on the day we spoke. He had agreed to meet me in a coffee shop in a midtown Manhattan hotel and seemed not the least bit reluctant to talk about his life as a short child, as an adolescent with a delayed onset of puberty, and as a middle-aged man whose height had topped out at five feet one. "No, this body doesn't dunk basketballs," he pointed out rather needlessly. "But there are other things it can do."

Despite his small stature and eyeglasses, despite the pen sticking out of his shirt pocket, Alan did not come across as shy or meek. He appeared vibrant, even muscular, and in very good physical shape. He wore a white shirt, black pants, white socks, and black shoes; indeed, he tends to see the world a bit in black and white as well, beginning with the issue of his stature, which in many respects dominated both his upbringing and his choices in his professional life.

Alan grew up in a small town in Connecticut, not far from New Haven. His parents were both immigrants from Lithuania and both of diminutive stature. His father, a country doctor, reached only four feet eleven, just a shade above the height that usually defines pituitary dwarfism, and his mother was four feet nine. Genetics alone seemed to have doomed him to a very low percentile on the growth chart. But perhaps the most difficult moment for Alan — and indeed one of the most tormenting passages for many boys — came during adolescence, for in addition to being small, he was also a late maturer. He attended excellent elementary and prep schools and gained entry to the Massachusetts Institute of Technology, where he majored in physical chemistry. Living out the dream of emulating his father's career — "All I wanted to be was a country doctor, like my dad" — he went on to medical school at Duke University and trained in pediatrics at Johns Hopkins School of Medicine. After many years of practice, he made no apologies for his own small stature — or, for that matter, anyone else's. "You know, some of us, believe it or not, are actually high school graduates," he said, with perhaps a tad too much practiced sarcasm. "And a lot of tall people are pretty fucked-up."

Despite a superb record of academic and professional achievement, it is the little things that Alan could not do as a child and adolescent that still stick in his mind. "I couldn't compete in Little League baseball," he said. "Nothing could be done. That's just the way things are." As he continued to talk about his upbringing, the conversation kept returning — probably because I kept steering it there — to adolescence. "You worked around the problems," he said. "Did I play basketball? Good grief, no! But I played ice hockey and wrestled."

As he spoke, I had the sense that I was hearing a conversation that Alan had had with himself many times. Indeed, I recognized its gymnastic rationalizations because I'd had that conversation with myself for many years. He went on, "I was short because of my family, and because I was delayed for puberty. Now, did it bother me? It must have. One place it bothered me, in high school and in college, was that dating was difficult. Do I remember the difficulty? Definitely. In the same intense way as I probably did then? No . . . ," he said, his voice trailing off. "It just never dawned on me that we might have done something."

Could he separate the effects of small stature from the delayed puberty and growth spurt? "They were conflated," he said with a laugh, "and I was oblivious [to the difference]."

"Alan," it turns out, is the real name of a real person who has thought a lot about stature, delayed puberty, and its impact on individual male psychology. He is Alan D. Rogol, a pediatrician specializing in endocrine disorders, who trained with the legendary American growth expert Robert M. Blizzard, has worked as a professor at the University of Virginia for many years, and consults with both the pharmaceutical companies that make human growth hormone and with families in which there are children, usually boys, experiencing the same frustrations he did growing up in Connecticut.

Rogol's own growth history, and his conflation of size and pubertal timing, is a perfect example of an overlooked truth about stature. There are two kinds of short — temporary and permanent. Permanent short stature is an indifferent roll of the genetic dice. If your parents are unusually short, as were Alan's, the odds are that you're going to be short, too. Indeed, growth experts have developed quite reliable formulas to predict a child's ultimate height based in part on the growth histories and adult heights of the parents. (There are notable exceptions: the father of Wilt Chamberlain, the first dominant seven-footer in the NBA, was five feet eight.) Temporary shortness has more to do with the tempo of growth and maturation, which is at its most variable and extreme during puberty. If you are destined to be a late-maturing boy, you at least temporarily inhabit the nether regions of the growth chart. Whether temporary or permanent, however, short stature during adolescence leaves a psychological mark. It plunges a boy — even a boy destined to be tall by the end of his growth — into the emotional turmoil of what is, literally and figuratively, a no man's land.

"Which is normal," Rogol asked me, "a fourteen-year-old boy who is six feet two and two hundred twenty-five pounds, or a fourteen-year-old who is four feet ten and eighty-eight pounds? The answer is both. Both are normal. One is a fourteen-year-old man, and the other is a fourteen-year-old boy. At the end of the day, at twenty years of age, they're essentially the same, but the trajectory is different, and the trajectory is different at a crucial time in a person's psychosocial development."

Having lived a particularly extreme version of both frustrations as a child — being short because of genes *and* late maturation — Alan now makes a living as a medical specialist counseling teenagers and their families, explaining the biological issues of delayed growth (known as constitutional growth delay) and sometimes monitoring their treatment with a drug such as human growth hormone. When I asked Rogol if adolescent boys are typically able to articulate the emotions they are feeling when their tempo of growth falls so far behind that of their peers, he shook his head. "It's tough," he said, "because they don't want to say anything in front of their parents." Ultimately, they end up in a doctor's office, he added, and these awkward consultations almost always peak toward the end of August. Teenage boys who have been short all their lives, who have been short all summer despite desperate hopes of having a growth spurt, come to growth specialists seeking some kind of miracle transformation by Labor Day. In today's world, these visits are largely driven by concerned, and sometimes demanding, parents, but Rogol said that he always makes a point of meeting with the child one-on-one to hear his perspective on the problem. Many of the boys are too tongue-tied to express their frustration, but one boy in particular, Rogol remembered, managed to blurt out his concerns in stark, almost vulgar terms.

"He was sitting on the examination table," Rogol recalled, "and I was asking him some general questions, and finally he just pointed down to his crotch and said, 'Doc, I need hair and balls down there by Monday.' That's the problem with hundreds of kids, but they can't articulate that. This kid could."

DEEP INTO *Fetus into Man*, James Tanner floats a provocative notion. He suggests that chronological age — that is, the age we celebrate at birthdays, the age by which we are granted admittance to all manner of societal activities, from school entry and grade level to obtaining a driver's license and drinking alcohol — is a very poor measure of physical development (to say nothing of emotional maturity), especially around the time of puberty. Citing the growth history of three fourteen-year-old boys — the first already finished with puberty, the second in the midst of its tumultuous changes, and the third still awaiting its onset — he says that it is "ridiculous" to consider the three boys to be of equal physical, psychological, and social maturation. He writes, "One simply should not talk of 'fourteen-year-olds': the statement that a boy is fourteen is hopelessly vague, for so much depends on whether he is an early or a late maturer."

As a culture, of course, we do that all the time, and have done so for centuries. According to Roman law, a boy reached the legal age of maturity at fourteen (girls achieved it at twelve). Many of the social structures of contemporary childhood, from school itself to extracurricular activities such as soccer leagues and dance classes (indeed, any activity demanding either physical or mental acumen), lump children together according to chronological age. Yet as an organizing principle for childhood activities, age has a particularly tenuous link to physical and mental development around the time of adolescence.

It's not that scientists and psychologists have been unaware of this discrepancy. Franz Boas, of course, harped on the profound importance of the tempo of growth more than a century ago. Indeed, by the 1890s, Boas appreciated that some boys have their growth spurts as early as nine or ten years of age, while late maturers don't begin to shoot up until age thirteen or fourteen. Boas's notions about differences in physiological maturity anticipated, by just a few years, Wilhelm Roentgen's report of the discovery of x-rays. As a result, a few visionary growth experts in the twentieth century struggled to use this new technology to find an alternative to chronological age that might more scientifically assess where a child was in terms of his or her development. The good news is that they ultimately developed a relatively accurate method to do so. The bad news is that ionizing radiation, in the form of x-rays, is required to perform this assessment. Called bone age, this measure is particularly important around the time of puberty, for it can help doctors distinguish between normal variations in growth delay and an abnormal delay that might reflect a medical problem.

In many cases, an x-ray of the hand tells a more accurate story about growth than a birth certificate. Typically, the skeletal bones proceed along a continuum of growth, maturation, and fusion that — barring any unusual diseases — is the same in every maturing human being. Through an extensive series of growth studies and experiments, doctors began to create "atlases" of bone growth in which the size, shape, and maturation of certain parts of the skeleton accurately corresponded to the stage of overall physical development, regardless of chronological age. To cite an extreme example, an early-maturing twelve-year-old boy might have bone growth nearly identical to that of a late-maturing fifteen-year-old boy. Children today do not routinely undergo an x-ray examination to determine their stage of growth (the old-fashioned stadiometer is perfectly adequate in most cases), but many American and British children in the past did endure repeated x-ray exposure, which enabled scientists to create skeletal growth charts. These charts are used today to assess cases of extremely early or late maturation. Beginning in the early decades of the twentieth century, growth experts at the Fels Research Institute in Yellow Springs, Ohio, used x-rays of the knees and other joints to determine the progression of growth, and the first practical bone atlas of the hand and wrist, published in 1937, grew out of that work.

But the use of bone age measurements in the clinic is largely a post–World War II phenomenon. In 1952 Nancy Bayley, the psychologist and senior expert at the Berkeley Growth Study, and Samuel R. Pinneau "first placed the prediction of adult height on a firm basis," according to Tanner, with their Bayley-Pinneau tables, which are still widely used. Two years earlier, William Greulich of Stanford University and Sarah Idell Pyle of the Cleveland-based Bolton-Brush Study used their studies of white children born between 1917 and 1942 in the United States to produce what has become the standard American bone atlas, which guides the assessment of skeletal maturity in twenty-eight distinct bones within the hand. In 1962 Tanner and Reginald Whitehouse introduced the Tanner-Whitehouse system, the third edition of which was published in 2001. (For what it's worth, Tanner told me that the British bone atlas has been selling particularly well in China and Japan — two nations where the secular trend, or trend toward greater average height within the population, has been especially robust since the middle of the twentieth century.) Bone age is now used not only by doctors assessing growth but also by baseball coaches and trainers. Former major-league pitcher Mike Marshall, for example, uses bone age measurements to assess the physical maturation of teenage pitchers who attend his baseball camp.

THE "PROBLEM" OF maturation, especially late maturation in boys, is not new — nor, apparently, is the suggestion that late maturation can have long-term effects on personality development and perhaps even artistic temperament. And its psychological ramifications are not limited to short boys. It can affect even average-size adults who, as adolescents, fell temporarily behind their peers in growth. Because the infatuation with height that swept Europe in the eighteenth century was so intense in Germany, and because the record keeping was so thorough and precise at one particular school, we have excellent biological data — indeed, a full-fledged adolescent growth chart — for a well-known late-maturing artistic rebel of that era: poet and dramatist Friedrich von Schiller.

Born in 1759, Schiller was sent at age thirteen to the Karlsschule, a military academy established and run by Karl Eugen, Duke of Württemberg. Housed in a former barracks, the Karlsschule won renown for both its military rigor and its progressive educational agenda. It was also a hotbed of anthropometric activity. In 1772, the year before Schiller entered, school officials commenced one of only two longitudinal studies of growth known to have been conducted anywhere in the world during the eighteenth century. The young men were measured two or three times a year, and each one's place in various school hierarchies was adjusted accordingly. Thus relative size formed an intrinsic part of their adolescent identities — and, significantly, it was not just short stature but also growth velocity that ultimately shaped these identities.

Schiller hated the Karlsschule. Part of his antipathy stemmed purely from class issues: the school segregated the sons of military officers (part of the upper class) from the sons of the bourgeoisie (to which he belonged). But part of it, Tanner suggests, may have been due to Schiller's late pubertal maturation — not his size per se, for he was actually taller than average, but the lag in his growth spurt compared to that of other boys. Thanks to records unearthed in the mid-twentieth century, we know that Schiller's height was about four feet eleven at age fifteen, and later estimates suggest that he did not reach his peak growth velocity until he was nearly seventeen. That was nine months behind the average for his bourgeois classmates and a full year behind the average for the blue bloods — even then, the upper class tended to mature more quickly and grow taller than the middle class. Since students typically lined up by height at the Karlsschule, Tanner imagines that "Schiller must have started further up the line than all his bourgeois contemporaries. But he sank progressively down the order during his fifteenth and sixteenth years; when 15.0 he was only slightly above the bourgeois average and actually below the average of the nobles. With puberty, but only then, he regained his place."

This jostling order in the queue may seem trivial, but it is precisely these quotidian rituals of school life — lining up, placement for school photographs, the sports in which one can, or cannot, participate — that reinforce a boy's self-consciousness about size and his awareness of place in a physical (and, ultimately, social) hierarchy that is particularly intense during adolescence. And, as in Schiller's case, you don't have to be short to feel the psychological burden of pubertal delay. The mere sensation of falling behind — in something as meaningless as one's place in line for a parade — can affect a child of almost any height.

Whatever the impact of his growth history, Schiller had barely left the Karlsschule when, at age twenty-one, he made his reputation as a Romantic firebrand with his first play, *Die Räuber,* in which a brilliant and disaffected young man abandons his noble upbringing, becomes a brigand, and embodies a kind of principled antiauthoritarian stance. Indeed, one's growth history may color one's adult — and even artistic — temperament. Writing of Pablo Picasso's short stature, his first serious lover, Fernande Olivier, observed that "he always regretted the lack of those few inches, which would have made him ideally proportioned." Similarly, Picasso's biographer John Richardson has suggested that Picasso's size influenced his art. "Whether or not this accounted for the artist's mammoth will," Richardson writes, "self-consciousness about it is reflected in his work. Heads out of all proportion to bodies, and features out of all proportion to faces, are only some of the devices that Picasso will use to conjure up monumentality."

A growing body of research is making the case that pubertal timing is one of the most significant opportunities for psychological trauma in adolescents, both boys and girls, with behavioral effects that ripple well into adulthood. The preliminary evidence suggests that early or late pubertal maturation may be as crucial to adult psychology as height or stature per se. Experts in human growth have long recognized the truism that early maturation in girls and late maturation in boys can have seriously deleterious effects (and that early maturation in boys and late maturation in girls often bestow considerable advantages). The fact that early-maturing girls often inhabit the same social environment as late-maturing boys (schools, churches or synagogues, and neighborhoods) only heightens the tensions and frustrations of these extremes. Despite much conventional wisdom about early and late maturers, however, the crucial link between pubertal timing and psychology has only recently been rediscovered.

OF ALL THE research on the psychological implications of early and late maturation, nowhere was the science more ambitious — and the results more steadfastly ignored for decades — than at the University of

California. In 1950 psychologist Nancy Bayley of the Berkeley Growth Study and her colleague Mary Cover Jones published a landmark paper in the *Journal of Educational Psychology* that, in a way, put male pubertal timing and emotional behavior on the same developmental map. Benefiting from the Berkeley study's longtime longitudinal observation of children who had now reached adolescence, Bayley and Jones focused on late-maturing boys and found that, as a group, they were considered less physically attractive and less well groomed yet more likely to be sociable and interactive than early-maturing boys. When the teenage boys in the study were asked to assess their own peers, the late-maturing boys were regarded as "more attention-getting, more restless, more bossy, less grown-up and less good-looking" than the early maturers. "Less good-looking" may easily reflect disparities in growth and physical size, for late maturers have delayed growth spurts, delayed sexual maturation, and delayed development of physical characteristics associated with adult appearance, including facial hair and jaw maturation. Nonetheless, this modest but pioneering study concluded that pubertal timing affected both "overt behavior" and "reputational status."

Reading such broad and imprecise psychological characterizations today, it's easy to suggest that the California researchers — in this and two significant follow-up studies — may have used antiquated research tools to single-handedly create, or at least confirm, much of the popular mythology about the psychological effects of early and late maturation. But for all the methodological chaff, there are also fascinating grains of wheat in this groundbreaking and underappreciated research.

In a 1957 paper, Jones, one of the pioneers of behavioral psychology, and Paul Henry Mussen assessed thirty-three boys, all age seventeen, from the related Oakland Growth Study and tested a number of hypotheses about the psychological makeup of early versus late maturers. They found that, compared to early maturers, late-maturing boys more often had feelings of inadequacy; "displayed strong motivations to escape from, or defy, their parents"; tended to be more dependent and require attention, or "succorance," as the psychological vocabulary of the day put it; and yet were "more sensitive to their own feelings" and more ready to face them. "Since these qualities are basic to the development of psychological insight," Mussen and Jones wrote of this self-awareness, "it may be inferred that late-maturers, as a group, are more likely to become insightful individuals." Late-maturing boys surprised the researchers by turning out to be just as self-confident, ambitious, and interested in individual achievement as the early maturers. Mussen and Jones published another follow-up study in 1958, which confirmed that late-maturing boys have strong needs for social affiliation ("particularly with the opposite sex") yet contradicted the earlier study by finding a greater tendency for aggressive behavior among late maturers.

These are very old studies, and, revisiting them today, one is struck as much by the archaic language, inferential armchair psychologizing (the work was heavily influenced by psychoanalytic theory), and the methodological limitations (the numbers of boys studied were quite small, and the psychological assessments were based on highly subjective rating systems). But Bayley, Mussen, and Jones had followed the children in the Berkeley and Oakland studies for many years, knew their personalities intimately, had tracked their physical maturation closely, and had a unique vantage point from which to reach conclusions about their social and emotional behavior. Because of the longitudinal nature of the studies, these findings have much more depth than an ordinary questionnaire study would have. More to the point, the Berkeley group realized that "physical status during adolescence — mediated through the sociopsychological environment — may exert profound and lasting influences on personality." That is exactly what much more recent research, using much more sophisticated instruments of measurement and a much more focused approach, has begun to show.

The Berkeley researchers tilled a difficult field that most other social scientists, with few exceptions, preferred to leave fallow. Although there were a few isolated attempts to look at the psychology of physical maturation in boys — notably a Swedish study in 1990 — it was only in the mid-1990s that researchers took another, closer, more systematic look at the psychological impact of pubertal timing. A fascinating study on teenage depression launched in Oregon confirmed, almost accidentally, what Mussen and Jones had first suggested: that pubertal timing could affect behavior well into adulthood.

Peter Lewinsohn, a psychologist at the Oregon Research Institute, had studied adolescent depression for many years, and, in collaboration with psychologists from Columbia University, he set up an ambitious longitudinal study at nine senior high schools in western Oregon, some rural and some in the urban setting of Eugene. The Oregon Adolescent Depression Project, which began with about seventeen hundred students, identified adolescents between the ages of fourteen and eighteen, assessed their psychological status during high school, and then continued to follow them through college and early adulthood. In the course of setting up the study, Lewinsohn added, almost as an afterthought, a few questions about pubertal status. For the first time in a large epidemiological survey, the prevalence of depression, anxiety, antisocial behavior, substance abuse, and eating disorders could be analyzed in the context of pubertal stage. In some respects, the results confirmed conventional wisdom; in others, they offered fresh and disturbing insights into the psychological costs of physical maturation.

The first interim report came out in 1997, with the provocative title "Is Psychopathology Associated with the Timing of Pubertal Development?" The short answer was yes. Compared to boys of average pubertal development, for example, the late maturers cut a broad swath through the landscape of serious psychological dysfunction. This included, in language that reflects specific textbook diagnoses of mood disorders, "more daily hassles, higher level of depression, more internalizing problem behaviors, more negative cognitions, more depressotypic attributional style, more self-consciousness, more emotional reliance on others, poorer coping skills, more conflict with parents, elevated hypomanic personality style, more parental dissatisfaction with grades, more tardiness at school and lowered homework completion."

"Wow!" Julia A. Graber, then at Columbia University and the lead author of the 1997 study, recalled thinking as she reviewed the results of that initial survey. "We found effects here to things that psychiatrists pay attention to!" Indeed, all those symptoms could be summarized as more depression and more anxiety, she said, but of a severe nature, "to the point where it's impairing someone's life."

That was not totally surprising — late maturation in boys had always been viewed, anecdotally, as a negative. What was surprising was that the early-maturing boys, with all their precocious muscle, also had considerable psychological baggage to carry. Compared to boys of average timing, the early maturers reported higher levels of depression, more emotional reliance on others, more physical illness, and greater use of tobacco. (On the distaff side, early-maturing girls reported elevated rates of psychopathology, including more depressive symptoms, lower self-esteem, more tobacco use, and higher rates of attempted suicide.)

As intriguing (and troubling) as these findings were, they nonetheless represented little more than a kind of adolescent snapshot — a funk, perhaps, or an episode of bad behavior caught at one moment in time. The larger scientific question was, did the negative psychological effects associated with pubertal timing persist into adulthood? Once again, a longitudinal study allowed researchers to track their initial observations to the next stage of life, and once again the answer was yes. Graber (now at the University of Florida), Lewinsohn, and colleagues went back and assessed the same Oregon high school kids several years later, when they were twenty-four years old, to find out how they were doing. Their study — "perhaps the first to report on timing and disorder in young adulthood" — came out in 2004, roughly half a century after Nancy Bayley first intimated that pubertal timing could affect long-term psychological health. And although the answer in 2004 was yes, it was a more interesting kind of yes than in 1997, because now the timing of puberty (and, implicitly, the growth spurt) could be linked to adult mental health.

In boys, pubertal timing was associated with several adult disorders. First, late maturers had "significantly higher lifetime prevalence rates of disruptive behavior disorders." In lay language, they tended to have severe problems dealing with authority on into adulthood — and, in a way, Graber explained, that involved "asserting one's rights and trampling on others' rights." And that wasn't all. They were twice as likely to have problems of substance abuse, they had lower self-esteem, and they had elevated depressive symptoms. As the authors put it, "Late maturation in men is associated with serious psychopathology during young adulthood."

Surprisingly, early-maturing boys found themselves in the same foundering boat. The 2004 follow-up study revealed that, as adults, they had significantly lower self-esteem compared to on-time boys and were more likely to be regular smokers. So, again, the time of physical maturation seemed linked to psychologically debilitating and self-destructive adult behaviors. (Similarly, early maturation in girls seemed to increase the risk of depression and anxiety in adulthood. Early-maturing girls also displayed greater difficulty in maintaining healthy relationships with family and friends and reported lower life satisfaction as young adults. In terms of adult achievement, only one significant association was found with late-maturing girls: they were more likely to have completed a bachelor's degree by age twenty-four.)

"All too often, people think adolescents have problems and that they'll all grow out of it," said Graber, who hopes to assess the Oregon men and women again when they reach their late twenties and thirties. "But the caution here is that people can have serious problems during adolescence, and those problems may have negative effects on where you're going later in life. We're seeing that [early or late] pubertal timing is [related to] serious psychopathological problems into adulthood and a serious pattern of dysfunction throughout . . . life." Indeed, it's hard to ponder these results without concluding that an average puberty — neither too early nor too late — might pose the least psychological challenge to a child. As Graber put it, "I think it's just good to be on time."

The Oregon Adolescent Depression Project represents a renascent scientific effort in the past decade or so to study the long-term psychological effects of pubertal timing. Even today, however, the social sciences largely attack these questions with pen and paper. When you read through the recent literature, you come across references to the Sensation Seeking Scale for Children (to measure a predilection for risky behavior) and the Pubertal Development Scale (a questionnaire filled out by both parents and children, although the degree of male pubertal development, as one paper concedes, "would not be accurately assessed or reported by parents"). Nonetheless, the message that emerges from recent research echoes Tanner's observations about how misleading chronological age can be. Pubertal stage, regardless of age, is strongly affiliated with behavioral problems such as alcohol and drug use that extend into adulthood.

More and more research, in line with the Oregon longitudinal study, supports the current thinking that time of pubertal maturation has long-lasting psychological effects on both boys and girls. In an Australian-American study, for example, boys and girls at roughly the midpoint of puberty (Tanner stage III) were twice as likely as late maturers to have tried tobacco, alcohol, or marijuana and had a twofold higher incidence of substance abuse. By late puberty (Tanner stage IV/V), there was a threefold higher incidence of tobacco, alcohol, or marijuana use, and more than a threefold higher incidence of substance abuse than in early puberty. Significantly, these results, collected by George C. Patton and his colleagues, were "independent of age and school grade level." In other words, the farther along the puberty railroad they were, regardless of age, the more likely they were to drink, smoke, and use drugs. As the authors concluded, "Puberty ushers in a phase of heightened risk for substance abuse."

The emerging picture is not pretty: early-maturing teens are more likely to suffer from depression, anxiety, and eating disorders; to indulge in risky sexual behavior; and to exhibit antisocial, even violent, activity. Many of these early experiments in living are major determinants of adult behaviors — especially bad behaviors.

The time of pubertal development is now seen as a significant risk factor in other adolescent behaviors as well, according to several studies published in the past ten years. A group at the University of Kentucky reported in 2002 that "pubertal stage, regardless of age, is associated with drug use risk." In this study, teenagers who rated higher in sensation-seeking behavior exhibited a greater use of cigarettes, alcohol, and drugs. The surprise was that sensation-seeking behavior correlated with pubertal maturation, not age. In 2001 the same group at the University of Kentucky reported that a late onset of puberty in boys was associated with decreased alcohol use. And a group at Indiana University found that an earlier onset of puberty in girls was associated with an increased risk of smoking. The same study found that a girl's age at menarche was associated with when she first tried alcohol and her pattern of alcohol consumption at age sixteen.

Although these studies are not perfectly consistent, the general message seems to be that early maturers, both boys and girls, are at increased risk to experiment with, and ultimately to regularly use, drugs, be it nicotine, alcohol, or marijuana. A separate body of evidence suggests that adult use — and sometimes abuse — of the same drugs stretches all the way back to an earlier onset of puberty. One study has even shown that adolescent bullies (in grades five through eight) started dating earlier than their peers, which was linked to their earlier pubertal development.

The new research also marks a subtle but potentially significant shift in thinking about these behaviors. Researchers are now saying that activities such as drinking and drug use are not simply the results of becoming older and undergoing shifts in school, family, and peer relationships. They may be the direct products of changes — biological in origin, but neurocognitive and behavioral in outcome — that stretch all the way back to pregnancy. Patton and colleagues, for example, note that experiments in animals such as rats show that pubertal changes (yes, rats experience puberty, but they reach it just a few months after birth) are marked by greater exploratory behavior and greater novelty seeking, activities linked to parts of the brain known to be affected by pubertal changes. The possibility that growth-related neural changes associated with puberty may themselves drive some of these behaviors is important. And the idea that a delay in puberty can cause social isolation or alienation — and, oddly, increased psychological insight — may be an inescapable social side effect of this biological delay.

Sorting through the complexities of physical maturation during a time of exceptional inarticulateness (on the part of teenagers) and unusual reticence (in their relationships with parents) is a daunting task. When I went back to look at my old junior high and high school yearbooks, I began with all the pictures that I was in. But then I decided to examine the yearbooks more closely. I began to scan every one of those little postage stamp–size photos of the students. After perusing page after page of the photos (there were more than twelve hundred kids in my high school class), I had a kind of photo epiphany. Physical size doesn't particularly stand out in a headshot, but physical maturation does. Some students, myself included, simply looked childish. This is not a behavioral characterization or a value judgment, but a physical assessment. We were — how else to put it? — unformed. Compared to the sharp, well-chiseled features of the man-boys, our faces were still trapped in the pudding of childhood. The bones hadn't begun to expand in that unmistakable adult manner that Tanner captured so vividly in the photographs he took of the orphans at Harpenden. There is a steady accretion of brow, flesh, and chin extension, to say nothing of the hint of shadow associated with facial hair, that is surprisingly apparent in some boys but inescapably absent in others. In girls, the distinction is equally striking. By seventh and eighth grade, most girls had acquired a maturity of facial development that the boys could only dream about (and, staring at those pictures, probably often did).

The pressures on the adolescent boy who lags in growth and pubertal development come from three directions: parents, peers, and within. Among boys, visits to pediatric endocrinologists peak during early adolescence; these visits are primarily driven by parents, according to doctors who typically see these boys. Mark Sperling, head of pediatric endocrinology at Children's Hospital in Pittsburgh, told me, "Often, parents think the children have a complex [about short stature], but I think it's the parents who have the complex." The exact opposite situation pertains to girls, where early maturation and above-average height are often perceived as problems.

Although adolescents obviously do not revert to biological jargon — "Your growth spurt is delayed, nyah, nyah, nyah" — the shorthand of hazing is quite sufficient. Words such as "runt" and "midget" convey the message perfectly. Once internalized, these messages only add to the pressure that a late-maturing, short-statured boy is already putting on himself.

As Alan Rogol put it when we spoke, "For a boy of fourteen, it's not about reading and writing. It's about girls and sports." How does a late-maturing boy cope with the issues of sports and girls? I'm tempted to say "involuntary abstinence," but that doesn't come close to capturing the sense of isolation these boys often feel.

Like people at all stages of life, late-maturing boys tend to think the grass is greener (or perhaps at least taller) on the other side of the pubertal fence. As I thought about puberty and early versus late maturation, I wondered how someone at the opposite end of the growth spectrum experienced this passage. Thumbing through my high school yearbook, I came across the picture of H. Thomas Andersen. In the picture, he has a goofy, amiable grin, and the way he leans forward in the photo reminded me of his cheerful, competitive, and occasionally aggressive personality. Although we weren't the best of friends, we did work together on the newspaper and had once competed together in a two-man twenty-two mile canoe race on the Fox River in Illinois. We were also a kind of Mutt and Jeff act, because while I was very short during adolescence, Tom was very tall. By the time he finished his growth spurt, which obviously came early, he stood six feet four. I hadn't seen or spoken to Tom since we graduated in 1969, but I managed to track him down in Eugene, Oregon, and decided to pay him a visit.

THE FIRST THING I noticed about Tom was not his height; it was his smile: it's permanently on high-beam. I was surprised at how youthful he looked, with a lean body (he rode his bicycle prodigiously), smooth, wrinkle-free face, and full head of still-blond hair. He greeted me at his home wearing khaki shorts and a yellow polo shirt. He was as garrulous and friendly as I remembered him being during our high school years.

As it turns out, Tom had been living for nearly twenty-five years in the same Arts and Crafts bungalow on the outskirts of Eugene, where he works as a lawyer specializing in labor cases. He proudly showed me his collection of Civil War books and memorabilia, his collection of antique maps, and several custom-made surfboards crafted by his younger son, Eli, under the brand name Ooligan. His sons had inherited the familial longitude — Eli was six feet seven and Ben was six feet nine. Tom was in every respect the proud father, the successful lawyer, and the gregarious and generous host — grilling a king salmon caught in British Columbia several weeks earlier by his wife, the adventure travel writer Jessica Maxwell, who also had baked a pie brimming with fresh Oregon blackberries for the occasion.

Before dinner, we repaired to Tom's study to talk about growth, height, and pubertal development. I hoped to hear not only what he had to say about his own adolescence but also, if he remembered anything about it, mine. As he settled his long frame into a chair, Tom admitted that there hadn't been a day in his life when he'd regretted being tall, with one exception: when he and his son climbed Mount Shasta in California during a period of high winds. "For the first time in my life," he said, "I wanted to be small and squat rather than big and tall." As far back as he could remember, he had towered above classmates and, he believes, received deferential treatment from teachers because he appeared more mature. They expected more from him, he said, and the mere expectation gave him added confidence. But life as a favored son of the altocracy, I learned, was not without its own unique problems.

As an early maturer in junior high school (he was six feet tall by ninth grade), Tom was the tallest boy in his class and, predictably, was picked to be on the basketball team. This "honor" brought him nothing but misery, because he wasn't especially talented at the sport. As many tall boys have learned, if you're big, people assume that you will be a good basketball player. "As you may remember," Tom said, "I was terribly clumsy. I was very awkward. I couldn't run down the court, I couldn't shoot layups off the right foot, and I couldn't jump high for rebounds. And after a while, the coach began to take out his frustrations on me."

Physical clumsiness is not unusual for tall, early-maturing boys. Another old friend of mine, Tom O'Neill, stands well over six feet tall and also experienced an early growth spurt. But far from enjoying the social dominance his height supposedly conferred, his growth forced him to quit sports such as baseball, at which he had previously excelled. "It was like I could not control what was going on, and I just became too clumsy, so I stopped playing sports for a while," he told me. Nelson, another friend, is also taller than six feet, but his above-average size during adolescence did not purchase immunity from the depredations of school bullies. He still recalls having to avoid them.

A turning point for Tom Andersen came during his freshman year in high school. Instead of playing a sport he seemed perfect for but was not (basketball), he went out for the swim team, and his physical awkwardness vanished in the water. As a freshman, he recalled, he finished very high in a statewide invitational swim meet at nearby Hinsdale Central, a school synonymous with scholastic swimming excellence in the Midwest. When he mentioned this, I remembered the buzz at school when word of his precocious weekend performance had spread. "I gained confidence because I had athletic success swimming and because of the support of my family," he told me. "But being tall was also an advantage."

Two qualities that Tom always displayed were that he didn't care what other people thought about him and he didn't mind challenging authority. He had a quirky and somewhat combative personality, and he was always getting into disputes with teachers. Memorably, he was suspended on the first day of school in 1966 for wearing "bizarre pants" — a hip-hugging pair of bell-bottoms with wide blue and white vertical stripes, which had been purchased on Carnaby Street in London over the summer. This represented the first cultural sighting of such garb in our insulated suburb of Chicago. Tom's behavior attracted even more attention because he was the son of a prominent local minister. Defiance of authority, aggressiveness, and mischievous behavior are, of course, classic behaviors of children of clergy, but they also are typical of early maturers.

Tom went on to star in swimming and cross-country; had the lead role in many high school theatrical productions; played the coveted role of our school mascot, Noil the lion; worked on the school newspaper; and in our senior year escorted the homecoming queen, Debi Allen, to the homecoming dance. When he dragged out our high school yearbook, he pointed out that he had more entries listed in the index than practically any other student. In the argot of economists, he had managed to accumulate a lot of human capital during his adolescence.

Was it because he was tall, or an early maturer? Height didn't hurt, he mused, but it was more than a matter of feet and inches, and more than a matter of Mother Nature's metronome. "I think I was confident because I had the unconditional love of my family, even when I got into trouble, which I did, a lot," he told me. "And athletic success gave me a lot of confidence." His size, of course, contributed to that success, but it was also connected to finding the right physical outlet for his enormous competitive energies.

While we were on the topic of human capital, I asked him what he remembered about me from those days. "I remember you as very short and tiny," he said. He also recalled a nickname, Ernie, which referred to the youngest, nerdiest sibling on the television show *My Three Sons*. "That's who you looked like," Tom said, "and you were about that size." I winced at the recollection; it had always seemed like one of those verbal tags that, though not rising to the level of bullying, stained one's adolescent existence as indelibly as a scarlet letter pinned to one's chest.

But then Tom surprised me by mentioning something else. "I also remember that you were a good singer," he said. "And I was envious of you because we were in freshman glee club and sophomore chorus together, but you were really good and got selected for the special smaller ensembles, with only four kids per part." There was an amusing, egocentric subtext to this memory. As Tom had earlier pointed out, with yearbook photos as prime exhibits, he had had the lead role in almost every school theatrical production — except for the ones that required singing. (His understudy for almost all the dramatic roles was David Hasselhoff, who tended to get the leading roles in musicals. Hasselhoff went on to become a famous television actor, starring in the series *Knight Rider* and *Baywatch*, and a well-known singer, especially in Europe.) Nearly forty years later, Tom was still reliving the competition.

"So you had skills," he continued, "and I knew you were smart. And you always seemed mature, which was not true of everyone." He mentioned another student who was small of stature and who also possessed a great singing voice. "But he was a dork," Tom pointed out. "He was so immature in so many ways."

So there we were, two graying, fifty-something males adopting the timeless vocabulary of the adolescent putdown. Garry Trudeau, it struck me, was right: you never outgrow your high school persona, at least among the kids who knew you way back when.

LISTENING TO TOM'S experience of tallness, pubertal maturation, and adolescent confidence was like hearing about an exotic foreign culture. In what felt like the physiological version of *Waiting for Godot*, I spent a good part of my adolescence in an existential wasteland, waiting for a growth spurt that was too little and too late. It was intensely frustrating and socially estranging. In retrospect, this preoccupation with physical size strikes me as a little exaggerated and, well, small-minded. At the time, however, I was convinced that physical size — not the horn-rimmed glasses, not the braces, not the braininess, not the awkwardness, not being new in town, not just adolescence in general — accounted for my alienation. Old zones of comfort, such as sports, didn't seem quite so much fun. Lagging size impaired my ability to compete in the sports I loved most, especially basketball and football. New areas of adolescent endeavor, such as dating, seemed as daunting and impossible as dunking a basketball. I rarely went on dates. Once, I went out with a girl who was a good deal taller than I was, and I recall the awkward calisthenics on her stoop just to be able to reach her lips: I had to stand on my toes to kiss her good night. It was the first and only time we went out, and that's what I remember most about that period — the awkwardness, the suppressed passion, the unformed me on the doorstep.

The overwhelming uncertainty, sexual insecurity, and lack of confidence persisted into young adulthood, and I'm convinced that much of the work of adult life, whether it comes through soul-searching, psychotherapy, or an alternate universe of experience, is to rewrite the sense of self that forms during these adolescent transitions. In the throes of this adolescent tumult, the urging (usually by parents) of self-acceptance might as well be in Urdu, so foreign is the concept. If my own experience is any guide, perhaps the trick is simply to hang on, as Tom did, until the storms die down.

One of the first obstacles to overcome on the road to self-acceptance is the often knee-jerk assessment of cause and effect. I don't doubt that many factors contributed to my distress, but a late-maturing boy, regardless of size, simply doesn't feel whole. When I went back and read the inscriptions in my junior high school yearbooks, I realized that some of the comments, especially from girls, reinforced the underlying sexual tension associated with small size. "You're my favorite boy under 4'," wrote one girl. "To a real cute little *nut!!*" wrote another. "To a cute pee-wee & fun to be with. Good luck always!" wrote a third. It wasn't malicious; indeed, the combination of treacle and insult is a time-honored form of adolescent sentiment. But reading these comments forty years later, I can't help but feel a little miniaturized by this backhanded female affection.

In the end, sports turned out to be my saving grace — though not quite the way they did for Tom, and not in a way I would have imagined. During my sophomore year in high school, my friend Scott Novotny asked me if I wanted to join the wrestling team. Not any team — the *varsity* team, at a large suburban high school in the Chicago area. My only previous exposure to wrestling was what I had done to my younger brother (when my parents weren't looking) and watching Bobo Brazil and Antonino Rocca on television with my Italian grandfather. In terms of high school wrestling, small size was my predominant, indeed, my only, qualification. Without starving myself or sweating off weight in a rubber suit (at least initially), I weighed ninety-five pounds. As it turned out, that was the lowest weight class in wrestling, which, unlike many sports, makes allowances for variation in size. The varsity team had been forfeiting every match at ninety-five pounds that year because the coach couldn't find anyone small enough to join the team. Any body, including mine, was better than no body. Or so they thought.

Exactly two weeks later, I found myself in a smelly gym at Proviso East High School, a prodigious factory of superb athletes just outside Chicago, wearing the spaghetti-strapped gold shirt and blue shorts of the visiting LaGrange Lions. I was such a novice, and the experience was so disorienting, that after I handed my glasses to Scott (who wrestled at the next weight level, 103 pounds), my teammates had to lead me, like a blind person led by a guide dog, to the center of the mat. Having no muscles (yet) and fewer moves than a teenage boy at a sock hop, I made short work of any athletic suspense. The kid from Proviso, who knew what he was doing, promptly took me down and started working me over. As he bulldozed my nose and right cheek across the most odoriferous patch of rubberized anaerobic mat I have ever had the misfortune to inhale, I began to have second thoughts about wrestling. He pinned me in about ninety seconds, eighty of which I spent staring at the ceiling and thinking, *How did I get into this?*

The experience was, if anything, even more humbling when the varsity team wrestled at home, for my school thoughtfully provided cheerleaders, whose advanced pubertal maturation only accentuated the gap between me and them. Not that sex is on your mind when someone is trying to drive your shoulders two feet below sea level, but it always seemed a surreal perversion of adolescent fantasies to have cheerleaders leaning, chest-first, over the edge of the mat and crying "Stand up, Steve!" when nearly a hundred pile-driving pounds of antagonism was at that exact moment trying to press me into the mat like a thumbtack.

And yet it was a terrific experience. In time I offered the team a better option than a forfeit — though not by much. In my entire two-year varsity career, I never won a match. I led some matches and lost some close ones, but I never had the referee raise my hand at the end. On the plus side, I never lost a junior varsity match, and I rarely lost a wrestle-off in practice. Perhaps the greatest, albeit perverse, satisfaction of my career was witnessing the weekly disbelief and disappointment on the face of the varsity coach when he received word that I had defeated my in-house rivals yet again. Truth be told, my heart was never totally in wrestling. Sometimes I would come home after two hours of wrestling practice and, in the icy chill of a midwestern winter, shoot baskets in the dark. Basketball was still my first love.

And looking back on it, maybe that was part of the problem. Although there's something to be said for refusing to give up an activity others say you are unsuited for, perhaps one of the most significant thresholds of emotional maturity is recognizing that you can't do something. Clinging to the dream of pursuing a basketball career when you are four feet eleven crosses the line between determination and self-denying, pain-inflicting stubbornness. Dreams die hard — but in this case, it had to die.

Much as I hated it, wrestling probably saved my adolescence. Being on a team is a form of belonging. The camaraderie was not only a kind of tonic but also a form of social vaccination. I can't remember any episodes of being picked on after I joined the wrestling team. (In all fairness, epidemiologists who study bullying note that it tends to decline after the middle school years.) Being even marginally proficient at something athletic conferred on me a certain amount of self-esteem. So too did the varsity letter I received as a sophomore. And being a little more buff in the mirror didn't hurt either. I spent an unseemly amount of time exploring the best poses to make myself look muscular, hoping to gain a psychological edge against opponents.

In the course of researching this book, I bumped into several short-stature or average-stature men who had selected size-independent sports such as wrestling, track, cross-country, swimming, gymnastics, and soccer as outlets for their athletic talents. Alan Rogol wrestled and lifted weights. Pediatric endocrinologist David Allen ran track and cross-country. Even my grade school colleague Albert Destramps went out for the wrestling team.

For the athletically inclined, these activities are crucial during puberty. They allow boys to participate, to acquire a specialized expertise, to compete, to belong to a community where effort (regardless of outcome) is appreciated. All those factors mitigate against the otherwise centrifugal social forces that push a late-maturing or inherently small adolescent boy toward isolation, alienation, bad behavior, and solitude. For boys who are not attracted to sports, other activities — theater, dance, music — provide similar opportunities for collegiality and nearly as much of an aerobic workout.

And this is where the economics study I discussed in chapter 9 brings surprising power to the issue of adolescent maturation. When I asked one of the study's authors, Andrew Postlewaite, why he thought adolescent height was so important to adult success, he was reluctant to jump to any conclusions — especially since he was in the midst of a follow-up study attempting to tease out the factors at play. But he did say this: "I do believe — and this is at the level of cocktail party conversation — that short teenaged boys seem to have less participation in sports, have less exposure to success, are less socially interactive. It may be that they don't participate because they've already not had success and withdrawn, or that they've already been excluded by that time."

No longer bound by high school measures of success, I felt obliged to raise an objection. The economist's measure of adult success — the higher wage — was not necessarily the only value worth considering. Human capital in the form of psychological insight, empathetic human interaction, and aesthetic achievement might be just as socially bankable as wages. By the criteria of the economists' paper, someone like Vincent van Gogh, who barely made a penny in his lifetime, possessed no human capital whatsoever.

Postlewaite made the reasonable point that "this paper is aimed at economists. If it was a psychology paper aimed at psychologists, I might be interested in other issues." But he went on to explain, from an economist's point of view, why the height-wage question is of fundamental importance. "We did look, just for our own interests, at measures of happiness. If you were shorter than average [as a teenager], you were more likely not to be married by age forty, and not being married by age forty is a category loosely called 'losers.' You earn less in wages, you're less likely to live as long — in most things you would measure, you would do worse than average." He also mentioned that in one of the data sets used in the study, several questions addressed self-esteem. "It does appear," he said, "that men who were shorter than average as teenagers had slightly lower than average self-esteem, so it appears there are some long-term effects of this.

"So we have a correlation: if you're shorter as a teenager, even if you grow to normal adult height, it has a lasting effect on your wage. But what is it about being short? It could be that nobody invites you to their birthday party, so you're a loser. The other possibility is you're invited but don't go, because you don't feel comfortable about yourself in that situation. These are two distinct situations, with two very different explanations. Participation in high school athletics is associated with higher wages, so the athletic component would seem to have some kind of a role. Is it that short teenagers don't go out for athletics, or that they would like to go out but are not successful? We don't know if it is participation in athletics or success in athletics [that is related to higher wages], and these end up being very difficult questions to sort out." But, he said, he believes it all comes down to self-esteem. And the reason this is so important to economists (not to mention psychologists and parents), he added, is that in understanding what happens to short boys during adolescence, we might learn something that will enhance everyone's human capital.

11

"MAN IN HIS PERFECTION"

Adolescent Boys and Male Body Image

> We are created in God's image, and God doesn't wanna
> be a weakling.
>
> — ANGELO SICILIANO

IN THE EARLY 1900S, the Brooklyn Museum of Art featured a gallery that typified museum offerings throughout the world prior to the advent of cheap jet travel and blockbuster art shows: a collection of plaster-cast replicas of the greatest hits of ancient Greek statuary. You can't see these ersatz classical statues anymore, because the museum eventually got rid of them. But they were still on the premises during the summer of 1909, when a group of young immigrants from an Italian settlement school in Brooklyn came to visit. Among the students was a slender, dark-eyed sixteen-year-old named Angelo Siciliano.

Angelo had been born in 1893 near Acri, a "populous townlet" located in the hilly, lawless interior of Calabria. Acri was notorious for a spectacular incident in 1806, when brigands from the nearby mountains descended on the town, chased most of its merchant class half naked into the countryside, and then dragged the burghers back to the main piazza, whereupon they were "spitted and sliced, and set to roast, amid the howling applause of the maddened people." Calabria was the southernmost province of the Italian mainland and had been part of Magna Graecia, the outermost collection of Greek colonies in the seventh and sixth centuries B.C. Crotone, just over the hill from Acri, had been the refuge of Pythagoras and home to Milo of Crotone, "the Greek Samson," whose legendary strength and skill as a wrestler captured six championships at the original Olympic Games.

But the teenage Angelo was apparently unaware of the cultural richness of his native land. In fact, this provincial son of immigrants claimed never to have set foot in a museum before the day of the school trip. In 1903, when Angelo was eleven, his family had joined the great wave of European immigration to the United States. The family was poor and broken; Angelo's parents had separated in Italy, and his mother had brought the family to New York, where they lived with Angelo's uncle in modest quarters on Front Street, near the foot of the recently constructed Brooklyn Bridge. Angelo attended a special school for immigrant children, where they learned to speak English and accustom themselves to the ways of American life, with hopes of ultimately attaining citizenship. Of his youth, Angelo later confessed to no greater distinction than eating, sleeping, and playing. "I was never sickly," he once said, "but on the contrary was rather strong, though not unusually so."

The transforming event in Angelo's life came on that class trip. "I did want to be strong and I hoped I would be," he wrote about a decade later, "but it went no further than that until one day our teacher, Mr. Davenport, took a number of us to the Brooklyn Museum of Art. I was interested in everything there, but most of all in the statuary, copies in plaster of ancient works of art. While the other boys were wandering about looking at other things, I remained studying the magnificent bodies of Hercules, the Dying Gladiator, the Wrestlers, the Discus Thrower, the Boxer and the rest of the splendid specimens of manhood."

Angelo was transfixed. He had always been fascinated by the notion of strength, but here strength was married to physical beauty, creating a form of bodily perfection that had been celebrated as the greatest achievement of Western civilization. Strength, he realized, could be a form of art, an expression of beauty. He couldn't believe that such men had ever existed, even though he had been born near the cradle of their creation. "I was only sixteen at that time, and I was too ignorant to know," he later admitted.

Angelo sought out Davenport and asked for an explanation. His teacher patiently explained that the ancient Greeks had worshiped a well-developed body and had encouraged boys to develop their physical gifts to the best of their abilities. He was the first to inform Angelo about Milo of Crotone and how he had become one of the most perfectly developed males of ancient times. He told the boy about the labors of Hercules and the public games of athletic skill and strength that had marked Greek culture. He said that the winners of these contests had achieved lasting fame.

All this came as a revelation to Angelo. As he later recalled, "I had it in my mind that the Greeks were a different and peculiar race of men, since they cared so much for physical perfection and we so little." He said to his teacher, "I suppose that no one could get to be as strong as that in these times."

"Most anybody can be strong," Davenport replied. "Anyone who is willing to work for it can obtain the same muscular development."

"Do you think that I could develop myself to be like one of these men?" Angelo asked. He half expected his teacher to laugh, but Davenport reassured him. "If you were willing to work hard enough, you could," the teacher said.

He went on to suggest that Angelo visit the gymnasium at the local YMCA. Angelo's family could not afford to give him the money to join the YMCA, but he would go to the gym to watch other men exercise, then return home and replicate the routines. He watched the men do squats, stretching exercises, and "the dip" (what we now call a pushup), then imitated the exercises at home until he was doing one hundred at a time. He even claims, improbably, to have fashioned a homemade set of barbells out of two twenty-five-pound rocks lashed to a broomstick. He became a fitness fiend, and it began to show in his increasingly chiseled physique. As he later put it, "I felt myself growing stronger perceptibly, and as I loved my strength I used to exhibit it to my admiring playfellows." As a stunt, he would lift neighborhood boys, one on each hand, above his head.

At the time, Angelo was a leatherworker, but a steady job was hard to come by. All the while, he continued to work out, and as his strength grew, so did his reputation. There was a time, several years after the trip to the Brooklyn Museum, when he happened upon a crowd in the street surrounding a car that had broken down. One of its tires was flat, but a jack could not be located to raise the car to change the tire. You can guess the rest of the story, which added to the growing mythology surrounding Angelo. It was around this time that a passerby, having marveled at Angelo's physique as he strolled down the street in the Rockaways, pointed out the wooden figure of Atlas that adorned a nearby building. The man observed that Angelo appeared to be as strong as the Greek god, who could bear the weight of the world. Soon after, Angelo started calling himself Atlas.

Eventually, Angelo found the perfect job — standing in a department store window demonstrating a mechanical chest developer. This satisfied his desire for constant bodybuilding exercise and his abiding taste for exhibitionism. While demonstrating the exercise device, he was spotted by a vaudeville strongman named Young Samson, who was looking for someone to perform strongman feats. Soon Angelo had a job in vaudeville and even ran his own performance company for a while. This led to strongman acts during the summer at Coney Island. When he got tired of "the stage," as he put it, he thought he could make more money posing for artists. He was soon making a very handsome living as a model.

By 1921 Angelo had become the dominant figure in the world of physical culture. Encouraged by friends, he submitted a series of photographs of himself to a contest to find "The World's Most Handsome Man." He won the competition unanimously, and the slow but inexorable transition in his persona was apparent in the $1,000 check made out to him by the organizers of the event: it read "Angelo Siciliano Atlas." By the end of the year, he had tweaked his stage name a little more, adopting the identity by which he would ever after be known: Charles Atlas.

In 1922, *Physical Culture* magazine held a similar competition at Madison Square Garden to select "The World's Most Perfect Human." Again, Angelo won. That same year, he and a physical culture enthusiast named Frederick W. Tilney formed a business partnership to market a bodybuilding system. With the help of Tilney, a British copywriter whose grasp of the English language undoubtedly exceeded that of his new Italian-born friend, Angelo began to churn out pamphlets, brochures, and magazine articles describing his discovery of physical culture and his approach to exercise. In little more than a decade, he had gone from admiring the physical beauty of Greek statuary in the Brooklyn Museum to posing for a new generation of sculptors. His likeness, from the neck down, appears in no less than seventy-five examples of public sculpture in the United States. You can see his torso, for instance, in the statue of George Washington in New York's Washington Square Park, the statue of Alexander Hamilton in front of the U.S. Treasury Building in Washington, D.C., and the male centaur in front of the state capitol building in Jefferson City, Missouri.

Angelo Siciliano, aka Charles Atlas, had come to embody the ideal male physical form of his time, and he knew it. "It may not seem quite modest to say so," he later wrote, "but I am known among artists as the Greek God, and I don't know of anything that gives me more pleasure, for I think the Greek God as shown in the old sculptures is so splendid to look at that to be likened to one is the highest compliment that could be paid me. It was from the old sculptures that I got my first ambition to develop myself because they seemed to me to show man in his perfection."

From the moment he was spotted in that department store window, however, Angelo had also fallen within the orbit of Bernarr Macfadden, the preeminent apostle of physical culture and one of the savviest impresarios of his age. By the time he began to recount his remarkable life in a series of autobiographical (and, one suspects, ghostwritten) accounts that appeared in physical culture magazines, the Charles Atlas story had become so marbled with marketing mythology that it's difficult to say what was true and what was concocted to help promote the Atlas brand. It may or may not be the case that, as Angelo noted in numerous interviews, he had been a ninety-seven-pound weakling who got beat up at the beach — the episode is not mentioned in any of the early writings. It may or may not be true that he got the idea for a program of isometric exercises — the kind in which muscles are positioned in opposition to each other, which he called Dynamic-Tension — by watching lions in the Prospect Park Zoo in Brooklyn. In some versions, it's the Bronx Zoo; in others, it's tigers, not lions. It nonetheless made a good story, and Angelo told it well. Recalling the incident for a *New Yorker* writer, he said, "The muscles ran around like rabbits under a rug."

But the "just so" stories of Angelo Siciliano's life underline a much larger point, at least in the context of boys and body size and male psychology: there are really two Charles Atlas stories. One is the biographical tale just recounted, of the earnest Italian immigrant who stumbled upon the idea of isometric exercises and created a program of muscular development that, to twenty-first-century eyes, is surprisingly modern in its particulars. Atlas insisted, for example, on the importance of good nutrition, and many of the foods he encouraged would not be out of place in the current Mediterranean diet: lots of fruits, whole grains, and protein (often in the form of steaks, which he loved). He cautioned against excessive definition of muscles — an argument, obviously, that has fallen on deaf ears in the modern bodybuilding culture. And as Atlas never ceased to tell the steady stream of writers who came to repackage his story, exercise was just one component of a larger philosophy that emphasized mental, emotional, and moral hygiene. He believed that an increase in strength diminished the likelihood that one would resort to physical aggression. "I may be mistaken," he wrote in 1921, "but I think that when a man knows he is strong and better able than most to take care of himself, he is less touchy and less disposed to quarrel." That, of course, was not exactly the message of the famous Charles Atlas advertisements — which brings us to the second tale.

The other Charles Atlas story, which is much more culturally interesting, entails the marketing of physical strength to boys who do not possess it, at precisely the age when they feel most insecure. Everything about the Charles Atlas enterprise was ahead of its time — the demographics of its target audience, its salesmanship, its psychological astuteness. In 1929, when the Charles Atlas bodybuilding "system" was straggling along, Tilney sold his share of the business to a young advertising man named Charles Roman. Roman shrewdly understood that the future of Dynamic-Tension did not lie so much in physical culture magazines, but in a younger generation of adolescents and young adults who were just becoming aware of their changing bodies, their emerging sexual selves, and the excruciating psychological pain experienced by losers in the mating game. There is no record that Atlas or Roman ever uttered the name Darwin, but they marketed their bodybuilding program based on factors that, at least in the animal world, often determine sexual selection: strength, physical agility, and beauty.

And where did they take this message? Comic books! You could hardly find a better vehicle for targeting adolescent boys than the cheap books chronicling the exploits of Superman, Batman, and a host of other superheroes. Indeed, the most famous advertisement ever to come out of the Charles Atlas enterprise — the ad that has forever embodied the blunt Darwinian appeal of bodybuilding and made "ninety-seven-pound weakling" an enduring and unflattering stroke of cultural shorthand, appeared in the form of a comic strip. Created by Roman and titled "The INSULT That Made a MAN Out of 'Mac,'" it compressed a universe of male insecurity into eight panels. The ad (there are several versions) shows a spindly young man on the beach with his girlfriend. Two toughs come up to the couple, kick sand in Mac's face, and walk off with the girl. Determined to win her back, Mac sends for his Dynamic-Tension kit, performs the exercises diligently, and returns to the beach, where he faces down his former antagonists and wins back his girl. "Oh, Mac! You ARE a real man after all!" she says.

This concise ad packs in as much drama and as many emotional twists as a Greek tragedy: physical weakness, sexual betrayal, humiliation, hard work, redemption, revenge, might makes right. Prior to the appearance of the ad, Charles Atlas had typically maintained, in interviews and in his own signed articles, that he had not been sickly and in fact had been "rather strong" as a young man. After the ad appeared, he began to describe an episode at Coney Island that sounded suspiciously similar to the Mac ad, in which two lifeguards came up and stole his girl. It may be a case of life imitating advertising.

In any event, the ad campaign was hugely successful. Within a year, Dynamic-Tension had acquired tens of thousands of adherents, and Atlas and Roman reportedly became overnight millionaires whose financial success easily weathered the stock market crash of 1929. Indeed, while so many companies were failing, Charles Atlas Ltd. opened offices in England and Brazil, translated its program into six languages, and claimed millions of subscribers. Despite changing fashions, demographics, and sophistication in the advertising medium, the brand has endured. Although Atlas himself died in 1972 and Roman in 1999, Charles Atlas Ltd. continues, and it continues for one reason above all: boys are, have been, and always will be insecure about their physical appearance and strength. Angelo Siciliano may have been among the first to notice (and exploit) it, but contemporary researchers are now arguing that boys have become every bit as self-conscious and psychologically fragile about body image as girls have been for generations.

I SENT AWAY for my Charles Atlas kit when I was about twelve. I can't say it changed my life, but then you didn't go to the beach much if you lived in the Midwest. For thirty dollars (I know the price because Atlas never changed it, at least from the 1920s into the 1960s), all I got was a small, thick booklet. No paraphernalia, no gear, just words. The booklet described a series of isometric exercises, which in fact enjoyed a bit of a fad in the 1960s. I remember standing at a bathroom sink in my underwear, lifting myself up on my toes and sucking in my breath repeatedly. It was a sight no mother, no sibling, not even a pet, should be forced to see. For all I know, the program may have worked, but I soon gave up on the exercises and went back to less strenuous activities, like reading comic books.

But Atlas and Roman were onto something. Their astute perception of adolescent male insecurity about strength and body image lives on today, in ways they could scarcely have imagined. The cartoonish pectorals and sinewy quads of superheroes have been supplanted by a much more graphic and exaggerated ideal of male physical development, and this updated ideal assaults teenage boys in all the places where they live mentally. You see it in the male models in teen fashion catalogs, which border on soft-core pornography. You see it in the films and TV shows that cater to teenage audiences, where you need a stopwatch to time the brief interval from the beginning of the show to the time a male protagonist starts peeling off his shirt. And you see it in gymnasiums all over the world, where teenage boys skip study hall after school to put in time on the Nautilus machine and lift weights. You even see it in the action figures that prepubescent boys play with. These toys have, in fact, inspired a scientific study shedding light on how something as innocuous as a plaything could help create the cultural context for serious psychopathology.

Several years ago, Harvard Medical School psychiatrist Harrison G. Pope Jr. and his colleague Roberto Olivardia compared the measurements of contemporary action figures such as Batman and GI Joe to earlier versions. They found that just as Arnold Schwarzenegger's generation of bodybuilders dwarfed Charles Atlas, plastic models have bulked up over the years. Pope and Olivardia measured the waist, chest, and biceps dimensions of the dolls and projected them onto an average-size, 5-foot-10 male. Batman, to cite one absurd tale of the tape, had the equivalent of a 30-inch waist, a 57-inch chest, and 27-inch biceps. Just to put this into perspective, Atlas in his prime had a 33½-inch waist, a 49¾-inch chest, and 16¾-inch biceps. And to put *that* into perspective, Joe Louis, a superb athlete and among the greatest heavyweight boxers of all time, had a 36½-inch waist and 15-inch biceps. It is not just that the physical dimensions of the toys are biologically impossible; it is that such bulk is unconnected to athletic ability or even physical coordination.

"People misinterpreted our findings to assume that playing with toys, in and of itself, caused kids to develop into neurotic people as they grew up, who abused anabolic steroids," Pope told me. "Of course that was not our conclusion. We simply chose the toys because they were symptomatic of what we think is a much more general trend in our society."

A number of studies in the past fifteen years — primarily of men, not boys — have suggested that body image disturbances, as researchers sometimes call them, may be more prevalent in men than previously believed and almost always begin in the teenage years. Katharine Phillips, a psychiatrist at Brown Medical School, has specialized in body dysmorphic disorder, a psychiatric illness in which patients become obsessively preoccupied with perceived flaws in their appearance — receding hairlines, facial imperfections, small penises, inadequate musculature. In an early study describing thirty cases of this "imagined ugliness," Phillips and her colleagues identified a surprisingly common condition in males; the symptoms include excessive checking of mirrors and attempts to camouflage imagined deformities, most often of the hair, nose, and skin. In some extreme cases, the Brown group reported, men suffering from the disorder believe they are so ugly or unattractive that they refuse to leave their homes — they become, in effect, body image agoraphobics. The average age of onset for body dysmorphic disorder, Phillips told me, is fifteen. It appears to be an aberrant form of adolescent self-consciousness.

Just as teenage girls have historically tended to feel they aren't thin enough, boys now show signs of feeling they aren't big and strong enough. Since roughly 90 percent of teenagers who are treated for eating disorders are female, boys still have a way to go in that area. But to hear some psychologists tell it, boys may be catching up in terms of insecurity and even psychological pathology. Since the early 1990s, evidence has emerged suggesting that a small but growing number of adult males suffer from these extreme body image disorders. The incidence of body dysmorphic disorder, for example, has been estimated at 1 to 2 percent of the U.S. population, both men and women — an astoundingly high number given that the disorder specifies serious psychopathology and not just self-consciousness. And as Harrison Pope and Geoffrey Cohane reported in 2001, the problem has become apparent in boys under eighteen years of age and is not unrelated to self-perceptions of size. "Although boys generally displayed less overall body concern than girls," they wrote, summarizing more than a dozen studies on the topic, "many boys of all ages reported dissatisfaction with their bodies, often associated with reduced self-esteem. Whereas girls typically wanted to be thinner, boys frequently wanted to be bigger."

"Basically, men in general are getting the same medicine that women have had to put up with for years, which was trying to match an unattainable ideal in terms of body image," Pope told me.

"The feminist complaint all along is that women get treated as objects, that they internalize that, and that it damages their self-esteem," said Kelly Brownell, director of the Yale Center for Eating Disorders. "And more and more, guys are falling into that same thing. They're judged not by who they are, but how they look."

Mary Pipher, a clinical psychologist and author of the groundbreaking book about teenage girls *Reviving Ophelia*, has noticed the same thing. "Boys are much more prone at this point to worry about being beefed up, about having muscles," she said. "As we've commodified boys' bodies to sell products, with advertisements that show boys as bodies without heads, we've had this whole business about focusing on the body." Families move around so often, she added, that teenagers "don't really know each other very well, so the only piece of information that's really accessible is your appearance."

Pope, an avid weightlifter, has created a cottage industry documenting both the psychological disorders of male body image and the cultural factors that contribute to it. He stumbled onto the issue in the mid-1990s while studying steroid use among male weightlifters. At that time, he discovered that 10 percent of the men "perceived themselves as physically small and weak, even though they were in fact large and muscular." At first researchers termed this syndrome reverse anorexia nervosa and started looking for more cases. Two years later, the Pope group renamed the disorder "muscle dysmorphia," a more specialized condition that involves an obsessive preoccupation with muscularity. Men who were clearly well developed and, by anyone's standards, exceedingly muscular repeatedly expressed the feeling that they were too small, too skinny, and too weak, to the point that their obsessive quest to build up their bodies began to interfere with work and relationships — in short, disrupting their entire lives. "It's very hard to document trends like this in quantitative terms," Pope told me, "because people who are insecure about their body appearance are unlikely to come out of the woodwork to confess that they're insecure about their body appearance. And so it is an epidemic which by definition is covert. But it clearly has become a much more widespread concern among men in the United States."

Phillips, Pope, and Olivardia recently coined the term "Adonis complex" to describe the growing male fixation with an ideal body image, which includes both size (in terms of muscles and strength) and appearance (in terms of hair, facial features, and rippling midriffs). These disorders are usually associated with adult males, but the insecurity has its roots in adolescence, they believe, and is entangled with issues we have already seen as crucial to male psychological development: height, overall size, pubertal timing, strength, and body shape.

In their more recent research, Pope and his colleagues created something called the "somatomorphic matrix," a tool that allows research subjects to manipulate proportions of muscularity and fat in a male image that appears on a computer screen. Men are asked to use the device to create a picture of various body images: how they imagine their own bodies look, how they think the "average" male in their culture looks, how they would ideally like to look, and what they think women would most desire in a male body. (There's an unexpected punch line to this research that I'll withhold until a little later.) The main point is that, using this device, young men in three Western cultures (Austria, France, and the United States) demonstrated similar degrees of dissatisfaction with their bodies. Typically, when asked to imagine their ideal body forms, the men, with a few clicks of a computer mouse, added an additional twenty-eight pounds of muscle to their physiques.

The somatomorphic matrix sounds like a uniquely high-tech tool for our image-conscious times, but it is in fact merely the latest in a very long line of such devices. The issue of body image always comes back to measurement, and if you want to know the roots of the Adonis complex, it is necessary to go back to the age of Adonis — or, more properly, the era when the myth of Adonis was revived after a long, medieval slumber, ensnared like Gulliver in a tangle of mathematical string.

LONG BEFORE STEROIDS, long before Charles Atlas, humans whipped out rulers to determine not only height but also something more exalted and elusive: the precise dimensions, reduced to pure numbers, of the ideal physical form. Greek culture celebrated male beauty, and in an effort to recapture that aesthetic, many of the first systematic measurements of the human form — the birth, in a way, of the field of anthropometry — date back to the Renaissance. The rulers were wielded not by doctors or scientists (strictly speaking), but by artists of a modern, scientific sensibility.

These artists — Leon Battista Alberti, Albrecht Dürer, and Leonardo da Vinci, to name the most prominent — sought a mathematical formula for, as one book put it, divine human bodily proportion. In search of that formula, however, many seekers did not bother measuring mere human beings. Rather (and here history presages the transformation of Angelo Siciliano), they measured classical statues — the ones that survived from antiquity and the more recent knockoffs. By the time this flurry of tape measure aesthetics had been completed, in a burst of quantification that extended from the fifteenth to the eighteenth century, Adolphe Quetelet, the founder of modern statistics, had proposed a formula to tame the numbers and define perfect human beauty. The way that formula has changed and become exaggerated in recent times helps explain why boys today face new pressures about body image.

James Tanner, who originally became interested in human growth through an obsession with body shape, or somatotyping, has written at length about the human fascination with perfect proportion. He locates the rebirth of interest in the subject to the rediscovery of Vitruvius. Though known primarily as an authority on architecture, Vitruvius devoted one of the ten books of his *De architectura* (On Architecture) to human proportion, and it features one of the most iconic images of the human body ever published: a naked man, standing with his legs spread apart and his arms outstretched to form an X, superimposed on a grid of tiny squares. Vitruvius's rule of human proportion, as it became known, inspired many copies, including the more famous image by Leonardo. The connection to architecture may at first seem odd but was part of the general reclamation of Greek ideals after the Dark Ages. Vitruvius believed, Tanner writes, that "the symmetry and proportion of a temple should truthfully reflect the symmetry and proportion of the human body." Just as the later history of statistics formed a double helix with eugenics, the early history of human aesthetics became entwined with mathematics, cartography, and instruments of measurement.

If there is a scholar laureate of this renewed celebration of proportion and geometric harmony and a fitting heir to Vitruvius, it was the Florentine architect and humanist Leon Battista Alberti, intellectual successor to Filippo Brunelleschi and godfather to many Renaissance artists. Alberti is best known among art historians as an architect of rigorous, almost excessively formal harmony and balance. But he also created a new city plan for Rome in the middle of the fifteenth century. In doing so, he not only codified the scientific and mathematical principles of perspective painting, which forever transformed the visual arts, but also sought to relate the geometry of physical proportions to the larger goal of classical harmony and ideal form. Around this time, Alberti wrote a small volume called *De statua* (On Sculpture). During his city planning stint in Rome, Alberti had used a cartographic instrument to plot out the proportions and locations of buildings in maps he created of the Eternal City, and he adapted the tool to begin "mapping" the proportions of the human body. This was of a philosophical piece with the habit of Florentine painters, who had adapted the grid technique of map projection to translate small sketches into the scale of wall-size frescoes. Based loosely on the astrolabe and called the *finitorum*, this instrument began to quantify the human form, and the echo of its measurements reached all the way to Charles Atlas.

In his quest to capture perfect beauty, Alberti created a uniquely customized sort of ruler, which he called the *exempeda*. Rather than employ one standardized ruler with which to measure all bodies, Alberti instead crafted a personalized ruler for each subject, which could be analyzed to reveal unique proportional relationships. Thus, adopting the Greek obsession with proportion, Renaissance scientists and doctors were less concerned with absolute size, as Tanner points out, than relative individual measurement. "[When] I took on the task of recording the *Dimensione* of man," Alberti wrote,

I proceeded to measure and record in writing not simply the beauty found in this or that body but, as far as possible, that perfect beauty distributed by Nature, as it were in fixed proportion, among many bodies; and in doing this I imitated the artist at Croton [Crotone, home of Milo] who, when making the likeness of a goddess, chose all remarkable and elegant beauties of form from several of the most handsome maidens, and translated them into his work. So we too chose many bodies, considered to be the most beautiful by those who know, and took from each and all their dimensions which are then compared with one another, and leaving out of account the extremes on both sides, we took the mean figures validated by the *exempeda*.

In other words, the mean, or average, was the ideal. The fiftieth percentile of any beautiful limb became the standard of perfection.

Leonardo, says Tanner, "incomparably illustrated his predecessor's ideas, and incorporated a good deal of Alberti, without acknowledgment, after the manner of the times, into his own treatise on painting." To complete a thread running back and forth between the artistic eruption of the Renaissance and the new math of bodily beauty, Leonardo did some of the illustrations for a book by his friend Luca Pacioli called *De divina proportione* (On Divine Proportion), which was published in 1509. The book provided additional data on the mathematics of classical beauty. When he was in his sixties, Pacioli apparently received a visit from a young painter from Germany who had traveled to Italy "to take lessons in secret perspective" and had learned of Pacioli's research. His name was Albrecht Dürer, and he began to apply the mathematics of proportion in the work that would gain him lasting artistic fame.

There was a parallel, less mathematical school of research pursued by other intellects and academics in the seventeenth century, and it involved measuring Greek statuary — and its widely disseminated copies — to derive the formula for classical beauty. The distance between toes, eyes, nostrils, and breasts; the thickness of forearms and calves; the location of abdominal indentations; the arc of distance from navel to shoulder, from nipple to chin, from hipbone to lower cheek of the buttocks — no dimension was too small, too obscure, to elude capture by the statue measurers. *Hercules,* the *Medici Venus,* and dozens of other statues from antiquity yielded to the ruler. The obsession of contemporary teenagers with their "six-packs" has nothing on the way the abdominals of Hercules were parsed as "he" appeared in Gérard Audran's 1683 book on human proportions. "This school," Tanner writes, "became institutionalized in the art academies of the eighteenth and nineteenth centuries, where it figured increasingly as the quest for Ideal Beauty."

But it was only a matter of time before the pursuit of beauty crossed paths with the arc of biology. Johann Gottfried Schadow directed the Berlin Academy of Art in the early nineteenth century, and it was in his hands that the aesthetic quest for the ideal body and the scientific quest to understand growth and physical size merged. Schadow was not only a prodigious statue measurer, but he began to apply his sculptor's compass to real human children as well, providing some of the very earliest measurements of actual human growth.

Toward the end of his life (he died in 1850), Schadow received a visit from another statue measurer, the young Belgian mathematician Adolphe Quetelet. In addition to his early contributions to the growth chart, Quetelet was an astronomer, meteorologist, and, most important, the founder of modern statistics. His philosophy, scrawled into the margin of a book, was "Numbers rule the world," and Florence Nightingale, an ardent admirer, called him "the author, inventor, Master of all the Science of Statistics, and of all of us." Quetelet the humanist obsessed about human beauty and proportions. Quetelet the mathematician vowed to use modern statistical methods to devise a formula that would forever define perfect physical beauty and the human form. He half succeeded, and in doing so established a line of inquiry that began as aesthetics and has now become an indispensable part of modern medicine, especially in the age of obesity.

Quetelet's efforts to reduce human beauty to a formulaic expression came out in a hugely influential book, *Physique sociale* (Social Physics), first published in 1835 (under a different title). There Quetelet laid out his vision of *l'homme moyen*, which is often translated as "the average man." Like Alberti, Quetelet believed that physical beauty lay in the mean — the average value of a set of physical measurements that described the human form. "An individual who combined in his own person all the qualities of the average man," Quetelet wrote in the 1835 edition of *Social Physics*, "would . . . represent all which is grand, beautiful and excellent." Quetelet not only established an aesthetic of average proportion, but he also inevitably established a statistics of *unaesthetic* deviation, exaggeration, even ugliness. "If the average man were completely determined," he wrote, "we might consider him as the type of perfection; and everything differing from his proportions would constitute deformity and disease; everything found dissimilar, not only as regards proportion and form but as exceeding the observed limits, would constitute monstrosity." In these remarks, we can see the first indication that statistical difference (or deviation) could be equated with a kind of deformity.

Quetelet surely believed that social physics represented his greatest gift to posterity, but it was another invention that has had a more powerful, and, arguably, a much more practical, impact on human affairs. In an effort to understand the proper proportion of muscle to body fat, Quetelet was the first to devise a ratio called the body mass index (BMI). To this day, it remains the principal measure to assess appropriate weight for height and obesity.

In this early application of statistics to the human body, we can easily see the initial creation of a narrow margin of error — in the psychological, not the mathematical, sense — between an acceptable body image and the many unacceptable shapes, sizes, and features to which the human race is inevitably, indeed genetically, prone. And yet by the time Quetelet died in 1874, the "average man" was just about to be overtaken in popular culture by the exaggerated man: well built, uncommonly strong, and rippling with Darwinian fitness in a world of Victorian weaklings. As the social historian John F. Kasson has pointed out, the advent of photography and, later, movies, showing images of real people with really big muscles, helped create a huge cultural following for Eugen Sandow, the Prussian-born bodybuilder known as "the perfect man." One of Thomas Edison's earliest movies featured the preening Sandow, who toured Europe and America in the 1890s and became the first truly popular strongman. Angelo Siciliano kept a picture of Sandow in his childhood bedroom.

By the turn of the twentieth century, dozens of physical culture "systems" competed to help men build their bodies. The explosion partly stemmed from the rediscovery of Greek culture and the Hellenic ideal. Sandow popularized the muscular body; Charles Atlas was adept at marketing it. Atlas did not necessarily offer the best program or the finest specimen, but his enterprise was especially pioneering because it was probably the first to marry body image and mass marketing. There were even political consequences to this outburst of physical culture. At the time Atlas and Charles Roman pitched their message to ninety-seven-pound weaklings in the 1920s, during an ugly confluence of anti-immigration fervor and eugenic enthusiasms, U.S. lawmakers were being urged to enact compulsory sterilization laws not only for criminals and the mentally disabled but also for a new and ill-defined category of social misfits known as weaklings.

Between the 1920s and 1970s, the manic pursuit of a sculpted body (and modern pharmacology) transformed the small subculture of weight-lifters and bodybuilders from the "naturals" of Atlas's generation to the behemoths of *Pumping Iron.* By the time that 1977 documentary came out, bodybuilders were so musclebound that they looked like anatomical dummies. "I think drugs have a *huge* part to do with that," said Roberto Olivardia, who noted that steroid use has increased dramatically in recent decades. "People from the earlier generation like Atlas wouldn't even be eligible for bodybuilding competitions now; they would be deemed too small." He suggested that broader cultural trends may have contributed to this transformation. As women attained greater equality with men during the 1960s and 1970s, he said, there was "almost this need for hypermasculine models for men to look up to. So it's not an accident that in the early 1980s Schwarzenegger and Stallone were the leading actors in this hypermasculine culture. It feels, historically, more desperate."

If you listen to the comments of the young Arnold Schwarzenegger in *Pumping Iron,* they mark — in their unapologetic manipulativeness and hubristic narcissism — a stark departure from the more genial self-confidence of Charles Atlas. But they are also true to their roots. When an interviewer in the film asks Schwarzenegger if he visualizes himself as a piece of sculpture, he quickly takes the bait. "Yes, definitely," he says. "Good bodybuilders have the same mind, when it comes to sculpting, that a sculptor has."

Just as in the days of Charles Atlas, mass media — especially advertising — has helped to promote the image of the ideal man, but he is anything but average these days. The images exert an enormous cultural influence on adolescent boys, as I discovered several years ago when working on a story for the *New York Times Magazine.* That was when I met a personable young man named Alex Bregstein.

ON A SWELTERING day in July, I joined Alex at his local gym in northern New Jersey. He had slept only three hours the night before and had then spent eight hours with preschool children at a summer camp where he was a counselor. But his first idea of relaxation after all that was to be lying on his back on an inclined bench, headphones pitching three-figure decibels of rock music into his ears as he gripped eighty-five-pound weights in his hands and then, after a brief pause to gather himself, muscled them into the air with focused bursts of energy. Each lift was accompanied by a sharp exhalation of breath, like the quick short stroke of a piston.

The first thing you should know about Alex is that he didn't need to create bursting biceps to make himself attractive. After spending just a little time with him, I could tell he was, at sixteen years old, bright, articulate, and funny in that self-deprecating teenage way that slyly conveys a great deal of self-awareness. However, about a year earlier, Alex had had a kind of epiphany. He had been seriously overweight, carrying 210 pounds on his five-foot-six frame, and he was hearing about it from schoolmates.

"Oh, man, was I *teased*?" he exclaimed. "Are you kidding? When I was fat, people must have gone home and thought of nothing else except coming in with new material the next day. They must have had *study groups* just to make fun of people who were overweight." And so, in April 1998, while on spring break with his family in Florida, Alex reached a point of no return in self-loathing as he stood in front of the mirror and eyeballed his shirtless torso. "I remember the exact, like, *moment* in my mind," he said. "Everything about that room is burned into my head, every little thing. I can tell you where every lamp was, where my father was standing, my mother was sitting. We were about to go out, and I'm looking in this mirror — me, with my gut hanging out over my bathing suit — and it was, like, who would want to look at this? It's part of me, and *I'm* disgusted! That moment, I realized that nobody was giving me a chance to find out who I was because of the way I looked."

Resolved to change things, Alex lost forty pounds in one month and started lifting weights. He still hung out with the computer geeks at school, but he also discovered a new physiological vocabulary (abdominals, triceps, quads) and a new workout ethic. Realizing that the first thing people knew about him was the way he looked, he made a conscious decision to make sure they would see something impressive. And what they began to see, after less than a year, was a young man with thick neck muscles, shoulders so massive that he couldn't scratch his back, and a chest that had been deliberately chiseled for the two-button look — what Alex referred to as "my most endearing feature."

As his spotter looked on, Alex lifted the eighty-five-pound weights three more times, arms quivering, face reddening with effort. Each dumbbell, I realized as I watched, weighed more than I had when I entered high school. Another half dozen teenagers milled around the weight room, casting glances at themselves and one another in the mirror. They talked of looking "cut," with sharp definition to their muscles, and of developing "six-packs," sculpted abdominals. While we talked between sets of Alexander's ninety-minute routine, his eyes wandered to the mirror again and again, searching for flaws, looking for areas of improvement. "The more you lift," he admitted, "the more you look in the mirror." Indeed, of all the muscles that get a workout in rooms like these, the most important may be the ones that move the eyes in restless, sweeping arcs of comparison and appraisal. "Once you're in this game to manipulate your body," Alex said, "you want to be the best." He likened the friendly competition in the room to a form of "whipping out the ruler."

A number of psychologists with whom I spoke about this phenomenon returned to the same point again and again: the cultural messages about an ideal male body, if not new, have grown more insistent, more aggressive, more widespread, and more explicit in recent years. And this is where today's body image concerns intersect with a larger, more complex, and in some ways timeless dilemma of male development that, while appearing to suffer from the triteness of pop psychology, also happens to be true: boys, like girls, are keenly aware of, and insecure about, their physical appearance. Boys, unlike many girls, do not talk about it — not with their parents, not with other adults, and not even among themselves, lest they be perceived as "sensitive," a code word for weak. William S. Pollack, a Harvard psychologist and the author of *Real Boys,* refers to this as the boy's code, and defines it as "what they can say and can't say, how they feel about their body self, how they feel about their self-image, how they feel about themselves in school."

Dan Kindlon, another Harvard researcher and the coauthor of *Raising Cain,* put it this way: "When you go to ask men questions about psychological issues, you've got two things going against you. One is emotional literacy. They're not even in touch with their emotions, and they're doing things for reasons of which they're not even aware. You're not getting the real story because *they* don't even know the whole story. And even if they did, a lot of them would underrepresent what the problem was, because you're not supposed to ask for help. If you can't ask for directions when you're lost in a foreign city, how are you going to ask for help about something that's really personal? Especially if you're an eighth grader."

If the concern about body image among boys is not exactly new, the anxiety feels fresh and confusing to each new generation of adolescent males dealing with these ever more insistent cultural messages. I heard it not only in Alex Bregstein but also among several groups of middle school boys in New York with whom I met to discuss the issue of male body image for the *New York Times Magazine* story. It obviously wasn't a scientific survey, but the students came from varied backgrounds: a public school, a private school, and an afterschool program at an urban YMCA. Even as they grappled to articulate what they felt, their voices — and their struggle to make sense of an emotionally loaded, constantly changing, and utterly confusing situation — came through loud and clear.

On one occasion, six public school teenage boys and I sat around a table on a warm afternoon near the end of the school year in Manhattan. I asked them to describe the feelings they had when they looked at themselves in the mirror. For sheer confused candor, it was tough to top the remark of M., a thirteen-year-old who was scheduled to start ninth grade in the fall. "I don't know," he said at first. "I can't even tell what stage of puberty I'm in. Some parts I'm sure about, but" — he added with an impish smile — "other parts, I'm not so sure."

We went around the table. Dwayne, mentioning that he appeared younger than his thirteen years, looked forward to the effect youthfulness would have later in life. Bernie, lean and a little more satisfied than the others, said he didn't want muscles and would never use steroids. James saw a chubby thirteen-year-old in his mirror. "I just want to be skinnier," he said plaintively. Adel, who had shot up six inches and gained twenty-four pounds in the previous fourteen months, monitored acne outbreaks with the avidity of a Drug Enforcement Administration agent. Willie, a powerfully built fifteen-year-old with impressive biceps, derived no solace from his solid athletic build. "When I look in the mirror, I wish my ears were bigger and my feet were smaller," he said. "I wear size eleven and a half shoes. My behind is big, too, but girls like it." In retrospect, perhaps the most interesting thing about the conversation was how the older, bigger boys dominated the discussion, while the younger, smaller boys deferred. It was an impromptu dominance hierarchy: size and physical maturation cued the conversation.

On another afternoon, I had lunch with a group of teenage boys from a private school who aired similar anxieties. One was that, as many psychologists know, boys don't like to confide in their parents — about body image or anything else. "Not that it's embarrassing," said Alex, a fifteen-year-old. "There are things that you say to your peers that they completely understand, but that if you say to your parents, they would *never* understand." Another theme was the hierarchical dominance of athletes in school cultures. "Like in the movies, jocks rule," said I., also fifteen. "When I was young," added Kyle, a fourteen-year-old, "and watched movies like *Revenge of the Nerds,* I thought, 'Is it really going to be like that?' And it really *is* like that!"

The idea of appearing seminaked in public so clearly terrified the boys that when I asked what they did when they took showers at school, they replied in unison, *"We don't take showers!"* Here, at least, was a definitive change from my days in a large public high school. Back then, most boys showered after gym class, although the showers, true, were often the scene of horrific ambushes and sneak humiliations. Many of today's teenage boys are so squeamish about body image that they either don't shower at all or enter the shower semidressed. At summer camp, Alex told me, boys showered in their bathing suits. The parent of a thirteen-year-old boy who attended a private school in the Boston area told me that all the boys wore boxer shorts in the shower.

"At camp, if you do swimming," a boy named Robert reported, "and climb out of the water, there are guys [standing there] who are just wearing trunks."

"I'm putting my shirt on," Alex said, "because I'm afraid."

"Are you afraid because of what the girls think or what the boys think?" Kyle asked.

"The girls," Alex replied. "It's mostly the girls."

And here is the deferred punch line. Harrison Pope's research on male body image found that although young men — college students in his study — thought that an additional twenty-eight pounds of muscle would make them look ideal, women who took a spin on the somatomorphic matrix selected "a very ordinary looking male body." Indeed, Pope and his colleagues pointed out that "in both the United States and Europe, there appears to be a striking discrepancy between the body that men think women like and the body that women actually like." Put another way, men are from Schwarzenegger, and women are from Quetelet.

So why is it that young men so badly misread what women want? Maybe it's because what they've been educated to regard as the ideal male body — in magazine ads, movies, and television shows — is meant not to look attractive to women, but rather to appeal to men.

*   *   *

POPE'S GROUP AT Harvard has studied extensively the impact of advertising on boys and male body image. It boils down to a slow, decades-long striptease on glossy, four-color paper.

In one study, for example, they compared ads in *Glamour* and *Cosmopolitan* between 1958 and 1998 and found that the percentage of "undressed men" (as they defined it, models whose lack of clothing "would be considered inappropriate if they were walking on a downtown street") rose from just a few images in the 1950s to between 25 and 35 percent of all male imagery by the 1990s. They also identified a distinct "inflection point" in the 1980s, when the frequency of such images rose sharply. (There appears to be a cultural component to this, because a follow-up study in 2005, using the same methodology, found that only 5 percent of the images of Asian males appeared underdressed in comparable women's magazines in Taiwan and that Taiwanese men appeared "much more comfortable with their body appearance" than their Western counterparts.)

Dan Kindlon similarly dates the shift in the media representations of the male body to the early 1990s. "Maybe fifteen years ago, there was a Diet Coke ad in which a construction worker takes off his shirt," Kindlon said. "He was really ripped, and you could see the muscles. Advertisers talk about that ad as a signal that there was a change in advertising. Ads now focus on baldness, on being thin and fit and huge, and advertisers are pushing that more and more and more."

Just as in the days of Charles Atlas, the "look" is established by the marketing department. In a famous car ad from the late 1990s, one manufacturer suggested that driving a minivan (instead of a sporty coupe) said everything you needed to know about the driver's masculinity. "You are what you drive" has long been a chrome and steel proxy for manhood. But the message has permeated even reasonably sacrosanct, apple-pie precincts of the American experience. During baseball's home-run frenzy in the late 1990s (a frenzy that, many suspect now, was fueled by the use of performance-enhancing drugs), Nike — as savvy a marketer as Charles Roman — ran a campaign with the tag line "Chicks Love the Long Ball." "Freud would have had a field day with that," Kindlon said with a chuckle.

The brilliance of marketing to adolescent male insecurity may have reached an early zenith with Charles Atlas, but it has become much more sophisticated in recent times. In men's fashion advertising, there has been a sequence of iconic visual images notable for being both risqué and explicit. Experts who follow historical trends in advertising have observed that Calvin Klein in particular has consistently pushed the envelope on tastefulness and sexual innuendo since the company's groundbreaking 1980 ad, when a fifteen-year-old Brooke Shields teasingly announced that nothing came between her and her Calvins. The ad that crossed the cultural Rubicon, however, was a Calvin Klein underwear ad in 1982 that introduced the homoerotic aesthetic to a mass market of young male consumers. Shot by fashion photographer Bruce Weber, the ad showed model Jeff Aquilon splayed on a boulder, in a pose that spoke much more of physical ecstasy than of fetching an undergarment from the sock drawer. A subsequent Calvin Klein ad, from 1992, showed model Mark Wahlberg (then known as Marky Mark) prancing around in the company's underwear. These were landmark images not only because they were so aggressive in depicting half-naked models but also because the bodies of these male models (just as the bodies of female models had for decades) set impossibly high standards for appearing chiseled and buff. An essential component of the 1992 ad, Roberto Olivardia told me, was the knowledge that Marky Mark was heterosexual. This in effect gave males cultural permission to linger over blatantly homoerotic imagery.

If there was any lingering question about the aesthetic informing this school of advertising, the answer came in 1995 in a series of commercials that critics took to calling Calvin Klein's "basement porn" campaign. These television spots, ostensibly selling jeans, featured a deliberately cheesy, amateurishly lit basementlike setting with cheap wall paneling. They began with an adult male voice posing questions to youthful and shirtless boys. The models were, of course, beautiful, but only in retrospect did you realize how toned and buff their bodies were — and how the ads made sure you noticed. In one commercial, the off-camera voice says, "You have a lovely body. Do you like your body?" In another, a boy who has both the looks and indifferent demeanor of a young James Dean sits on a ladder, wearing jeans and a white T-shirt. The dialogue is so creepy that when I first screened the ad at home, I became nervous because my children, though only toddlers at the time, were in the room.

"You got a real nice look," an adult male voice says off-camera. "How old are you?"

"Twenty-one," the boy says. (He looks so much like a teenager, however, that a subsequent U.S. Department of Justice investigation was launched to establish his age, which was indeed twenty-one.)

"What's your name?"

"August."

"Why don't you stand up?"

When the boy complies, the man continues, "Are you strong?"

"I like to think so."

"You think you could rip that shirt off of you?" The boy pulls down on the T-shirt with both hands and suddenly rips it off his body, revealing an extremely lean and well-developed chest. "It's a nice body!" the man exclaims. "Do you work out?"

"Uh-huh." The boy nods.

"Yeah, I can tell."

The ad hit all the desired notes — youthfulness, desirability, strength, manhood, working out, the lascivious undertones of "real nice look" — and hinted at others, including rough sex, pederasty, and homoerotic attraction. "The style, the look, the leering tone, even the 'chicken hawk' voice-over — Klein mimicked, closely, the style and tone of cheap basement gay pornography," said Bob Garfield, a columnist for *Advertising Age* and a longtime critic of what he calls Klein's "shockvertising" approach. Roberto Olivardia, who has studied the impact of advertising on body image, pointed out another connection with gay culture. He suggested that advertising's increasing fascination with buff bodies "probably had to do with the AIDS epidemic, that looking thin was not a good thing."

If it is true, Garfield speculated, that these commercials influence how boys think about their bodies, it reflects in part "the opening up of gay culture, where male objectification has almost nearly the effect that the objectification of females has had for time immemorial for women." Which, in a way, returns the story full circle to those Greek gods whose form Angelo Siciliano so admired at the Brooklyn Museum. No culture so thoroughly exalted the male form as the ancient Greeks.

How much do these social cues actually inform the behavior of boys? Consider a very portable version of this trend: the shopping bags used by the teen clothier Abercrombie & Fitch, with its photographs of half-clad, musclebound models. Not coincidentally, Bruce Weber, who photographed some of the early Calvin Klein ads, went on to create some Abercrombie & Fitch marketing campaigns. The ads have come a long way from old Mac on the beach, yet the message is remarkably constant, and, like a lot of shrewd advertising, it works. "When you hear girls gawking at Abercrombie & Fitch about how hot the guy is on the bag — that makes an impression," Alex Bregstein told me. "If I look this way, I've got my foot in the door."

WHAT, ULTIMATELY, IS the impact of adolescent concerns about body image? From the rather more extensive literature on girls and self-image, it is clear that the somatic self-consciousness that develops during adolescence can become a lifelong pathology, a sink of enormous emotional energy and thought, a hair shirt for the insecure mind. As researchers increasingly study males, they are uncovering a number of similar body-related psychological disorders in men, many of which seem to have their origins prior to adulthood. Consistent with the general theme tracing the interplay of physical size and personal psychology, a lot of habits that originate in adolescence — including the corrosive behavior of self-doubt and positive behavior of self-esteem — seem to persist into adulthood.

In addition, not every boy relies solely on weightlifting and working out to achieve "the look." According to the University of Michigan's Monitoring the Future research project, a broad-based national survey of adolescent drug use behaviors and attitudes, approximately 3.3 percent of boys in grade twelve — and, surprisingly, 1.7 percent of girls at the same grade level — have tried anabolic steroids at least once. Previous surveys have suggested that 6 percent of high school boys have used steroids. The overall rate in kids in grades eight through twelve translates, said Charles Yesalis, an expert on steroid use at Pennsylvania State University, into a minimum of one million adolescents using steroids to bulk up. "It has gone up substantially in recent years, especially in girls," Yesalis said. "The figure we used to use was five hundred thousand, but now we talk about a million kids having used anabolic steroids at one time or another. And common sense tells you that's an underestimate." Success in sports is not the sole motivation for this rising use. "About one-third of the kids are *not* interscholastic athletes," Yesalis pointed out. Why do they do it? "To look better." A large percentage of users try steroids before age sixteen, Yesalis said, and some as early as seventh grade. If one includes the use of legal over-the-counter dietary supplements such as creatine, he added, the incidence of use skyrockets into the millions.

It's also clear that adolescent insecurity about body image begets increasing body work in adulthood. Recent figures on cosmetic surgery indirectly confirm the anecdotal sense that men are going to greater lengths to improve their appearance. Women still account for a majority of the procedures (about 83 percent in 2004), but the number of men undergoing cosmetic surgery rose more than 600 percent between 1994 and 2004. (The most common male procedures are nose jobs, hair transplants, blepharoplasty [eyelid surgery], and liposuction.) A handful of short-stature men who are otherwise medically normal and healthy are beginning to opt for limb lengthening, an elaborate orthopedic procedure previously reserved for dwarfs and people with severe congenital bone and joint anomalies. Alfred Grant, a surgeon at the Comprehensive Center for Skeletal Dysplasias & Growth Disorders at the Hospital for Joint Diseases in New York, said that the surgery involves severing bones in the legs and arms and then — with the use of metal rings, pins, and adjustable struts — maintaining a millimeter of distance between the bone ends, which naturally fill in the gap. Over the course of months, with the bones moved incrementally apart on a daily basis, patients opting for the surgery typically gain about eight centimeters (about three inches) in height. Limb lengthening has become an increasingly common cosmetic procedure in China and elsewhere in Asia, where employment ads typically include height requirements.

If this new male preoccupation with appearance seems to herald a dubious, regressive form of equality — now boys can become as psychologically and physically debilitated by body image concerns as girls have been for decades — it also reflects a particularly superficial swing of the cultural pendulum. Alex Bregstein admitted as much to me. "I tell you, it's definitely distressing," he said back in 1999, "the fact that as much as girls get this anorexic thing and they're going through these image things with dolls and stuff, guys are definitely doing the same." True, he admitted, his social life at the time we had this conversation had never been better. "But in a way it depresses me," he added, "that I had to do this for people to get to know me."

When I tracked Alex down five years later, his perspective had changed. Now an economics major in college, he had grown three more inches, and a severe rugby injury had forced him to view his body and his image in a different light. "I lift, but not as feverishly," he said. "It's still a part of my life, but not central. Getting through the injury and getting back in shape, and choosing things that were reasonable to do, it started to be, like, I don't need to feel perfect or amazing, I just need to feel accomplished in what I can do. It was a real turning point." He no longer felt compelled, he added, to search, "for more strength in all the wrong places."

12

THE EMPEROR'S NEW MEDICINE CABINET

Human Growth Hormone and Height Augmentation in Children

> Today, it is acknowledged that the non-growth-hormone-deficient child's central concern is identical to that of the child with [growth hormone deficiency]; namely, "I am short and I would like to be taller" . . . If "enhancement" refers to a desire for a child to be taller than he would be if left alone, then all children involved in this debate are seeking enhancement.
>
> —DAVID B. ALLEN AND NORMAN FOST

ON JUNE 10, 2003, a group of medical experts convened by the U.S. Food and Drug Administration (FDA) gathered in a Bethesda, Maryland, hotel to consider a new use for human growth hormone (hGH) in children. There was a wonderful moment in the afternoon discussion that boiled down decades of scientific study and social fretting about this remarkable drug to a simple question regarding human height and human happiness. Paul D. Woolf, chief of medicine at Crozer-Chester Medical Center outside Philadelphia, confessed a nagging uncertainty about the link between height and well-being, so much so that he posed an unusual question about the psychological impact of added inches.

"What is a clinically significant increase in height?" Woolf asked, wondering aloud how much more height a child needed to attain before he or she felt emotionally better. "Is it one inch, two inches, five inches, eight inches? I don't know."

In 1988 Eli Lilly, the Indianapolis-based pharmaceutical giant, had begun to collect data in hopes of providing an answer to just that question. The company set out to prove that hGH could be used to treat children with a condition known as idiopathic short stature (ISS), which essentially means patients who are unusually short for unknown (idiopathic) medical reasons. The potential market for this new application was huge. According to the way Lilly and the FDA defined short stature, as children at or below the 1.2 percentile on the growth chart, the company estimated that approximately 400,000 children between the ages of seven and fifteen would fit the description. (To put that number in perspective, experts believe that fewer than 8,000 children received growth hormone treatment from its initial clinical testing in the early 1960s through 1985.)

By the time of the FDA advisory committee meeting in 2003, Lilly had distilled reams of clinical information into several succinct and compelling messages in its bid to win government approval. During a long morning session, company representatives and leading pediatric endocrinologists who consulted for Lilly presented results from a randomized and placebo-controlled test of growth hormone, a trial that pitted the drug against injections of salt water. Although the drug did increase the height of children with ISS, the amount of the increase was surprisingly modest. In Lilly's "pivotal trial," height increased by 3.7 centimeters, roughly 1½ inches, after four years of thrice-weekly injections. In a second trial in Europe, height increased by 7 centimeters, about 2½ inches, at higher and more frequent doses. The company also presented vast amounts of data to establish that the drug was safe. Since a genetically engineered version of growth hormone had first been approved by the FDA in 1985, an estimated 200,000 patients worldwide had been treated with the drug, with no evidence of serious or long-term side effects. By the usual criteria of drug approvals, Lilly had clearly established that the drug was safe and effective.

What the company had failed to establish, at least in the minds of many members of the FDA advisory committee, was whether the drug actually made a difference — that is, whether it was "clinically meaningful," as doctors like to put it — to short but normal children. You might think that the company would be able to present a clear justification for using a medication that costs, on average, twenty thousand dollars a year over many years of use, but that was not the case. In the briefing document submitted to the FDA, Lilly cited the research of psychologist David Sandberg and growth expert Linda Voss to support its contention that "short children may be subject to juvenilization, teasing, bullying, exclusion from activities and peer groups and impairment of the normal progression toward independence." But Lilly also admitted, in a line buried elsewhere in the briefing document, that neither of its two main studies "provided evidence of potential benefits in quality of life or psychological well-being." Try as it might (and Lilly spent a lot of money on the trial), the company had found no evidence that short children whose height increased after using the drug were better off psychologically. And that uncertainty, those unconnected dots between physical size and emotional well-being, is what moved Paul Woolf to search for some correlation between the two. What, he wanted to know, is a clinically significant increase in height?

No one — not doctors, regulators, parents, or perhaps even children — can answer that question, at least for anyone else. And yet an enormous amount of emotional, financial, and societal resources are devoted to finding an answer. The FDA ultimately did not come to grips with it on that day in 2003. If you read the transcript of the advisory committee hearing and if you talk to members of that panel, as I did, you come away with the clear impression that many of the experts, probably the majority, remained unconvinced that hGH was, in the words of committee chairman Glenn Braunstein, "clinically meaningful" to children who are unusually short but otherwise medically normal. Yet on that afternoon in June 2003, the advisory committee voted 8–2 to recommend approval, and a month later the FDA announced that it had approved Lilly's application.

There are a couple of ways to read the FDA's decision. To many bioethicists, who have followed the amazing twists and turns of the growth hormone story for nearly half a century, the FDA approval for short but medically normal children represented a significant step across an invisible social threshold: the use of biological agents in children not to treat disease, but to alter physical appearance. No one argues with the use of growth hormone to treat children with serious growth disorders, such as growth hormone deficiency (GHD) and Turner's syndrome in girls; in those cases, hGH normalizes growth, and the drug is clearly life-altering in the best possible way for many patients. But the ISS approval opened the door to treatment of not just *growth* problems, which are medical, but *height* problems, which are social. "I think the FDA got it completely wrong when they approved growth hormone for idiopathic short stature," said Joel Frader, a doctor and ethicist in the Medical Humanities and Bioethics Program at Northwestern University. He called the FDA decision "tragic" because it "medicalized short stature and turned it into an illness." That echoed the sentiments of Alan Rogol, a pediatric endocrinologist who has both treated short children with growth hormone and consulted for the drug companies. "With all sorts of talking and fancy statistics," he said of Lilly's FDA presentation, hGH "*was* [shown to be] safe and effective, although effective per buck not very much at all. But that's all you've got to show."

From the point of view of the drug companies, they were merely giving people what they wanted — and medical consumers wanted a lot of growth hormone. In 2004, the first full year after the FDA approved expanded use of the drug, sales of growth hormone went up across the board. Sales of Pfizer's Genotropin totaled $736 million, up 53 percent from the previous year. Eli Lilly sold $430 million of its Humatrope, up 16 percent. Genentech sold $354 million of its Nutropin, up 10 percent. Novo Nordisk sold about $379 million of its Norditropin, up 9 percent. And Serono sold $268 million of its two versions of growth hormone (one targeted toward adults), up 20 percent. Nor is all growth hormone going to kids who are at or below the 1.2 percentile. A news dispatch out of Texas described a Dallas doctor who defended the use of growth hormone in a child at the twenty-fifth percentile. Once a drug is approved, of course, doctors can use it any way they see fit.

So sales of growth hormone now exceed $2 billion a year, and much of it is used to augment the height of short, but normal, children without any compelling evidence to date that a gain in height translates into a gain in psychological well-being. As Glenn Braunstein said in explaining his vote recommending approval, "My conclusion about the clinical importance is that it really has to be defined by the patient and the parents." Later, in an interview, he made clear that he viewed the treatment of ISS as a form of "cosmetic endocrinology" — and, possibly, a waste of money. "I see this very much like plastic surgery for young women who are very distraught because they have small breasts," he said. "If you're making someone go from five-one to five-four to make them feel better about themselves, then I think it's very worthwhile." Still, he had misgivings about the government or health insurance companies covering the enormous cost of what is essentially a drug for self-esteem. "I think that money could be better spent on better prenatal care for pregnant women, better vaccines, and other forms of preventive medicine," he said.

WHEN I MENTIONED to Camille Weichlein, the mother of an adolescent boy who had been treated with growth hormone, that some doctors and regulators had doubts about the psychological value of such treatment, she sounded genuinely shocked. "Oh, my gosh," she said in disbelief. "In another twenty years, it will be different, because growth hormone has completely changed my son's life. Not just how he perceives himself, but how his peers perceive him. It's changed *everything.*" She went on to recall how her older son, Jon, had been teased and bullied during much of his childhood in a community in western New York State. People at school had called him shortie, and during those years, his mother added, "he had just been *horribly* distressed." Since being treated with growth hormone, he not only had grown eight inches but also had grown more confident, performed better in school, and even made the football team at his high school. "This has benefited him tremendously," she said.

That kind of testimonial is not unusual. When the FDA panel considered growth hormone for short but normal kids in 2003, they heard from a young man named Deno Andrews, whose mother, Mary Andrews, ran the Magic Foundation, an advocacy group devoted to families with children who have growth disorders. Deno approached the podium on his knees to make a point. "On my knees, today, I stand two inches taller than the first endocrinologist told my mother that I would ever reach as an adult," he said. "However, I was treated successfully with growth hormone, as you guys can see. And I reached a very normal adult final height." He too recounted a litany of childhood traumas and tribulations: he was called names, picked last on sports teams, and in general was "singled out because of my height." He began to perform poorly academically because "the last place in the world I wanted to be was at school." He also, it turned out, had worked nearly three years for a pharmaceutical company selling growth hormone and admitted that Lilly was one of the companies that funded the Magic Foundation. But his main point was to push for approval of the drug. "Is it right to treat idiopathic short stature with growth hormone?" he asked the committee. "I say the answer is yes. It is as right as getting corrective lenses for eyesight that is abnormal. It is as right as an insurance company paying to repair a dent in a car. It is as right as getting a tutor or extra help at school for a child who isn't performing well." He concluded by borrowing a line from his mother: "Children have only a short time to grow, and a lifetime to live with the results."

For an earlier generation of families — including Andrews, who was treated in the late 1970s for classic growth hormone deficiency — there is little doubt that the drug made a difference. It especially made a difference for children who were severely short, well below the first percentile on the growth charts, and usually suffering from an inability to make or use their own growth hormone. But, as mentioned earlier, the definition of severe short stature tends to be statistical rather than medical; many children who are severely short have nothing obviously wrong with them medically. One of the best ways of thinking about severe short stature came up in a conversation with Stephen Chernausek, a pediatric endocrinologist in Cincinnati. "You can look at someone and say, 'This person is short, but he's normal short,'" Chernausek said. "Or you can walk down the street and you may see someone who is so short that you do a double take and say, 'Wow, I wonder what's wrong with them?' That's what we're talking about here." For many years, the severely short couldn't be treated. And then growth hormone arrived, and it was truly a miracle drug.

In 1956 Robert M. Blizzard, a physician at Johns Hopkins School of Medicine, treated a poorly growing three-and-a-half-year-old child with growth hormone derived from the pituitary glands of cows. That initial attempt failed, but in 1958 Morris Raben at Tufts University reported the first successful use of human growth hormone. Because it was derived from human cadavers, the drug was exceedingly rare. Pathologists needed to collect 365 pituitary glands to isolate enough hormone to treat one child for one year. Soon, Blizzard recalled, a black market in pituitary harvesting developed to satisfy the demand of frenzied families. Market forces have always been part of the growth hormone story — and not always for the prettiest of reasons.

As a result, the government moved in to establish the National Hormone and Pituitary Program in 1963. This agency, overseen by the National Institutes of Health and run by Blizzard, coordinated the harvesting of growth hormone from human cadavers and monitored its equitable distribution and use. In those early years, regulators accounted for every drop of the drug. Veteran pediatric endocrinologists such as

Leslie Plotnick at Johns Hopkins remember picking up vials of the precious hormone at the Trailways bus station in Baltimore and keeping meticulous notes in logbooks that recorded each and every injection. "You had to submit data on each patient," she recalled, and once a child reached a height of five feet, "you had to stop." Still, only a few thousand children with severe growth failure received treatment, because of the tight supply. In 1963 Blizzard predicted that with more ample supplies, the drug could become as popular and as widely used as cortisone. It's still too early to say if he was right or wrong.

Then tragedy struck. In the spring of 1985, several patients receiving cadaver-derived growth hormone in the United States and Great Britain came down with a rare and devastating neurological disorder known as Creutzfeldt-Jakob disease (CJD). Essentially a form of mad cow disease, the outbreak of CJD had been caused by contaminated growth hormone. James Tanner, who coordinated the British distribution of growth hormone, still recalls the phone call from Blizzard, his American counterpart, confirming this horrific development. "Bob and I were in contact all the time," Tanner said. "And my recollection was that he rang me and he said, 'Jim, a terrible thing has happened here.' And I said, 'You've got a case of CJD, too?' 'Exactly.' 'What are we going to do?'" The United States and Britain simultaneously ordered a halt to all treatment. Eventually, more than two dozen former patients worldwide died of the disease transmitted by contaminated growth hormone.

Just as modern medicine seemed to have visited, with the best of intentions, a terrible tragedy upon an already beleaguered pediatric population, modern technology rode to the rescue. One of the first human genes cloned during the birth of recombinant DNA technology in the 1970s was the one for human growth hormone. Although the circumstances of that achievement remained a bit murky at the time (and would later provoke several high-profile, multimillion-dollar lawsuits), medical need easily superseded academic etiquette. Genentech, the pioneering biotech company in South San Francisco, began testing its genetically engineered version of hGH in 1981. When the CJD crisis broke, the company sent a letter to the FDA offering to supply recombinant growth hormone to the pediatric endocrinology community for free. In October 1985, the FDA approved the genetically engineered version of the drug. Within a year, however, after the immediate crisis had passed, patients were paying as much as $10,000 to $15,000 a year for a drug that the government had previously distributed for free. And limitless supplies of the drug also strained the traditional definitions of normal variation and disease when it came to height. As Alan Rogol famously noted, "Short stature became a disease when unlimited amounts of growth hormone became available."

I tried to speak to patients and families about these expanding uses, especially in short but otherwise normal children. A few families were willing to cooperate; many were not. When I asked leading pediatric endocrinologists if they would put me in touch with their patients, they almost invariably did not respond. There are probably multiple reasons for this reticence. Doctors are, rightly, fiercely protective of their patients' privacy, and recent federal legislation about medical privacy has only strengthened the firewall between patients and the public. But I have been writing about medical matters for two decades, and as a general rule, I've found that patients representing a broad spectrum of serious illnesses have been more than willing to speak publicly about their medical experiences, and doctors have been happy to put me in touch with them. I've witnessed open-heart surgery with the patient's consent, and I've been in the examining room when one cancer patient learned the devastating news that his disease had progressed and there was nothing further to be done. The situation with patients on human growth hormone, especially ISS patients, strikes me as being rather different. Parents did not return phone calls; doctors did not proffer patients the way they often do. Part of this reluctance no doubt derives from the fact that most of the patients are children. Still, something about that wall of reticence made me think that there was more to it, something akin to ambivalence about publicly acknowledging one's use of the drug.

Another possibility is that, in many circumstances, hGH treatment of short but medically normal kids may not make much of a difference — either physically or psychologically — to the children or to the adults they become. One of the striking aspects of Eli Lilly's presentation to the FDA was how modest the gain in height was for ISS children after many years of treatment. By a variety of measures, including the use of dozens of statistical approaches, the height gain on average amounted to one to two inches. Alan Rogol called that "marginally effective" and reiterated his belief that "the biggest side effect from growth hormone use is unmet expectation." The bottom line, he said, is that if a normal child is short to begin with, he or she is still going to end up in the "short bin" after treatment. And perhaps that reality helps explain the absence of data proving that growth hormone is a psychological boon to short but normal kids. To children who respond well, it undoubtedly makes a difference. To the many in whom the response is modest or even nonexistent, the disappointment can be excruciating. It all goes back to Paul Woolf's question: What is a clinically significant increase in height?

One of the most revealing moments during the 2003 FDA hearing came when Eli Lilly attempted to answer this question. Judith Ross, an endocrinologist at Jefferson Medical College in Philadelphia, stepped forward to present data from a psychological study of the children who had been recruited into Lilly's randomized, placebo-controlled trial of growth hormone. The results were not just unconvincing. Glenn Braunstein, chairman of the committee, later termed the data "horrible." More than a year after the FDA gave its approval, Ross and her collaborators on the Lilly-sponsored study published their results in a leading endocrinology journal, concluding that the data "do not support the use of [growth hormone] treatment for idiopathic short stature to improve psychological dysfunction." In an earlier study, European researchers could find no significant differences in the quality of life between adults who had been treated with growth hormone as children and a control group of adults (equally short as children) who had not — except that those who had been treated with hGH had a romantic partner less often than those who had not been treated.

Some studies even suggest that the animating idea behind growth hormone use in short but normal children — that it will improve psychological dysfunction — may be fundamentally flawed. In 2004 researchers from the Wessex Growth Study in England updated the results of that large, ongoing, community-based longitudinal survey of short but medically normal children and once again found that short kids were no different than others in terms of psychological health and well-being.

There are several possible explanations for the seeming discrepancy between the anecdotal woes of individual children and the findings of well-controlled scientific studies. Deno Andrews, the young man who testified before the FDA panel, for example, took pains to undermine the credibility of those studies. He said that children who are bothered by their height don't trust psychological surveys and tend not to answer questions truthfully about their emotional condition. He even admitted that he had lied to researchers. David Sandberg, one psychologist who has conducted such surveys, suggested another possible reason why treatment with growth hormone might improve, at least anecdotally, the well-being of some ISS patients. "Is this," he asks, "a placebo effect?" This may sound like a rather outrageous suggestion, but perhaps an even more outrageous point is that, to date, there is no compelling evidence to contradict it.

"We're really having to confront the issue of 'Does the emperor have any clothes?' when we're talking about this whole issue," said David B. Allen, a pediatric endocrinologist at the University of Wisconsin who, with the bioethicist Norman Fost, wrote an influential 1990 paper titled "Growth Hormone Therapy for Short Stature: Panacea or Pandora's Box?" "The underlying assumption has always been that if you're outside the normal range when it comes to height — just like you're outside the normal range with your blood calcium level or thyroid level — there should be some ramifications of that. And the presumption has been that there are psychological, sociological, and economic ramifications, and some of that has been borne out. But in terms of the psychological disability, it's really been the case that the more we've looked, the less we've found. We've gotten as far as we have without people really asking this question: Okay, you've made people taller, but what does that mean?"

IN OCTOBER 2004, fifteen years after the two Wisconsin doctors submitted their paper for publication, I went to Madison to discuss all this with Allen, who works in a busy pediatric endocrinology clinic on the fourth floor of the university hospital. He turned out to be a lean, compact, and cheerful man with high cheekbones and a youthful face. His wiry build suggested the cross-country runner he had been since high school, and his relatively short stature (he said that he "used to be five feet eight") suggested that his familiarity with some of the psychological issues associated with small size were not entirely academic. But the conversation unfolded in a series of unexpected surprises, both professional and personal, beginning with the very first question.

If you accept the argument that severe short stature (on the order of the third percentile or lower on the growth chart) represents a psychological disability, an argument Allen and Fost made in 1990 and reiterated over the next decade, it logically follows that anyone who displays that certain degree of shortness should qualify for growth hormone, simply as an issue of equitable access for all. And indeed, during the 1990s, the FDA had approved the use of growth hormone for a number of childhood illnesses, citing the argument that it would be unfair to deprive these children of the drug when they were just as short as kids who were growth hormone deficient. So hadn't Fost and he, I asked, essentially made the bioethical case for relaxed standards, in a way legitimizing far greater use of growth hormone? Allen was horrified by that suggestion.

"It's interesting that you used the term 'relaxed,'" he said, looking anything but laid-back as he tensed up in his chair, "because our interpretation of our whole approach to this has been almost the antithesis of relaxed. The driving force behind our argument has always been equitable distribution of growth hormone and appropriate targeting of growth hormone. The whole purpose of the paper in 1990 was to raise people's awareness of the ethical issue — that if you go on to show that growth hormone is effective in other, non–growth hormone deficient situations, there's going to be no rational argument to restrict it from those individuals, except based on heights. In other words, you're going to be treating the disability and not the disease." That is precisely the argument that Eli Lilly took to the FDA, and it's apparent from the transcript of the meeting that it convinced many members of the advisory committee.

But there was a second, companion part of Allen and Fost's argument — the Pandora's box part, if you will — that was conveniently jettisoned by the drug industry, FDA regulators, and others. "If you accept [the equitable access argument]," Allen continued, "then you *need* to have guidelines to restrict the use of growth hormone, because it really does become a Pandora's box in that situation." What makes it a Pandora's box, he continued, is not that more children start using it, but that fewer and fewer *stop* using it once they attain a normal height. In other words, patients may begin using growth hormone as a legitimate medical therapy, but once they reach a height that is within the normal range, continued use of the hormone would no longer be for medical purposes. Instead, it would be a form of pharmaceutical enhancement. Allen paused as he made this point, leaning over the table in his office. "That argument has been, I think, for fifteen years not understood," he said, shaking his head. "I mean, I think people have always looked at that 'Panacea or Pandora's Box?' article and taken away the message that you did."

The point may be subtle, but it inches society into a territory we don't often occupy: the "business" of normality, where personal psychology and the growth chart meet modern drug economics. In the years since the cautionary appearance of Allen and Fost's article, the FDA had gradually expanded the uses of growth hormone largely because it increased the height of children. Thus it was approved for use in children with chronic kidney disease and girls with Turner's syndrome in 1995, children with the rare Prader-Willi syndrome in 2000, and children who are small for gestational age (and failed to catch up properly by age two) in 2001. Bit by bit, approval by approval, the drug is well on its way to becoming an example of what Duke University philosopher Allen Buchanan has called an "expansive biotechnology." New, limitless supplies of a drug, Buchanan has argued, "break down the conceptual boundaries we draw between disease and health, between health care and other services, between treatment and enhancement, between what social justice requires and what individuals should be free to choose, and between what we regard as fate and what we regard as subject to individual or social choice." Slowly but surely — and the process is still early in what may be a very long evolution — height is becoming not an issue of genetic fate, but rather a biological option, like an accessory we might choose for a car. This is true regarding not only growth hormone but also illicit appearance-altering substances such as steroids and licit second-generation, height-augmenting drugs such as insulin-like growth factor-1 (IGF-1), which entered the increasingly crowded market in 2005.

The choice to augment one's height is obviously a very personal decision, rooted in very specific circumstances, and that point was brought home to me during my conversation with David Allen when it took a surprising turn. As we talked, Allen allowed that he was not a stranger to the emotional issues of short stature. He told me that he had faced teasing because of small stature when he attended school and had sought refuge in a sport that did not require a behemoth's physique: running. "I think that could well have sustained me through that really difficult time," he admitted. I asked where he grew up, and he mentioned the western suburbs of Chicago. I asked which one, and it quickly became apparent that we had attended the same high school, about five years apart. His older sister, Deborah, was the homecoming queen of my high school class; she was my friend Tom Andersen's date! I could almost feel the synapses sizzling in my brain as this coincidental turn in the conversation rustled deep memory circuits and transported me back to my adolescent days.

THERE IS A picture of Debi Allen in my high school yearbook, showing the moment she learned — hands to face, body contorted in ecstatic disbelief — that she had been selected homecoming queen for the class of 1969. Just glancing at the photograph, I felt like my face was pressed against a window, looking in on people and events I had always experienced as an outsider and triggering memories of the cliques of athletes and cheerleaders, greasers and proto-heads, jerks and nerds. Debi and I sat right next to each other in the picture of the National Honor Society (she was not only beautiful but also sharp as a tack). As usual, I was in the front row because of my height. The faces, the names, and my constricted body language (halfway to rigor mortis, in that misguided adolescent attempt not to look goofy) brought back memories of the culture of high school society, of the canyon that separated early-maturing boys from late maturers, of fitting in versus feeling left out.

Staring at my adolescent angst preserved in yearbook amber, I was struck by how one's psychological vulnerabilities at this most vulnerable of developmental times might be manipulated — "treated" — with a drug that promotes greater height. Yet the urge to see that physical difference, and to believe in its psychological impact, is so powerful, so widespread in some emotionally distraught children (not to mention their parents) that it is not at all hard to imagine all the juvenile fingers struggling to pry open Pandora's box. As David Allen put it, "Everyone wants to be taller."

But it is not just the fingerprints of children and parents that we find on the growth hormone story. Health economists have calculated its cost in dollars per inch gained; bioethicists have debated ad nauseam whether its use is medical or cosmetic; scientists have published a vast literature on the effects of its use; and academic economists such as Andrew Postlewaite (see chapter 10) have even calculated whether an investment in hGH therapy would be worthwhile in terms of lifetime earnings. At this wild intersection of psychological desire and pharmaceutical availability, growth hormone becomes a fascinating mirror of who we are as biological creatures, what we want to be, what we are willing to do, and what risks we are willing to take — as individuals and as societies — to satisfy that desire.

I've looked into that mirror myself. As someone who felt beleaguered by short stature, I've often wondered how I would have reacted if presented with the possibility of growth hormone treatment. I wouldn't have met all the criteria for idiopathic short stature — I was down there around the first percentile, and Lord knows it felt like an oppression, but I was growing normally. I probably wouldn't have needed it, and certainly didn't deserve it, especially in an era when the drug was so rare and the need so great among those with genuine medical problems. Even today the third percentile, where I resided during part of my adolescence, does not meet current FDA recommendations for hGH treatment. But I also know — and this has long been part of the growth hormone story — that families often shop around until they find a doctor willing to prescribe it. Even ten years ago, in 1996, 40 percent of all hGH use was off-label, or for purposes other than the medical criteria stipulated by the FDA.

Would I have been tempted to use hGH? In principle, sure. Even a couple of extra inches would have felt huge in those days. But the more I thought about the treatment — not just the daily injections but also the idea that I *needed* injections, that I was somehow sick or abnormal — the more I wondered if I might have ended up feeling maimed, psychologically rather than physically, by growth hormone therapy. As an adolescent, I couldn't and shouldn't have been trusted with thinking about potential side effects. As a parent (and as an adult who writes about the drug industry occasionally), I can tell you that I would now have great reservations about potential long-term side effects, especially when treating a fundamentally healthy child. I asked my parents about it a few years ago, and my mother confessed that she wouldn't have been thrilled about the idea. "That would have been a real, *real* hard decision," she told me. "I'd have to have had a guarantee that there was no risk whatsoever in the long term. But I don't think I would have done it, I really don't."

That being said, extensive use of growth hormone in tens of thousands of children has not, to date, suggested any serious long-term side effects. But here's the crucial and cruel paradox: by the time boys really feel themselves falling behind because of their physical size — around middle school and early high school, when the separation between early and late maturers becomes painfully obvious — it's usually too late to derive much benefit from hGH.

"It's the *delay* in growth that brings people to us," Allen told me. "In our practice, we virtually never use growth hormone to treat the twelve-year-old or eleven-year-old short-stature individual. We use other growth-promoting agents — weak oral androgens and things like that. Because eventually, those kids normalize. You know, there's nothing wrong with their system, other than that it's markedly delayed. But by the time you get to junior high, the pressures to grow build. Everybody else is growing, and the disparity grows. If you look at the distribution of when kids get started on growth hormone in this country, you'll see that there's a huge blip right in the area that you're talking about — the ten-, eleven-, twelve-year-old child. I mean, that is the most common age for kids to get started on treatment. But is it necessary? For the majority of kids, it's not necessary. And do they stop treatment as soon as they go into puberty and start growing on their own? Well, no, they don't. Most of them continue on treatment."

This brings us back to the growth charts that James Tanner produced in the 1960s — charts that make clear that even late maturers will, in most circumstances, end up perfectly normal. Those charts have been supplanted in England, Tanner told me, by charts that are distributed for free by either drug companies that make growth hormone or growth foundations supported by some of those companies. Indeed, the definition of normal height has now been ceded, at least partially, to the very companies that will benefit from increased sales of growth hormone. In 2004 Eli Lilly began distributing its revised chart, which includes that ominous red line at the 1.2 percentile. What makes that line so insidious, as Michael Freemark pointed out in an editorial in the *Journal of Clinical Endocrinology and Metabolism,* is that by increasing the height of children who are currently below the line with growth hormone, we are merely creating a new population of children who fall into the bottom percentile and who are thus potentially eligible for treatment. "This may be the only circumstance," he wrote, "in which treatment of one group of children creates illness in another previously healthy group."

MORE AND MORE parents are going to have to confront these issues, because more and more children are going to qualify, at least statistically, for growth hormone treatment — and more of it is going to be available, quite possibly at cheaper prices. In 1985, at the time of the CJD crisis, Genentech was the lone manufacturer. Now there are six companies competing in the U.S. market, including a generic company (Teva), which has, according to doctors in the field, slashed the cost by as much as a third. Limitless supplies of the drug, falling prices, and mounting social pressure to augment a child's height in order to give him every possible advantage in life — the ingredients are there for a dramatic expansion in use, including ever wider applications of what has been termed cosmetic endocrinology.

Since growth hormone appears to be on its way to becoming a lifestyle drug — an elective treatment designed to make appearance a little better and life a little easier — it's fair to ask the $64,000 devil's advocate question: What's so wrong with that? How is growth hormone any different from, say, a nose job? And why shouldn't parents, whose definition of nurture might easily include maximizing their children's opportunities for self-realization and happiness, increase their kids' height in a world that, like it or not, places extraordinary value on appearance?

Here are a couple of thoughts. In children with growth failure — with a demonstrable deficiency in their own ability to manufacture growth hormone — there's no argument; the drug is replacing something that's absent and allowing these children to grow more normally, more toward their genetic potential. For them, and for other children with physiological problems related to grown, hGH is truly a miracle drug. What about kids who are exactly the same size but don't have any deficiency in growth hormone? From the point of view of social equity, it's hard to argue that they should be denied treatment when other equally short children qualify. Doctors are currently looking for other points of dysfunction in the molecular pathway that leads to growth, and perhaps there will be more precise and sophisticated diagnostic tests in the future (although I'm always a little leery about these intense molecular searches for disease markers that are motivated, at least in part, by commercial interests). But I have reservations about using hGH in such children, as do some experts, for medical reasons.

It's one thing to replace a hormone that isn't there to begin with; diabetics have been doing that with insulin for nearly a century. But in children who make sufficient growth hormone and still don't grow, you're dumping extra hormone into the system. These so-called supraphysiologic doses may take a subtle but cumulative toll on the body over time and end up having side effects that may not become apparent for years. Similarly, growth hormone elevates the level of IGF-1. There's no evidence to date that IGF-1 has caused illness in children (people have been looking), but the molecule has been identified as a player in the complex series of steps that lead to certain cancers. In a recent paper, Adda Grimberg, a researcher at Children's Hospital of Philadelphia, examined the possible role of growth hormone and IGF-1 in cancer. She explained the results as follows: "When you look at the evidence to date, there's no strong evidence that growth hormone and IGF-1 cause cancer. But there is certainly accumulating evidence that they fuel the fire."

That needs to be part of the risk-benefit analysis, and it is with Grimberg's patients; she always schedules a special session with families to review potential benefits and potential risks. As she points out, there are also risks to *not* treating short stature in certain circumstances, such as the long-term cardiac damage in growth hormone–deficient kids. But risk-benefit calculations are tricky, especially at a time when everyone has become justifiably sensitized to the issue of long-term, unexpected side effects. If I were battling a life-threatening illness, I don't suppose that slight hint of trouble would matter much. In an otherwise normal child, however, even that slight risk looks a little different. Every family has its own method of weighing those risks and benefits, of course, but given the uncertain psychological benefits and the relatively modest height gains that come with growth hormone use in children with ISS, those risks would give me pause.

For the sake of argument, let's assume that there are not any deleterious long-term side effects of growth hormone treatment. What's the downside for short but normal kids? One reasonable response is a related question: What's the upside? The drug can cost upwards of $20,000 a year for many years, there are no proven psychological benefits to patients, and if you're small when you start the treatment, you're almost certainly going to be small when you stop. Two other problems might derive from the use of growth hormone as a so-called lifestyle drug. One is broadly societal, and the other is deeply personal.

Growth hormone is very expensive, even for a short but otherwise normal child, and somebody has to pay for it. If insurance companies or the government pay, that means I have to pay, too. I'm not terribly keen on shouldering the cost of this treatment, especially since medical dollars are precious and there are so many more pressing medical needs: vaccines, childhood well visits, preventive medicine in general. If, however, families must pay out of their own pockets, it means that all the lofty talk about equitable distribution of the drug (a major point in Eli Lilly's pitch to the FDA) is hooey. Only the wealthy will be able to take advantage of the drug, and only wealthy kids will enjoy the presumed advantage of greater height. As it is now, the vast majority of patients are white males of above-average socioeconomic background.

I'm actually more concerned about possible psychological implications. A friend of mine has a theory about mass-market drugs and unintended consequences. He believes that the class of drugs known as SSRIs (selective serotonin reuptake inhibitors), such as Prozac, has quietly but insidiously transformed the nature of our electoral politics. Why? Because the widespread use of these and other mood enhancers, which take the edge off anxiety and frustration, might have the unintended collateral effect of dissipating voter discontent. In a similar vein, maybe drugs such as human growth hormone inadvertently dissipate an essential quality of human existence, even as they redress a physical shortcoming. Maybe they leach away a bit of our persistence, our determination. In a different sense, maybe they preserve the thinness of our skin. As a general rule, I don't like the idea of telling other people how they should confront and deal with their unhappiness, and I certainly empathize with the unhappiness that tyrannizes a child who feels unusually short. But I keep wondering if, with that minimal gain of inches, we might also be diminishing ourselves in some deep and fundamental way.

PART V

STATURE AS METAPHOR

13

COLLEGE AND BEYOND
The End of Physical Growth

> Pygmies are pygmies still, though percht on Alps;
> And pyramids are pyramids in vales.
> Each man makes his own stature, builds himself.
> Virtue alone outbuilds the Pyramids;
> Her monuments shall last when Egypt's fall.
>
> — EDWARD YOUNG, *Night Thoughts*

MANY HIGH SCHOOL graduation speeches sag under the weight of ponderosity, but the following episode is a classic of this genre. The speaker, class valedictorian at a high school in California, used the occasion to extol the value of books over athletics. Smaller than most of his fellow graduates and notably dour, Ronald minced no words about a culture that elevated the status of physical strength over cultivation of the mind. "The secret of getting a medal like this is books, not sports," he said. "The student who wastes his time on athletics rather than study shows only ignorance." Revenge of the ninety-seven-pound weakling? Hardly. The remarks provoked a walkout of the entire graduating class. By the time Ronald had finished speaking, the only person left in the audience was his mother.

But the story doesn't end there. Reality often steps on the toes of youthful ideals, and when Ronald entered Clayton College the following fall, he was forced to eat his words in a bid to capture the heart of his coy, dismissive heartthrob, whom we'll call Mary. Convinced that he would never win her hand if he remained a sickly, empathetic, uncoordinated swain, he abandoned his studies and took up collegiate athletics. He arrived in his dorm room with full football gear. He tried out for the baseball team — although his unfamiliarity with the game aroused considerable suspicion, especially when he opted to wear catcher's gear while playing third base. He tried out for the track team — but when he failed at the pole vault, failed spectacularly at the hurdles, and was outrun by two small boys playing tag during a sprint, he didn't make that team either. Confronted by the dean of the college over his miserable academic performance, Ronald confessed that he was doing it all to win the affections of his inamorata. "I took up athletics because the girl I love thinks I'm a weakling," he explained. "I love her and would do anything to please her!"

At the last minute, the dean ordered the crew coach to make Ronald the coxswain on the team. "His size and weight are perfect," the dean exclaimed, "and he has brains." Not only did Ronald's ingenuity engineer a victory against Clayton's archrivals in crew, salvaging his self-esteem, but he had an unusual opportunity for valor when he learned Mary was being held hostage in her room by a towering, locker room goon. Applying the very physical skills that had aroused so much ridicule earlier, Ronald dashed like a broken-field runner through the crowd after the race; he leaped over hedgerows; he grabbed a laundry pole and vaulted into Mary's second-floor window, then barraged the rival jock with fastballs and batted balls. And, of course, he got the girl; they ended up getting married.

An earlier generation would have immediately recognized the plot line of one of Buster Keaton's funniest movies, the 1927 silent film *College*. Hardly anyone watches it now, but in its brilliant physical comedy and its redemption of physical competence in moments that really count, I find it a wonderful evocation of issues that arise toward the end of the process of growth: the maturation of the body into adult physicality; the fitful transition to adult sexual behavior; and the increasing adult appreciation that intangible factors such as character, ingenuity, and determination often overcome physical limitations, whether of size or skill. Just watching the slight but muscular Keaton hurtle toward his destiny as an athletic and romantic hero, in one of the most exhilarating chase scenes in film history, is a reminder that as boys grow into men, size matters less and less, just as passion, persistence, intelligence, and compassion matter more and more. And it is indeed the college years, roughly from ages seventeen to twenty-one, that mark the beginning of a significant transition. Physical size and athletic prowess are still important, but they need no longer be the sole, or even the predominant, factors shaping self-esteem and mating success. Stature ceases to be measured only in feet and inches.

Growth largely ceases for boys (and girls) between the ages of eighteen and twenty-one, at least for adolescents from middle- and upper-socioeconomic backgrounds. Late maturers continue to grow, and people who have been undernourished or seriously ill may gain two centimeters (about three-quarters of an inch) in height per year as late as age twenty-seven. But once the growth plates are sealed, no major changes in height are in store. For adult males in the United States, the average height is slightly less than five feet ten. In Japan it is five feet seven, and in the Netherlands it is nearly six feet one.

But there are two very important points to bear in mind about the physical stature of young adults. The first is timing. Although two different boys may end up at exactly the same adult height, an early-maturing boy, whose growth spurt occurs at age twelve, will probably enter adulthood carrying a different set of psychological luggage than a late-maturing boy whose growth spurt is delayed until age fifteen or sixteen. In terms of height, the final destination is not always as important as how quickly, or slowly, you get there. The second important point in a sense contradicts the first: once a man reaches adult height, size begins to matter much less. Buster Keaton's "Ronald" made much the same point in his valedictory address, though it's probably just as well no one was around to hear it. "Future generations depend upon brains and not jumping the discus or hurdling the javelin," he said. "What have Ty Ruth or Babe Dempsey done for Science?" Yogi Berra couldn't have put it better.

This final stage of growth is not an overnight process. Although changes in height are unlikely, other physical changes persist for six or seven years after adult height is reached. In fact, growth experts have begun to speak of a distinct postpubertal growth phase known as the transition period, during which tissues continue to mature and a person fills out while attaining peak bone mass, peak muscle mass, and greater strength. This transition also involves, at the neural level, changes in brain volume that continue into the mid-twenties, and at the reproductive level, a slow social and sexual maturation that similarly extends well beyond the age of fertility. As growth expert Barry Bogin has pointed out, girls are often sterile for two or three years after menarche and do not become truly mature reproductively until, on average, age nineteen. Boys begin producing sperm around age fourteen, yet "few boys successfully father children until they are into their third decade of life."

The last throes of physical growth can be accompanied by changes that resemble nothing so much as an internal psychological makeover, achieved through a combination of emotional maturation, life experiences, and, I suspect for many people, some form of psychotherapy. Whatever the route, the destination is self-acceptance, and in coming to terms with one form of physical imperfection (psoriasis), John Updike offers a road map of how to get there. "My war with my skin," he writes in *Self-Consciousness*, "had to do with self-love, with finding myself acceptable, whether others did or not." I'll spare the reader details of this fumbling, bumbling period of self-acceptance in my own life. Suffice it to say that, just as the recent research suggests, I lugged a considerable amount of psychological baggage from my adolescence, and those insecurities — many rooted in the physical, and indeed sexual, uncertainties I first encountered during puberty — were superimposed on the normal fumbling, bumbling phase of young adulthood, as men struggle to understand what they want in a mate and what they can offer to a mate while imagining a family and a professional trajectory. For me this makeover took years, and, like all makeovers, it requires constant maintenance and occasional overhauls.

Borrowing once again from Garry Trudeau's "inner shrimp" idea, the challenge in the adult years for men of short stature is to relinquish, emotionally, the persona of the "inner shrimp" that you used to be in order to become fully the person you are now. It's easy to apply a ruler to determine a person's height in inches, but it is extraordinarily complex and difficult to translate those inches into the qualitative values by which we all measure our lives: contentment (if not happiness), compassion, security, freedom from fear and anxiety, respect, a sense of self-worth, psychological resilience, confidence, and the unique humane values we bring to our families, our relationships, and our work. All of those values are cultivated during childhood, although we do not mark them on a chart. But growing up small made me realize that the things we value most in adulthood are very much shaped by the adversities we confront during childhood — physical size and stature being just a couple of the possibilities — and how we equip ourselves to deal with them during those tumultuous years. Perhaps another way of saying this is to restate the challenge posed to me one day by the psychologist David Sandberg: "What do you tell *your* children?" he asked.

To answer that question, I first have to tell you what Sandberg told me, because no one, according to a number of pediatric endocrinologists with whom I spoke, has achieved a better understanding of the psychology of the short-stature child than this University of Buffalo researcher. At the same time, no one has reached conclusions about short stature that so contradicted what I knew in my schoolboy bones.

DAVID SANDBERG SHOULD have been on top of the world when I met him in the fall of 2004. I found him hunched over a cup of coffee in a greasy-spoon diner on the Upper West Side of Manhattan, an earnest and friendly-faced man, but also a little wary and, as it turned out, quite reasonably beleaguered. He had just published his most recent research in the respected journal *Pediatrics,* and all his colleagues were buzzing about it. It had been picked up by the *New York Times* and other publications. David Allen, the pediatric endocrinologist at the University of Wisconsin, had told me that Sandberg's work had the potential to force many of his colleagues to rethink their basic assumptions about short stature and its medical treatment. Sandberg had been arguing, with some pretty good data, that short stature was *not* a psychologically disabling condition. In a large, well-designed study, he and his colleagues had shown that, contrary to conventional wisdom, the short kids were all right.

Sandberg is not, technically speaking, an expert in endocrinology. Indeed, if he is associated with any area of expertise, it is usually the psychology of individuals with intersex — that is, people who have, to varying degrees, the physical characteristics of both males and females. But he has always been just a step removed from hormone biology. Born in Montreal and raised by Jewish immigrants from eastern Europe, Sandberg graduated from Bar-Ilan University in Israel with a major in psychology. He obtained his doctorate at Concordia University in Montreal, where he studied the effect of hormones on animal behavior. When he "got tired of being bitten by rats," he switched over to the study of hormones in humans, eventually doing postdoctoral research at Columbia University. His adviser at Columbia, Heino F. L. Meyer-Bahlburg, was a psychologist who did pioneering studies on intersex individuals but also had written a chapter on the psychology of short stature for one of the leading textbooks in child psychiatry. Sandberg was being groomed to become a clinical psychologist and ultimately worked two years as a child clinical psychologist at North Shore University Hospital on Long Island, specializing in stature, before moving to Buffalo in 1990.

Short stature was then — as it continues to be now — the single most common reason for medical referrals to a pediatric endocrinology clinic. Sandberg, having just arrived in Buffalo, thought it would be great to add a psychosocial component for the pediatric patients who came to the endocrinology clinic there. "I fully expected, when I started, to find that children, when they were referred, would have very severe problems in adjustment," he said. "That's what all the literature said. There was a commonality to the findings of these studies — that they were shy, depressed, stigmatized, and juvenilized. So when I got to Buffalo, I decided to establish a clinical service where there would be both a medical piece and a psychosocial piece. If there were any problems at the point of entry, we could start to intervene."

But the short kids who came to the clinic in Buffalo didn't always live down to their reputations as shy, moody, unhappy youngsters. Sandberg and his psych colleagues met with every single child who came in the door for a consultation, some 552 consecutive patients referred to the clinic between 1990 and 1997, and they assessed every one psychologically, following the exact same protocol. "That had never been done before," he told me, "and I found that these kids seemed to be doing, overall, very well."

They were, to be sure, not immune to the typical stresses endured by short children. The majority had been teased about their size, and two-thirds complained of being treated as younger than they actually were. "But in terms of behavioral and emotional adjustment," Sandberg said, "they were difficult to differentiate from norms." In other words, although short stature inevitably brought greater stress into the lives of many children, most seemed to be able to handle it; only a few manifested behaviors suggesting deeper psychological problems. Sandberg and his colleagues wrote up those initial findings and published them in 1994.

That same year, one of the drug companies that makes growth hormone sponsored a meeting, and Sandberg presented the data from his 1994 paper. "I said, 'Here, look, these kids look better than anybody thought.' And the complaints were, 'Oh, but it's when they're adults that you see the problems. Nobody will want to marry them, or they'll be doing terrible in business, or they can't be president.' I had the feeling that the goalposts were moving."

The story has remained essentially unchanged over the past decade. Indeed, if anything, the evidence may have gotten stronger that short stature, in and of itself, does not necessarily doom a child to a lifetime of emotional scarring. In the belief that many of the previous studies attributing a psychological handicap to short stature were biased in the way they cherry-picked children who showed up in clinics, Sandberg and his colleagues decided to fan out into the local community. They set up another large, well-controlled study of hundreds of schoolchildren in grades six through twelve in the Buffalo area. The students didn't know that the study was about height. They were told that they had been chosen to be the director of a class play. They were given thumbnail sketches of various characters in the drama — "a good leader," "teases others too much," "gets picked on," and so forth — and asked to cast the play by selecting classmates who best fit the roles.

If short stature is a ticket to social prejudice and psychological purgatory, which has been the animating idea behind the expanded use of growth hormone in the past fifteen years, you would have expected the shortest children in the Buffalo study to be lining up to collect their Tonys in victimhood: they would have been nominated by classmates for every beleaguered role — getting picked on, behaving shyly, acting withdrawn, being left out. But that, surprisingly, was not the case. Sandberg and his colleagues concluded that a child's stature, whether tall or small, male or female, had "minimal detectable impact" on his or her social standing among schoolmates. The only discernible social impact was that shorter children were more likely to be considered "younger-looking." At least in this setting, even extremely short children (around the first percentile) made friends and earned the respect of their peers as well as kids of average size did.

Nor, it turns out, was this an isolated finding. Linda D. Voss, an epidemiological nurse with the Wessex Growth Study in England, had reported similar results in British children. Again, these were not kids who had turned up at a growth specialist's office, but rather kids who were part of a large longitudinal study in a general population. With a few exceptions, such as the finding noted earlier (see chapter 5) that small children are more likely to be bullied, the Wessex study has consistently reported that children of short stature are, on average, well-adjusted psychologically and show no signs of handicap or disability. An update published by the Wessex researchers in 2004 extended their findings to young adults who had been short as children and reported that "no significant differences in personality functioning or aspects of daily living were found which could be attributable to height."

These findings, of course, fly in the face of widespread medical assumptions, of a $2-billion-a-year industry devoted to increasing the height of short but normal children, and, not incidentally, of my own experiences while growing up. The studies were well designed; they were peer reviewed; they were published. But were they true? And what did they mean?

"IT'S A NO-BRAINER," Sandberg was saying, nursing a cup of watery coffee. "Everyone wants to be taller. If you're five-ten, you want to be six-two. People have done those studies, and both men and women earn less money if they're not as tall. So it's a no-brainer to say 'Do you want to be taller?' They all say yes. But," he continued, shaking his head, "we give too much weight to people who say 'I want to be taller.'" Especially, he added, when they come to doctors seeking growth hormone. "People show more discrimination when they're buying cars," he grumbled, "than when they are entering these treatments."

At this point in the conversation, my gut was grumbling a bit, too, dubious about Sandberg and his findings. They contradicted everything I thought I knew, at the level of emotional knowledge and truth, about life on the lower slopes of the growth chart, and they went against everything the parents of short kids typically say about the stigma of small size — in testimony before the U.S. Food and Drug Administration, on their foundation Web sites, and in anecdotal statements to reporters like me.

There's nothing mysterious or mischievous about why parents are willing to consider a powerful drug to treat their short but otherwise normal children. They have read the same studies linking short stature to psychological stigma. More to the point, they have listened to the utter despair of their children as they sink into social and emotional isolation. They want, as any loving parent would, to create a haven against such obvious pain and give their children the best chance for a happy and fulfilling life.

The pharmaceutical companies have always been eager to foster this impression, too, although they are careful not to state it as scientific fact. When Eli Lilly went before the FDA in 2003 to defend its growth hormone, for example, several company representatives alluded to the notion that short stature is associated with psychological stigma. They did not dwell on the issue, however, or cite any studies or proof, because their own very expensive, randomized, and placebo-controlled study had failed to produce any data showing psychological benefit to children who received growth hormone. (The Lilly-sponsored study, published in the *Journal of Clinical Endocrinology and Metabolism* in 2004, a year after the FDA approved the drug, unambiguously concluded, "The data do not support the use of [growth hormone] treatment for idiopathic short stature to improve psychological dysfunction.")

Sandberg's findings nonetheless seemed to provoke a great deal of controversy. Pinchas Cohen, a pediatric endocrinologist at the University of California at Los Angeles, cited a number of methodological weaknesses in the work in an analysis on the BioCritique Web site. He argued that Sandberg made a mistake in assessing the psychological makeup of kids at or below the fifth percentile, as this was a more generous definition of "short stature" than the usual clinical definitions. Although this is true, from a social point of view it doesn't make much difference if 97 percent or 95 percent of your peers are bigger. Short is short, and severe short stature is a very arbitrary medical condition. More to the point, the Sandberg paper analyzed a small subset of kids at or below the first percentile, and the results were the same.

In a broader sense, Cohen echoed doubts about the ability of contemporary psychological research to probe these issues. When I spoke with him, he referred to questionnaires, of the type used by Sandberg (and virtually every other researcher in the social sciences), as "toilet paper." Charmian Quigley, a Lilly physician, also got in a dig at Sandberg when I asked her about the psychological research. She noted that Sandberg had focused on a population that was not the same as the children eligible for growth hormone treatment, and she reminded me, in passing, that one of the children who had testified before the FDA advisory committee had asserted that children tend to lie on questionnaires. Jerry Avorn, a leading medical epidemiologist at Harvard's Brigham and Women's Hospital, also made the point that a lot of psychological research is terrible. "I would think that a thoughtful layperson might have a better handle on this than a psychologist or a quality-of-life guru," he said.

But there is plenty of support for Sandberg's research, too. Alan Rogol, who is now secretary of the largest professional association of pediatric endocrinologists in the United States, told me, "David Sandberg's data are pretty damn strong that kids, as a group, are not severely hampered psychologically by short stature." The studies by Sandberg and Linda Voss in England, he added, "are less ivory tower and academic, and more on the ground. I think they are probably a more realistic picture of what's going on." Robert Blizzard, the dean of American growth studies (now retired), said, "I have great respect for Sandberg's work, and I have great respect for David. The work he's doing is work that needs to be done."

Over many years of science writing, I've learned to distrust gut feelings, my own and those of others. Indeed, on countless occasions, I've been told by scientists that they designed an experiment with a hypothesis (which might be thought of as a kind of experience-based, working prediction), only to discover a result that completely contradicted their expectations. Well-executed science is the only thing that can test and ratify (or refute) first impressions, gut feelings, and all the other forms of intuitive knowledge that we fervently believe to be true in the absence of firm evidence. And Sandberg's work is, generally speaking and despite the objections, good science.

But what is at stake in this research is something, as should be clear by now, bigger than just the biomedical issues raised by short stature. The research also speaks to concepts of self: how we know what we know; why we believe what we believe about the narrative of our lives; how we can pathologize and medicalize personal problems; and how personal history, with its internalized perceptions of hardship, so often settles on a single, surpassingly neat cause for all its messy effects. Our perceptions of ourselves rely not only on the reflection in the mirror but also on all the other things in the background of that reflection — the environment, the context, the nurture of our respective worlds. In the case of stature, the issue is not just our shortness or, in a broader sense, our difference from others; it's also how we cope with that difference, what we make of it, how we're supported as we struggle with the adversity, and how we summon the resources to survive a socially challenging situation, learn from it, and emerge from the experience even stronger. Some of these larger issues leapt out of Sandberg's data.

One of the first points he wanted to make is that today's version of "short" is different from the version in times past. A child who is seriously short (well below the first percentile), is failing to grow, and otherwise fits diagnostic criteria, he said, should receive growth hormone. Period. At one point, he took pains to say, "I'm not against the use of growth hormone at all. I'm just questioning the assumptions behind its use."

He continued, "But if a child is at the fifth percentile, the pediatrician has been trained to measure the kid, and if you're tracking his growth and everything is well, then it's fine. You know, somebody's got to be down there. But if a child has problems under those circumstances, if twenty of one hundred parents are concerned, you're going to get a disproportionately large number of poorly performing kids who are going to be referred [to a pediatric endocrinologist]. So you're going to get an enriched population of kids coming to pediatric endocrinologists with problems." If you are performing a study of the psychological effects of short stature and use that population, Sandberg suggested, your study will automatically begin with a bias that tilts the conclusion to psychological disability.

His second point is that the child referred to the clinic is far more likely to be a boy than a girl. This may seem like an obvious and innocuous fact, but think about it for a moment. Are boys more biologically "prone" to being short than girls? Of course not. Shortness, for both boys and girls, is defined by statistics. Does this rate of referral reflect something other than a medical malady? Sandberg argues that it does. "The rate of referral of boys versus girls is as much as three to one," he said. "Since we define short stature within gender, there are the same number of short girls as short boys. But far more boys are referred to clinics. Which should be a tip-off to the endocrinologist about where the 'disease' is. Where does the energy come from to organize a trip to a pediatric endocrinologist? Who makes the appointment?" Sandberg continued, "I wonder if the urgency of the parents has to do with the concern that their short boys are not *real* boys."

The demographics of growth hormone use also are racially skewed, according to Sandberg and many doctors. The patients tend to be not only boys but white middle- and upper-class boys. Children in families of lower socioeconomic status or without insurance tend not to see pediatricians for well visits, and consequently they (and minorities in general) are underrepresented in specialty clinics. In addition, many health insurers will not pick up the tab for treating short but normal kids.

Sandberg wanted to make a larger point about desire and enlightened choice: how you ask the question — about height or anything else — changes the answer you're likely to get. He said that researchers have shown that when you ask a child (or his parents) if he wants to be taller, the answer is simple and unqualified: yes. When you ask if the child wants to be taller even if it would mean having to take a medicine every day for the rest of his life, the numbers drop. When you ask if the child wants to be taller even if it would cost him a couple of years of life expectancy down the road because of potential long-term side effects, the numbers drop even further. At a certain point, these questions stop being a medical algorithm and become a practical exercise in personal philosophy. Or, as Sandberg chose to frame the issue, "Which is a more meaningful way to ask about happiness?"

I understood where Sandberg was coming from; I just wasn't sure he'd gotten far enough to get a good glimpse of the dark side of being short. I mentioned sports, for example — that I had excelled as a younger boy and simply couldn't compete (and was discouraged from competing) in football, baseball, and basketball as I got older because I was smaller than the other boys. I mentioned that the baseball coach at my junior high school had refused to let me try out for the team because I was too small — even though I'd been a Little League all-star (okay, alternate all-star) the year before in a different town.

"I was never involved in sports," Sandberg admitted, "but you say it was a real stressor. That assumes that the baseline of adolescent development is happiness, as if nobody else has anything they're dealing with. But there's lots of data to show that that's not the case. Let's say you're fifteen years old and of average height and you have a younger brother who is taller. He's a better athlete and gets onto teams, and you get bent out of shape and complain that it's not fair. And it becomes a focus. You feel cheated.

"But what happens if some of this variability contributes to the choices you make? If you were a basketball player and six-five, would you be a writer? You know, that gets lost in it — how variety might open us up to different experiences."

He recalled, "I was a skinny kid, not with any athletic prowess. My parents were immigrants from Poland, and I was the first generation, and grew up in Montreal. The situation was ripe for misattribution. I grew up feeling that I didn't quite belong and didn't know why. And those things stick with you, they stay with you . . . But if we're talking about kids with short stature, there's going to be as much variation in how they adapt to it and have success . . . as in any other group."

Sandberg said that how a child adapts to being short might have a lot to do with the feedback he gets from family members. In some families, he said, height may not be "a salient issue." "I have the feeling that there are families that, when [height becomes an issue], they teach the kid to have more chutzpah and blow it off," he explained. "If you have a kid with a certain temperament, he won't get bent out of shape."

IN AN EARLIER life, I would have blown off Sandberg's arguments as insensitive, snooty, and out of touch. In the society of children — and in the even more rigid and unforgiving society of adolescence — there is always an emotional price to pay for being different, and the price may be even higher when you are physically small in a very physically conscious world.

But as I sat at the table with him, glancing out at the early-morning passersby on Broadway — each so different in shape and size, each with a physical and emotional history as unique as a fingerprint — I found that I couldn't completely disagree.

As certain as I had been that short stature was the defining factor of my youth and adolescence, I was now certain — grudgingly certain, but certain nonetheless — that reaching this conclusion was a convenient way to compartmentalize and compress all the ill-fitting aspects of adolescence into one neat package. It was like an emotional compactor — I dumped all the insecurity and angst of my teenage years into one bag and squeezed until they fit. The Nobel Prize–winning psychologist Daniel Kahneman and his colleague David Schkade, in discussing the kind of attributions people make, have described what they call a "focusing illusion" in the way people assess life satisfaction. Their experiments have shown a tendency to focus on, and give more weight to, a single explanation, while in the process neglecting other potential contributing factors. "We predict similar effects for any determinant of life satisfaction," Schkade and Kahneman wrote, "which depends on so many factors that focusing attention on any one of them will inevitably cause an exaggeration of its impact."

There's no way to gild an unopened lily: being a late bloomer, living through delayed maturation, and feeling left out and on the sidelines is a drag. Critics have attacked Sandberg's work by suggesting that the problems of small size don't truly emerge until a child, especially a boy, is on the cusp of puberty. That criticism is well taken, but it doesn't diminish or distract from the larger point of Sandberg's research, which is that a large proportion of small children seem to have the emotional, psychological, and even physical wherewithal to weather the storm of delayed growth and small size. "Storm," in fact, is an appealing metaphor, because storms blow over, and as long as you have shelter, you'll be okay. The shelter in this case, of course, is emotional and almost always familial.

Some children don't have that wherewithal, and in those cases, pharmaceutical intervention may well be appropriate. But, as Sandberg suggests — indeed, as the vast literature on human growth has repeatedly and surprisingly suggested — the environment, or context, is terrifically important. And if it's important physically, it surely must be important psychologically. In families where attention and empathy are in short supply, a child might not develop the inner resources to weather the storm. In families where the parents, especially the father, subtly convey concern (or, worse, disappointment) about a boy's size, the child can easily internalize that disapproval, and it will become part of the way he thinks about himself.

This came home to me during a conversation I had with Dr. Selna Kaplan, a pediatric endocrinologist at the University of California, San Francisco, and one the pioneers in treating children with growth hormone. She was no stranger to social bias during her own upbringing, when she vowed to attend medical school despite being discouraged from doing so because she was a woman. In recalling this history, she mentioned the support of her family, and the remark contrasted sharply with what she had told me, just moments earlier, about some of the families who bring their children to her for medical consultations about short stature. The fathers, she said, seem especially disappointed by the size of their sons.

My conversation with David Sandberg also made me think about the long-term side effects of behavioral adaptations. I had argued that being small had forced me to adapt my behavior to "survive" adolescence — not in the Darwinian sense of life-or-death survival, of course, but in a more psychosocial sense of adjusting one's behavior to endure the social duress of the teenage years. At first I considered these changes merely maladaptive, because they had constrained the ways in which I had engaged with the world. But in acknowledging that context is very important, I can also see that some of those strategies shaped my adult behavior — indeed, many of my professional skills — in a useful way. They have proved to be indispensable tools to a writer.

For instance, growing up smaller than average, I learned to pay very close attention to the emotional signals other people give off; back then it was to avoid looming confrontation, but being attuned to these signals has other uses now. Growing up smaller than average, I learned to talk fast and keep people off balance with jokes; then it was to defuse potentially awkward or dangerous situations, but now I know that a sense of humor and a little verbal aggressiveness go a long way toward equalizing social disparities in adult situations, too. Growing up smaller than average, I learned that there could be a price to pay for being assertive; then it convinced me to blend into the background, but now I see that it also encouraged me to be a good listener. Growing up smaller than average (and occasionally suffering physical and verbal abuse because of it), I learned to empathize with others; then it was just a way for commiseration to find some company, but now I realize that the wrong situation can turn anyone into a victim of social prejudice, injustice, or sheer cruelty. Growing up smaller than average, I learned to keep a low profile and not attract too much attention; then it was a way of making myself less of a target, but now it helps explain my outsider mentality — distrusting organizations and institutions, being fiercely attached to family and less inclined than most to accept conventional or popular wisdom.

Like all children and adolescents, with their unique landscapes of problems and challenges, I developed behaviors that I carried into adulthood, clutching them like a bag lady defending her most prized possessions. Some have proved useful, some less so. Some are immensely helpful in certain circumstances but nearly disastrous in others. All are part of the person I've become. Perhaps it's a cliché, and a cold-hearted one at that, but if personality and character are tempered in the crucible of experiences (especially difficult experiences), then resorting to a drug like growth hormone in nonmedical circumstances strikes me as being a little like lowering the temperature of that tempering process. It might make adolescence easier, but it might make adulthood harder.

"As a predictor of adults and how they are doing, which is better, adult height or the family?" Sandberg said finally, as the waitress brought us the check. "There's no question in my mind which it is. It's the family." He continued, "Height is a lightning rod, and if this kid is having other problems — he lives in a neighborhood with a bully, whatever — the problems are overdetermined. In child psychology, there's not one problem. In the kids I see in the psychology clinic, there's financial stress in the home, marital stress — *and* they're short. But when they come to the clinic, the problem is they're short."

PERHAPS THE MOST difficult daily task for any parent is to discern that line — ever shifting, often written in invisible ink — where growth pains stop being healthy and begin to take a toll. At what point does adversity stop building character and start eroding self-confidence and determination? At what point does parental shelter become overprotection? At what point does struggle cease to educate and serve only to demoralize? Like many parents, I can't give an exact answer to these questions, except to say that I think about them all the time, and that the answer most certainly does not reside in the kind of parenting where a father habitually addresses his child, as one doctor told me, as Shrimp.

Some research has taken on, gingerly, familial factors other than size that may contribute to a child's psychological distress. In 1999 a group of Dutch researchers compared young adults who had consulted pediatric endocrinologists as children because of height (and in whom no growth problems were identified) with young adults in the general population who had been of similar stature while growing up but who had not sought medical intervention. Adults in the first group attributed major life problems to their short stature, such as finding a mate or landing a job; adults in the second group, of matched height, reported no day-to-day problems. Jan Busschbach and colleagues concluded, "It seems that the problems of patients with idiopathic short stature who present themselves to endocrinologists may not directly be related to their short stature. This would suggest that therapy should not focus too much on the short stature itself, but should treat the problems associated with short stature as symptoms of more general distress."

Parents may be the elephant in the examining room. If they accept a child for who and what he is and devote their energies to cultivating the kind of coping skills that will equip any child to deal with the frustrations and setbacks we all encounter throughout life, the odds are that there will never be a psychological reason to visit that examining room in the first place. If, however, a boy's size becomes the focus of conversation and concern, the child often will pick up on that. And if the focus is on physical qualities that a child doesn't possess, such as normal height, harping on those qualities can undermine a child's sense of self. Families cannot protect children from all the insults of the outside world, but they must offer refuge from, and first aid for, those insults.

So what would I tell my children about size and stature?

I would tell them, first and foremost, that there is a point in one's life where size ceases to matter. I no longer think of myself as small, and haven't for a long time. There's no magic cutoff point, no particular Tanner stage or age when this change occurs. Rather, it is a bumpy trip through a hilly and uneven landscape, where you can't see your destination until you're practically there. In *The Education of Henry Adams,* the author suggests that any path that arrives is the right one. Some paths take longer than others, and I think my personal path to the point where size didn't matter probably took me on an especially roundabout journey. I dated late, married late, and had children late. But the timing doesn't matter as much as the doing. And height issues don't bother me at all anymore. It doesn't bother me that my wife is a good three inches taller than I am. It didn't even bother me that the photographer at my wedding asked my wife to sit, with me standing behind her, for our formal portrait, as if this physical disparity might foreshadow some other, darker inequity. As my sister-in-law recently remarked, "If it mattered, you wouldn't have gotten married in the first place." Exactly.

I would tell them, if they were being teased (about stature or anything else), that it *is* unfair; there's no point in pretending that teasing doesn't hurt. But I'd try to give them tools that would help them blunt the sting of such verbal assaults. I would tell them, as most bullying experts suggest, that they should tune out the abuse and, if need be, change the scenery by walking away. If they felt up to it, I'd even encourage them to volley the teasing with a clever turn of phrase. I'm not suggesting that they respond in kind. Rather, I'd encourage them to say something that would make two things clear: that they weren't bothered by the insult and that they retained a sense of humor about it. Easier said than done, I know. But developing even a slightly thicker skin during one's childhood will also serve one during adulthood, with the teasing, criticism, and more substantial setbacks that are an inevitable part of life.

I would make sure they know they are loved and esteemed. In speaking to growth experts, one quality repeatedly came up in connection with children who had learned to cope: the strength of a child's social life, especially familial. It may not be apparent, or even seem helpful, in the midst of the storm, but the security of unconditional love seems to lend some enduring emotional ballast that helps a child find his or her equilibrium in the midst of the difficulties.

I would tell them not to worry too much if they happened to be smaller than average, or even very small. I think one of the most difficult moments in parenting comes when a child is despondent or undermined by a physical shortcoming, real or imagined, that cannot easily be "fixed" — not just height, but body shape, facial characteristics, raw athletic skill, and so on. Pouring gallons of adult reason onto these wounds tends just to keep them fresh and wet. So it's important not to make too big a deal of it. Much more than parents acknowledge, kids can pick up the most indirect and subtle parental concerns. My children are not even in double digits, and they can parse a parental monologue down to its hidden agenda in a matter of seconds. And this leads to what might be called the Heisenberg principle of parental concern, after the twentieth-century physicist who showed that the velocity and direction of a subatomic particle can be altered by the sheer act of scientific inquiry. Similarly, a child's reaction to an issue such as stature can easily be swayed by constant, seemingly indirect adult inquiry. If a child hears the same flavor of question over and over again — "Do you think you get picked on at school because of your size?" or even the more neutral "Is there anything you want to tell us about gym class?" — it begins to reinforce the message that there may be a problem.

I would tell them to examine their feelings, understand what they think, and stick to their guns. Parents should do everything they can to empower a child with the serenity and strength of his or her own judgments, in anticipation of those moments — more frequent as a child matures and enters adolescence — when peers become more important than parents. I've always thought that if you wait until peer pressure becomes an issue, it's too late. If children are constantly encouraged to trust their own sense of self, it's less likely that they will oblige their tormentors by responding with self-doubt. As Eleanor Roosevelt once observed, "No one can make you feel inferior without your consent." My wife and I have always believed in the utmost importance of cultivating independence of mind and strength of character in a child as early as possible, so that the child grows comfortable expressing opinions and reaching decisions that may contradict the nearest authority figure, whoever (parents or peer group) that may be. It's also important for them to learn that they are free to walk away from any situation that feels improper (such as participating in a campaign of bullying) and that they should try to act on the moral imperative to assist those who are weaker, disadvantaged, or victimized by bias.

I would urge them to participate in school or other community activities. Participation instantly enrolls a child in a subculture and creates a cohort, a like-minded group; it leads to peer acceptance; it forces one to learn social skills of interaction, negotiation, and cooperation; and it almost automatically ensures that the child will belong, tightly or at least peripherally, to a community. I would urge them to find a sport or an activity that is suited to their size and talents. Many accomplished men with whom I spoke during the preparation of this book — pediatric endocrinologists such as David Allen and Alan Rogol, even the high school teacher down the block — told me that they had found an outlet in size- and skills-appropriate sports. Physical activity is essential to the growth of bones and overall good health, but other activities also help build human capital.

I would tell them that there will always be moments — like the one described by Garry Trudeau, curled up in his father's lap — when utter helplessness outstrips any rational argument a parent can muster. At times like these, words will fail, so hugs and gentle reassurances, not sermons, may be the best medicine. They won't make the hurt go away, but they can be applied liberally, like a balm, to ease the pain. Try as we might to minimize the hurt, we ultimately cannot assure our children a life free from conflict and challenge. Any variation from the norm can feel like an oppression and bring on suffering. But each variation is an opportunity to remind our children that they are anything but average and, as Buster Keaton demonstrated at the end of *College,* they can rise to the occasion when it really, truly counts.

Finally, I would tell them that height says nothing about the character of an individual, but it says a great deal, as we will shortly see, about the character and values of a society.

14

THE TALLEST PEOPLE ON EARTH

Historical Anthropometry and
the Standard of Living

> White men like to dig in the ground for their food. My people
> prefer to hunt the buffalo as their fathers did. White men like
> to stay in one place. My people want to move their tepees here
> and there to the different hunting grounds. The life of white
> men is slavery. They are prisoners in towns or farms. The life
> my people want is a life of freedom. I have seen nothing that
> a white man has, houses or railways or clothing or food, that
> is as good as the right to move in the open country, and live
> in our own fashion.
>
> — SITTING BULL

O N A SUNNY MONDAY morning in June, Richard Steckel, an
economic historian at Ohio State University, emerged from the Bowling
Green subway stop in lower Manhattan and joined me at the entrance to
the Smithsonian Institution's National Museum of the American Indian.
As he made his way across the cobblestone square, Steckel hardly looked
the part of an academic pariah and economics revolutionary. He was of
average height (by now, one of my first pieces of business in any conversation with an expert in the field was to establish his or her height; he was
five feet ten) and perhaps above-average girth, with a broad face and
short, gray-flecked brown hair. We didn't have a destination in mind, but
as we wandered through the museum's superb collection of artifacts, we
found ourselves lingering in front of a large watercolor and ink drawing dating from the 1880s. The scene depicted the Battle of the Little
Bighorn. It had been painted by Standing Bear, who as a seventeen-year-
old had participated in the battle.

While most museumgoers (including me) predictably search for the likeness of George Armstrong Custer in the tableau, Steckel saw in it a crystallization of all the invisible factors that can contribute to a unique quality of life, and that quality revealed itself in a single characteristic of the figures peopling the painting: their height. Indeed, he spoke about things so unexpected, so removed from the literal depiction of this famous clash between Native American civilization and encroaching U.S. interests, that several museum visitors paused and did a double take at the illustration. Standing in the middle of the gallery, Steckel spoke about the nutritional advantages of long-term breast-feeding. He mentioned the high-protein diet of the Plains tribes and their "excellent dental health." He pointed out that the use of horses reduced their "work effort" — the sheer amount of energy expended by members of a particular society — and may have allowed tribes to disperse quickly at the first sign of epidemic disease. Finally, as he stepped closer to the drawing and peered at it more intently, he began to point out individual Lakota Sioux warriors who appeared to be as tall as, or taller than, their American adversaries.

"When you look at this one," he said, indicating a warrior in the thick of the action, "this guy is bigger than this soldier. And this guy is about the same," he said, pointing out another tall Native American. The guard shot a worried look our way when Steckel wondered aloud about the possibility of obtaining some calipers to measure the figures more precisely. The point, he continued, was that "the natives are certainly depicted at least as physical equals. It's not the shrimps versus the giants."

Was it by naif accident or with mythologizing intent that a number of the Sioux warriors in the drawing indeed appeared to be taller than the European Americans whose heights they were about to shorten by the five or six millimeters that mark the thickness of a human scalp? The simplicity of Standing Bear's style suggests that artistic license may have informed the disparity of size between the Native Americans and American soldiers in the illustration. But researchers have unearthed evidence arguing that it was anything but artistic license. Scott Carson, one of Steckel's colleagues, managed to track down height data from the muster rolls of Custer's 7th Cavalry. These soldiers averaged 170.9 centimeters in height, slightly more than 5 feet 7 inches, which is an inch or two shorter than the average height of the tribes they fought.

I went to view the Native American collection with Steckel, who is also a scholar at the National Bureau of Economic Research, for a specific reason. Using exceedingly accurate measurements of the height of Native Americans collected in the nineteenth century, Steckel and Joseph M. Prince, a colleague at the University of Tennessee, have argued that the Plains tribes were on average among the tallest people in the world at the time — taller than native-born white Americans, taller than Europeans, taller than virtually any national group for whom reliable data exists. "How did apparently 'poor' tribes become the tallest in the world?" Steckel and Prince asked. Pointing out that "height and health are known to be sensitive to inequality," they suggested that egalitarian values, a steady food supply, and "social and economic fluidity" allowed these Native American nomads to build a stronger social safety net than their European American contemporaries. In short, Steckel and Prince argued, they had a higher standard of living.

The study of the Plains tribes, first published in 2001 and bolstered by follow-up data assembled during the summer of 2004, reflects one of the more audacious conclusions to have emerged from a relatively recent, intellectually ambitious, and once-scorned field of interdisciplinary research known as historical anthropometry, which is based on the physical measurement of human beings (or their remains) from distant historical epochs. Steckel, if not the founder of the field, was there at its inception. Back in 1979, he was among the first academics to publish a modern anthropometric study of historical significance, about the heights of African American slaves. This also accorded him the honor of being among the first economic historians to encounter the disbelief (not to say derision) of social scientists as they first assessed this biological form of economic history. Since then, Steckel and other proponents of this growing field have made the provocative argument that the average height of a society — not the inevitable human variations that occur due to genetic differences, but the aggregate height of many members of a given population, all averaged out — offers a window onto that society's quality of life, its values, and its overall welfare. They argue, in fact, that the health and welfare of a society may best be gauged not by monetary numbers such as average income or gross domestic product, but by the communal commitment and collective ability to care for the young, resist disease, and maximize the salutary effects of good nutrition. All those factors help a given society to maximize the genetic potential of its people, and that maximized potential translates into a single salient characteristic: greater average height.

Moreover, since traditional economic measures such as income are usually not available for societies in the distant past, the collection of height data may provide a unique, and unusually revealing, perspective on a historical culture, whether Italian city-states of the Renaissance or European nations after the Industrial Revolution or equestrian nomadic tribes that wandered the North American plains in the nineteenth century. And it may have implications — not always flattering ones — for contemporary societies such as ours. Growth experts have long known, for example, that the average height of certain cultures has increased dramatically since World War II. In 1982 James Tanner and his colleagues reported this "secular trend" in Japanese men, whose height increased noticeably between 1957 and 1977. Researchers in the Netherlands similarly revealed that since the end of World War II, Dutch men have become, on average, the tallest people in the world. Just as significant, the average height of Americans has stagnated for the past half century. Steckel is among a handful of anthropometric economists in the world actively trying to figure out why.

THE BASIC PRINCIPLE of modern anthropometry smells, at first, more like an academic gimmick than a serious method of intellectual inquiry. The word "anthropometry" itself has floated around for centuries. The Belgian mathematician and growth expert Adolphe Quetelet gave the idea an official academic sheen with his 1870 book *Anthropométrie*. And well before the era of modern biology, a connection had been drawn, shakily, between stature and environment. As the French scholar Julien-Joseph Virey succinctly observed early in the nineteenth century, "Misery produces short people."

A latter-day French scholar, Emmanuel Le Roy Ladurie, is generally credited with pioneering the idea of collecting and studying height data in the hope that such information would lead to inferences about historical times. Ladurie examined nineteenth-century French military archives, which included height data, and in 1969 began to publish his findings on the physical stature, geographic mobility, and "delinquency" of young Frenchmen enlisted in the army. The American school of historical anthropometry arose out of different academic and historical concerns. In 1974 Robert W. Fogel, an economic historian at the University of Chicago, and his colleague Stanley L. Engerman of the University of Rochester published a hugely controversial book about the economics of African American slavery. *Time on the Cross* argues, among other things, that the nineteenth-century slave economy was more efficient than previously believed. Fogel and Engerman make the point, for example, that it was in the economic interests of plantation owners to treat their indentured workers relatively well in terms of food and shelter, or their productivity would diminish. At the time of its publication, the book triggered an enormous backlash against the historians and their thesis, and the modern use of anthropometry grew out of that controversy.

The notion that the measurement of height could in any way influence the course of this raging debate, or any other historical controversy, seems ludicrous at first. But some of Fogel and Engerman's original research was based on shreds of information contained in nineteenth-century ship manifests — essentially bills of lading for human cargo, used on slave ships plying the routes between southern coastal cities. After the U.S. Congress abolished the African slave trade, authorities required ship captains to keep logs of any slave transported between coastal cities, in an effort to thwart smuggling. These simple handwritten documents listed slaves by name and physical characteristics, including height. Fogel discovered that thousands of these documents were stored at the National Archives.

One of Fogel's graduate students at the time was Richard Steckel, who was working on a dissertation about the relative fertility of slaves and southern whites when the backlash to *Time on the Cross* erupted. Steckel grew up outside Rochester, New York, and obtained a degree in economics from Oberlin College in 1966 before going to the University of Chicago. The only hint of a previous interest in growth or height, he recalled, came when he was ten years old and his father, a psychiatrist in the New York State mental health system, came home one day with several two-month-old calves that were small and sickly because they had been mistreated and malnourished from birth. It was Richard's job to see if they could be nursed back to health and normal size. "And by gosh but if after another four months or so, they were back to normal," he recalled over lunch on the day we visited the Native American museum. "That was my first experience of catch-up growth, and is probably what got me interested in this field." While working on his dissertation, Steckel knew that

Fogel and Engerman had used the ship manifests to study the pattern of slave migration to the American West. "That was their intent from the beginning, and the heights just happened to be there," Steckel said. "But the heights are there to identify the slaves. They're there to prove they weren't smuggled in."

In 1974, when he joined the faculty at Ohio State, Steckel discovered he had a research assistant with not quite enough to do. "I remembered the slave manifests," he said. "So I put this research assistant to work coding the data . . . not having in mind a specific agenda." That came soon enough. By the time Steckel had collected and analyzed enough data to make several astonishing claims, he too ran into a fierce line of resistance from mainstream economists. Indeed, he entered this academic fray with only one blocker running interference for him, but it was a good one: Jim Tanner.

"The question of interest for me," Steckel recalled, "and one that had come up in the slave debates, was the age of slaves at menarche [that is, the age at which menstruation first occurs]. When could they have first had children? Because the assumption was, by some people, that slave women had children early and often. I was intrigued. And nobody had any data on age at menarche for slaves. I had found that age at first birth was nineteen and a half or twenty for the larger farms. Well, if menarche was as late as seventeen or seventeen and a half, as some data suggested, they could have had children about as early as would have been biologically possible."

With that question in mind, Steckel began to collaborate with James Trussell, a Princeton professor and one of the world's leading demographers. Trussell was conducting research in London at the time, and as soon as he learned that Steckel had data on slave heights from thousands of ship manifests, he walked over to the Institute of Child Health and spoke to its director, James Tanner, about it. This was a crucial juncture, because Tanner informed Trussell that the peak of the adolescent growth spurt served as an excellent predictor of age at menarche. Growth studies in Europe had reliably established that menarche occurred twelve to eighteen months after the peak of adolescent female growth. So Steckel and Trussell realized that by averaging the heights of slave women by age and plotting the time of their maximum growth spurt from the ship manifests, they could, improbably, estimate the age of menarche. This allowed them to make the bold assertion that slave women, contrary to conventional wisdom (and consistent with a claim made by Fogel and Engerman in *Time on the Cross*), abstained from having children for a number of years after they were capable of conception. Steckel and Trussell had reached this conclusion by 1976, but the paper — with its profound counterintuitive findings on the reproductive behavior of African American slaves — did not appear until 1978 in the *Journal of Interdisciplinary History*.

Tanner's role in the inception of this field was far from incidental. During the mid-1970s, after Trussell's initial contact, Steckel began a correspondence that grew into a significant mentorship, not only for his own career but for the entire field of economic history. He sent letters requesting background on growth data to Tanner, who at the time was completing two of his opuses on human growth, *Fetus into Man* (1978) and *A History of the Study of Human Growth* (1981). No one in the world knew more about the biological significance and interpretation of human height data, and when Steckel began to share the slave height data with Tanner in the spring of 1976, the British scientist became extremely excited. Here was a source of historical data on height that had not previously been tapped, and it promised to shed light on several boiling historical debates.

At a meeting in England many years later, Steckel asked Tanner why he had been so interested in the historical data. "Well," Tanner replied, "you know, Rick, I think we've learned about all we can from growth studies, measuring heads and bodies. We have huge amounts of data. We know the patterns of human growth. What's important now are the social relationships between anthropometrics and society." Indeed, one of the key lessons to have emerged from the systematic, broad-based growth studies of the nineteenth and early twentieth centuries was that average height measurements of discrete groups — urban poor, upper-class private school students, military recruits, children from impoverished parts of southern Europe — revealed the degree of nurture in a social environment. Height, oddly enough, was an excellent shorthand for understanding the role of environment in growth, which easily translated into a different, more profound measure: how well a society takes care of its children.

So Steckel sent Tanner drafts of his early papers. He learned, through

Tanner and his London associates, the statistical tricks necessary to smooth height data, guard against bias, and make it credible. Soon Fogel, who would later share a Nobel Prize with Douglass North for founding the new economic history, was calling Tanner, too, and he began gathering height data in 1977, studying the relationship of average height to illness and mortality in Europe and the United States during past epochs. Tanner, for his part, became an honorary member of the University of Chicago circle.

The reaction to the paper on slave fertility, Steckel said, established a pattern that has held true ever since: people at first refused to believe it. I have to admit that I was one of those people when I first encountered the field. The key point of objection is this: doesn't a person's height derive more from genetics than from the environment? The answer is yes, one person considered at a time. But historical anthropometry typically deals with thousands of height measurements, and although genetics strongly determine the height of an individual, the environment emerges as the predominant factor when you average the heights of a great number of people, especially in localities and circumstances where the environment is not especially nurturing. Critics have raised other issues, too. Are the measurements accurate? How large a sample are the researchers dealing with, and how representative are the ship manifests of the entire population of African American slaves?

As Steckel sifted through the shipping records, he noticed that about half of the height measurements were to a fraction of an inch — "which suggests," he said, "a fairly high degree of care." Since human slaves represented, lamentably, a kind of merchandise, you could argue that the measurements were as commercially precise as when farmers weighed grain or merchants counted widgets. Steckel conceded that there was some "height heaping," in which measurements were rounded up or down to the nearest half or whole foot. But there are statistical tricks to check for ways that such heaping can distort the data, and Tanner and his colleague Michael Preece had taught the American researchers how to smooth out those wrinkles in the measurements.

Steckel initially pored over some 1,400 ship manifests, amassing the heights of some 50,000 slaves (the database is now up to 30,000 manifests and 146,000 slave measurements), and this led to the next controversial paper. By 1981 — though, again, it wouldn't be published until later, in 1986 — Steckel had enough of the ship data to show that adult male slaves were, on average, nearly the same height as native-born white Americans. What made this surprising is that slave children were, on average, severely stunted — "comparable," Steckel said, "to the smallest children ever measured." Steckel's findings inevitably led to three startling historical ideas. First, stunted childhood growth suggested that slave owners made an economic decision not to feed children particularly well, since they had yet to demonstrate any economic return on such an investment. Second, the adult heights of the male slaves suggested, despite this clear-cut retardation in early growth, phenomenal catch-up growth by the time they reached mature height. And third, this spectacular catch-up growth could only have been achieved if slaves received abundant nutrition during their later growth spurts. In other words, once they had proved their economic worth through work, they were probably very well fed. These speculations about the economic behavior of long-dead nineteenth-century slave masters rested on centuries of bedrock knowledge about the biology of human growth.

However solid their statistical basis, Steckel's findings almost derailed his career. When he came up for tenure review at Ohio State in 1979, he told me, the provost wanted to fire him. Steckel's entire tenure committee threatened to resign, including the chairman of the economics department. Grudgingly, the administration granted him tenure as an assistant professor. "So that's how I got started in this business," Steckel said. "I almost didn't. And I had the faith — let me put it this way — because I had these conversations and correspondence with Tanner, who said, 'Yes, this works.' And I was impressed with him as a person, you see. I read his stuff. This makes sense. He knows what he's doing. He has a great reputation. And it just confirmed in me, 'Well, either this is going to work and I'm going to have a career, or it's not.'"

If there was a turning point, both in Steckel's career and for the new field he championed, it may have occurred in 1982, when mainstream economists still expressed serious reservations about using height data to reach sweeping historical conclusions. So Steckel conspired to bring Tanner to the United States to attend the annual meeting of the Economic History Association. "He knew we were struggling, that the historians, the economists, may not understand," Steckel told me. First Steckel organized groups of pediatricians in Columbus and Cincinnati to subsidize a series of lectures by Tanner in Ohio. Then he dragged Tanner along to Baltimore for the Economic History meeting, where Tanner appeared as a discussant on a Steckel paper. This paper made the preposterous argument (since confirmed) that the average height of nineteenth-century Americans, despite an unprecedented economic expansion, dipped in the mid-nineteenth century.

"Nobody could believe it," Steckel recalled of the reaction. "'This can't be true. And therefore the methodology is wrong, because we all know that heights are genetically determined anyway.' Well, for people who grow up in affluent circumstances, that's true. If you live in an optimum environment, all differences in height are genetic, one hundred percent. What they hadn't seen were very poor, very deprived people, in developing countries or in history. Tanner had, you see. And Tanner understood the medical side of this, and he was kind of authoritative and very calm and very direct."

He was more than that. "I got up and said that, to any auxologist, this was ABC," Tanner told me. "From my point of view as a growth specialist, this was all very simple stuff, nothing controversial about it, very straightforward. But to historians, it was not only controversial, but ridiculous."

"There were still skeptics in the audience," Steckel said, "but that imprimatur — the fact that he would come and do this — had a big impact on thinking in the field. By the mid-1980s, you really didn't have to explain yourself in the journals anymore."

In 1986 Steckel finally published his study on the heights of slaves, with all its sociological and economic implications. About the same time, another doctoral student from Fogel's group at the University of Chicago, the Hungarian-born and American-bred John Komlos, created a dynamic research center at the University of Munich that has since spearheaded a number of important anthropometric studies. Among his methods was sifting through European military logs for height data that he could use to assess historical trends. Between the first slave study in 1979 and the mid-1990s, the "new anthropometry," as Steckel likes to call it, gained momentum and respect. Steckel and others began to use height and other new techniques to probe deeper into the past. By analyzing skeletons — the length of thighbones, the pattern of skull formation, markings on teeth — economic historians could glimpse the standard of living in medieval societies. And then, while all this was going on, some very new, yet very old, data emerged that have helped us understand living conditions in North America more than a century ago — the world as it was before Little Bighorn.

IN 1982, RICHARD L. Jantz, a well-known physical anthropologist at the University of Tennessee, contacted people at the American Museum of Natural History in New York with an obscure question. Did they know the whereabouts of some research material collected by Franz Boas around the turn of the century?

The question prompted a search of the premises, and in a closet that had not been cleaned for perhaps half a century, officials found several large boxes. They contained original data sheets of fieldworkers who had fanned out all over North America in the 1890s to measure a vanishing breed of human subject: some fifteen thousand Native Americans, from Cheyenne to Sioux, Bella Coola to Tsimshian. "The records went to the American Museum, nobody knows when," Jantz recalled. "But probably in the early 1940s, shortly before Boas died, and were never heard from again."

We met Boas in chapter 2, when he accepted an offer from G. Stanley Hall to run the anthropology department at Clark University. As it turns out, Boas remained in Worcester for only two years (time enough to launch some of the most far-reaching studies on the biology of human growth). He left in 1891 to accept the job of heading the anthropological section for the World's Columbian Exposition of 1893, to be held in Chicago. A superb physical anthropologist and a self-described "unregenerate idealist," Boas almost single-handedly used his science to correct the racial and eugenics misinterpretation of nineteenth-century anthropometry. Boas felt strongly the need to document various cultures, in part to refute ethnic stereotypes that were fulminating in American society at the end of the nineteenth century.

The World's Columbian Exposition project was, in Jantz's estimation, "an astonishingly ambitious program." More astute about statistics than many of his contemporaries, Boas knew that he needed a massive number of measurements to detect small physical variations. So beginning in 1891, he trained a cadre of more than fifty amateur anthropometrists and dispatched them to the plains, the Midwest, the Pacific Northwest, and the Northeast to measure Native Americans and document their cultures. The fieldworkers returned with their little worksheets, having recorded the height, to the millimeter, of some 15,000 individuals belonging to more than 200 tribal groups, including 2,500 Plains Indians, primarily Sioux and Crow. The measurements were "arguably the most important" historical data the field had seen, according to Jantz, and represented "some of the highest quality historic records available." Boas computed the mean size (height and skull dimension) of 4,000 individuals by hand, with pencil and paper. But aside from producing a little-known paper, written in German and published in 1895, he never did anything with the data. Jantz and a colleague have challenged Boas's interpretation of some data, specifically his anthropometric studies of immigrants; Jantz told me that Boas was not "entirely honest scientifically at all times." But as for the quality of the Native American data, there is little disagreement among experts. "In terms of his data collection, and the idea that conclusions should be based on data, Boas was light-years ahead of people that were his contemporaries," Jantz said.

Following the discovery of the Boas trove, Jantz translated all of the information into a computerized database. To anthropometric researchers, it was a gold mine. The Plains tribes ranged from the Assiniboin in the north to the Kiowa and Comanche in the south. As they assembled the measurements of adult men in each tribe and plotted out the results, Steckel and Prince were surprised to see that average heights were higher in the middle of the plains than at either the northern or the southern extreme. They were even more surprised to see that the average height of the central Plains tribes — the Crow, Sioux, Arapaho, and Cheyenne — topped 172 centimeters, or nearly 5 feet 8 inches, on average. The Cheyenne (although the number of adult men measured was relatively small) headed the list with an average height of 176.7 centimeters, or slightly less than 5 feet 10 inches.

Steckel and other historians were simply stunned that a nomadic people could be so tall. Tanner was stunned, too. He instantly appreciated the fact that such an average height, if accurate, meant that North America's shrinking and beleaguered Native American tribes were nonetheless taller on average than nineteenth-century Englishmen, taller than native-born Americans of European stock, taller than virtually any national or ethnic group in the nineteenth century, with the possible exception of Australians. "And the very tallest ones," Steckel told me, "were as tall as, almost as tall as, modern Americans. You know, they were 176, 177 centimeters. Which is absolutely remarkable." When Steckel and Prince first announced their findings in 1999, they boldly claimed that these nineteenth-century Native Americans were "the tallest in the world."

Were Boas's measurements credible? "Absolutely," said Jantz when I asked him recently. Indeed, as Steckel told me, "He was known as a great data collector. He was well skilled, and he knew how to train people to take measurements." Were there enough measurements to derive meaningful conclusions? The sample Steckel and Prince used included 1,123 adult men — not ideal in terms of numbers if you're studying a group of living people, but remarkably substantial for a historical cohort long dead. Was there any corroborating evidence? Steckel began to comb the nonscientific literature for clues. He discovered that George Catlin, the itinerant nineteenth-century painter of the American frontier, had commented on the tall stature of the northern Cheyenne in his journals. Although this hardly qualifies as hard scientific data, Catlin wrote that there was "scarcely a man in the tribe, full grown, who is less than six feet in height." Another anecdotal source is Laura Ingalls Wilder's *Little House on the Prairie,* in the chapter titled "The Tall Indian."

But the most important questions were, what could explain such tallness, and what living conditions could nourish that kind of growth? During his work on American slaves, Steckel had developed a concept he calls "net nutrition." It builds on theories of economic measurement proposed by the British economist Amartya Sen and represents an attempt to measure standard of living in a nontraditional way. Steckel's method assesses the overall balance of nutrition in a given society — not only the quality and amount of available food but also the metabolic demands that lifestyle places on the diet, whether through work (farming or, in the case of nomadic tribes, moving around) or exposure to disease. By these measures, Steckel made a surprising argument: the Plains tribes, especially the children, enjoyed a better standard of living than, say, urban children in industrialized societies of the mid-nineteenth century.

"Let's think about how the urban poor of the mid-nineteenth century, the lives of their children, were so different from the lives of children in the Plains," Steckel said. "Certainly one is continuity of the food supply. Here" — he gestured toward the Little Bighorn illustration — "we have abundant protein that makes its way down. It's superabundant, you see. That's the thing. The limiting factor is how much you can carry with your horses. And, indeed, an index of wealth is horses. Even the poor tribes would have at least one horse per person. And so you could carry shelter, the tepees. You could carry two or three months of food. And you didn't have to walk. A lot of energy is expended in walking, and so that is a hardship for hunter-gatherers. It shows up as degenerative joint diseases of the hip and the knees. Remarkably, it starts appearing in the older children of the hunter-gatherers, and that's early.

"Now, breast-feeding probably went on longer as well for these groups," he continued. "That does tend to hold down fertility, but it also provides additional nourishment. If the urban mother has to go to work or is away from the child, then the child is supplemented with food that was probably contaminated." And contamination is the least of it. As Tanner notes in his history of growth, infants and young children in nineteenth-century England were often sedated by their working and absentee parents (or by their caretakers) with a broad range of over-the-counter narcotics. Sold as patent medicines with names like Godfrey's Cordial and Mrs. Wilkinson's Soothing Syrup, these elixirs contained ingredients such as opium, laudanum, and morphine and, on top of everything else, stunted the children's growth.

"So the general environment in which urban people lived was contaminated with waste, bacteria spread by flies, parasites, and the like, which frankly you're not going to find out here," Steckel said. "I would say, therefore, that the exposure to disease is quite a bit lower for children of the plains, with the exception of the occasional episodes of smallpox and measles that came through. The disease element for urban children [was worse], not only because of congested households, congested cities, waste in the streets, waste in the home, [and] clothes that were only occasionally washed. But back in those days, in urban areas, it would have been diphtheria, scarlet fever, and whooping cough — you know, very serious diseases that could take months to get over. I think there was more of that in the cities." The bottom line: "I think the Native [American] kids here in the plains had an advantage."

As we regarded the illustration of Little Bighorn, Steckel listed what he called his leading suspects to explain this surprisingly high standard of living. "The Plains tribes were well nourished," he said. "You see, with horses they could easily hunt for buffalo, which provided this huge reservoir of protein, and from which you could make housing. You had not only abundant protein, which is key — I mean, experiments have shown the importance of protein to the growth of children — but a lot of diverse plant resources, through trade and through gathering. They devised a way of storing meat — the pemmican. You dry buffalo meat, mix it with berries and so forth, bracket it in animal skin, and let it dry into pillow-sized food packs — dried, spiced food that would last through the winter. So they obviously had a good diet. They moved, so they weren't living with parasites in accumulating waste. And they learned, too, how to avoid epidemics. When the first sign of smallpox would appear, they would disband. So their technology was very adaptable to the environment. It is remarkable. They didn't have a deep biological understanding of what was going on in these epidemics, but they knew dispersion. With horses, and with food that they could carry and knowledge of the terrain, they could disperse and meet up three weeks later. It was not a disaster at all, you see?"

Steady food, portable shelter, utter mobility, a primitive but service-able understanding of epidemiology, knowledge of the terrain and how to use it — these factors do not typically figure into most economic as-sessments of quality of life, as Steckel likes to point out. Yet they define a highly successful culture, even as it found itself losing its food supply, its maneuverability, and its very terrain under the relentless press of Mani-fest Destiny. "Certainly they were withering numerically," Steckel con-ceded. "But that's the incredible achievement. Because in the face of all this strife and turmoil, you can produce culture — you know, artifacts like this," he said as he waved his hand to encompass a roomful of, well, museum-quality clothing, sculptures, ceramics, handicrafts, and other items. "The fact that there *is* all this art establishes a minimum standard of living way above subsistence. Here was a rich culture. And it was sup-ported by adapting so well to the ecological environment."

BEFORE WE GET too carried away with the "height as destiny" argu-ment, it's important to point out some obvious limitations in this school of thought. Richard Jantz, for example, is uncomfortable with the degree to which genetics are excluded as an explanation for average height. "The general operating hypothesis is that height will respond to environmen-tal circumstances, and it does," he says. "But they tend to leave out the ge-netic component." He's right, and papers in the field of anthropometry generally ignore any detailed analysis of the relative contribution of ge-netics to height data. Having said that, however, if there's any message that's come out of recent genetic studies, it's how deeply engaged genes are in conversation with the environment. In that regard, the work by

Boas, Tanner, and other growth experts in the twentieth century offered early clues that environment (or, if you will, nurture) can modify, tweak, or even stunt the power of genes (nature), especially in human development. Given the fact that modern medicine recognizes a form of growth failure known as "psychosocial stunting," it's clear that even a negative emotional environment can blunt the action of genes.

The other major problem with modern anthropometry is an inherent limitation in its explanatory power. Whenever Steckel attempted to interpret the heights of the Plains tribes, he reverted to a tentative vocabulary of "I think" or "we believe." In other words, he doesn't know — and can't know — for sure why the Plains tribes were taller and what their height means. Indeed, clear-cut, definitive explanations for disparities in height among historical populations are largely unknowable. All those thoughts about high-protein diets and low-risk disease exposure are reasonable, well-informed, provocative speculations — but speculations nonetheless. Even if the operating hypothesis for all these studies is correct, they may merely raise questions that can never be definitively answered.

However, I'm more forgiving of physical measurement as an index of cultural health than I was when I first encountered these studies — not just because a huge amount of painstaking biology backs them up but also because they offer such a potentially powerful way of examining questions of enormous social and historical importance. If Steckel and the other new anthropometry experts are right, height not only provides a unique window onto past cultures, but it also challenges traditional measures of well-being in our own societies today. Because growth and adult height exquisitely reflect the health of children at precise, well-known "sensitive periods" of development, height studies also become an inferential index on how a society regards the welfare of its children — their care, their nutrition, their hardiness and ability to resist disease. To that end, Steckel and a large international consortium of researchers have been pushing the idea further back in time. Using an admittedly "modest sample" of skeletons from northern Europe, Steckel recently proposed that average heights in the early Middle Ages may have exceeded those in the seventeenth and eighteenth centuries by more than two inches. Meanwhile, the international collaboration recently completed a large project measuring skeletons and other fossilized data to extend height and health studies thousands of years into the past for populations throughout the Western Hemisphere. An even more ambitious program to look at worldwide historical trends using skeletal data is on the drawing board.

All these studies may help biologists understand a contemporary, and very compelling, puzzle in the field of anthropometry — the fact that the average height of native-born American males (that is, men born in this country, not immigrants) has barely changed in birth cohorts since the 1950s. This stagnation in growth is in sharp contrast to trends in Europe, even though the genetic endowment is quite similar. In their book *Worldwide Variation in Human Growth*, James Tanner and Phyllis Eveleth document the increase in average heights of men and women in many industrialized countries during the twentieth century, especially after World War II. In the United States, however, the population's average height has remained essentially flat.

This stagnation in height is an ominous hint, in the view of Steckel and others, that social inequality and poor health care may be taking their toll on vast numbers of American children — an unfolding demographic tragedy that may be disguised by our focus on more traditional economic indicators such as average income and gross national product. In 2004 John Komlos and Marieluise Baur noted that "the Dutch, Swedes, and Norwegians are the tallest, and the Danes, British, and Germans — even the East Germans — are also taller, towering over the Americans by as much as 3–7 centimeters." They went on to venture the hypothesis that "this adverse development is related to the greater social inequality, an inferior health care system, and fewer social safety nets in the United States than in Western and Northern Europe, in spite of higher per capita income."

The last time I visited Steckel, he sat in his office at Ohio State University on a Saturday morning, crunching numbers from a large longitudinal study of American children, searching for patterns in the height data and explanations for those patterns. He hadn't found any yet, but he wasn't deterred. "I believe in the power of this work," he said, "that it can tell a very interesting story."

15

FINAL HEIGHT
Heightism Deconstructed

He who can take no interest in what is small will take false
interest in what is great.

— JOHN RUSKIN, *Modern Painters*

ONE HOT DAY IN the summer of 2005, I found myself standing nervously in a hallway of the third-floor endocrinology clinic at
Children's Hospital of Philadelphia. As Adda Grimberg, a physician and
researcher at the hospital, cast an expert eye on the proceedings, her
colleague Terri Lipman invited me to stand under the wall-mounted
Holtain stadiometer to measure my height. This wasn't one of those
flapdoodle devices you often see in the offices of pediatricians and family practice doctors, with a scale to measure weight and a limp-wristed,
wobbly appendage to measure height. Rather, it was a precision-tooled,
exquisitely accurate British device — a by-product of the Harpenden
Growth Study, in fact — that moved up and down with quiet, well-oiled
clicks.

"Can I keep my shoes on?" I asked, with perhaps more than a trace of
desperation in my voice.

"No shoes!" Grimberg said with a laugh. "That can be an inch or two right there."

"I can use all the inches I can get," I replied. That, alas, has been a lifetime refrain.

As I moved into place, Lipman issued instructions — "Feet, buttocks, back, and head against the wall," she said in a voice as firm as the grip with which she held my chin in an upright position. Then she lowered the shelflike arm of the stadiometer. The machine clicked as the arm grazed the crown of my head.

Although I hadn't been formally measured in decades, I had decided to travel to Philadelphia to learn my final height. Final height describes how tall you are when you have finished the growth process, although many growth experts prefer the term adult height (as pediatric endocrinologist Paul Saenger once put it, "Final height is when you're in the casket"). Despite the finality of the word "final," there's room for a little squish in the definition. Some people add a millimeter or two per year well into their twenties, and several decades later they almost inevitably discover they've misplaced a few millimeters, too. So final height is a somewhat relative term.

Even though I'm in my sixth decade — happily enveloped in family affairs, secure in my personal and professional life — the measurement of my height still taps into primordial feelings of insecurity and anxiety. Where will I fit on the curve of that great vertical splay of humanity? What will it mean — not only for me (for whom the question is, at this point, somewhat anticlimactic), but for my children (for whom it has a bit more urgency)? And does the resulting number say anything about the intrinsic *me* beyond the obvious increments of physical measure? Digging into the archives of adolescent neuroses, I wondered, Will it make me feel small all over again?

Lipman kept firm hold of my chin as she lowered the arm of the stadiometer. She wrote "166.8 cm" in my notebook. Then she repeated the procedure two more times, as growth experts are taught to do. The second and third measurements were both 166.9 centimeters. We would average the numbers and consult the chart.

In an age when functional MRI images of the brain can detect patterns of thought, DNA fingerprints can detect patterns of inheritance, and exquisitely sensitive blood tests can detect the molecular residues of lifestyle, the measurement of height seems like a quaint throwback to the medicine of mustard plasters and bloodletting. But as should be abundantly clear by now, height is nature's picture window on the process of growth, and growth is probably the single clearest index to a child's health. And yet doctors take this measurement so much for granted that it is routinely done wrong.

One of the reasons I went to Philadelphia to be measured is that I knew it might not be done well in a lot of other places. Several years ago, Lipman and her colleagues at the University of Pennsylvania essentially audited the accuracy of childhood height measurements as they were performed at more than fifty family practice centers in the United States. Approximately 70 percent of those measurements were wrong. In a randomized, controlled fashion, the researchers went on to show that when general practitioners were properly trained to do height measurements, the rate of accuracy improved dramatically.

The mismeasure of children, in this country and presumably throughout the world, represents a significant public health issue. It could easily lead doctors to overlook a potential growth problem or, conversely, worry about one when none exists. This is especially true with girls. Grimberg and colleagues published a study in 2005 showing that boys were referred to growth specialists twice as often as girls, even though more than 40 percent of the girls who were referred had real medical problems related to growth, as opposed to only 15 percent of the boys. Mismeasurement also introduces a huge potential for error when calculating a child's growth velocity, or rate of growth, a calculation that is essential to deciding whether growth is abnormal, whether that growth should be corrected by treatment with drugs, and, increasingly, whether a child is likelier to develop serious diseases in adulthood. And finally, some of us do need every inch we can get. When you consider that years and years of growth hormone treatment may add only an inch or two to one's final height and that countless people may have surreptitiously added that much to their heights on driver's licenses and identification cards (I'm not naming any names), it's clear that the mismeasurement of children also has a psychological and cultural impact. After all, the determination of one's percentile on the growth chart represents a kind of test for which the final score is unrelated to preparation, ability, or merit.

We moved to an examining room to translate the centimeters into feet and inches and to consult the chart. After looking over the data for several suspenseful moments, Lipman announced, "You're five feet five and three-quarters inches."

Damn, I thought to myself, not even five feet six! I'd been shedding millimeters as rapidly as hair.

"That puts you," she continued, "between the fifth and tenth percentiles." Among all adult males in the United States, the average, or median, height is a little more than five feet nine, while for females it is slightly more than five feet four. The currently accepted cutoff for normally short versus abnormally short is at the third percentile, which is five feet four for men and four feet eleven for girls.

As the three of us stood in the examining room chewing over the data, such as they were, I asked if my numbers were normal. "Good question," Grimberg said with a laugh. "We like to say that anything between the fifth and ninety-fifth percentiles is normal, but it's totally arbitrary. How do you decide what is short? It's a social thing, an ethnic thing, a financial thing." She went on to make what later impressed me as the essential point: it is crucial for children, parents, and even doctors to stay focused on normal *growth* as the central issue, because when growth is normal, height really doesn't matter. As soon as the focus shifts to height, it flings open that Pandora's box of issues, from familial dynamics and peer relationships to potential drug treatment to the social costs of medical care to the cultural attitudes toward height as a pervasive but often flawed biomarker of intrinsic competence, sexual attractiveness, and evolutionary merit. "You can see two kids with exactly the same growth chart," she said, "and have two completely different encounters with the families." One family will be gunning for growth hormone; the other will be relieved that there is nothing medically wrong with the child. In Grimberg's opinion, it all boils down not to height, but to a person's — that is, a child's — ability to cope with the stresses of being short.

"But I think there's no question that there's discrimination against short people in this culture," Lipman chimed in from the other side of the room. By this point in the odyssey, I was ready to take a more critical look at that bias.

IN 1995 THE *Economist* published a long, stylish, and very witty essay called "Short Guys Finish Last," which argues that discrimination against people of short stature is as pronounced, pernicious, and widespread as any of the other, more familiar forms of discrimination that are proscribed by law, including those based on race, religion, and gender. It's a beautifully written piece that deploys all the familiar evidence of bias in politics, employment, compensation, respect, and sexual attractiveness. The article mentions the well-known auxological chestnut that in all but three American presidential elections during the twentieth century, the taller man won. It mentions the 1980 survey showing that more than half of the chief executive officers at Fortune 500 companies were six feet or taller. It notes that taller people typically receive a larger salary than those under six feet tall. It even comes with its own warning label: short men are advised to "proceed at their own peril. What follows will depress them."

The *Economist* piece has been hailed as a classic distillation of the problem of heightism. It's been posted on Web sites for "little people" and on the excellent Short Persons Support home page (www.shortsupport.org) and has become a touchstone for SHRIMPs (Severely Height-Restricted Individuals of the Male Persuasion). I do want to unpack several of the arguments and burrow a little deeper into what is being said — and what might have been left unsaid.

The article mentions, for example, a 1984 experiment in which two hundred mothers of preschool children were asked to rate the social and cognitive abilities of nineteen-to-twenty-month-old toddlers, based solely on photographs in which the toddlers varied in height. The mothers rated the large boys as more competent than average-size or small boys. (The same effect was seen, to a lesser extent, when the mothers rated similar photos of girls.) Why any parent would presume to understand the social and cognitive ability of a child on the basis of photographic evidence is a mystery to me. Does this suggest, as the article implies, that "as boys grow, the importance of height is drummed into them incessantly"? Or is there another possible explanation? One could argue that this study conflated size with maturation, even though the researchers tried to control for that possibility. Especially between birth and age two, when a child's growth velocity is typically higher even than during the pubertal growth spurt, size is indeed a biomarker of competence and ability, because it is tightly correlated with greater development. A larger child will in all likelihood be an older child, and during the toddler years, as any parent can tell you, an older child — even a slightly older child — will, having benefited from mere weeks of learning, demonstrate astonishing leaps in competence and ability. In other words, the results of this study may not tell us as much about societal attitudes toward height as they seem to. Rather, they may reflect a natural inclination to associate greater size with more advanced development in very young children. It's a subtle point, but one that illustrates how careful researchers must be in separating apparent bias from quite logical confounders.

The article also mentions the research of Henry Biller and Leslie Martel, authors of the 1987 book *Stature and Stigma,* which remains one of the best compendiums of research and literature on the psychology of stature. Much of that book is devoted to a review of psychological issues investigated prior to 1985, but it concludes with a bit of original research: a survey of several hundred college students, both men and women. The study found that men of short stature (between five feet two and five feet five) came up short on a variety of subjective measures. They were, as the *Economist* notes, "less mature, less positive, less secure, less masculine; less successful, less capable, less confident, less outgoing; more inhibited, more timid, more passive; and so on." I asked David Sandberg about this, because he has published widely on the social perceptions of short children, in well-designed, peer-reviewed papers. The first thing he said was, "Well, all those students, even the short ones, were at Brown University. They attended an Ivy League school, so they couldn't have been doing too bad."

These findings, whether of toddlers or college students, reflect social preferences based on factors that are, in every sense of the word, superficial. That, of course, is the essence of a bias. But embedded in the *Economist* article, as in many other accounts, are some foundational premises about that bias. One is that, quite simply, the bias may be acceptable, even justified. Another is that the bias somehow reflects a biological truth — indeed, that it exists as a modern residue of evolution — and therefore that natural selection prefers humans, like all species, big and tall.

First, is height discrimination justified? Are taller people actually more competent and confident? The quickest response is the boilerplate reply to any suggestion of societal bias: people are people, not types. Some tall people are confident and some undoubtedly are not, just as some small people are verbally aggressive and others are not. In any event, the measurement of qualities such as confidence and security is always very tricky. In animal research, for example, scientists have spent decades assessing the role of size in fighting competence, but have only recently recognized that elusive qualitative factors such as "persistence" have significant impact on outcomes. What does it mean, for example, that women in both Western cultures and China rate stature high among the desirable qualities of a potential mate? What especially does it mean in societies where the divorce rate is about 40 percent? Perhaps it means that sexual selection in humans is not all it's cracked up to be. Perhaps it means that tall stature in particular, and appearance in general, is not a particularly good predictor of enduring domestic or emotional happiness, to say nothing of the long-term relationships that scientists increasingly argue are key to reproductive success in humans. Perhaps it means that the desire for a taller mate reflects, at some level, a potential spouse's own emotional insecurities. And perhaps it suggests that any evolutionary advantage attached to a tall male spouse might well be undone by the rupture to kinship support and familial cooperation that occurs in a broken family. Because human childhood and adolescence is so long and so crucial to intellectual and psychosocial maturation, constancy in what the ethologists call pair bonding is probably more important in humans than in almost any other animal species. After all, it prepares the next generation for *its* mating choices.

Since we're obviously breaking eggs to make a few rhetorical omelets, let me raid the henhouse and push this argument a little further. What exactly does it mean to say that someone is confident or has high self-esteem? We can obviously accept self-esteem at face value: the person has wedded self-knowledge to a sense of inner security, has reached an enviable comfort zone with his or her values and temperament, and knows and likes himself or herself in a way that allows, as much as is humanly possible, the fulfillment of his or her potential. If that is the case, more power to them. This is the kind of swagger and sway we all would desire. But I wonder, more on the basis of anecdotal experience than of the psychological literature, just how much the notion of self-esteem tells us in this context. The armchair psychologist in me would argue that it is just as likely that some people only appear confident, that self-esteem is merely the outerwear for unearned arrogance or a particularly insufferable form of self-delusion. We all know people who have a higher opinion of themselves than what, for lack of a better term, objective reality might otherwise suggest. By standard measures, these people may well rate very high in self-esteem; by more critical analysis, their self-esteem may be misplaced and socially costly. Indeed, self-esteem can often produce a kind of collateral emotional damage. We all know self-confident people who are also so self-centered that they are indifferent to the emotional and social cues around them. Indeed, in many work and interpersonal situations, open-mindedness, conciliation, negotiation, and perhaps even a dollop of self-doubt might be more useful than supreme self-confidence. At a time when psychobabble has become the white noise of our culture, self-esteem has become one of the most misleading indices of psychological health. And the fact that tall people are perceived to be more confident and to have greater self-esteem may have absolutely nothing to do with their long-term desirability as leaders and mates.

Similarly, what exactly does it mean that CEOs tend to be tall? Does it suggest that tallness is a marker for leadership or decisiveness or business acumen? I am unaware of any research that makes that case. Rather, tallness may be a marker for social entitlement (because children from middle- and higher-socioeconomic backgrounds have historically grown a little more quickly and seen more of their genetic growth potential enabled by a generous environment) and perhaps for the kind of social dominance that begets deferential treatment, which is something many tall men begin to notice around puberty. When Phillip Lopate speaks of the "noblesse oblige" of tall men, he implies not only privilege but the expectation that it will be recognized.

The most interesting research about the adult mindset of the short-stature male remains the rare longitudinal study that looks at height throughout a person's life. Forget the boardroom; forget even the college locker room. Instead, focus on the high school cafeteria, the grade school homeroom, and possibly even the crib. In 1994, as the *Economist* article notes, David Blanchflower and James Sargent of Dartmouth College made a preliminary pass at some of the same data that informed Andrew Postlewaite and colleagues' 2004 study. (Remember that Postlewaite and his colleagues found a connection between height at age sixteen and earning power; see chapter 9.) This was the first report (albeit not quite as robust as Postlewaite's) to suggest that a boy's height during adolescence affected his wages as an adult, with tall teenagers earning more.

If something is indeed happening during adolescence, at least two other things might be true. First, as has already been argued in this book, the income gap may have as much to do with pubertal timing and early versus late maturation as it does with height, in which case height is a kind of red herring for a different psychodevelopmental turmoil. Postlewaite and colleagues believe that they controlled for pubertal timing in their study, but experts on puberty point out that the strategy the researchers used was indirect and may not have fully captured the impact of early versus later maturation. Second, adolescent psychology, not height, might be the truly important target of intervention — and that intervention might just as easily (and more cost-effectively) be psychological therapy as height-augmenting pharmacology. The sensitivity of the adolescent years might also argue for more aggressive adult oversight and intervention during this critical period. That view is supported, at least in part, by research by David Sandberg and the Wessex Growth Study in England showing that short children in early to late adolescence show few if any signs of psychological dysfunction and in fact are difficult to distinguish from normal-size children by standard measures. Finally, in the past several years, there has been a little research suggesting that the income gap between big and small adults may have very early origins — possibly fetal origins. A group in Finland, collaborating with David Barker, whom we met in chapter 1, has published an epidemiological study indicating a correlation between low birthweight and adult socioeconomic measures, including lower wages. All of this research suggests that the connection between adult height and salary is much more complicated than one might initially think. As Dan Silverman, one of Postlewaite's collaborators, has said, figuring out what it is about adolescence, or adolescent size, that so strongly affects adult earning power is an enormously difficult problem. "Ultimately, I think it's going to be a pretty tough nut to crack," Silverman noted.

ALL WELL AND good, you say, but so what? It's clear that a bias in favor of tall people is deeply ingrained in the human psyche and probably reflects an ancient evolutionary predilection. As the *Economist* piece points out, "Mating opportunities are, at least in evolutionary terms, the ultimate prize of status," and it goes on to cite examples from "traditional cultures" to suggest that tall men typically dominate in tribal affairs. "Among anthropologists," the article notes, "it is a truism that in traditional societies the 'big man' actually is big, not just socially but physically." The not-so-subtle implication is that perhaps the bias is not really a bias at all. Perhaps the perceived mating success and status of taller, bigger individuals reflects a deep biological truth, forged in the crucible of evolutionary time.

The evolutionary importance of size has long been an issue of fascinating biological debate. In the nineteenth century, an American paleontologist named Edward Drinker Cope formulated what has become known as Cope's rule. Many people know the first part of Cope's rule: over the huge gulps of evolutionary time, measured in millions of year, natural selection tends to select for increasing size within a species. Few people talk about the second part of the rule: larger species, at least on the basis of the fossil record, are more likely to go extinct. In more recent times, analysis of the fossil record and expanded use of databases has suggested that, indeed, species tend to evolve to be larger. But this has in turn begged a very big question: If species tend to evolve to be larger, why isn't the earth overrun by behemoths of every stripe?

The answer, implied by life all around us and yet still beyond the snare of scientific proof, is that there are countervailing selective forces that tug evolution in the other direction, valuing smaller size. One of the reasons we haven't figured out the evolutionary advantages of smaller size may be that we simply haven't bothered to look for them very carefully. In an extensive review of the scientific literature, the Swiss biologist Wolf U. Blanckenhorn has suggested that "research biases" partially explain the lack of work exploring the evolutionary advantages of smaller body size, adding that "demonstrations of the disadvantages of large body size are relatively uncommon in the literature, even though they are crucial for explaining why we are not surrounded by gigantic organisms."

The most profound advantage of small size, in terms of human evolution, was suggested by Charles Darwin. "In regard to bodily size or strength," he wrote in *The Descent of Man*,

> we do not know whether man is descended from some small species, like the chimpanzee, or from one as powerful as the gorilla; and, therefore, we cannot say whether man has become larger and stronger, or smaller and weaker, than his ancestors. *We should, however, bear in mind that an animal possessing great size, strength, and ferocity, and which, like the gorilla, could defend itself from all enemies, would not perhaps have become social; and this would most effectually have checked the acquirement of the higher mental*

qualities, such as sympathy and the love of his fellows. Hence it might have been an immense advantage to man to have sprung from some comparatively weak creature. [Italics added.]

Boiled down to its speculative essence, what Darwin seems to be saying is that there would have been greater selective pressure on smaller, weaker hominids to develop intelligence, cooperation, and other advanced social skills — along with the brainpower necessary to remember and execute those mental skills in order to compensate for the absence of sheer size and brute force. If, as the evolutionary record clearly shows (and as Darwin obviously appreciated), larger relative size confers social and sexual dominance in most species, what makes humans unique is that evolution has bestowed on us cognitive and emotional capacities that can temper and, in circumstances where culture (in every sense of the word) flourishes, create alternatives to the "law of battle" that governs social relations and hierarchies in so many other species. It is worth noting that, according to primatologists, both gorillas and chimpanzees are stronger than humans. The upper body strength of chimps, for example, allows them to dominate humans in physical encounters. It may also be worth noting that the bonobo, an Old World primate distinguished by its pacific social cooperation and matriarchal social organization, was originally known by another name. At the time of its discovery in the 1930s, the bonobo was more commonly known as the pygmy chimpanzee.

I read that passage from Darwin over the phone to primatologist Frans de Waal. He wasn't familiar with it, but he considered it "very insightful" and went on to talk about the role of size in the evolution of human intelligence and sexual selection. He noted, for example, that when our human ancestors first left the forest to inhabit the African savanna, they were not so much predators as prey. Thus, out of self-protection, these early hominids had to adjust their social structures to create greater group cohesion. "Once you have a highly cooperative society," de Waal said, "size helps a little, but in terms of predators, there's probably a higher premium on being fast, being able to run to the nearest tree." He conceded that "within the group, it's probably to your advantage to be big and strong, for status. Females who attach to males are going to look for that." But, as so much of de Waal's research on apes suggests, the story is always a little more complicated than a simple evolutionary advantage of greater size. In pair-bonding species such as humans, he continued, "females are selecting for all sorts of other things. Is the male easy to live with? Is he a good protector? Does he provide food? As soon as the female settles in with the male, then being dominant is not the only thing. And this has been playing out for several million years. So in our human lineage, we've had quite a long history of developing family relations, and once you settle into that social structure, then male characteristics other than big and strong are going to count."

If Darwin was correct (his interesting suggestion has provoked, as far as I can tell, surprisingly little experimental inquiry or theoretical comment), the relative smallness and weakness of smaller human ancestors might be responsible for nothing less than the birth of civilization.

LET ME SPIN out this idea a little more, because it not only expands on the evolutionary implications of small physical size among humans, but it also leads us to consider values related to social skills that are rarely, if ever, addressed in studies on earnings per inch, questionnaires about sexual attractiveness, or surveys of business leadership. Perhaps the metrics used in the vast literature that explores the advantages of tallness miss the biggest evolutionary point of all. How do you measure the value of complex social skills relationally and longitudinally, over an extended period of time? How do you measure the social value of sympathy, one of the higher evolutionary traits mentioned by Darwin? How do you measure the value of the love of one's fellows? How do you measure something like cooperation?

The answer may be that the complexity of our brains has become more important, over evolutionary time scales and in the social context of complex and sophisticated human communities, than the physical size of our bodies. The farther removed we are from the "law of battle," as Darwin put it, the less size may matter as an absolute, and the more social cooperation emerges as a value — perhaps the key value — for survival of the fittest. De Waal has emphasized again and again the importance of cooperative behavior in primates. In *Our Inner Ape,* he rails against the simplicity of the "selfish gene" model and stresses how central cooperation is to complex social structures. With the advent of advanced brain imaging techniques, scientists have begun to pinpoint neural activity related to cooperation, and the initial findings suggest that cooperation is hard-wired into our brains — indeed, is linked to classic neural circuits of reward and satisfaction. In a 2002 article in the journal *Neuron*, for example, researchers at Emory University in Atlanta reported on an experiment in which women were asked to play the Prisoner's Dilemma while their brains were being scanned in a functional MRI machine. This is a classic laboratory game in which cooperation between two players results in the maximum benefit for both. In this experiment, scientists were able to observe that the act of cooperation in the game activated the pleasure pathway in the brain. In neural terms, it felt good to cooperate, to suppress the impulses of self-interest.

There have been other, similar findings that underpin what has been called the biology of altruism, but the main point is that humans — at least some humans — are wired to derive pleasure from cooperation, which in a way may be what Darwin had in mind when he spoke of "the love of his fellows." And I'm tempted to speculate on how physical size — especially smaller than average physical size — might be linked to cooperation, not necessarily in the evolutionary sense, but perhaps more in the way developmental size can shape behavior.

Take emotional cooperation, for example. Although there's at best modest evidence in support of it, researchers such as Nancy Bayley and Mary Cover Jones suggested half a century ago that late pubertal development (with its concomitant delay in the growth spurt) seems to produce personalities that are more emotionally attuned to themselves and to other people. This observation is rooted in an archaic, personality-based psychology of the 1950s, but these were astute educational psychologists who knew their subjects extraordinarily well, and I suspect there's something to their insight.

To the extent that the suggestion may be true, my guess is that it's not necessarily an altruistic instinct. A lot of that emotional intelligence probably has to do with being able to read social cues quickly and accurately, especially during childhood and adolescence, in a bid to avoid conflict, physical confrontation, and perhaps humiliation. Indeed, this instinct probably has a lot in common with fear conditioning. But there may be social value in those developmental experiences. Growing up small, you tend to develop particularly acute antennae to pick up these signals. So the impulse is not without self-interest. But understanding another person's emotional weather — what might be causing it, how it is changing — is part and parcel of this behavior and is the psychological substrate upon which we develop cooperative and altruistic qualities such as sympathy, empathy, and concern, which can affect the duration of a relationship, which in turn can affect the quality of parenting, which in turn may affect the reproductive success of our offspring as they attempt to send *their* genes hurtling into the future. Primatologists make the point that one of the most sophisticated social skills in animals is the cognitive ability to understand another creature's pain or distress. Part of the emotional openness I'm attributing to smaller stature no doubt stems from the developmental experience of victimhood: if you've been teased, verbally abused, discriminated against, or physically attacked or humiliated for no particular reason, you are more likely to sympathize with the tribulations of someone else in a similar situation. Again, this is not a virtue of small size; it is the involuntary diploma we receive for being different.

Consider social cooperation. We all know bullies in the workplace; they demand rather than elicit cooperation, and they are singularly tone-deaf to the social and emotional implications of such a crudely demanding environment. If you have grown up on the small side, you probably do not have much experience in getting your way in social or workplace situations by intimidation, coercion, or sheer physical will. Instead, in the desire to avoid conflict and defuse confrontational situations, you have spent a lifetime developing skills for getting along, seeking solutions, finding the middle ground, and including as opposed to excluding. You can draw on these skills in the workplace. But cooperation should not be confused with accommodation. Small people are no different from other mature, self-interested adults who want to get their way; they strategize just like everyone else to win in social situations. They just know that one option rarely available to them is to throw their weight around, so they have to be a little more socially sophisticated (or, perhaps, manipulative) than that. They cultivate skills such as persuasion, logic, patience, and negotiation to win an argument. They understand that cooperation, at a fundamental level, means equality and partnership, which is a very hard social idea to accept in any dominance hierarchy, whether in the highlands of Central Africa or in the boardrooms of Wall Street. Indeed, ethologists are increasingly making the point that although primates may achieve dominance through physical attributes such as size and strength, they *maintain* dominance only through social negotiation. And for the same reasons that small people are so sensitive to emotional exclusions, they are more likely to be much more sensitive to social inequities. If you have ever been excluded, discriminated against, or ridiculed as a member of a class, an ethnic group, or a religion, you are much quicker to recognize the same dynamic when it applies to someone else. Equal opportunity, after all, is a touchstone of cooperation.

Let us consider the "higher mental qualities," as Darwin put it. Cooperation requires both mental agility and behavioral restraint. Just as the short kid or geek who is also a precocious motor mouth has become a cliché in countless teen movies, it is doubtless a cliché to mention here that growing up on the small side is a powerful inducement to hone your verbal skills; probably the most well-developed muscle in a small adolescent is the tongue (assuming, of course, that you are the beneficiary of favorable genetic and environmental resources). When you can't rely on strength or size for conflict resolution — when you are the "weaker," in Darwinian terms, in a physical confrontation (or even a looming physical confrontation) — you must rely on other, less violent forms of aggression. One is verbal reasoning; another is humor. It's always been my impression that growing up on the small side encourages the development of a sense of humor and quick, nimble repartee. Is that cooperation in the technical sense? Probably not. There's as much animosity embedded in wit as there is a willingness to get along. But the recent work by Barry Bogin and John Locke suggests that there is in fact evolutionary value in these compensating adolescent behaviors: verbal dexterity improves mate selection, they believe, and enhances our reproductive success.

As for behavioral restraint, it is probably no accident that in the 2002 brain study mentioned earlier, one of the two brain regions that lit up dramatically during cooperation was a chunk of neural tissue above the eyes known as the orbitofrontal cortex. This forehead extension of the brain represents the location of a vast increase in neural real estate in humans as compared to other mammalian species, including primates such as chimpanzees. Indeed, some neuroscientists consider it one of the defining anatomical hallmarks of the human species. And one of the orbitofrontal cortex's principal functions, scientists now believe, is to control impulses.

Last but not least — certainly for the continued evolution of the species — let us consider sexual attraction and cooperation. From the perspective of popular culture, concepts such as the alpha male and dominance hierarchy have probably obscured our evolving notion of what mating success means in human biology. For the vast majority of species, reproductive success boils down to mating, producing offspring, and turning them loose — immediately in the case of many species; after some degree of dependency and nurture in others. But one of the major themes of primate biology in recent years has been that reproductive success in humans does not rely solely on physical dominance, and — to an extent unique among all animal species — does not end with mating and childbirth. Human reproductive success requires sustained and committed social nurture over many, many years in order to ensure that our offspring will send *their* genes — along with a remnant of ours — farther into the future. And the nature of that social nurture probably has little to do with physical size.

Much has been made of tall stature as a positive and sexually appealing attribute in contemporary mating. A recent article in the *New York Times Magazine* reported that women seeking sperm donors refuse donations from men who are less than five feet nine in height. It turns out that those women may be using a relatively poor marker in their search for genetic fitness. The desire for a tall mate may be the behavioral equivalent of a vestigial organ — something that once may have had evolutionary value in more primitive epochs but appears less useful in our current environment. In terms of reproductive success, size appears to matter less as an animal society gets more socially complex. As we've seen, many animals concoct alternative mating strategies. Researchers who study primates have lately come to realize that lower-ranking males who engage in affiliative behaviors — grooming and other social interactions — seem to elicit female choice. If reproductive success entails more than copulation, as it clearly does in humans, then an entirely different suite of skills comes into play. In *The Evolution of Primate Behavior*, Alison Jolly makes the point that evolutionary pressures in humans uniquely select for "quick thinking, social responsiveness, cooperation, manipulation, and memory and foresight for events in the past and the future." None of those traits requires a big body, and yet they seem to make us more successful, more adaptable, *fitter* creatures. Jolly writes, "Mental agility buffers environmental change, and has replaced reproductive agility."

Hence it is becoming harder to figure out just what role height (or size) plays among all the physical traits that contribute to sexual selection. If a recent report in *Nature* is to be believed, evolution has paid attention to traits other than size all along. A team of researchers headed by Robert Trivers, the Rutgers University professor who helped to put the "biology of altruism" on the map, added a new and fascinating wrinkle to the physical side of sexual selection: physical movement, specifically dance. In a long-running study based in Jamaica, Trivers and his colleagues established that dancing ability, independent of all other aspects of a young man's visual appearance, made a measurably positive impression on women, in part because dance reveals bodily symmetry, and bodily symmetry may be a particularly good marker for developmental stability — that is, it suggests (as does height) that a male's biological growth and maturation have been normal and healthy. As the authors note, "Dance in Jamaica seems to show evidence of sexual selection and to reveal important information about the dancer." I once attended a dance concert at a Dance Theater Workshop in New York with its founder, David White. At one point during the performance, David leaned over and whispered to me, "You know who the best dancers are? The short ones. A low center of gravity belongs to the small." Movement, perhaps even more than size, signals balance, symmetry, and health.

I'd like to say two things here. One, I've always been a pretty good dancer. And two, it didn't do me much good for the better part of my early adulthood. I may have been revealing important information about myself, but I don't think I was particularly receptive to information traveling the other way. Perhaps that lingering sense of feeling less complete, less physically mature in adolescence, made me cling to the old self-image I possessed as a young teenager — as I suspect many small or late-maturing men do — rather than allowing me to transmit (and receive) updated information as my adult self. The little adolescent chip in my brain reminded me that junior high school girls thought of me as a "cute little *nut*"; the girl I adored in high school went out with college guys. My voice wasn't deep enough; my beard wasn't full enough; my inseam wasn't long enough. And, like a lot of men, tall as well as short, I internalized those insecurities and embraced them so fiercely that I couldn't, for a long time, even hear the warblings of sexual attention when they finally came my way. Eventually, I learned that all those qualities of cooperation we've just discussed — altruism, emotional sensitivity, sense of humor, sense of equity — contribute a great deal to sexual attractiveness, too.

When I say I confused sexual maturity with sexual worthiness, I mean to suggest that the residue of adolescent uncertainty led me to believe that I couldn't compete sexually, couldn't provide satisfaction as my more developed (more muscular, taller, or more mature) male peers. I learned of the errors in my self-appraisal in part because a number of my girlfriends (when I finally had any) confessed to making the same mistake in their mate selections: the physical size of the box, in effect, revealed nothing about the quality of the merchandise inside. That's not to say tall or strong men are always insensitive oafs or that short men are always charming and egalitarian. It's just that there isn't much correlation — at least in the minds of my girlfriends — between the outward appearance and the inner reality. In support of this point, I cite no less authoritative a source than the film *Revenge of the Nerds,* in which Betty Childs, the prettiest cheerleader in school, thinks she's just had sex with her jock boyfriend, Stan, but discovers that her partner was a geek named Lewis, who wore a mask to hide his identity.

> BETTY: Oh, Stan! That was wonderful. You did things to me you've never done before. [Lewis removes his mask.] Ach, you're that nerd!
> LEWIS: Yeah . . .
> BETTY: Oh, God, you were wonderful.
> LEWIS: Thanks.
> BETTY: Are all nerds as good as you?
> LEWIS: Yes.
> BETTY: How come?
> LEWIS: Because all jocks think about is sports. All we ever think about is sex.
> BETTY: What's your name?
> LEWIS: Lewis.
> BETTY: Lewis, would you meet me after the pep rally tonight?

Granted, there's more than a little wish fulfillment in that passage, but there's also a kernel of truth. The ultimate test of evolutionary fitness is surviving to reproductive age and getting one's genes into the next generation. Heightism suggests a collective, unconscious sexual selection for tallness, a kind of proxy vote by natural selection for larger size. But as we've seen in the animal literature, alpha males often turn off their dates, and females don't always find larger size and dominant behavior sexy. The more sophisticated cognition becomes, the more female sexual selection may be based on qualities other than large size (tallness) and physical domination — qualities that might advertise a mate who will stick around and share the burden of raising those children. If Darwin was right, there must be some selective advantage to intelligence, compassion, "the love of his fellows" — and possibly, by extension, smaller size. Humans, in fact, may be in the midst of an evolutionary experiment in which those aggressive, fast-talking, smart-alecky, compassionate, Napoleonic wannabes are sending plenty of their equally selfish genes into the future, too. And given the results we've had with tall presidents of late, I'm ready for a short one.

Okay, I admit it; I've been generalizing shamelessly for pages. Maybe my infatuation — maybe *everybody's* infatuation — with size is misplaced. It matters, yes, but it's not the only thing that matters. In terms of human growth, it often matters only temporarily. And there are reasons to argue that, given the evolving social complexity of human civilization, it is destined to matter less and less. In their work on the focusing illusion, Daniel Kahneman and David Schkade pointed out that it's easy to exaggerate the importance of a single issue when assessing the quality of one's life. In their experiments, Kahneman and Schkade addressed the specific issue of where one lives, but the issue could just as easily have been stature, obesity, facial appearance, ethnicity, race, or whatever. The moral of their research is that "nothing you focus on will make as much difference as you think."

I, of course, attributed all my woes and unhappiness as an adolescent to small stature, as if there weren't plenty of other possible reasons for the emotional bumps of those tumultuous years. If you've paid attention, however, you've probably noticed that the dateline on my various childhood traumas and tribulations kept changing: Pennsylvania, Massachusetts, Michigan, Illinois. My family moved around a lot; that undoubtedly contributed to my sense of psychological displacement. I blamed height, of course, and I know that feeling must have persisted into college, because I recall a conversation with a professor about how socially alienated I felt, still a mouse while others were mating like rabbits. His reply was a global (albeit anecdotal) rejoinder to heightism, to the *Economist* article, to the whole issue of sexual selection and selfish genes. "I have two words for you," he said. "Carlo Ponti." For those who may not recognize the name, Ponti is a small, almost dwarfish, and not conspicuously handsome Italian film producer. His wife is, and has been since 1957, Sophia Loren.

Darwin may or may not have been right, but I like to think that there was at least a little biological wisdom in the role he projected for smaller, weaker humans in the evolution of the species — in its encouragement of the higher mental qualities and behavioral virtues we associate with civilized life. There's a widely accepted bit of epigrammatic sophistry that's made the rounds recently, which holds that life is just an adult version of high school with money. It sounds amusingly astute, but it reflects a surprisingly narrow — dare I say *small?* — notion of what life is about.

Not long ago, I attended a banquet with three Nobel laureates from the sciences. Two of them were distinctly smaller than average in size, and the other, though tall, spoke with almost painful self-deprecation about his awkward and out-of-sorts adolescence. As I looked around the table, assessing these three men as physical specimens, I found it difficult to imagine them near the top of any teenage dominance hierarchy. I couldn't picture them dating the high school homecoming queen, heading a fraternity, or even employing the classic C-student social skills said to be the passport to success in adult society and commerce. By the standards of adolescent society, it was about as pathetic a collection of human capital as you could imagine. Nonetheless, these men had managed to change the world — indeed, *reconfigure* the world, from its fundamental knowledge to its lifesaving medicines — with their "higher mental qualities" and, along the way, make it a little more civilized.

EPILOGUE
"If They Get a Good Nipple . . ."

> The world of living things, like the world of things inanimate,
> grows of itself, and pursues its ceaseless course of creative
> evolution. It has room, wide but not unbounded, for variety
> of living form and structure, as these tend towards their
> seemingly endless but yet strictly limited possibilities of per-
> mutation and degree: it has room for the great and for the
> small, room for the weak and for the strong. Environment and
> circumstance do not always make a prison, wherein perforce
> the organism must either live or die; for the ways of life may be
> changed, and many a refuge found, before the sentence of un-
> fitness is pronounced and the penalty of extermination paid.
>
> — D'ARCY THOMPSON, *On Growth and Form*

THE MASSIVE SOW, five hundred pounds of promissory bacon
and mother's milk, rolled on her side and began grunting in a guttural,
snuffly rhythm, which is a pig's way of announcing that for the next minute or two, and not much longer, she will be lactating. Instantaneously,
thirteen piglets started squealing and swarmed over her belly, fighting for
a nipple. Up until that moment, I had never given a moment's thought to
the origin of the word "piggyback," but it came vividly to life in the noisy,
shoving, rooting scrum of thirteen eager mouths angling for access to the
two rows of nipples, an upper and lower deck of nourishment, that lined
the mother's belly. Some literally rode the backs of others; some bur-
rowed under the squirming mass, suggesting a distant kinship with moles.

This is survival at its most elemental for baby pigs. These piglets were
only ten days old, and almost all of them were the same size, about five

pounds. But in each of the five litters arrayed in the barn, there was always one little pig that was littler than the rest. The runt. And in every case, the runts threw themselves into the scrum, fighting for nourishment, wriggling toward a teat, getting trampled or shouldered out of the way, diving back in, giving as good as they got.

"Amazing," said John Crispino, the pig farmer, who has witnessed this springtime ritual for thirty-five years and has never lost his sense of amazement.

We're not much of an agrarian society anymore, but "runt of the litter" has survived as a potent metaphor. It speaks not just of size; it equates small size with diminished prospects, undesirability, perhaps even abandonment. But I wanted to see exactly what life was like for the runt of a litter, so one day in April, I drove up to visit Crispino at his pig farm in upstate New York.

As the sow continued to huff and grunt, Crispino pointed out the runt near the back of the sow's belly. The little fellow had his eyes closed and his ears tucked back in a brief moment of streamlined ecstasy. "In that case," John said, shaking his head with an "I told you so" laugh, "he fought for a good nipple, and he got it."

Crispino takes very good care of his animals — vast trays of bagels were drying in his garage, because he thinks they're particularly good feed for very young pigs — and in fact had been up late the night before trying to nurse one of the runts, which hadn't been eating and finally died. "I put him on a nipple," John explained as we walked back to the barn, "but he just wasn't growing."

Clichés die hard. These little pigs have more in common with the Olivia of children's literature than the mud-wallowing creatures of popular imagination. They are of the faintest, rosiest pink, with a short, pristine coat of soft hair. When they're not scrambling for a teat, piglets are nosy, curious newborns. Nobody picks on the runt. Mostly, they wander around the pen or plop down under heat lamps, which keep them warm. They tend not to scrap or fight, and then only if a pig from one litter gets mixed in with another litter. So powerful is their sense of smell that the outsider is sussed out by scent, not size or appearance. And if the runt of the litter gets enough nourishment to survive those first few days, he (or she) will never catch up in size, according to Crispino, but he may well have a bigger heart than his larger companions.

"See, [the runts] can't compete with the bigger pigs," he was saying as another sow began grunting and her piglets began swarming over her belly. "They just have a disadvantage. If there's a bigger pig, he'll take whatever nipple he wants. They'll win sometimes. But when the runts get a little bigger? If they decide to fight, he'll win — or, if it's a she, she'll win. They're very scrappy and aggressive. They've got to fight for it every time. That's the way it is."

Runts, as it turns out, may not grow as large as their littermates, but they'll grow. They may not have all the advantages of size, but they can compete — indeed, they may have the advantage of attitude to compensate for their lack of size. And there was something that John Crispino said that struck me as having as much metaphorical weight as being a runt: "They will compete," he said, "and they will grow, if they get a good nipple."

If they get a good nipple . . .

If the nipple stands not only for nourishment of the literal nutritional sort but also for nurture in general, for environment in the largest possible sense, for all the kinds of sustenance we can draw on as growing creatures, then what's true of the runt is undoubtedly true of all of us, regardless of size. If we get a good nipple, we will compete. We will grow. We will be fine.

I should have remembered that before I called my old grade school nemesis, Albert Destramps.

AS I PREPARED to call Albert, whom I'd neither seen nor heard from since we mixed it up on those cold mornings on the playground in 1962, I had a curious mix of feelings. On the one hand, I was exhilarated at having tracked him down in a small town in southeastern Massachusetts, although finding him was more a matter of luck than detective work. He'd moved away from Whitinsville, the town where we attended sixth grade, but had later moved back to a nearby village. At the same time, I felt a guilty twinge of voyeurism, dropping down out of the blue, searching for signs of how his life, like mine, might have been shaped by biological size and childhood events. As I heard his voice — still a fine, delicate tenor, after all these years — I explained who I was and why I was calling. I mentioned that I had been short while growing up. "Tell me about it!" he replied instantly. In other words, I had the right Albert Destramps. I was even prepared to be a little saddened by a life whose trajectory I had perhaps, in a small, boyish, and bullying way, deflected into an orbit of frustration and limitation.

I could have saved myself the trouble.

First of all, Albert didn't remember me. That was neither surprising nor insulting; it had been more than forty years, and my family had lived in Whitinsville for exactly nine months, barely enough time to gestate a friendship or, for that matter, a lasting animosity. Second, Albert was not scarred by his small stature, although it had been a prominent feature of his childhood. Four decades removed from the playgrounds of our youth, he was still the feisty, scrappy, self-described wiseass I recalled from elementary school.

As he filled me in on a bit of his background, I realized that personal history was exactly the sort of thing that children never bother to find out about their friends (or victims) as they're chasing and tackling and pounding them. Albert was originally from Woonsocket, Rhode Island, which is about fifteen miles from Whitinsville, and it turns out that our fathers had worked for the same company, a large textile mill called Whitin Machine Works. He told me that his parents divorced when he was two years old, and that he had lived with his father, stepmother, and older sister. When he was in fourth grade, he continued, he had missed a month of school while doctors ran tests on him at a hospital in Worcester, Massachusetts, "to try to find out why I was so small." They couldn't find any medical reason for his short stature, but it was dramatic. In seventh grade, right in the middle of middle school, at the peak of bullying and cruelty, he was three feet eleven. I asked if he had ever been a candidate for human growth hormone therapy. He said, "I have no idea." That made sense. His workup in Worcester would have been in 1960. Just two years earlier, Dr. Morris Raben of Tufts University had pioneered the first attempt to use growth hormone in small-stature children, and at the time, the hormone was incredibly rare.

I can't say Albert's life was a triumph of indomitable spirit over physical adversity. He was held back a year in high school because, he explained, he was something of a class clown and flunked English. At age sixteen, he moved to Boston to live with his mother's new family. He never attended college, and although he eventually trained as an electronics technician at a technical school, he described his work history as "wandering from job to job every few years." In 1986 he moved to a village near where we had both gone to school; his wife was a senior scientist at one of the larger biotech companies in the Boston area. They did not have children. At the time I touched base with him, he said he was between jobs.

When you hear a personal history like this, you naturally wonder whether the effects of physical size and the tormenting events of childhood were somehow father to the man. Was he teased? "Oh, yeah," Albert recalled. "Especially in junior high school. But there were two factions in school. One was the tough kids, then the other kids. I used to hang out in the middle. But sometimes the tough kids were on my side and would protect me, because they liked me. I was a wiseass, but I was also spunky. And for my size, I was also pretty fast."

Aside from the teasing and minor scraps, the only real fight he'd had was in high school. "This was the year I moved to Boston," he recalled. "There was a kid who was picking on me. He must have been a head taller and about thirty pounds bigger. He liked to think of himself as a bully [and was always bothering me]. One day I was walking down the hall and — *bam*! He slugged me in the shoulder. I was getting tired of this, so I walked up to the kid, jabbed my finger in his chest, and said, 'Got a problem? You want to fight?' I told him I would fight him, as long as it was on my terms, in my place. He said yes, and I said, 'Meet you in the wrestling room.'"

It turns out that Albert, too, was a wrestler, and he had a winning record on the junior varsity team at Brookline High School. "I pinned him two times in about two minutes," Albert recalled. "He never came back to school the next year. It was kind of humiliating to be beaten up by the class shrimp." The more he talked, the more it became clear that Albert had no problem with self-esteem. His "inner shrimp" had the roar of a lion, and he insisted that his childhood on the receiving end of taunts and teasing had had no lasting effect. "I'm of the opinion that good things come in small packages," he said. "I might be little, but don't underestimate the little guy."

Oh, and he remembered that schoolyard game perfectly. In fact, he recalled many more details than I did. He remembered that it was called relievio (probably a variation of that well-known game). He remembered that the lone boy in the middle at the start of the game sometimes called out the name of a classmate as the person he had to tackle.

"Do you remember who you tackled most in the sixth grade?" I asked eagerly.

"No," he replied.

"It was me."

"That was a long time ago," he said. And so it was.

SIZE MATTERS, JUST as genes matter, to the growth of children, the development of boys, and the shaping of male psychology. Since the discovery of the double helix structure of DNA in 1953, the discovery of genetic engineering in 1973, and the completion of the Human Genome Project in 1999, we have been inundated with an exhilarating but also indoctrinating flood of information about the roles of genes in human biology, including the biology of growth and physical size. So much so that one might easily forget that genes, for all their power, are still shaped by the environment in which they act. If not, natural selection, evolution, and the current manifestations of humankind we see all around us would make no sense.

Call it nurture, call it the nipple, call it whatever you wish — the environment is beginning to reemerge, after half a century of DNA-mania, as an equal partner in the biology of humans. This is hardly news. Indeed, the oldest experiments (although they are possibly apocryphal) in the field of psychosocial stunting go back to the twelfth century. King Frederick II of Sicily, convinced that an infant's acquisition of language was innate, managed to obtain and then isolate several newborns, forbidding any human speech or sound in their presence. The infants, though well nursed, ended up profoundly stunted and eventually died. The potential genetic ramifications of this kind of misanthropic nurture came home to me during a conversation with Richard Tremblay, the Canadian expert on physical aggression.

"It's amazing what we're learning now," he said. "It's not the genes in themselves. It's how they are expressed and the affect of the environment on the expression of the genes." He mentioned that a woman who smokes during pregnancy, for example, will affect the expression of the genes that are forming the brain of her child, and that by reducing the stress that prompts some pregnant women to smoke in the first place, you can indirectly control the activity of fetal genes.

But it goes far beyond mechanical behaviors such as smoking. "The quality of the relationship between a mother and a child has a major impact on the expression of the genes," he continued. "So that love, simply, affects how genes are expressed." He mentioned the work of Michael Meaney, a colleague at McGill University in Montreal, who has for twenty years been exploring the molecular biology of mother and child relationships — especially what happens when mother rats lick the rat pups when they're born. "They first showed that the more the rats are licked, the longer they live," Tremblay said. "And the puzzle was, how can you explain this? They published a paper in 2004 showing that the licking affects the expression of genes, especially in the hypothalamus-pituitary axis, the stress system. If you're not licked, these genes are not expressed. And so your stress system is not functioning properly, and your life will be shorter because your stress system is not working well. And we're pretty sure that it's the same thing with the parent-child relationship early on. A major part of the problems in the long run with children who have been abused and neglected — it's not the abuse in the sense of the psychological aspect of it. It's more the genetic impact — the impact of the environment on gene expression."

The implications, as Tremblay was quick to point out, are profound, because they suggest that fundamental social interactions — parenting, formal education, peer relationships, and even psychotherapy — exert their effects, at least partially, through the manipulation of genes. "Listen, what we're doing here is showing that your work as a psychotherapist or your work as an educator is probably more powerful [than what we are doing as scientists] — is probably, in that sense, more dangerous in terms of negative effect. If you're not doing the right thing, you can have long-term consequences. So it's not only the biologists who can do wrong. The people that are interacting with others can have long-term impact."

In terms of parenting, of child-rearing, of physical interactions with bullies in early childhood, of indirect verbal confrontations with bullies in later childhood, of a vast array of human social interactions, this is an enormous thought: that social activity, depending on its quality and timing, can be affirming or hostile to the healthy functioning of one's genes. So it's not a matter of just getting a nipple; it's getting a *good* nipple, in every sense. Environment matters just as much as size, because it either enhances or undermines the latent power of our genetic inheritance. When I embarked on this book project, I dwelled on memories of physical confrontations and episodes from my youth. As I finish it, my memories have shifted to a different form of experience, namely nurture: my father's presence at every sporting event in which I participated, my mother's fierce and unyielding advocacy for my educational opportunities, the love of grandparents and extended family, and daily acts of nurture and support too distant and dim to recollect fully. Who knew that, at some level, nurture was a form of genetic engineering?

And in a larger ecological sense, who suspected that small size was an expression, however involuntary, of good citizenship on an endangered planet? Bigger people place a greater burden on the environment. As Wolf Blanckenhorn has observed (as have many others), larger animals, be they humans or bivalves, require more metabolic energy (that is, food) to keep going, and they place greater demands on the environment. Put bluntly, they consume more food, take up more space, generate more waste (and pollution), and use up a greater share of our finite and increasingly precious resources. From the point of view of macroecology, which has become a very important word to scientists, they are a drag and a drain. Smallness, in terms of people, but also in terms of a guiding philosophy, is probably better for the planet and, in strictly evolutionary terms, better for its future.

And this point leads me to an especially pleasant obligation: allowing James Tanner to have the final word. "It is not certain," he wrote in 1981, "that growth up to the maximum size permitted by the genes is essential for the full expression of a person's intellectual and cultural potential . . . On a limited Earth with a scarcity of energy available to its inhabitants, we must suppose that nature, at least, prefers small people to big ones."

NOTES

Introduction: "Squirt"

PAGE

1   *British bulldog:* The playground game occurred during the winter of 1962–63 at what was then known as the Hill Street School in Whitinsville, Massachusetts. The school no longer exists. One of the boys, Albert Destramps, confirmed the nature of the game in a telephone interview, Feb. 7, 2005.

4   *"for the rest":* Garry Trudeau, "My Inner Shrimp," *New York Times Magazine,* Mar. 31, 1996, p. 76.

    "all the children": Garrison Keillor, *News from Lake Wobegon,* Minnesota Public Radio (see "Lake Wobegone," Wikipedia.org/wiki/Lake_Wobegon).

    average Dutch citizen: For Dutch heights, see B. Bilger, "The Height Gap," *The New Yorker,* Apr. 5, 2004, pp. 38–45. For a recent account of pygmies, see P. Salopek, "Who Rules the Forest?" *National Geographic,* Sept. 2005, pp. 74–99.

5   *"We both knew":* Trudeau, "Inner Shrimp," p. 76.

7   *Physical aggression in humans:* For research on physical aggression, see chapter 5.

8   *as much as an inch taller:* This fact has been known for nearly three hundred years. In 1724 observations to that effect were published in the *Proceedings of the Royal Society,* submitted by a parish clergyman named Joseph Wasse. Cited in James M. Tanner, *A History of the Study of Human Growth* (Cambridge: Cambridge University Press, 1981), p. 101.

9   *"It's a no-brainer"*: David Sandberg, personal interview, Oct. 22, 2004, New York.

12   *"keeps you thinking"*: John Updike, *Self-Consciousness: Memoirs* (New York: Knopf, 1989), p. 45.
     "An overvaluation of the normal": Ibid., p. 47.

13   *"small and uncannily rodent-like"*: L. Grove, "A Mag-nate for Parody by Bushnell," *New York Daily News*, June 13, 2005, p. 24.
     "I'm into low costs": J. P. Williams, quoted in R. Johnson, "Red State Humor Turns Blue," *New York Times*, June 13, 2005, p. C-1.
     "stood on the shoulders": Sir Isaac Newton, quoted in W. Gratzer, "Feet of Clay," *Nature* 433 (Feb. 10, 2005): 575–76.
     "The remark . . . is generally": Gratzer, "Feet of Clay," p. 575.
     In the very first sentence: "Rabbit Angstrom, coming up the alley in a business suit, stops and watches, though he's twenty-six and six three. So tall, he seems an unlikely rabbit." John Updike, *Rabbit, Run* (New York: Fawcett, 1960), p. 5.
     "To be tall": Phillip Lopate, *Portrait of My Body* (New York: Anchor, 1996), p. 22.
     "is taller by almost": Jonathan Swift, *Gulliver's Travels* (New York: Norton, 2002), p. 24. In an instance of science imitating satire, anthropologists in 2004 reported the discovery of unusually small, "Hobbit-like" human skeletal remains on the Indonesian island of Flores, which is, ironically, not far from where Swift located his hypothetical Lilliput in 1699. See J. Diamond, "The Astonishing Micropygmies," *Science* 306 (Dec. 17, 2004): 2047–48, and Swift, *Gulliver's Travels*, p. 14.

14   *reached back to Tacitus:* For Tacitus and the military roots of heightism, see chapter 9.
     "the secret self": Leslie Fielder, *Freaks: Myths and Images of the Secret Self* (New York: Simon & Schuster, 1978).
     "We didn't lie": *Freaks*, Tod Browning, director, 1932.
     dwarf subjects: On Isabella d'Este and the role of dwarfs in European courts, see Betty M. Adelson, *The Lives of Dwarfs: Their Journey from Public Curiosity Toward Social Liberation* (Piscataway, N.J.: Rutgers University Press, 2005), pp. 11–21.
     Las Meniñas: In *Looking at Pictures*, Kenneth Clark describes the inherent fascination that freaks of nature held for Velázquez. In the painting, the Infanta Doña Margarita balks at being painted and her ladies in waiting (*las meniñas* in Spanish) have brought two dwarfs, Maribárbola and Nicolasito, to entertain her. Clark writes that Maribárbola "affronts the spectator like a blow from a muffled fist" and speculates that Velázquez had a "strange and poignant relationship" with the dwarfs and buffoons depicted in so many of his paintings. "No doubt it was part of his duties to record the likenesses of these Court favorites," Clark notes, "but in the main Velasquez room of the Prado there are as many portraits of buffoons as there are of the royal family (nine of each). Surely that goes beyond official instructions and expresses a strong personal preference. Some of his reasons may have been purely pictorial. Buffoons could be made to sit still longer than royal persons, and he could look more intensely at their heads. But was there not also the feeling that their physical humiliations gave them a reality which his royal sitters lacked?" (*Looking at Pictures* [New York: Holt, Rinehart, and Winston, 1960], pp. 38–40).

15   *Several monarchs attempted:* For dwarfs, see Adelson, *Lives of Dwarfs*, p. 11, and Tanner, *History of the Study*, p. 121. For giants, see Nancy Mitford, *Frederick the Great* (New York: Harper & Row, 1970), p. 26, and James M. Tanner, "A Short Walk

Through the Garden of Auxological Delights," in *Human Growth in Context,* ed. F. E. Johnston, B. Zemel, and P. B. Eveleth (London: Smith-Gordon, 1999), pp. 3–4.

John Hunter and his agents: See W. Moore, *The Knife Man: The Extraordinary Life and Times of John Hunter, Father of Modern Surgery* (New York: Broadway Books, 2005), pp. 199–215. I am grateful to Nelson Smith for bringing this account to my attention. The Hunterian Museum at the Royal College of Surgeons in London displays many of Hunter's anatomical specimens, including the skeleton of Byrne (who reportedly measured eight feet four inches when he died in 1783) and that of Caroline Crachami (a Sicilian dwarf who measured twenty inches at death). For background on the collection, see www.rcseng.ac.uk/services/museums/collections.html.

"acquisitions": "An African Pygmy," *Zoological Society Bulletin,* Oct. 1906, pp. 1–2. Also see P. V. Bradford and H. Blume, *Ota Benga: The Pygmy in the Zoo* (New York: St. Martin's Press, 1992). For an account of the Midget Village and other dwarf exhibitions in the 1930s, see M. Raabe with D. Kinske, *Memories of a Munchkin: An Illustrated Walk Down the Yellow Brick Road* (New York: Back Stage Books, 2005), pp. 27–47. In the film *The Wizard of Oz,* Raabe played the Munchkin coroner who declares the Wicked Witch of the West dead.

The Littlest Groom: See D. Bianculli, "Worst Television of the Year," *New York Daily News,* Dec. 29, 2004, p. 80. Bill Paolantonio, the program's executive producer, called the show a "celebration of diversity," but most TV critics shared the view of Ray Richmond, who accused Fox of "successfully lowering the standards of reality to the level of bedrock," adding that the show "embodies wretched taste on so many levels that it's difficult to convey it fully." Reuters, "Fox's Planned Dwarf Dating Show Sparks Controversy," MSNBC, Jan. 30, 2004, www.msnbc.msn.com/id/4100620/ (accessed Feb. 20, 2006); Ray Richmond, "'Littlest Groom' an SNL Skit Come to Life," MSNBC, Feb. 17, 2004, www.msnbc.com/id/4292766/.

The tallest presidential candidate: See, for example, J. Mathews, "The Shrinking Field," *Washington Post,* Aug. 3, 1999, p. C-1. The heights of all the presidents are given at www.uvm.edu/~tshepard/tall.html.

16 *A fascinating study:* Nicola Persico, Andrew Postlewaite, and Dan Silverman, "The Effect of Adolescent Experience on Labor Market Outcomes: The Case of Height," *Journal of Political Economy* 112 (2004): 1019–53.

"writing about growth hormone": David B. Allen and Norman C. Fost, "Growth Hormone Therapy for Short Stature: Panacea or Pandora's Box?" *Journal of Pediatrics* 117 (1990): 16–21.

"Bond always mistrusted": Ian Fleming, *Goldfinger* (New York: Penguin, 1959), pp. 28–29.

U.S. Food and Drug Administration: See P. Callahan and L. Abboud, "A New Boost for the Vertically Challenged," *Wall Street Journal,* June 11, 2003, p. D-1. On bioethicists' opposition, see J. Lantos, M. Siegler, and L. Cuttler, "Ethical Issues in Growth Hormone Therapy," *Journal of the American Medical Association* 261 (Feb. 17, 1989): 1020–24.

17 *thousands of men:* See C-C Ni, "Stature of Limitations in China," *Los Angeles Times,* Mar. 31, 2005, p. A-1. In a story reporting similar trends in Singapore, a doctor is quoted as saying that most patients undergoing limb-lengthening surgery "seem to be coming from the entertainment industry" ("Small but Increasing Number of

Singaporeans Go Under Knife to Be Taller," *Channel News Asia*, Jan. 26, 2006, www.channelnewsasia.com/stories/singaporelocalnews/views/190637/1/html).

"over nine feet": 1 Samuel 17. For other details of the David and Goliath story, see *The New Oxford Annotated Bible*, 3rd ed., ed. M. D. Coogan (New York: Oxford University Press, 2001), pp. 425–27. Goliath's height of "six cubits and a span" was "about nine and one-half feet."

18   *"the secret of life":* James Watson, *The Double Helix* (New York: Atheneum, 1968), p. 197.

Human Genome Project: A. Allen, "The Disappointment Gene: Why Genetics Is So Far a Boondoggle," *Slate*, Oct. 18, 2005, www.slate.com/id/2128292/?nav=navoa.

19   *"physical stature is greater":* Quoted in J. Komlos, M. Hau, and N. Bourguinat, "The Anthropometric History of Early-Modern France" (working paper, University of Munich, 2001). (For a slightly different translation of this famous passage, see Tanner, *History of the Study*, p. 162.)

British film documentary: Seven Up, Paul Almond, director, 1964; *7 Plus Seven*, Michael Apted, director, 1970; *21 Up*, Apted, 1977; *28 Up*, Apted, 1984; *35 Up*, Apted, 1991; *42 Up*, Apted, 1998; and *49 Up*, Apted, 2005.

20   *One of many recent studies:* A. Raine, C. Reynolds, P. H. Verables, S. A. Mednick, and D. P. Farrington, "Fearlessness, Stimulation-Seeking, and Large Body Size at Age Three Years as Early Predispositions to Childhood Aggression at Age Eleven Years," *Archives of General Psychiatry* 55 (Aug. 1998): 745–51.

How could mere height: See R. H. Steckel, "Historical Perspective on the Standard of Living Using Anthropometric Data," in *What Has Happened to the Quality of Life in the Advanced Industrialized Nations?* ed. E. N. Wolff (Northampton, Mass.: Edward Elgar, 2004), pp. 257–74.

"If you are asking": James M. Tanner, personal interview, Sept. 29, 2004, Dunkeswell, Eng.

21   *Research has shown:* On British children during the Industrial Revolution, see Tanner, *History of the Study*, p. 156. On French males and Napoleonic wars, see Vernon Kellogg, "Eugenics and Militarism," *Atlantic Monthly*, July 1913, pp. 99–108. On postwar Japanese males, see Phyllis B. Eveleth and James M. Tanner, *Worldwide Variation in Human Growth*, 2nd ed. (Cambridge: Cambridge University Press, 1990), pp. 111–12, 206. On height of Americans, see C. L. Ogden et al., "Mean Body Weight, Height, and Body Mass Index, United States, 1960–2002," *Advance Data from Vital and Health Statistics* 347 (Oct. 27, 2004): 1–18.

23   *When I wondered:* See J. G. Kingsolver and D. W. Pfennig, "Individual-Level Selection as a Cause of Cope's Rule of Phyletic Size Increase," *Evolution* 58 (2004): 1608–12. For a book-length treatment of related issues, see John Tyler Bonner, *The Evolution of Complexity by Means of Natural Selection* (Princeton, N.J.: Princeton University Press, 1988).

24   *"Clearly, something happens":* Andrew Postlewaite, quoted in Natalie Angier, "Short Men, Short Shrift: Are Drugs the Answer?" *New York Times*, June 22, 2003, p. 12.

I've often wondered: See Stephen S. Hall, "Short Like Me," *Health*, Jan./Feb. 1996, pp. 98–106.

Recent psychological studies: See, for example, J. Ross et al., "Psychological Adaptation in Children with Idiopathic Short Stature Treated with Growth Hormone or

Placebo," *Journal of Clinical Endocrinology and Metabolism* 89 (Oct. 2004): 4873–78.

25 *"I think it had"*: Paul Simon, quoted in L. F. Martel and H. B. Biller, *Stature and Stigma: The Biopsychosocial Development of Short Males* (Lexington, Mass.: Lexington Books, 1987), p. 8.

1. *"Chunky": Gestation and Birth*

30 *In 1938 two British scientists:* See James M. Tanner, *Fetus into Man: Physical Growth from Conception to Maturity,* 2nd ed. (Cambridge: Harvard University Press, 1990), pp. 41–42. The original article is A. Walton and J. Hammond, "The Maternal Effects on Growth and Conformation on Shire Horse–Shetland Pony Crosses," *Proceedings of the Royal Society B,* 125 (1938): 311–35.

31 *The advent of ultrasound:* See B. B. Goldberg, "Obstetric US Imaging: The Past 40 Years," *Radiology* 215 (2000): 622–29, and Stephen S. Hall, *Mapping the Next Millennium* (New York: Random House, 1992), p. 148.

mécomètre: See James M. Tanner, *A History of the Study of Human Growth* (Cambridge, Cambridge University Press, 1981), p. 478.

By the 1860s: Ibid., pp. 262–63.

highest at five months' gestation: Tanner, *Fetus into Man,* pp. 38–39.

Peak weight gain: Ibid., p. 41.

32 *Spectacular photographs:* For more recent images of developing fetuses, see L. Nilsson and L. Hamberger, *A Child Is Born,* 4th ed. (New York: Delta, 2003), and Alexander Tsiaras, *From Conception to Birth: A Life Unfolds,* text by Barry Werth (New York: Doubleday, 2002).

formal echo-portraits: S. Lubell, "The Womb as Photo Studio," *New York Times,* Sept. 23, 2004, p. G-1. These prenatal photo sessions may come at an unsuspected cost. Recent research by neuroscientists at Yale University has raised the possibility that ultrasound scans may disrupt the normal and necessary migration of neural cells in the developing fetal brains of unborn mice. Scientists are now looking to see if the same thing occurs in monkeys. See J. Giles, "Ultrasound Scans Accused of Disrupting Brain Development," *Nature* 431 (Oct. 28, 2004): 1026.

"period of the embryo": Tanner, *Fetus into Man,* p. 36. Given the continuing public debate about embryo research and when life begins, it is worth noting that Tanner, one of the leading twentieth-century experts on human biology, writes that the period of the embryo "is considered to begin two weeks after fertilization and ends eight weeks after fertilization" (p. 36). During this "hazardous period," about two-thirds of fertilized eggs either fail to implant in the uterus or spontaneously abort, "usually without the mother knowing anything has happened" (p. 37).

The earliest phase: K. L. Moore and T.V.N. Persaud, eds., *Before We Are Born: Essentials of Embryology and Birth Defects,* 5th ed. (Philadelphia: W. B. Saunders Company, 1998).

Upon the grid: For a layperson's account of development by organ system, see D. Sanghavi, *A Map of the Child: A Pediatrician's Tour of the Body* (New York: Holt, 2003).

homeobox genes: See Stephen S. Hall, "Head Stuff and Tail Stuff," in Hall, *Mapping the Next Millennium,* pp. 193–214.

"tool kit genes": Sean B. Carroll, *Endless Forms Most Beautiful: The New Science of Evo Devo* (New York: Norton, 2005). This is not only a lucid description of the master genes that control early development, it also explains how these genes have been profound agents of change in the shape, structure, and size of countless organisms, including humans, over time.

33   *Then it's all building:* For general benchmarks of gestation, see Tanner, *Fetus into Man,* pp. 38–40. For the creation of 100,000 neurons, see Tsiaras, *From Conception to Birth,* p. 9.

By this time: Recent research by Fred Gage and his colleagues at the Salk Institute in La Jolla, California, has identified neural stem cells that promote the creation of new neurons under certain conditions in adults. It remains unclear how many new brain cells can be created, but it appears possible to increase the number of cells in the brain by at least a little, and this may be true in other organs as well, such as the liver and muscles. See Fred H. Gage, "Neurogenesis in the Adult Brain," *Journal of Neuroscience* 22 (Feb. 1, 2002): 612–13.

During the last ten weeks: Tanner, *Fetus into Man,* p. 40.

34   *In 2004 doctors at Loyola:* "At 8.6 Ounces, She's Littlest Survivor," *New York Daily News,* Dec. 21, 2004, p. 34; Loyola University Health System, "Loyola Discharges Smallest Surviving Baby in the World," news release, Feb. 8, 2005.

Studies have shown: Tanner, *Fetus into Man,* pp. 43–47.

But a longitudinal study: M. Hack et al., "Chronic Conditions, Functional Limitations, and Special Health Care Needs of School-aged Children Born with Extremely Low-Birth-Weight in the 1990s," *Journal of the American Medical Association* 294 (July 20, 2005): 318–25. More popular accounts of this research include D. Grady, "Very Premature Babies Are Still at Risk, Researchers Find," *New York Times,* July 20, 2005, and R. Rubin, "Tiniest Babies More Likely to Have Problems," *USA Today,* July 20, 2005, p. 5-D.

If children are small: Tanner, *Fetus into Man,* pp. 44–46.

35   *"I'll get the map":* This and all other quotes, unless otherwise noted, are from David J. P. Barker, personal interview, Oct. 2, 2004, East Dean, Eng. The atlas Barker fetched was M. J. Gardner, P. D. Winter, and D.J.P. Barker, *Atlas of Mortality from Selected Diseases in England and Wales, 1968–1978* (Chichester, Eng.: Wiley, 1984).

36   *"epidemiological studies":* D. Barker, "The Midwife, the Coincidence, and the Hypothesis," *British Medical Journal* 327 (Dec. 20, 2003): 1428–30. This provides a good background account of the original epidemiology.

"This decay must betoken": Ibid., p. 1428.

37   *in the* Lancet: For the original report of the Hertfordshire data, see D. J. P. Barker, P. D. Winter, C. Osmond, B. Margetts, and S. J. Simmonds, "Weight in Infancy and Death from Ischaemic Heart Disease," *Lancet* ii (1989): 577–80.

Barker hypothesis: For detailed accounts of the Barker hypothesis from its main proponent, see D. J. P. Barker, *Mothers, Babies and Health in Later Life,* 2nd ed. (Edinburgh: Churchill Livingston, 1998), and Barker, *The Best Start in Life: How a Woman's Diet Can Protect Her Child from Disease in Later Life* (London: Century, 2003). For a good lay account, see Ellen R. Shell, "Interior Designs," *Discover,* Dec. 2002, pp. 49–53, and Ellen R. Shell, *The Hungry Gene: The Sci-*

ence of Fat and the Future of Thin (New York: Atlantic Monthly Press, 2002), pp. 173–90. For current thinking of fetal programming, a good recent summary can be found in Peter Gluckman and Mark Hanson, *The Fetal Matrix: Evolution, Development, and Disease* (Cambridge: Cambridge University Press, 2004).

"As a group": Barker, *The Best Start*, p. 67.

A clinic run: Tanner, *History of the Study*, pp. 96–97.

Some twenty thousand infants: Ibid., pp. 255–56.

38 *A reduced rate:* See Tanner, *Fetus into Man*, p. 43.

First, they looked: For results in other populations, see Barker, *The Best Start*, for Finnish (pp. 63–64), Dutch (pp. 81–83), Indian (p. 71), and American (p. 69) studies.

39 *"irreversibly"*: W. Y. Kwong, A. E. Wild, P. Roberts, A. C. Willis, and T. P. Fleming, "Maternal Undernutrition During the Preimplantation Period of Rat Development Causes Blastocyst Abnormalities and Programming of Postnatal Hypertension," *Development* 127 (2000): 4195–202. See also T. P. Fleming et al., "The Embryo and Its Future," *Biology of Reproduction* 71 (2004): 1046–54. For a recent popular summation of prefertilization events in the oocyte that may affect later embryonic development, see Stephen S. Hall, "The Good Egg," *Discover*, May 2004, pp. 30–39.

40 *In 2005 Barker and colleagues:* D.J.P. Barker et al., "Trajectories of Growth Among Children Who Have Coronary Events as Adults," *New England Journal of Medicine* 353 (Oct. 27, 2005): 1802–9.

"The faster growing sex": Barker, *The Best Start*, p. 53.

41 *At first there was:* See David Sharp, review of *The Fetal Matrix* by Gluckman and Hanson, *RedNova*, Mar. 29, 2005, www.rednova.com/modules/news/tools.php?tool=print&id=139257 (accessed July 21, 2005), and C. Mooney, "From Womb to Tomb," *SAGE Crossroads*, June 16, 2003, www.chriscmooney.com/articles.asp?year=2003. For more detailed criticisms of the hypothesis, see R. Huxley, "Commentary: Modifying Body Weight Not Birthweight Is the Key to Lowering Blood Pressure," *International Journal of Epidemiology* 31 (2002): 1051–53.

"The importance of events": "The Fetal Origins Hypothesis — Ten Years On," editorial, *British Medical Journal* 330 (May 14, 2005): 1096–97.

"Mounting evidence": Matthew W. Gillman, "Developmental Origins of Health and Disease," *New England Journal of Medicine* 353 (Oct. 27, 2005): 1848–50.

"catch-up growth": J. G. Eriksson et al., "Catch-up Growth in Childhood and Death from Coronary Heart Disease," *British Medical Journal* 318 (1999): 427–31.

incidence of kidney failure: D. T. Lackland et al., "Low Birth Weights Contribute to High Rates of Early-Onset Chronic Renal Failure in the Southeastern United States," *Archives of Internal Medicine* 160 (2000): 1472–76.

future earning power: D. J. P. Barker et al., "Infant Growth and Income 50 Years Later," *Archive of Disease in Childhood* 90 (2005): 272–73.

42 *It is as if:* Patrick Bateson et al., "Developmental Plasticity and Human Health," *Nature* 430 (2004): 419–21.

"For our hunter-gatherer": Sharp, book review.

In one Norwegian study: Tanner, *Fetus into Man*, p. 45.

"Leaving the uterus early": Ibid., p. 46.

Experts have calculated: Ibid., pp. 46–47.

"considerable portion": Ibid., p. 45.

43   *38 percent:* Hack et al., "Chronic Conditions."
      Swedish babies: Tanner, *Fetus into Man,* p. 43.
      This state-sponsored system: G. Critser, *Fat Land* (Boston: Houghton Mifflin, 2003),
      pp. 36–37. For a more extensive account of puericulture, see P. M. Stearn, *Fat History: Bodies and Beauty in the Modern West* (New York: New York University Press,
      1997), pp. 156, 195–201.

2. "Longitude" and "Pondus Absolutum": A History of the Growth Chart

45   *"We're already seeing":* This and all other quotes, unless otherwise noted, are from
      James M. Tanner, personal interview, Sept. 29, 2004, Dunkeswell, Eng. For additional background on Tanner's career, plus his assessment of many other key figures in the study of human growth, see James M. Tanner, "A Short Walk in the
      Garden of Auxological Delights," in *Human Growth in Context,* ed. F. E. Johnston,
      B. Zemel, and P. B. Eveleth (London: Smith-Gordon, 1999), pp. 1–14. See also Stephen S. Hall, "With His Bells and Curves, Human Growth Science Grew Up," *New
      York Times,* Mar. 1, 2005, p. F-3.

47   *"biology, psychology, and sociology meet":* See James M. Tanner, *A History of the
      Study of Human Growth* (Cambridge: Cambridge University Press, 1981), p. 490.

48   *He dropped a note:* During the September 2004 interview, Tanner related that
      Medawar, in an article prepared for a D'Arcy Thompson Festschrift, had argued
      that there was no such thing as an adolescent growth spurt. Tanner, in correcting
      this obvious mistake, made a lifelong friend. "Peter, I may say, was an older brother
      of mine," Tanner told me. "That was the relationship we had. Very close."
      "to give a course": Tanner, *History of the Study,* p. 490.
      "Few people in England": Ibid., p. 349.
      "was the obvious": Ibid.

49   *A French nobleman:* Ibid., pp. 102–6.

50   "perhaps the greatest polymath": Stephen Jay Gould, introduction to D'Arcy Thompson, *On Growth and Form,* ed. J. T. Bonner, abr. ed. (Cambridge: Cambridge University Press, 1992), p. ix.

51   *"If parents would once":* Percy Boulton, quoted in Tanner, *History of the Study,*
      p. 194.
      "descriptive geometry": Tanner, *History of the Study,* pp. 231–33.
      "the question was the same": Ibid., pp. 394.

52   *"I began the experiments":* Christian Friedrich Jampert, quoted ibid., p. 89.
      "The amount of growth": Ibid., p. 90.
      "in those [measurements]": Ibid.
      J. G. Roederer initiated: Tanner, *History of the Study,* pp. 96–97.

53   *One of them is:* Ibid., pp. 122–41.

54   *Quetelet tailored:* Ibid., pp. 130–36.
      Cross-sectional studies: On the differences between cross-sectional and longitudinal studies, see James M. Tanner, *Fetus into Man: Physical Growth from Conception
      to Maturity,* 2nd ed. (Cambridge: Harvard University Press, 1990), pp. 10–14.
      "mere averages": Charles Roberts, quoted in Tanner, *History of the Study,* p. 179.

55   *Not only did Galton:* See Martin Brookes, *Extreme Measures: The Dark Visions and
      Bright Ideas of Francis Galton* (New York: Bloomsbury, 2004); D. V. Kevles, *In the*

Name of Eugenics: Genetics and the Uses of Human Heredity (New York: Knopf, 1985); and Tanner, *History of the Study,* pp. 180–85.

Percentiles and standard deviations: In the clinical literature, much of the variation in human growth is rendered not in percentiles, but in standard deviations (SDs). Once the mean (average) of height, for example, has been established in a population, there is a statistical formula to determine degrees of variation from that average. One SD above and below the mean captures roughly two-thirds (about 68 percent) of the entire population and corresponds to about the sixteenth and eighty-fourth percentiles. In this case, the SD is typically written as 1 SD (indicating the eighty-fourth percentile) or −1 SD (sixteenth percentile). For heights that lie farther from the mean, 2 SDs corresponds to slightly less than the ninety-eighth percentile and −2 SDs corresponds to slightly more than the second percentile. Most pediatric endocrinologists consider anything from 2 to −2 SDs to fall within the normal height range. In 2003, when the FDA approved growth hormone therapy for short but normal children, the cutoff for approved use was −2.25 SDs, which equals the 1.2 percentile.

56 *"We do not know":* Francis Galton, quoted in Tanner, *History of the Study,* p. 181.

"a simple and clear statement": Tanner, *History of the Study,* p. 394.

notably in Boston: Bowditch, later dean of Harvard Medical School, is credited with launching North American studies by reporting a survey of twenty-five boys and girls in 1872; see ibid., pp. 185–96.

57 *"small in stature":* C. R. Pierpont, "The Measure of America," *The New Yorker,* Mar. 8, 2004, pp. 48–63.

In August 1888: Tanner, *History of the Study,* pp. 234–35.

"the father of child study": Ibid., p. 234.

"His vast domain": Ann Hulbert, *Raising America: Experts, Parents, and a Century of Advice About Children* (New York: Knopf, 2003), p. 37.

"a firm champion": Tanner, *History of the Study,* p. 234.

by the time the train: Boas described negotiations with Hall in a letter to his wife dated Sept. 3, 1889. In R. P. Rohner, ed., *The Ethnography of Franz Boas* (Chicago: University of Chicago Press, 1969), pp. 111–13.

Shortly after arriving: For the Worcester longitudinal growth study, see Tanner, *History of the Study,* p. 236, and Douglas Cole, *Franz Boas: The Early Years, 1858–1906* (Seattle: University of Washington Press, 1999), pp. 141–44.

58 *"have their anatomies felt":* Cole, *Franz Boas,* p. 142.

head length and breadth: For some results from the study, see Franz Boas and Clark Wissler, "Statistics of Growth," in *Report of the Commissioner of Education for 1904* (Washington, D.C.: Government Printing Office, 1905), pp. 25–48.

"tempo of growth": Tanner, *History of the Study,* p. 235.

"Though he couched it": Ibid.

"young children grow": Franz Boas, quoted ibid., p. 240.

"He found that the shorter": Tanner, *History of the Study,* p. 240.

59 *If that were Boas's:* For Boas's seminal papers on human growth, see Franz Boas, "The Growth of Children," *Science* 19 (May 6, 1892): 256–57; Franz Boas, "The Growth of Children — II," *Science* 19 (May 20, 1892): 281–82; Franz Boas, "The Growth of Children," *Science* 20 (Dec. 23, 1892): 351–52; and Franz Boas, "The Relation Between Physical and Mental Development," *Science* 93 (Apr. 11, 1941): 339–42. The early papers represent the impenetrable algebra.

Published in 1898: Tanner, *History of the Study,* pp. 241–42.

60   *Coming so soon:* See also Stephen Jay Gould, *The Mismeasure of Man* (New York: Norton, 1981), for a good discussion of how physical measurement could assume pernicious social implications. Boas addresses the issue of eugenics in Franz Boas, *Anthropology and Modern Life* (1928; reprint, New York: Dover, 1986). Boas's original findings, however, have recently come under challenge; see C. S. Sparks and R. L. Jantz, "A Reassessment of Human Cranial Plasticity: Boas Revisited," *Proceedings of the National Academy of Sciences* 99 (2002): 14, 636–39.

      "Boas's findings": Tanner, *History of the Study,* p. 250.

      At age seventy-two: Boas's later work, such as "The Relation Between Physical and Mental Development" *Science* 93 (1941), reflects his lifelong search for links between tempo of growth and mental traits. While admitting that data linking physical and mental development were "very scanty," Boas nonetheless cited his own data comparing skeletal growth and intelligence quotient and concluded, "A study of the data collected shows an unexpectedly high relation between intelligence quotient and stature" (p. 341).

61   *"were already taller":* Franz Boas, quoted in Tanner, *History of the Study,* pp. 246–247.

      "each individual has": Ibid., p. 249.

      Two other American scientists: James Tanner, "Brief Biographies," in *Cambridge Encyclopedia of Human Growth and Development,* ed. S. J. Ulijaszek, F. E. Johnston, and M. A. Preece (Cambridge: Cambridge University Press, 1989), pp. 447–54.

      One of the biggest surprises: Tanner, *History of the Study,* p. 393.

      "reflects what is happening": Ibid., p. 395.

62   *"Innocent of any academic training":* Ibid., p. 350.

      "He dealt with": Noel Cameron, telephone interview, Jan. 27, 2006.

      "Every measurement": Tanner, *History of the Study,* p. 350.

63   *The errors that occur:* See Linda D. Voss et al., "The Reliability of Height Measurement (the Wessex Growth Study)," *Archives of Disease in Childhood* 65 (1990): 1340–44, and Terri H. Lipman et al., "A Multicentre Randomised Controlled Trial of an Intervention to Improve the Accuracy of Linear Growth Measurement," *Archives of Disease in Childhood* 89 (2004): 342–46.

      To this day: For the initial results on puberty that emerged from the Harpenden study, see James M. Tanner, *Growth at Adolescence* (Oxford: Blackwell, 1955).

      an unusual "tempo-conditional": For the basic paper on growth standards, see J. M. Tanner, R. H. Whitehouse, and M. Takaishi, "Standards from Birth to Maturity for Height, Weight, Height Velocity, and Weight Velocity: British Children 1965," *Archives of Disease in Childhood* 41 (1966): 454–71, 613–35.

      Unlike the cross-sectional charts: For current U.S. growth charts, see R. J. Kuczmarksi et al., "CDC Growth Charts: United States," *Advance Data from Vital and Health Statistics* 314 (2000): 1–27. The charts are available at www.cdc.gov/growthcharts.

64   *"He's absolutely right":* Alan D. Rogol, telephone interview, Dec. 7, 2004.

      "Those charts": Leslie Plotnick, telephone interview, Apr. 19, 2005.

65   *He has been particularly critical:* See Tanner's comments on the original 1977 U.S. growth charts in Tanner, *History of the Study,* p. 393.

      Other scientists have agreed: For a history of the national charts and their international applications, see M. de Onis and R. Yip, "The WHO Growth Chart: Historical Considerations and Current Scientific Issues," in *Nutrition in Pregnancy and Growth*, ed. M. Porrini and P. Walter (Basel: Karger, Bibliotecha Nutritio et Dieta, 1996), pp. 74–89. For a discussion of the drawbacks of the cross-sectional charts, see M. de Onis, C. Garza, and J-P. Habicht, "Time for a New Growth Reference," *Pediatrics* 100 (Nov. 1997): E8, and M. de Onis and A. W. Onyango, "The Centers for Disease Control and Prevention 2000 Growth Charts and the Growth of Breastfed Infants," *Acta Paediatrica* 92 (2003): 413–19.

"cross-sectional charts should": Cameron interview.

66 *"certainly affects":* David Sandberg, personal interview, Oct. 22, 2004, New York.

67 *"I think it would be helpful":* David B. Allen, personal interview, Oct. 7, 2004, Madison, Wisc.

In the fall of 2004: A copy of the "Lilly chart," provided by David Allen, clearly shows that it is based on the CDC chart.

3. A Brief Interruption for a Bicycle Accident: The Growth of Bones and the Creation of Height

69 *"Micaela's fracture was near":* David M. Scher, personal interview, Aug. 24, 2004, New York.

All bone begins: For general background on the growth of bone, see James M. Tanner, *Fetus into Man: Physical Growth from Conception to Maturity* (Cambridge: Cambridge University Press, 1990), pp. 31–35. For more recent reviews of the molecular understanding of bone development, see G. Karsenty, "The Complexities of Skeletal Biology," *Nature* 423 (May 15, 2003): 316–25, and H. M. Kronenberg, "Developmental Regulation of the Growth Plate," *Nature* 423 (2203): 332–36. For a wonderful, though obviously dated, discussion of the mechanical strength of bones, see "On Form and Mechanical Efficiency," in D'Arcy Thompson, *On Growth and Form*, abr. ed., ed. J. T. Bonner (Cambridge: Cambridge University Press, 1992), pp. 221–67. Some of the same material is covered (and updated) in T. A. McMahon and J. T. Bonner, *On Size and Life* (New York: Scientific American Library, 1983).

70 *Beginning at age ten:* The figures for growth at each growth plate come from David M. Scher.

71 *Putting weight on bones:* On the role of mechanical forces in bone growth, see C. Ruff, "Growth in Bone Strength, Body Size, and Muscle Size in a Juvenile Longitudinal Sample," *Bone* 33 (2003): 317–29. On the effect of mechanical forces on stem cells, see M. F. Pittenger et al., "Multilineage Potential of Adult Human Mesenchymal Stem Cells," *Science* 284 (1999): 143–46.

72 *"necessary to maximize":* S. Khosla et al., "Incidence of Childhood Distal Forearm Fractures over 30 Years: A Population-Based Study," *Journal of the American Medical Association* 290 (Sept. 17, 2003): 1479–85.

until they die: Barry Bogin, telephone interview, Dec. 13, 2005.

throughout their lives: Susan Alberts, telephone interview, Feb. 2, 2005.

Once the bones fuse: Growth hormone can still be used in adults to promote muscle mass and reduce fat; once the bones fuse, however, it no longer affects skeletal growth.

73   *"It's been known"*: Sundeep Khosla, telephone interview, Mar. 11, 2005.
     Yet another possible explanation: B. Pennington, "Doctors See a Big Rise in Injuries as Young Athletes Train Nonstop," *New York Times,* Feb. 22, 2005, p. A-1. Among the injuries mentioned were stress fractures, growth plate disorders, and cracked kneecaps.

4. The Invention of Childhood: Growth from Ages Two to Ten

77   *"Although a prolonged":* Theodosius Dobzhansky, *Mankind Evolving: The Evolution of the Human Species* (New Haven, Conn.: Yale University Press, 1962), p. 58.

79   *Jerry Spinelli's novel:* Jerry Spinelli, *Wringer* (New York: HarperCollins, 1997). This book explores peer pressure among nine- and ten-year-old boys.
     "If you look at a group": Richard E. Tremblay, telephone interview, Mar. 4, 2005.

80   *A longitudinal study found:* A. Raine, C. Reynolds, P. H. Venables, S. A. Mednick, and D. P. Farrington, "Fearlessness, Stimulation-Seeking, and Large Body Size at Age 3 Years as Early Predispositions to Childhood Aggression at Age 11 Years," *Archives of General Psychiatry* 55 (Aug. 1998): 745–51.
     In some growth charts: See James M. Tanner, *Fetus into Man: Physical Growth from Conception to Maturity,* 2nd ed. (Cambridge: Harvard University Press, 1990), pp. 13, 15.
     children tend to settle: See the remarks of William Tamborlane, M.D. (p. 295) and Ron Rosenfeld, M.D. (p. 228), Food and Drug Administration, Center for Drug Evaluation and Research (CDER), Endocrinologic and Metabolic Drugs Advisory Committee Meeting, June 10, 2003 (transcript), www.fda.gov/ohrms/dockets/ac/03/transcripts/3957T1.htm.
     gaining on average: See Tanner, *Fetus into Man,* pp. 15–21, 56–57.

81   *Richard Scammon rediscovered:* See James M. Tanner, *A History of the Study of Human Growth* (Cambridge: Cambridge University Press, 1981), p. 265–66, and Tanner, *Fetus into Man,* pp. 6–7. The data first appeared in Richard E. Scammon, "The First Seriatum Study of Human Growth," *American Journal of Physical Anthropology* 10 (1927): 329–36, and was later published in Richard E. Scammon, "The Measurement of the Body in Childhood," in J. A. Harris, C. M. Jackson, D. G. Patterson, and R. E. Scammon, *The Measurement of Man* (Minneapolis: University of Minnesota Press, 1930), pp. 173–215. The Montbeillard data are discussed therein on pp. 175–76.
     "over six feet tall": Peter Medawar, *Pluto's Republic* (New York: Oxford University Press, 1984), p. 228.

82   *"The more one goes over":* Nancy Bayley, "Individual Patterns of Development," *Child Development* 27 (Mar. 1956): 45–74.
     mid-childhood growth spurt: See Barry Bogin, *The Growth of Humanity* (New York: Wiley-Liss, 2001), p. 84, and Tanner, *Fetus into Man,* p. 6.
     There are seasonal: See Tanner, *Fetus into Man,* p. 145.
     One British study: See W. A. Marshall, "Evolution of Growth Rate in Height Over Periods of Less Than 2 Years," *Archives of Disease in Childhood* 46 (1971): 414–20.
     a graph created by: See Tanner, *History of the Study,* pp. 264–67.
     The painter Raphael: See ibid., p. 60.

83 *The thymus:* See Tanner, *Fetus into Man,* p. 17, and C. A. Janeway, P. Travers, M. Walport, and M. Shlomchik, *Immunobiology: The Immune System in Health and Disease,* 5th ed. (New York: Garland, 2001), pp. 230–31.

 dentition: See Bogin, *Growth of Humanity,* pp. 81–83.

84 *cephalic index:* See Stephen J. Gould, *The Mismeasure of Man* (New York: W. W. Norton, 1981).

 That impulse found: On the Porter school surveys and Boas's counterargument, see Tanner, *History of the Study,* p. 219.

85 *"We want to be able":* Bayley, "Individual Patterns," p. 45.

 Many growth-related medical problems: See *The Merck Manual,* 17th ed., M. H. Beers and R. Berkay, eds. (Whitehouse Station, N.J.: Merck Research Laboratories, 1999), 2241–45, 2377–80, and Tanner, *Fetus into Man,* pp. 222–39.

 The availability of limitless: This summation is based on personal interviews with David Allen, University of Wisconsin; David Sandberg, University of Buffalo; and James M. Tanner.

 And the final irony: See Tanner, *Fetus into Man,* p. 15.

86 *In the race to puberty:* See ibid., pp. 56–57.

 "must represent the small": Ibid., p. 57.

 The "typical" girl: For recent U.S. data on when the pubertal growth spurt begins for boys and girls, see S. S. Sun et al., "National Estimates of the Timing of Sexual Maturation and Racial Differences Among U.S. Children," *Pediatrics* 110 (2002): 911–19.

87 *The vast majority:* On mouse and other animal reproduction, I relied on William F. Crowley Jr., telephone interview, May 5, 2005. On primate "childhood," see Bogin, *Growth of Humanity,* pp. 81, 84, and Frans de Waal, *Our Inner Ape: A Leading Primatologist Explains Why We Are Who We Are* (New York: Riverhead, 2005), p. 109.

88 *"The prolongation":* Tanner, *Fetus into Man,* p. 23.

 "There must be more": Barry Bogin, telephone interview, Dec. 13, 2005. See also Barry Bogin, "Adolescence in Evolutionary Perspective," *Acta Paediatrica* Suppl. 406 (1994): 29–35.

 resting metabolic rate: Bogin, *Growth of Humanity,* p. 81.

89 *Bogin and linguist John Locke:* John L. Locke and Barry Bogin, "Language and Life History: A New Perspective on the Development and Evolution of Human Language," *Behavioral and Brain Sciences,* in press for June 2006. An online version is available at www.bbsonline.org/preprints/Locke-06252004/Referees/Locke.3.pdf (accessed Apr. 14, 2006). On the role of physical growth in the development of human language, see Locke and Bogin, "Language and Life History."

 In 2004 researchers: see H. Coqueugniot et al., "Early Brain Growth in *Homo Erectus* and Implications for Cognitive Ability," *Nature* 431 (Sept. 16, 2004): 299–302.

 "It took childhood": Sharon Begley, "Childhood May Separate Humans from Apes," *Wall Street Journal,* Sept. 16, 2004, p. B-1.

5. The Bully Inside Me: The Consequences of Being a Bully

91 *I can still picture:* The bullying incident with Jimmy took place at the Goucher Street School in Westmont, Pennsylvania, just outside Johnstown, in the fall of

1962. Aspects of the sixth-grade class and its tensions were confirmed by the teacher, Anne Fattman (telephone interview, Jan. 30, 2006), and a classmate, Stephen Aronoff (telephone interview, Jan. 25, 2006).

93 *difference in general:* Helen Sweeting and Patrick West, "Being Different: Correlates of the Experience of Teasing and Bullying at Age 11," *Research Papers in Education* 16, no. 3 (2001): 225–46.

"There was absolutely": Jim Finkelstein, telephone interview, Jan. 19, 2006.

94 *Pieter Bruegel's 1560 painting:* See W. S. Gibson, *Bruegel* (New York: Oxford University Press, 1977), pp. 17, 85, for a description of the depicted games.

Bullying is far older: For a more recent example of how little attention bullying attracted in the past, see Arnold Gesell and Frances L. Ilg, *The Child from Five to Ten* (New York: Harper and Brothers, 1946). Gesell and Ilg were affiliated with the famed Clinic of Child Development at Yale University School of Medicine. This standard text on childhood development from the 1940s contains only two fleeting references to bullying (pp. 120, 150).

When a sixteen-year-old: "Funeral for Alberta Boy Bullied at School," *CBC News,* June 13, 2001, http://cbc.ca/cgi=bin/templates/view.cgi?/news/2001/06/13/boy_bullied010613.

In cases where bullying: For Curtis Taylor and the Norwegian cases, see Hara Estroff Marano, "Big. Bad. Bully," *Psychology Today,* Sept. 1995, pp. 50–82. For more background on the early Scandinavian studies and how the Norwegian tragedy affected them, see Dan Olweus, *Bullying at School: What we know and what we can do* (Malden, Mass.: Blackwell, 1993).

95 *"A student is being bullied":* Olweus, *Bullying at School,* p. 9.

96 *The Scandinavian researchers found:* Ibid., p. 13.

"It is the younger and weaker": Ibid., p. 15.

"the school is without doubt": Ibid., p. 21.

Despite certain limitations: Research on bullying is often bedeviled by a number of limitations, not the least of which is methodology. Almost all of the national surveys are based solely on questionnaires — that is, students fill out forms with standardized questions. In addition, some studies are often quite small, and they are almost always cross-sectional as opposed to longitudinal. Longitudinal studies measure changes over time in the same children, whereas cross-sectional studies measure a cross section of children of various ages at the same time. Since tempo of growth — and therefore physical size — may be a crucial component of bullying, the shifting fortunes of the adolescent bully and the adolescent whipping boy often are missing in cross-sectional analyses. Finally, there are many contradictions between studies, as the incidence of bullying varies widely from culture to culture and from locality to locality.

published a paper in 2000: L. D. Voss and J. Mulligan, "Bullying in School: Are Short Pupils at Risk? Questionnaire Study in a Cohort," *British Medical Journal* 320 (Mar. 4, 2000): 612–13.

97 *"passive bullies" or "henchmen":* Olweus, *Bullying at School,* p. 34.

"cyber bullying": See Stop Bullying Now!, a helpful Web site sponsored by the U.S. Health Resources and Services Administration, www.stopbullyingnow.hrsa.gov, and A. Harmon, "Internet Gives Teenage Bullies Weapons to Wound from Afar," *New York Times,* Aug. 26, 2004, p. A1.

Olweus reported in 1993: Olweus, *Bullying at School,* pp. 14–16.

98 *"Thus it is not the infant's":* Saint Augustine, quoted in Richard E. Tremblay, "The

Origins of Youth Violence," *ISUMA (Canadian Journal of Policy Research)* 1 (Autumn 2000): 19–24.

"may have written": Tremblay, "Origins of Youth Violence," p. 23.

99 *"I started to work":* This and all other quotes, unless otherwise noted, are from Richard E. Tremblay, telephone interview, Mar. 4, 2004. For an excellent summation of research on physical aggression over the past one hundred years, see Richard E. Tremblay, "The Development of Aggressive Behavior During Childhood: What Have We Learned in the Past Century?" *International Journal of Behavioral Development* 24, no. 2 (2000): 129–41.

100 *"Fortunately, because of":* Tremblay, "Origins of Youth Violence," p. 19.

If children do not learn: For a brief summation, with relevant citations, of the adult behaviors associated with juvenile bullying, see "What We Know About Bullying," Stop Bullying Now! Tremblay itemizes the same adult sequelae in "Origins of Youth Violence," p. 23.

A very large study: R. B. Cairns et al., "Growth and Aggression: I. Childhood to Early Adolescence," *Developmental Psychology* 25 (1989): 320–30.

101 *"the process of socialization":* Tremblay, "Origins of Youth Violence," p. 20.

By age seventeen months: Tremblay, "Development of Aggressive Behavior," p. 134.

In the first twenty-four months: For standard physical developmental milestones, see, for example, Penelope Leach, *Your Baby and Child: From Birth to Age Five* (New York: Knopf, 1992), and James M. Tanner, *Fetus into Man: Physical Growth from Conception to Maturity,* 2nd ed. (Cambridge: Harvard University Press, 1990), pp. 15–18.

"The frequency and complexity": Tremblay, "Origins of Youth Violence," p. 22.

"Learning to wait": Ibid., p. 22.

102 *In a fascinating:* A. Raine, C. Reynolds, P. H. Venables, S. A. Mednick, and D. P. Farrington, "Fearlessness, Stimulation-Seeking, and Large Body Size at Age 3 Years as Early Predispositions to Childhood Aggression at Age 11 Years," *Archives of General Psychiatry* 55 (Aug. 1998): 745–51.

"children with increased height": Ibid., p 750.

In an innovative follow-up: A. Raine, K. Mellingen, J. Liu, P. Venables, and S. A. Mednick, "Effects of Environmental Enrichment at Ages 3–5 Years on Schizotypal Personality and Antisocial Behavior at Ages 17 and 23 Years," *American Journal of Psychiatry* 160 (Sept. 2003): 1627–35.

this time focusing: R. E. Tremblay et al., "Physical Aggression During Early Childhood: Trajectories and Predictions," *Pediatrics* 114 (2004): 43–50.

103 *"the intergenerational transmission":* Ibid., pp. 43–50. See also D. S. Nagin and R. E. Tremblay, "Parental and Early Childhood Predictors of Persistent Physical Aggression in Boys from Kindergarten to High School," *Archives of General Psychiatry* 58 (2001): 389–94.

104 *That is when researchers:* T. R. Nansel, M. Overpeck, R. S. Pilla, W. J. Ruan, B. Simons-Morton, and P. Scheidt, "Bullying Behaviors Among U.S. Youth: Prevalence and Association with Psychosocial Adjustment," *Journal of the American Medical Association* 285 (2001): 2094–100.

"When we went": Mary Overpeck, telephone interview, Feb. 10, 2005.

106 *"provocative victims":* Olweus, *Bullying at School,* p. 33.

"In a number of cases": "Preventing School Shootings: A Summary of a U.S. Secret Service Safe School Initiative Report," *National Institute of Justice Journal* 248

(2002): 10–15. The report states: "In a number of cases, bullying played a key role in the decision to attack. A number of attackers had experienced bullying and harassment that were longstanding and severe. In those cases, the experience of bullying appeared to play a major role in motivating the attack at school." For accounts of the possible role of bullying in the Columbine incident, see H. Kurtz, "Columbine Bully Talk Persists," *Denver Rocky Mountain News,* Aug. 26, 2000, http:// Denverrmn.com/shooting/0826colu3.shtml/ (accessed Apr. 8, 2006), and J. Kass, "Witnesses Tell of Columbine Bullying," *Denver Rocky Mountain News,* Oct. 3, 2000, denver.rockymountainnews.com/shooting/1003col14.shtml (accessed Aug. 1, 2005).

107   *a clear-cut pecking order:* See D. Conley, *The Pecking Order: A Bold New Look at How Family and Society Determine Who We Become* (New York: Random House, 2004).

108   *"little midget":* R. Grover, "How Eisner Saved the Magic Kingdom," *Business Week Online,* Sept. 30, 2005.

     "girlie men": J. M. Broder, "Schwarzenegger Calls Budget Opponents 'Girlie Men,'" *New York Times,* July 19, 2004, p. A-11.

     John Bolton . . . has left: see D. Jehl, "3 Ex-Officials Describe Bullying by Bolton," *New York Times,* May 3, 2005, p. A-11.

     "managers bullied subordinates" B. Carey, "Fear in the Workplace: The Bullying Boss," *New York Times,* June 22, 2004, p. F-1.

109   *One of the finest:* Jonathan Eig, "Violent, Unhappy and Brief — The Life of a School Bully," *Wall Street Journal,* Nov. 20, 2002, p. A-1. See also letters in response to the article, *Wall Street Journal,* Nov. 29, 2002, p. A-15.

     "I always assumed": Jonathan Eig, telephone interview, Sept. 9, 2005.

     "if kids stood up": Ibid.

6. Runts, Sneaks, and Dominators: Size, Aggression, and Animal Behavior

110   *"Nature red in tooth":* in Frans de Waal, "Peace Lessons from an Unlikely Source," *Public Library of Science — Biology* 2 (Apr. 2004), pp. 434–36.

     "an accident of history": Ibid.

111   *Contaminated meat:* On the tuberculosis outbreak, see R. Tarara et al., "Tuberculosis in Wild Olive Baboons, *Papio Cynocephalus Anubis* (Lesson), in Kenya," *Journal of Wildlife Disease* 21 (1985): 137–44, and R. Sapolsky and J. Else, "Bovine Tuberculosis in a Wild Baboon Population: Epidemiological Aspects," *Journal of Medical Primatology* 16 (1987): 229–34.

     "I was very attached": Robert M. Sapolsky, personal communication, Jan. 25, 2005.

     "the troop of my youth": Ibid.

     "By 1986": Robert M. Sapolsky and Lisa J. Share, "A Pacific Culture Among Wild Baboons: Its Emergence and Transmission," *Public Library of Science — Biology* 2 (Apr. 2004): 534–41.

112   *"a chronic state of stress":* Sapolsky and Shore, "Pacific Culture," p. 536. They suspect that other changes in community behavior, including increased levels of social grooming and a general decrease in dominance interactions, helped to reduce levels of stress.

pathological physiological state: For the role of stress in a variety of physiological settings, see Robert M. Sapolsky, *Why Zebras Don't Get Ulcers: The Acclaimed Guide to Stress, Stress-Related Diseases, and Coping,* 3rd ed. (New York: Owl Books, 2004). See also Robert M. Sapolsky, "The Trouble with Testosterone," in *The Trouble with Testosterone and Other Essays on the Biology of the Human Predicament* (New York: Scribner, 1997).

"the biggest, nastiest": Natalie Angier, "No Time for Bullies: Baboons Retool Their Culture," *New York Times,* Apr. 13, 2004, p. F-1.

at least through 2004: Robert M. Sapolsky, personal communication, Apr. 14, 2006.

113 *the earliest, shrewlike mammals:* See A. Weil, "Living Large in the Cretaceous," *Nature* 433 (Jan. 13, 2005): 116–17. Contrary to prevailing thought, Weil speculates that the size of mammals in the Cretaceous period, larger than previously thought, may have created evolutionary pressures for making dinosaurs even larger.

115 *Lorenz was the dominant:* See Konrad Lorenz, *On Aggression* (New York: Harcourt, Brace & World, 1966); Desmond Morris, *The Naked Ape: A Zoologist's Study of the Human Animal* (New York: McGraw-Hill, 1967); and Niko Tinbergen, "On War and Peace in Animals and Man," *Science* 160 (June 28, 1968): 1411–18. Tinbergen's work also appears in a large collection of essays on the intersection of biology and behavior edited by A. L. Caplan, *The Sociobiology Debate: Readings on Ethical and Scientific Issues* (New York: Harper and Row, 1978).

"But research takes": Tinbergen, "On War and Peace," p. 1418. Another example of the explicit link between ethology and fears of nuclear catastrophe can be found in Lorenz: "An unprejudiced observer from another planet, looking upon man as he is today, in his hand the atom bomb, the product of his intelligence, in his heart the aggressive drive inherited from his anthropoid ancestors, which this same intelligence cannot control, would not prophesy long life for the species" (Lorenz, *On Aggression,* p. 49).

"There is a huge literature": Robert W. Elwood, personal communication, Jan. 4, 2005.

116 *evolutionary biologist:* R. D. Alexander, "Aggressiveness, Territoriality, and Sexual Behavior in Field Crickets," *Behavior* 17 (1961): 130–223.

loser effect: On the winner and loser effects, see, for example, Y. Hsu and L. L. Wolf, "The Winner and Loser Effect: Integrating Multiple Experiences," *Animal Behavior* 57 (1999): 903–910. See also L. A. Dugatkin and R. L. Earley, "Individual Recognition, Dominance Hierarchies, and Winner and Loser Effects," *Proceedings of the Royal Society of London* B 271 (2004): 1527–40, and L. A. Dugatkin and M. Druen, "The Social Implications of Winner and Loser Effects," *Proceedings of the Royal Society of London* 271 (2004): S488–89. For the winner effect in mammals, see T. O. Oyegbile and C. A. Marler, "Winning Fights Elevates Testosterone Levels in California Mice and Enhances Future Ability to Win Fights," *Hormone Behavior* 48 (2005): 259–67.

"Crickets have a general": Richard Dawkins, *The Selfish Gene,* rev. ed. (New York: Oxford University Press, 1989), p. 81.

117 *pecking order:* For origins of pecking order, see Lorenz, *On Aggression,* p. 44.

"individuals lower in the order": Dawkins, *The Selfish Gene,* p. 82.

among prison inmates: Richard Tremblay, telephone interview, Mar. 4, 2004.

The prodigious increase in brain size: See, for example, P. Currie, "Muscling in on Hominid Evolution," *Nature* 428 (2004): 373–74.

118 *"If you are a monkey"*: Dawkins, *The Selfish Gene*, p. 82.

"My research suggests": Joseph LeDoux, personal interview, Jan. 27, 2005, New York. For an extensive discussion of emotional memory and the circuitry of fear in the mammalian brain, see Joseph LeDoux, *The Emotional Brain* (New York: Simon and Schuster, 1996).

recent research: B. Mitra et al., "Stress Duration Modulates the Spatiotemporal Patterns of Spine Formation in the Basolateral Amygdala," *Proceedings of the National Academy of Sciences* 102 (2005): 9371–76.

a recent paper: Paul J. Whalen et al., "Human Amygdala Responsivity to Masked Fearful Eye Whites," *Science* 306 (Dec. 17, 2004): 2061.

119 *"In a typical combat"*: J. Maynard Smith and G. R. Price, "The Logic of Animal Conflict," *Nature* 246 (Nov. 2, 1973): 15–18.

120 *"not far from what"*: Dawkins, *The Selfish Gene*, p. 75.

"this means": Ibid., p. 77.

"not very realistic": Ibid., p. 78.

Recognizing these real-world: For papers on contests designed with "asymmetry" — defined as "some intrinsic feature such as size" — see J. Maynard Smith, "The Theory of Games and the Evolution of Animal Conflicts," *Journal of Theoretical Biology* 47 (1974): 209–21; G. A. Parker, "Assessment Strategy and the Evolution of Fighting Behavior," *Journal of Theoretical Biology* 47 (1974): 223–43; and J. Maynard Smith and G. A. Parker, "The Logic of Asymmetric Contests," *Animal Behavior* 24 (1976): 159–75.

"Large size is not": Dawkins, *The Selfish Gene*, p. 80.

121 *That muscle-bound version*: For a spirited response to the aggression studies and the idea of "selfish genes," see Frans de Waal, *Our Inner Ape: A Leading Primatologist Explains Why We Are Who We Are* (New York: Riverhead, 2005), pp. 1–2, 21–22. De Waal's main argument is that the focus on fighting ability in dominance hierarchies misses the larger point, repeatedly shown in his and others' primate studies, that social dominance is at least as dependent on cooperative skills as on physical superiority, and that there are numerous subversive mating strategies to achieve reproductive success other than physical dominance.

122 *In a devilishly clever*: R. W. Elwood, K. E. Wood, M. B. Gallagher, and J.T.A. Dick, "Probing Motivational State During Agonistic Encounters in Animals," *Nature* 393 (May 7, 1998): 66–68. A follow-up study raises "disquieting questions" about the assumptions underlying much of the game theory approaches. For example, a quality such as persistence may be an unexamined factor in the resolution of fights. See P. W. Taylor and R. W. Elwood, "The Mis-measure of Animal Contests," *Animal Behavior* 65 (2003): 1195–1202.

"Field observations": Christopher Linn and Terry E. Christenson, "Body Size Affects the Ability of Male Spiders to Travel to Female Webs," abstract presented at the annual meeting of the Animal Behavior Society, 2000. See also Christopher D. Linn, "The Effect of Male Size on Travel Ability in the Golden Orb-Weaving Spider *Nephila clavipes:* Implications for Sexual Size Dimorphism" (master's thesis, Tulane University, 2001).

123 *the convict cichlid*: Simon Beeching, Amanda B. Hopp, and Ginger L. Ruffner, "Sex Differences in Mate Size Preference in the Convict Cichlid, *Cichlasoma nigrofasciatum,*" abstract presented at the annual meeting of the Animal Behavior Society, 2000. See also S. C. Beeching, C. Wack, and G. L. Ruffner, "Female Convict

Cichlids (*Archocentros nigrofasciatus*) Prefer to Consort with Same-Sized Males," *Ethology, Ecology & Evolution* 16 (2004): 209–16.

"The large males": Bill Sellers, personal communication, Jan. 4, 2005. For a fascinating popular account of Abernethy's research on female-dominated mandrill troops, see Natalie Angier, "In Mandrill Society, Life Is a Girl Thing," *New York Times,* May 23, 2000, p. F-1.

124   *Researchers at Purdue:* Richard D. Howard, J. Andrew DeWoody, and William M. Muir, "Transgenic Male Mating Advantage Provides Opportunity for Trojan Gene Effect in a Fish," *Proceedings of the National Academy of Sciences* 101 (Mar. 2, 2004): 2934–38, and Richard D. Howard, telephone interview, April 20, 2006.

125   *"Dominance rank":* This and all other quotes, unless otherwise noted, are from Susan C. Alberts, telephone interview, Feb. 2, 2005.

"queue-jumpers": See Susan C. Alberts, Heather E. Watts, and Jeanne Altmann, "Queuing and Queue-Jumping: Long-Term Patterns of Reproductive Skew in Male Savannah Baboons, *Papio cynocephalus,*" *Animal Behavior* 62 (2003): 821–40.

126   *"There are two":* Sapolsky, personal communication.

an evolutionary biologist: Joan Roughgarden, *Evolution's Rainbow: Diversity, Gender, and Sexuality in Nature and People* (Berkeley: University of California Press, 2004).

127   *dominance hierarchies:* For an extensive discussion of dominance hierarchies in primates, see B. B. Smuts, D. L. Cheney, R. M. Seyfarth, R. W. Wrangham, and T. T. Struhsaker, eds. *Primate Societies* (Chicago: University of Chicago Press, 1987). See also Bill Sellers, "Primate Behavior," lecture, University of Wisconsin Primate Lab, www.leeds.ac.uk/chb/lectures/anthl_11.html.

Anyone who thinks: Y. Takahata, M. A. Huffman, S. Suzuki, N. Koyama, and J. Yamagiwa, "Why Dominants Do Not Consistently Attain High Mating and Reproductive Success: A Review of Longitudinal Japanese Macaque Studies," *Primates* 40, no. 1 (Jan. 1999): 143–58. In addition to the 1 in 160 success rate of an alpha male, this paper details many complexities of macaque behavior that mitigate against the simple expectation that dominant males will achieve the greatest reproductive success. For example, DNA paternity testing of a macaque troop living in captivity at the Primate Research Institute in Japan showed that "there was no correlation between male rank and the number of offspring sired" (p. 148).

"do not choose males": Ibid., p. 152.

128   *painstakingly documents:* Frans de Waal, *Chimpanzee Politics: Power and Sex Among Apes,* rev. ed. (Baltimore: Johns Hopkins University Press, 1998), pp. 77–135.

"High-ranking individuals": Frans de Waal, "Primates — A Natural Heritage of Conflict Resolution," *Science* 289 (July 28, 2000): 586–90. The same general point is made in much greater detail in de Waal, *Peacemaking Among Primates* (Cambridge: Harvard University Press, 1989).

7. "To Grow Hairy": Puberty, or the Schuss

131   *an enterprising medical historian:* S. F. Daw, "Age of Boys' Puberty in Leipzig, 1727–49, As Indicated by Voice Breaking in J. S. Bach's Choir Members," *Human Biology* 42 (1970): 87–89.

132   *about three years later:* James M. Tanner, *A History of the Study of Human Growth*

(Cambridge: Cambridge University Press, 1981), p. 95. Tanner refers, with faint praise, to the Daw study as the "only one which throws a small and perhaps uncertain light on the age of puberty in boys in the early eighteenth century."
"Because their adolescent growth": Barry Bogin, "Adolescence in Evolutionary Perspective," *Acta Paediatrica* Suppl. 406 (1994): 29–35.
the word "puberty": Ibid., p. 29.

133   *Schuss:* Tanner, *History of the Study*, p. 139.
even adolescent baboons: Jeanne Altmann and Susan C. Alberts, "Growth Rates in a Wild Primate Population: Ecological Influences and Maternal Effects," *Behavioral Ecology and Sociobiology* 57 (2005): 490–501. These field observations of a wild population of savannah baboons (*Papio cynocephalus*) showed that in baboon "childhood," as in human childhood, the growth trajectory was fairly constant — "individuals generally remained consistently large-for-age or small-for-age throughout development" — but that sexual maturity occurred earlier in animals where food resources were plentiful. There was also a maternal aspect to size and early "puberty": high-ranking females, as well as females who had borne offspring more than once, had relatively large-for-age offspring, which in turn predicted an earlier age for sexual maturation.

134   *"one of the great mysteries"*: Stephanie B. Seminara et al., "The GPR54 Gene as a Regulator of Puberty," *New England Journal of Medicine* 349 (Oct. 23, 2003): 1614–27. For general aspects of the biology of puberty, see James M. Tanner, *Fetus into Man: Physical Growth from Conception to Maturity*, 2nd ed. (Cambridge: Harvard University Press, 1990), pp. 58–74; James M. Tanner, *Growth at Adolescence* (Oxford: Blackwell, 1955); and Barry Bogin, *The Growth of Humanity* (New York: Wiley-Liss, 2001), pp. 87–93.
"the longest, closest": Nicholas Wade, *The Nobel Duel: Two Scientists' 21-Year Race to Win the World's Most Coveted Research Prize* (New York: Anchor Press, 1981), p. 3.
"In endocrinology": This and all other quotes, unless otherwise noted, are from William F. Crowley Jr., telephone interview, May 5, 2005.
The new, molecular version: For the general sequence of hormonal secretion and signaling in puberty, see Tanner, *Fetus into Man*, pp. 84–89, 95–99, 100–103.

135   *"a mysterious period"*: Crowley, quoted in Seminara et al., "GPR54 Gene," p. 1622.
a two-year-old girl: William F. Crowley Jr. et al., "Therapeutic Use of Pituitary Desensitization with a Long-Acting LHRH Agonist: A Potential New Treatment for Idiopathic Precocious Puberty," *Journal of Clinical Endocrinology and Metabolism* 52 (1981): 370–72. For the first five patients treated this way, see F. Comite et al., "Short-Term Treatment of Idiopathic Precocious Puberty with a Long-Acting Analogue of Luteinizing Hormone-Releasing Hormone," *New England Journal of Medicine* 305 (Dec. 24, 1981): 1546–50.

136   *"early-morning and spontaneous"*: Andrew R. Hoffman and William F. Crowley Jr., "Induction of Puberty in Men by Long-Term Pulsatile Administration of Low-Dose Gonadotropin-Releasing Hormone," *New England Journal of Medicine* 307 (Nov. 11, 1982): 1237–41.

137   *Even then, it took:* For the research on GPR54 and its relation to kisspeptin, see Seminara et al., "The GPR54 Gene," and M. Shahab et al., "Increased Hypothalamic GPR54 Signaling: A Potential Mechanism for Initiation of Puberty in Primates," *Proceedings of the National Academy of Sciences* 102 (Feb. 8, 2005): 2129–34. A team of French-based researchers also uncovered this genetic pathway to pu-

berty at about the same time; the key publication is N. de Roux et al., "Hypogonadotropic Hypogonadism Due to Loss of Function of the KiSS1-Derived Peptide Receptor GPR54," *Proceedings of the National Academy of Sciences* 100 (Sept. 16, 2003): 10972–76. For a good background account of these discoveries, see G. Vogel, "A Powerful First *KiSS-1*," *Science* 309 (July 22, 2005): 551–52.

138 *"Their finding is":* Sergio R. Ojeda, telephone interview, July 26, 2005.

As in other areas: See Cheryl L. Sisk and Douglas L. Foster, "The Neural Basis of Puberty and Adolescence," *Nature Neuroscience* 7 (Oct. 2004): 1040–47. This is an excellent, up-to-date review of research on the molecular mechanics of puberty.

"the individual must": Ibid., p. 1041.

139 *"Whatever it is":* Tanner, *Fetus into Man,* p. 102. Sisk and Foster echo Tanner: "We are left with the simple recognition," they write, "that there is a maturational component in the juvenile that makes puberty unique. Such a view leads to the concept of an innate developmental clock that times the unfolding of primary genetic programs and produces the internally derived signals that in turn determine the responses to both internal and external permissive signals" (Sisk and Foster, "The Neural Basis," p. 1041).

passage in every human life: Although the terms "puberty" and "adolescence" are used interchangeably in casual conversation, scientists draw a subtle but important distinction. "Puberty is the period during which an individual becomes capable of sexually reproducing," write Cheryl Sisk and Julia L. Zehr. "Adolescence is the period between childhood and adulthood, encompassing not only reproductive maturation, but also cognitive, emotional and social maturation" (C. L. Sisk and J. L. Zehr, "Pubertal Hormones Organize the Adolescent Brain and Behavior," *Frontiers in Neuroendocrinology* 26 [2005]: 163–74).

atlas of pubertal change: For a brief background history of the Harpenden Growth Study, see Tanner, *History of the Study,* pp. 349–56. For another evolutionary view of adolescence, see Bogin, "Adolescence in Evolutionary Perspective."

140 *the Tanner stages:* The first "rough draft" of the pubertal stages were discussed in Tanner, *Growth at Adolescence,* but a more definitive version appeared in two parts: W. A. Marshall and J. M. Tanner, "Variations in Pattern of Pubertal Changes in Girls," *Archives of Disease in Childhood* 44 (1969): 291–303, and W. A. Marshall and J. M. Tanner, "Variations in the Pattern of Pubertal Changes in Boys," *Archives of Disease in Childhood* 45 (1970): 13–23. See also Phyllis B. Eveleth and James M. Tanner, *Worldwide Variation in Human Growth,* 2nd ed. (Cambridge: Cambridge University Press, 1990), pp. 161–175. In a retrospective account of this work, Tanner noted that excellent studies had preceded and followed the British studies, and he attributed the enduring popularity and impact of the Harpenden results to the fact that "ours was the only one in the period 1950–1980. Also our photographs were of better quality than others, and it was this fact that led to our photos of the stages of pubertal development in breasts and pubic hair being widely reproduced and adopted. (Much later, these stages got referred to in the U.S. as 'Tanner stages,' a wildly inappropriate attribution, since all we did was tidy up Reynolds and Wines [researchers at the Fels Research Institute in Ohio], who themselves took their descriptions from the German literature of the 1930s and earlier)" (James M. Tanner, "This Week's Citation Classic," *Current Contents* 43 [Oct. 28, 1985]: 16).

"All I did": James M. Tanner, personal interview, Sept. 29, 2004, Dunkeswell, Eng.

"bottle-sharing": Tanner, *History of the Study,* p. 353.

"One of the results": James M. Tanner, History of the Study, p. 354.

The Tanner stages still influence: For a good survey of various pubertal measures and why the Tanner stages are likely to endure, see J. C. Rockett, C. D. Lynch, and G. M. Buck, "Biomarkers for Assessing Reproductive Development and Health: I. Pubertal Development," Environmental Health Perspectives 112 (Jan. 2004): 105–112. The authors note that "it seems unlikely that current biomarkers of reproductive development and health will be displaced, at least in the near to mid-future. For example, the use of Tanner staging is a simple and inexpensive method of assessing pubertal development. Though it has its faults, such as being a subjective method, it is probably still the best choice for use in large longitudinal cohort studies such as the NCS [National Children's Study]."

In boys, the first: On pubertal changes in boys, see Tanner, Fetus into Man, pp. 58–63.

As we get into: For recent American data on the age of onset for the pubertal stages in boys and girls, see S. S. Sun et al., "National Estimates of the Timing of Sexual Maturation and Racial Differences Among US Children," Pediatrics 110 (Nov. 5, 2002): 911–919. Although there is some evidence that children, especially girls, are entering puberty earlier now than in previous generations, the data from large-scale surveys is still contradictory on this point. Marcia E. Herman-Giddens and colleagues have reported that the age of onset of genital and pubic hair growth in boys has been "younger than in past studies" (Marcia E. Herman-Giddens et al., "Secondary Sexual Characteristics in Boys: Estimates from the National Health and Nutrition Examination Survey III, 1988–1994," Archives of Pediatric and Adolescent Medicine 155 [Sept. 2001]: 1022–28). Adam M. Karpati and colleagues have suggested that "boys of this generation may be maturing more rapidly than did boys in the past (Adam M. Karpati et al., "Stature and Pubertal Stage Assessment in American Boys: The 1988–1994 Third National Health and Nutrition Examination Survey," Journal of Adolescent Health 30 [Mar. 2002]: 205–12). But two large studies have concluded that, with the exception of non-Hispanic black girls and boys, who tend to mature earlier, American children have been completing their sexual development at approximately the same ages as previous studies (see S. S. Sun et al., "National Estimates," and W. C. Chumlea et al., "Age at Menarche and Racial Comparisons in U.S. Girls," Pediatrics 111 [Jan. 2003]: 110–13).

Delayed puberty is: William F. Crowley Jr., personal communication, Mar. 12, 2006.

141 They observed exactly: On the development of axillary and facial hair, see Tanner, Fetus into Man, p. 62.

142 "often during sleep": Ibid. Crowley points out, however, that sperm can be detected in the urine of boys beginning at around ages eight to ten.

For the record: See David M. Friedman, A Mind of Its Own: A Cultural History of the Penis (New York: Penguin, 2003), p. 123.

In 1992 a research team: For a general discussion of the background of the NIMH's longitudinal study (including its implications for the diagnosis of early-onset schizophrenia), see Paul Thompson, "Brain Deficit Patterns May Signal Early-Onset Schizophrenia," Psychiatric Times, Aug. 2002.

"second wave of neural development," Ibid.

"The number of nerve cells": Jay N. Giedd, telephone interview, Jan. 5, 2006.

143 In several recent publications: Jay N. Giedd, "Structural Magnetic Resonance Imaging of the Adolescent Brain," Annals of the New York Academy of Sciences 1021

(2004): 105–9, and N. Gogtay et al., "Dynamic Mapping of Human Cortical Development During Childhood Through Early Adulthood," *Proceedings of the National Academy of Sciences* 101, no. 21 (May 25, 2004): 8174–79. For a more general discussion of pubertal brain development, see Daniel R. Weinberger, Brita Elevag, and Jay N. Giedd, "The Adolescent Brain: A Work in Progress" (Washington, D.C.: Campaign to Prevent Teen Pregnancy, 2005).

"important for controlling": Giedd, "Structural Magnetic Resonance," p. 105.

But researchers have discovered: See Sarah W. Bottjer, "Developmental Regulation of Basal Ganglia Circuitry During the Sensitive Period for Vocal Learning in Songbirds," *Annals of the New York Academy of Science* 1016 (2004): 395–415.

144   *"I'm betting there is":* Cheryl Sisk, personal communication, Jan. 6, 2006.

   During the first year: See Tanner, *Fetus into Man*, pp. 65–74.

   The main drivers: See ibid., pp. 89–92, 100–103.

145   *"It has been said":* Ron G. Rosenfeld, "A Tale of Two Centimeters," *Journal of Pediatrics* 146 (Jan. 2005): 10–11.

146   *"boy stops growing":* Tanner, *Fetus into Man*, p. 67.

   "After birth": Aristotle, quoted in Tanner, *History of the Study*, p. 7.

   It is as apparent: If it is often a burden for boys to be of small stature, in many eras it was an insufferable burden for girls — or, more accurately, for their parents — to be too tall. In my interview with Tanner, he told me that one of the most unpleasant interludes of his professional career occurred when he ran a clinic for tall girls for several years. "I hated it so much that I managed to get out of it after a while," he said. Why? "Because of the parents," he replied. "Specifically, the mothers. The mothers would come in — and it's a pretty general thing, I gather, from talking to other people — they'd come in with this rather attractive, rather shy, very tall, willowy, nice-looking daughter, and then there'd be the mum, who of course was towering over her, because she was fully grown. And the mum would go on about this girl being so awfully tall, and she's got to stop growing straightaway. The girl would sit, battered, you know, and thinking, quite rightly, she was going to be given some fearful drug. Those were the days you gave them a huge dose of estrogen, you know. And it *partly* worked. And if I then did a prediction, I'd say, 'But look, you know, five feet ten is a very nice height . . . But what's wrong with five feet eleven, really?' And [the mum would] say, 'It's perfectly dreadful! I don't mind what you do, but you've got to stop it,' and all this. And even some would say, 'Chop off some of her legs.'" Needless to say, no one got her legs chopped off, but this discussion with Tanner shows how social attitudes about height can creep into medical discussions.

147   *"Maturity is a high price":* Tom Stoppard, at www.whatquote.com.

   "Adolescence became": Bogin, "Adolescence in Evolutionary Perspective," p. 34.

   Bogin and linguist John Locke: John L. Locke and Barry Bogin, "Language and Life History: A New Perspective on the Development and Evolution of Human Language," *Behavioral and Brain Sciences* (Cambridge: Cambridge University Press, 2006).

   "small talk": Frans de Waal, *Our Inner Ape: A Leading Primatologist Explains Why We Are Who We Are* (New York: Riverhead, 2005), p. 187.

   Decked out in: The Lancer (Bloomfield Hills, Mich.: Bloomfield Hills Junior High School, 1965).

8. Belittled: The Consequences of Being Bullied

151 *"Bummer of a birthmark"*: Gary Larson, *The Prehistory of the Far Side: A 10th Anniversary Exhibit* (Kansas City: Andrews and McMeel, 1989), p. 257.

small of stature: According to contemporary records still on file at the school, my height on October 8, 1965, was 57 inches (4 feet 9 inches), and my weight was 82½ pounds (B. Morman, Lyons Township High School, LaGrange, Ill., personal communication, June 28, 2005.)

many of the recent research findings: See, for example, Helen Sweeting and Patrick West, "Being Different: Correlates of the Experience of Teasing and Bullying at Age 11," *Research Papers in Education* 16, no. 3 (2001): 225–46. Sweeting and West found that teasing and bullying were more likely to be directed at children who performed poorly academically, were "less physically attractive," overweight, or had a physical disability. Race, height, and physical maturity did not emerge as important factors of victimhood. For another summary of factors associated with victims of bullying, see L. D. Hanish and N. G. Guerra, "Children Who Get Victimized at School: What Is Known? What Can Be Done?" *Professional School Counseling* 4 (2000): 113–19.

154 *"Oh, Jesus"*: This and all other quotes are from Ken Monti, telephone interview, Jan. 30, 2006.

155 *"Short boys . . . were more"*: Linda D. Voss, "Bullying in School: Are Short Pupils at Risk? Questionnaire study in a Cohort," *British Medical Journal* 320 (Mar. 4, 2000). Apropos of bullying during adolescence, this study noted that many short students felt that bullying began in junior high school. Voss wrote, "More short pupils also report a degree of social isolation — the result, or possibly the cause, of their victimisation. These data are important since the Wessex growth study has previously found few significant psychological problems that could be attributed to short stature." For a more global critical examination of potential disadvantages of short stature (usually in school), see Linda D. Voss, "Short Normal Stature and Psychosocial Disadvantage: A Critical Review of the Evidence," *Journal of Pediatric Endocrinology and Metabolism* 14, no. 2 (2001): 701–11.

"It is an interesting paradox": Richard E. Tremblay, "The Development of Aggressive Behavior During Childhood: What Have We Learned in the Past Century?" *International Journal of Behavioral Development* 24, no. 2 (2000): 129–41.

156 *Beginning in the 1980s:* Richard E. Tremblay et al., "Testosterone, Physical Aggression, Dominance, and Physical Development in Early Adolescence," *International Journal of Behavioral Development* 22, no. 4 (1998): 753–77. See also L. M. Broidy et al., "Developmental Trajectories of Childhood Disruptive Behaviors and Adolescent Delinquency: A Six-Site, Cross-National Survey," *Developmental Psychology* 39 (2003): 222–45.

157 *"We suggest that"*: Tremblay et al., "Testosterone," p. 772.

"Children probably learn": Ibid., p. 772.

158 *"If you are socially dominant"*: Richard E. Tremblay, telephone interview, Mar. 4, 2005.

159   *research on female nonhuman primates:* S. B. Hrdy and G. C. Williams, "Behavioral Biology and the Double Standard," in *Social Behavior of Female Vertebrates,* ed. S. B. Hrdy and G. C. Williams (New York: Academic Press, 1983).

      researchers in Finland: K. M. J. Lagerspetz, K. Björkqvist, and T. Peltonen, "Is Indirect Aggression Typical of Females? Gender Differences in Aggressiveness in 11- to 12-Year-Old Children," *Aggressive Behavior* 14 (1988): 403–14.

      Recent research looking: See M. D. Overpeck et al., "Pubertal Status and U.S. Adolescent Male Bullying," abstract, annual meeting of American Public Health Association, 2004.

      e-bullying: See T. Bahrampour, "Message Is Clear in N. Va.: IM 'Threats' Can Bring Teens Trouble in an Instant," *Washington Post,* May 29, 2005, p. A-1.

      "Body size isn't it": Mary Overpeck, telephone interview, Feb. 10, 2005.

160   *"I think the victims":* Ibid.

      In the spring of 2004: For accounts of the case, see S. Shifrel, "Jury Strikes 195G Blow for Bullied Queens Boy," *New York Daily News,* Apr. 28, 2004, p. 4, and D. Barry, "A Boy, a Bully, and Cries Unheard," *New York Times,* May 1, 2004, p. B-1.

161   *If you dip:* For the role of physical size, appearance, and disability as factors in victimhood, see Sweeting and West, "Being Different." For overprotective mothers, see Dan Olweus, *Bullying at School* (Malden, Mass: Blackwell, 1993), p. 33.

      Paille-au-Nez: F. Markham, *Napoleon* (New York: Mentor, 1963) p. 18.

      two prominent Canadian: Wendy M. Craig and Debra J. Pepler, "Observations of Bullying and Victimization in the School Yard," *Canadian Journal of School Psychology* 13 (1997): 41–60. See also Debra J. Pepler and Wendy M. Craig, "A Peek Behind the Fence: Naturalistic Observations of Aggressive Children with Remote Audiovisual Recording," *Developmental Psychology* 31 (1995): 548–53. For bullying inside the classroom, see W. M. Craig, D. Pepler, and R. Atlas, "Observations of Bullying in the Playground and in the Classroom," *School Psychology International* 21, no. 1 (2000): 22–36, and R. S. Atlas and D. J. Pepler, "Observations of Bullying in the Classroom," *Journal of Educational Research* 92, no. 2 (Nov./Dec. 1998): 86–99.

162   *"naturalistic observations":* Pepler and Craig, "A Peek Behind the Fence."

      "occurred regularly": Craig and Pepler, "Observations of Bullying," p. 41.

      "not aware of": Atlas and Pepler, "Observations of Bullying in the Classroom," p. 94.

      "Adults intervened": Craig and Pepler, "Observations of Bullying," p. 56.

      60 percent of secondary: Olweus, *Bullying at School,* p. 20.

163   *study of Dutch schoolchildren:* M. Fekkes, F.I.M. Pijpers, and S. P. Verloove-Vanhorick, "Bullying Behavior and Associations with Psychosomatic Complaints and Depression in Victims," *Journal of Pediatrics* 144 (Jan. 2004): 17–22.

      "vulnerabilities associated": K. S. McKenney et al., "Psychosocial Consequences of Peer Victimization in Elementary and High School — An Examination of Post-traumatic Stress Disorder Symptomatology," in *Child Victimization,* ed. K. A. Kendall-Tackett and S. M. Giacomoni (Kingston, N.J.: Civic Research Institute, 2005), p 15.

      "long-term neuronal changes": See C. Holden, "Bullied Mice Implicate Brain's Reward Pathway in Mood Disorders," *Science* 311 (Feb. 11, 2006): 759; see also O. Berton et al., "Essential Role of BDNF in the Mesolimbic Dopamine Pathway in Social Defeat Stress," ibid., pp. 864–68.

One of the leading factors: Robert M. Sapolsky and Lisa J. Share, "A Pacific Culture Among Wild Baboons: Its Emergence and Transmission," *Public Library of Science — Biology* 2 (Apr. 2004): 534–41, and Robert M. Sapolsky, personal communication, Jan. 25, 2005.

Antibullying programs: See "Olweus Bullying Prevention Program," www.samhsa. gov, and Stop Bullying Now!, www.stopbullyingnow.hrsa.gov.

164   *behavioral guidelines:* All quotes are from *Citywide Standards of Discipline and Intervention Measures* (New York: New York City Department of Education, 2003), p. 16.

"notoriously unreliable": Ann Hulbert, "Elephant in the Room: America's Flawed New Antibullying Movement," *Slate,* Oct. 23, 2003, www.slate.com/id.2090186.

165   *"The antibullying crusade":* Ibid.

"taking a lot of harmless": John Leo, "Study on Bullying Mixes Serious and Trivial Statistics," syndicated column, May 13, 2001, www.townhall.com/opinion/columns/johnleo/2001/05/13/166400.html. For another unsympathetic take on recent school antibullying campaigns, see M. Labash, "Beating Up on Bullies," *Weekly Standard,* Feb. 24, 2003, www.weeklystandard.com/content/Public/Articles/000/000/0002/247mogt.asp?pg=1.

"Scandinavian wusses": Hulbert, "Elephant in the Room."

"culture of cruelty": Ibid. For an alternative view of the culture of cruelty, see Dan Kindlon and Michael Thompson, *Raising Cain: Protecting the Emotional Life of Boys* (New York: Ballantine, 1999), pp. 72–93.

"imagination": Frans de Waal, *Our Inner Ape: A Leading Primatologist Explains Why We Are Who We Are* (New York: Riverhead, 2005), p. 4.

bullying often plays: D. L. Hawkins, D. J. Pepler, and W. M. Craig, "Naturalistic Observations of Peer Interventions in Bullying," *Social Development* 10 (2001): 512–27.

166   *One study has reported:* S. Leff, "Bullied Children Are Picked On for Their Vulnerability," *British Medical Journal* 318 (Apr. 17, 1999): 1076. Of ninety-seven victims of bullying who sought a school health consultation, thirty had a physical disability such as a cleft palate, spinal deformity, or hemiplegia. See also Sweeting and West, "Being Different," p. 234.

9. The Prussian Curse: Heightism, or the Birth of the "Altocracy"

168   *varsity basketball team: Tabulae* (LaGrange, Ill.: Lyons Township High School, 1998), pp. 112–13, and George Knue, personal communication, Mar. 20, 2006.

170   *their sad lot:* James Compton Burnett, *Delicate, Backward, Puny and Stunted Children: Their Developmental Defects, and Physical, Mental, and Moral Peculiarities Considered as Ailments Amenable to Treatment by Medicines* (London: Homeopathic Publishing Company, 1895). Despite the expansive title, this slim volume is essentially a brisk recitation of case studies of children who were small for gestational age or who failed to grow and then were treated using homeopathy.

Frederick William of Prussia: For accounts of the life and times of both Frederick William and his son, see Robert Ergang, *The Potsdam Führer: Frederick William I, Father of Prussian Militarism* (New York: Columbia University Press, 1941); Robert B. Asprey, *Frederick the Great: The Magnificent Enigma* (New York: Ticknor and

Fields, 1986); Giles MacDonough, *Frederick the Great: A Life in Deed and Letters* (New York: St. Martin's Press, 1999); and Nancy Mitford, *Frederick the Great* (New York: Harper & Row, 1970).

"a short, fat": Asprey, *Frederick the Great,* p. 9.

171 *"an almost pathological"*: in Ergang, *The Potsdam Führer,* p. 84.

Taller soldiers have longer: See James M. Tanner, *A History of the Study of Human Growth* (Cambridge: Cambridge University Press, 1981), pp. 98–99. For a discussion of the military advantage of height in eighteenth-century warfare, see pp. 472–73.

"gigantomania": Ergang, *The Potsdam Führer,* p. 88.

"the tallest men ever": James M. Tanner, "A Short Walk through the Garden of Auxological Delights," in *Human Growth in Context,* ed. F. E. Johnston, B. Zemel, and P. B. Eveleth (London: Smith-Gordon, 1999), p. 4.

172 *"with transfer fees"*: Tanner, *History of the Study,* p. 98.

"Thus an officer of small stature": Ergang, *The Potsdam Führer,* pp. 84–85.

"one and only vice": Edith Simon, s.v. "Frederick the Great" in *Encyclopedia Britannica* 15th ed.

"oddest whimsy": Mitford, *Frederick the Great,* p. 21.

"They were an obsession": Ibid.

173 *political currency:* On the "market value" of eighteenth-century military giants, see Asprey, *Frederick the Great,* pp. 8, 126, and Tanner, *History of the Study,* p. 98.

"tall men for four": Asprey, *Frederick the Great,* p. 28.

"Nor have certain male": Charles Darwin, *The Descent of Man* (1879; New York: Penguin, 2004), p. 47. Darwin's sources on the success of the breeding program were probably incorrect; as his cousin Francis Galton correctly showed some years later, such matches would likely have produced smaller offspring, a phenomenon known as "regression to the mean" and consistent with Mitford's assertion that the children were of normal size.

"an expensive luxury": Simon, "Frederick the Great."

174 *"to reflect Goethe's"*: Tanner, *History of the Study,* p. 99.

the birth of anthropometry: See ed. John Komlos, *Stature, Living Standards, and Economic Development: Essays in Anthropometric History* (Chicago: University of Chicago, 1994).

175 *Inter-Departmental Committee on Physical Deterioration:* See Vernon Kellogg, "Eugenics and Militarism," *Atlantic Monthly,* July 1913, p. 99–108.

176 *"their physical characteristics"*: Tacitus, *The Germania,* trans. Harold Mattingly (New York: Penguin, 1970), p. 104.

"In every home": Ibid., p. 118.

"These are no love-locks": Ibid., p. 133.

"For myself, I accept": Ibid., p. 104.

"can never have dreamed": Harold Mattingly, ibid., p. 154.

"Those who preserve": Julius Caesar, quoted in Tanner, *History of the Study,* p. 469.

177 *"The young men are slow"*: Tacitus, quoted in Tanner, *History of the Study,* p. 468.

"Written in A.D. 98": Tanner, *History of the Study,* p. 468.

"comely tallnesse": Levinus Lemnius, quoted ibid., p. 25.

178 *"Nobility of soul"*: Johann Augustin Stoller, quoted in Tanner, *History of the Study,* p. 75.

"Nowadays we are soft": Julien-Joseph Virey, quoted in Tanner, *History of the Study,* p. 120.

179 *"Human height":* Louis-René Villermé, quoted in Tanner, *History of the Study,* p. 162.

The book provides: For variation in height according to population, see Phyllis B. Eveleth and James M. Tanner, *Worldwide Variation in Human Growth,* 2nd ed. (Cambridge: Cambridge University Press, 1990), pp. 205–7.

"You tell me": Alan D. Rogol, personal interview, July 22, 2004, New York.

Numerous histories: See, for example, Asprey, *Frederick the Great,* pp. 23, 47, 68.

180 *"soft silk robes":* Ibid., p. 21.

the beheading of: Ibid., pp. 69–70, and MacDonough, *Frederick the Great,* p. 35.

"in former years": Stoller, quoted in Tanner, *History of the Study,* p. 74.

"Impressions received": Frederick the Great, quoted in Asprey, *Frederick the Great,* p. 1.

"It is a question": Ibid., p. 124.

181 *This is hardly the place:* Since Napoleon's height is such a cultural signifier, it is not surprising that a robust debate continues over his actual size. On the basis of a rather extensive autopsy (see Paul Johnson, *Napoleon* [New York: Viking, 2002], pp. 180–81), it was widely believed that his adult height was 5 feet 2 inches, but there are claims that this stature reflects the incorrect translation of the French *pieds* into feet and inches. According to this point of view, Napoleon was actually 5 feet 6½ inches. For a flavor of the ongoing debate, see Ask Yahoo!, ask.yahoo.com/ask/20030724.html, and T. Holmberg, "First-Hand Descriptions of Napoleon," www.napoleon-series.org/research/c_description.html.

"in order to make": Kellogg, "Eugenics." The other facts about the height of French recruits also are from Kellogg.

"bellicosity": Johnson, *Napoleon,* p. 5.

182 *Napoleon complex:* Alfred Adler, *The Individual Psychology of Alfred Adler: A Systematic Presentation in Selections from His Writings,* ed. H. L. Ansbacher and R. R. Ansbacher (New York: Harper & Row, 1964), p. 36. Adler initially made the Napoleonic connection in a 1908 paper titled "Aggressionstrieb." In a discussion of compensation and the "aggression drive," he writes: "A further haven for the aggression drive is politics with its innumerable possibilities for activity and logical interpretation of any attack, Napoleon being the favorite hero" (ibid., p. 36).

Peter Gay points out: See ed. Peter Gay, *The Freud Reader* (New York: Norton, 1989), pp. 394, 665.

"one of the most blatant": John Kenneth Galbraith, quoted in Leslie F. Martel and Henry B. Biller, *Stature and Stigma: The Biopsychosocial Development of Short Males* (Lexington, Mass.: Lexington Books, 1987), p. 38.

"inherent disadvantages": Martel and Biller, *Stature and Stigma,* p. 9.

a survey of men: Ibid., p. 6.

least satisfied were: Ibid., p. 6.

183 *"All other things":* S. Fisher, quoted ibid., p. 6. For other early research correlating height with positive social values, see ibid., pp. 1–9.

According to a survey: L. Deck, "Short Workers of the World Unite," *Psychology Today* 5 (1971): 102.

one of the classics: D. Kurtz, "Tall Hiring Tale," *Wall Street Journal,* Nov. 25, 1969, p. 1.

"significantly more": William Graziano et al., "Height and Attraction: Do Men and Women See Eye to Eye?" *Journal of Personality* 46 (1978): 128–45.

Malcolm Gladwell polled: Malcolm Gladwell, *Blink: The Power of Thinking Without Thinking* (New York: Little, Brown, 2005), pp. 86–88.

184 *As a recent example:* T. A. Judge and D. M. Cable, "The Effect of Physical Height on Workplace Success and Income," *Journal of Applied Psychology* 89 (2004): 428–41. For earlier studies of the relationship between height and earnings, see G. Heineck, "Up in the Skies? The Relationship Between Body Height and Earnings in Germany" (working paper, Department of Economics, University of Munich, 2004), www.econhist/de/heineck/gh_Dateien/height-earn.pdf; and Martel and Biller, *Stature and Stigma,* pp. 37–39.

"open the black box": Judge and Cable, "The Effect of Physical Height," p. 438.

Even the Barker hypothesis: See D.J.P. Barker, J. G. Eriksson, T. Forsén, and C. Osmond, "Infant Growth and Income 50 Years Later," *Archives of Disease in Childhood* 90 (2005): 272–73.

185 *"height premium":* This and all other quotes are from Nicola Persico, Andrew Postlewaite, and Dan Silverman, "The Effect of Adolescent Experience on Labor Market Outcomes: The Case of Height," *Journal of Political Economy* 112 (2004): 1019–53. One caveat about this study: according to some psychologists with whom I spoke, the NLSY data set is weighted toward poorer socioeconomic factors, so that may have had an impact on some of the interpretations.

186 *"There's something going on":* Dan Silverman, telephone interview, Jan. 19, 2006.

187 *Growth Booster Plus:* This height-augmentation supplement is advertised on various Web sites. See, for example, www.growtall.com.

altPenis.com: This is a Web site about "penis enlargement, penis size," and related issues. See www.altPenis.com.

10. Timing Is Everything: Early and Late Pubertal Maturation

191 *"I was always small":* This and all other quotes are from Alan D. Rogol, personal interview, July 22, 2004, New York.

193 *father of Wilt Chamberlain:* see J. Taylor, *The Rivalry: Bill Russell, Wilt Chamberlain, and the Golden Age of Basketball* (New York: Random House, 2005), p. 44.

194 *"ridiculous":* James M. Tanner, *Fetus into Man: Physical Growth from Conception to Maturity,* 2nd ed. (Cambridge: Harvard University Press, 1990), p. 75.

"One simply should not": Ibid.

195 *According to Roman law:* See James M. Tanner, *A History of the Study of Human Growth* (Cambridge: Cambridge University Press, 1981), p. 12.

bone age: For a brief history of bone age and skeletal atlases, see J. M. Tanner, M.J.R. Healy, H. Goldstein, and N. Cameron, *Assessment of Skeletal Maturity and Prediction of Adult Height (TW3 Method),* 3rd ed. (London: W. B. Saunders, 2001). In the preface to the first edition (1962), Tanner et al. noted that bone age is "essential in any (perhaps misguided) attempts at treating short children by giving anabolic steroids. It also serves in the school years as the basis for the prediction of adult height and it is on this basis (and not by ex-cathedra assertions) that young people with an unusual but not pathological degree of growth delay may be rationally reassured as to their normality and future" (p. v). See also Tanner, *A History of the Study,* pp. 322–23, 329.

196   *"first placed the prediction":* Tanner et al., *Assessment of Skeletal Maturity.*
       Tanner-Whitehouse system: Ibid.
       baseball coaches and trainers: Murray Chass, "A Call for Smarter Use of Arms Falls on Deaf Ears," *New York Times,* Aug. 21, 2005, p. D-2.

197   *Born in 1759:* On Schiller at the Karlsschule, see Tanner, *History of the Study,* pp. 106–12.
       "Schiller must have started": Tanner, *History of the Study,* p. 110.

198   *"he always regretted":* Fernande Olivier, quoted in John Richardson, *A Life of Picasso,* vol. 1, *1881–1906* (New York: Random House, 1991) p. 310.
       "Whether or not": Richardson, *Picasso,* p. 49.

199   *In 1950 psychologist:* Mary C. Jones and Nancy Bayley, "Physical Maturing Among Boys as Related to Behavior," *Journal of Educational Psychology* 41 (1950): 129–48.
       In a 1957 paper: Paul H. Mussen and Mary C. Jones, "Self-Conceptions, Motivations, and Interpersonal Attitudes of Late- and Early-Maturing Boys," *Child Development* 28 (June 1957): 243–56.

200   *another follow-up study:* Paul H. Mussen and Mary C. Jones, "The Behavior-Inferred Motivations of Late- and Early-Maturing Boys," *Child Development* 29 (Mar. 1958): 61–67.
       "physical status during adolescence": Mussen and Jones, "Self-Conceptions," p. 254.
       a Swedish study: T. Andersson and D. Magnusson, "Biological Maturation in Adolescence and the Development of Drinking Habits and Alcohol Abuse Among Young Males: A Prospective Longitudinal Study," *Journal of Youth and Adolescence* 19 (1990): 33–41.

201   *almost as an afterthought:* Peter M. Lewinsohn, telephone interview, Apr. 26, 2005. For his earlier work on adolescence and depression, see P. M. Lewinsohn et al., "Adolescent Psychopathology: I. Prevalence and Incidence of Depression and Other DSM-III-R Disorders in High School Students," *Journal of Abnormal Psychology* 102 (1993): 133–44.
       first interim report: See J. A. Graber, P. M. Lewinsohn, J. R. Seeley, and J. Brooks-Gunn, "Is Psychopathology Associated with the Timing of Pubertal Development?" *Journal of the American Academy of Child and Adolescent Psychiatry* 36 (1997): 1768–76, and J. A. Graber et al., "Is Pubertal Timing Associated with Psychopathology in Young Adulthood?" *Journal of the American Academy of Child and Adolescent Psychiatry* 43 (June 2004): 718–26.
       "more daily hassles": Graber et al., "Is Psychopathology," p. 1772.
       "Wow!": This and all other quotes, unless otherwise noted, are from Julia Graber, telephone interview, Apr. 14, 2005.

202   *"perhaps the first":* Graber et al., "Is Pubertal Timing," p. 724.
       "significantly higher lifetime": Ibid., p. 722.
       "Late maturation in men": Ibid., p. 724.

203   *"would not be accurately":* C. A. Martin, T. H. Kelly, M. K. Rayens, B. R. Brogli, A. Brenzel, W. J. Smith, and H. A. Omar, "Sensation Seeking, Puberty, and Nicotine, Alcohol, and Marijuana Use in Adolescence," *Journal of the American Academy of Childhood and Adolescent Psychiatry* 41 (Dec. 2002): 1495–1502.

an Australian-American study: On pubertal development and substance abuse in Australia and Washington State, see G. C. Patton, B. J. McMorris, J. W. Toumbourou, S. A. Hemphill, S. Donath, and R. F. Catalano, "Puberty and the Onset of Substance Use and Abuse," *Pediatrics* 114 (Sept. 2004): 300–306.

204 *"pubertal stage, regardless":* Martin et al., "Sensation Seeking," p. 1501.

decreased alcohol use: C. A. Martin et al., "Adolescent and Young Adult Substance Abuse: Association with Sensation-Seeking, Self-Esteem and Retrospective Report of Early Pubertal Onset. A Preliminary Examination," *International Journal of Adolescent Medicine and Health* 13 (2001): 211–19.

a group at Indiana University: D. M. Dick, R. J. Rose, R. J. Viken, and J. Kaprio, "Pubertal Timing and Substance Abuse: Associations Between and Within Families Across Late Adolescence," *Developmental Psychology* 36 (2000): 180–89.

adolescent bullies: For the relationship between pubertal timing and the behavior of bullies, including dating, see J. Connolly et al., "Dating Experiences of Bullies in Early Adolescence," *Child Maltreatment* 5 (2000): 299–310.

experiments in animals: Patton et al., "Puberty and the Onset," p. 300–301.

205 *"Often, parents think":* Mark A. Sperling, telephone interview, May 31, 2005.

207 *"For the first time":* This and all other quotes are from H. Thomas Andersen, personal interview, Aug. 15, 2005, Eugene, Ore.

"It was like": Thomas J. O'Neill, personal interview, Feb. 15, 2005, Washington, D.C.

213 *the economics study:* Nicola Persico, Andrew Postlewaite, and Dan Silverman, "The Effect of Adolescent Experience on Labor Market Outcomes: The Case of Height," *Journal of Political Economy* 112 (2004): 1019–53.

"I do believe": This and all other quotes are from Andrew Postlewaite, telephone interviews, Apr. 13, 2005, and Jan. 19, 2006.

11. "Man in His Perfection": Adolescent Boys and Male Body Image

215 *"We are created":* Charles Atlas (Angelo Siciliano), quoted in P. Norman, "But Ladies, I Am Seventy-six Years Old," *London Sunday Times Color Supplement,* Oct. 19, 1969, p. 26.

a collection of plaster-cast: I am indebted to Edward Bleiberg, associate curator of Egyptian, classical, and Near East art at the Brooklyn Museum of Art, for information on the early history of the plaster statuary. I also consulted museum archives on the 1985 acquisition of the pieces and their disposition.

"populous townlet" and brigandage episode: Augustus J. C. Hare and St. Clark Baddeley, *Cities of Southern Italy* (New York: E. P. Dutton, 1911), p. 221.

216 *Milo of Crotone:* For a history of Milo, see H. W. Janson, *History of Art* (New York: Abrams, 1962), pp. 445–46, and *Encyclopedia Britannica,* 15th ed., s.v. "Magna Graecia." A nineteenth-century visitor to Crotone, the Scottish writer Craufurd Tait Ramage, noted: "The descendants of that Milo, whose feats of strength are among the wonders of our boyish days, stood before me. It was in vain that I looked round to discover the athletic forms and brawny muscles of former times" (ed., Edith Clay, *Ramage in South Italy* [Chicago: Academy, 1987], p. 129).

"I was never sickly": Angelo Siciliano (Chas. Atlas), "Building the Physique of a 'Greek God,'" *Physical Culture,* Nov. 1921, www.sandowplus.co.uk/competition/Atlas/atlasindex.htm (accessed Jan. 20, 2006). There is a vast literature, and equally

vast mythology, surrounding the Charles Atlas story, but this account, in Siciliano's own words and in the very early years of his business, has the advantage of being somewhat less exaggerated than subsequent versions and closer in time to the events described. I have relied on this for other biographical details as well. For a more official version, see Charles Gaines, *Yours in Perfect Manhood, Charles Atlas: The Most Effective Fitness Program Ever Devised* (New York: Fireside, 1982). This account is "based on the recollections of Charles P. Roman."

218 *a physical culture enthusiast:* For Tilney's role in launching the business, see G. Anderson, "Frederick W. Tilney, 1895–1977," www.sandowplus2.co.uk/Tilney/tilneyintro.htm. Also at this site, see Tilney's autobiography, *Young at 73 and Beyond,* in which he describes how he formed a mail-order business with Atlas in 1922.
His likeness: See S. Robertson, "Muscles by Mail," *Family Circle,* Jan. 20, 1939, and "Atlas Was Right All Along," *Life,* Apr. 17, 1964.

219 *"It may not seem":* Siciliano, "Building the Physique," p. 40.
who got beat up: See obituary of Charles Atlas, *New York Times,* Dec. 24, 1972, which recounts the beach episode. Atlas never mentioned the incident in any of his autobiographical writings, including ones with clear marketing intent, until around the time the ads first appeared.
"The muscles ran around": R. L. Taylor, "Self-Made Man — and Body," *The New Yorker,* Jan. 3, 1942, pp. 21–27.

220 *"I may be mistaken":* Siciliano, "Building the Physique," p. 39.
a young advertising man: For background on Charles Roman, see E. Pace, "Charles P. Roman, Associate of Charles Atlas, Dies at 92," *New York Times,* July 20, 1999, p. B-9. According to Jeffrey Hogue, who now heads the Charles Atlas enterprise, early coupon advertisements asked respondents to check a box if they were younger than fourteen years of age. Roman reportedly refused to sell the Dynamic-Tension system to anyone younger than fourteen, believing that the price was too high (telephone interview, Feb. 15, 2006).
Created by Roman: For online versions of "The Insult That Made a Man Out of 'Mac,'" see, for example, www.charlesatlas.com and www.sandowplus.co.uk/Competition/Atlas/Adverts/adverts.htm.

221 *"rather strong":* Siciliano, "Building the Physique."
Charles Atlas Ltd.: See M. Newman, "Hey, Skinny! Charles Atlas Lives!" *New York Times,* May 31, 2001, p. B-1.

222 *contemporary action figures:* See Harrison G. Pope Jr. et al., "Evolving Ideals of Male Body Image as Seen Through Action Toys," *International Journal of Eating Disorders* 26 (1999): 65–72.
Atlas in his prime: See "The World's Most Handsome Man," *Physical Culture,* Oct. 1921, pp. 19–22.
Joe Louis: See www.boxinginsider.net/stats_tott.php?vo=77.

223 *"People misinterpreted":* This and all other quotes, unless otherwise noted, are from Harrison G. Pope Jr., personal interview, June 3, 1999, Belmont, Mass.
"imagined ugliness": Katharine A. Phillips et al., "Body Dysmorphic Disorder: 30 Cases of Imagined Ugliness," *American Journal of Psychiatry* 150 (1993): 302–8.
The average age of onset: Katharine A. Phillips, telephone interview, July 18, 1999.
The incidence of body dysmorphic disorder: Roberto Olivardia, personal communication, Apr. 14, 2006.
"Although boys generally": Geoffrey H. Cohane and Harrison G. Pope Jr., "Body

Image in Boys: A Review of the Literature," *International Journal of Eating Disorders* 29 (2001): 373–79.

224 *"The feminist complaint":* Kelly Brownell, telephone interview, May 28, 1999. For background on girls' perception of body image and cultural messages in general, see C. Gilligan, *In a Different Voice: Psychological Theory and Women's Development* (Cambridge: Harvard University Press, 1982); M. Pipher, *Reviving Ophelia: Saving the Selves of Adolescent Girls* (New York: G. P. Putnam, 1994); and N. Wolf, *The Beauty Myth: How Images of Beauty Are Used Against Women* (New York: Morrow, 1991).

224 *"Boys are much more prone":* Mary Pipher, telephone interview, May 18, 1999.

"perceived themselves": Harrison G. Pope Jr. et al., "Muscle Dysmorphia: An Underrecognized Form of Body Dysmorphic Disorder," *Psychosomatics* 38 (1997): 548–57.

"muscle dysmorphia": K. A. Phillips et al., "Body Dysmorphic Disorder: An Obsessive-Compulsive Spectrum Disorder, a Form of Affective Disorder, or Both?" *Journal of Clinical Psychiatry* 56, Suppl. 4 (1995): 45–51.

225 *"Adonis complex":* For a book-length treatment of the Adonis complex, see Harrison G. Pope Jr., Katharine A. Phillips, and Roberto Olivardia, *The Adonis Complex: The Secret Crisis of Male Body Obsession* (New York: Free Press, 2000). For a good integration of body image and scientific issues, see Nancy Etcoff, *Survival of the Prettiest: The Science of Beauty* (New York: Doubleday, 1999).

"somatomorphic matrix": Harrison G. Pope Jr. et al., "Body Image Perception Among Men in Three Countries," *American Journal of Psychiatry* 157 (Aug. 2000): 1297–1301. For a review of recent studies involving body image issues in boys under age eighteen, see Cohane and Pope, "Body Image in Boys."

the first systematic measurements: On the measurement of the human form and the contributions of Vitruvius and Alberti, see James M. Tanner, *A History of the Study of Human Growth* (Cambridge: Cambridge University Press, 1981), pp. 32–45, and Janson, *History of Art*, pp. 135, 320–21, 329–32.

226 *"the symmetry and proportion":* Tanner, *History of the Study*, p. 33.

227 *"[When] I took on":* Leon Battista Alberti, quoted ibid., pp. 38–39.

228 *"incomparably illustrated":* Tanner, *History of the Study*, p. 40.

"to take lessons": Ibid., p. 41.

"This school": Ibid., p. 57. Tanner also provides the history of the statue measurers.

229 *"Numbers rule the world":* Adolphe Quetelet, quoted ibid., p. 123.

"the author, inventor": Florence Nightingale, quoted in Tanner, *History of the Study*, p. 141.

"An individual who combined": Quetelet, quoted in Tanner, *History of the Study*, p. 128.

"If the average man": Ibid.

230 *Eugen Sandow:* See John F. Kasson, *Tarzan, Houdini, and the Perfect Man: The White Male Body and the Challenge of Modernity in America* (New York: Hill and Wang, 2001), pp. 21–76.

political consequences: See D. Kevles, *In the Name of Eugenics* (New York: Knopf, 1985), p. 132; E. Black, *War Against the Weak: Eugenics and America's Campaign to Create a Master Race* (New York: Four Walls Eight Windows, 2003), pp. 250–52; and C. R. Pierpont, "The Measure of America," *The New Yorker*, Mar. 8, 2004, p. 57, all on the "anti-weakling" rhetoric of the proponents of eugenics legislation.

231 *"I think drugs"*: Roberto Olivardia, telephone interview, Jan. 24, 2006.
"Yes, definitely": Arnold Schwarzenegger, *Pumping Iron,* George Butler and Robert Fiore, directors, 1977.

232 *"Oh, man"*: Alex Bregstein, quoted in Stephen S. Hall, "The Bully in the Mirror," *New York Times Magazine,* Aug. 22, 1999, pp. 30–35, 58, 62–65. All quotes from Bregstein and the other boys, unless otherwise noted, are from this article.

233 *"what they can say"*: William S. Pollack, personal interview, June 1, 1999, Newton, Mass. See also William Pollack, *Real Boys: Rescuing Our Sons from the Myths of Boyhood* (New York: Random House, 1998).
"When you go to ask": Dan Kindlon, personal interview, June 2, 1999, Cambridge, Mass. See also Dan Kindlon and Michael Thompson, *Raising Cain: Protecting the Emotional Life of Boys* (New York: Ballantine, 1999). Useful observations on the emotional development of boys can also be found in M. Gurian, *The Wonder of Boys: What Parents, Mentors and Educators Can Do to Shape Boys into Exceptional Men* (New York: Tarcher, 1996), and J. Garbarino, *Lost Boys: How Our Sons Turn Violent and How We Can Save Them* (New York: Free Press, 1999).

234 *"Not that it's embarrassing"*: This and all other quotes from the private-school boys are from a meeting on the Upper East Side of Manhattan, June 22, 1999.

235 *"a very ordinary looking"*: Pope et al., "Body Perception Among Men," pp. 1300–1301.

236 *In one study:* H. G. Pope Jr., R. Olivardia, J. J. Borowiecki III, and G. H. Cohane, "The Growing Commercial Value of the Male Body: A Longitudinal Survey of Advertising in Women's Magazines," *Psychotherapy and Psychosomatics* 70 (2001): 189–92.
a follow-up study: C-F. J. Yang, P. Gray, and H. G. Pope Jr., "Male Body Image in Taiwan Versus the West: Yanggang Zhiqi Meets the Adonis Complex," *American Journal of Psychiatry* 162 (Feb. 2005): 263–69.
"Maybe fifteen years": Kindlon, interview.
"Chicks Love": Nike advertisement, 1998. By the 2006 baseball season, when accusations of steroid use hounded home-run hitter Barry Bonds, public sentiment had shifted dramatically; fans at spring training games held up signs reading CHICKS DON'T DIG CHEATERS (*New York Daily News,* Mar. 10, 2006, p. 90). In terms of the portrayal of the human body in television commercials, especially by sporting goods companies such as Nike, a surprising parallel can be seen between many contemporary ads and the visual sensibility of *Olympia* (1938), Leni Riefenstahl's documentary about the 1936 Olympics in Berlin.
"Freud would have": Kindlon, interview.

237 *"basement porn"*: For a brief history of homoerotic advertising, including the dialogue in the ad cited, see Hall, "Bully in the Mirror."
"You got a real nice look": Ibid.

238 *Department of Justice investigation:* See Pierre Thomas, "Calvin Klein Ads Cleared," *Washington Post,* Nov. 16, 1995, p. D-7.
"The style, the look": Bob Garfield, telephone interview, July 9, 1999. For an account of the furor over the Calvin Klein ads, see Stuart Elliott, "Will Calvin Klein's Retreat Redraw the Lines of Taste?" *New York Times,* Aug. 29, 1995, p. D-1.
"probably had to do": Olivardia, interview.
"the opening up": Garfield, interview.
the teen clothier: For an account of the Abercrombie & Fitch campaigns, see S.

Elliott, "Abercrombie & Fitch Extends a Print Campaign to TV," *New York Times,* Aug. 6, 1999, p. C-5.

239   *Monitoring the Future research:* L. D. Johnston et al., "Monitoring the Future: National Results on Adolescent Drug Use, Overview of Key Findings, 2004" (University of Michigan and National Institute on Drug Abuse, Bethesda, Md., 2005), pp. 38–39. On the adolescent use of steroids and body image drugs, see also G. Kanayama et al., "'Body Image' Drugs: A Growing Psychosomatic Problem," *Psychotherapy and Psychosomatics* 70 (2001): 61–65.
      The overall rate: Charles Yesalis, telephone interview, Feb. 24, 2005.

240   *Recent figures on cosmetic surgery:* American Society of Plastic Surgeons Web site, www.plasticsurgery.org.
      limb lengthening: Alfred Grant, personal interview, Dec. 22, 2004, New York.

241   *"I lift, but not":* Alex Bregstein, telephone interview, Mar. 11, 2005.

12. The Emperor's New Medicine Cabinet: Human Growth Hormone and Height Augmentation in Children

242   *"Today, it is acknowledged":* David B. Allen and Norman Fost, "hGH for Short Stature: Ethical Issues Raised by Expanded Access," *Journal of Pediatrics* 144 (May 2004): 648.
      "What is a clinically": Paul D. Woolf, quoted in Food and Drug Administration, Center for Drug Evaluation and Research (CDER), Endocrinologic and Metabolic Drugs Advisory Committee Meeting, June 10, 2003, transcript (hereafter FDA transcript), www.fda.gov/ohrms/dockets/ac/03/transcripts/3957T1.htm. See also Stephen S. Hall, "The Short of It," *New York Times Magazine,* Oct. 16, 2005, pp. 54–59.
      In 1988 Eli Lilly: For background on Eli Lilly's clinical trial for idiopathic short stature, see Lilly Research Laboratories, "Briefing Document: Endocrinologic and Metabolic Drugs Advisory Committee, June 10, 2003: Humatrope (somatropin [rDNA origin] for injection) for Non–Growth Hormone Deficient Short Stature" (hereafter "Briefing Document"), pp. 16, 22–24, www.fda.gov/ohrms/dockets/ac/03/briefing/3957B1_01_Lilly-Humatrope.pdf; and the remarks of Gregory Enas (pp. 17–18) and Raymond Hintz (pp. 29–30), in FDA transcript.

243   *The potential market:* See FDA transcript, pp. 81–82. Lilly officials stated at the time that they believed the number of actual users of hGH among this population would probably be 30,000 to 40,000.
      To put that number: For estimates of hGH use prior to 1985, see J. E. Fradkin et al., "Creutzfeldt-Jakob Disease in Pituitary Growth Hormone Recipients in the United States," *Journal of the American Medical Association* 265 (Feb. 20, 1991): 880–84. This study examined a "possible cohort" of 8,157 persons and confirmed that 6,284 received growth hormone through the National Hormone and Pituitary Program between 1963 and 1985.
      reams of clinical information: For results of Lilly's clinical trials of hGH for idiopathic short stature, see "Briefing Document," pp. 31–80, and FDA transcript, pp. 30–54.
      "pivotal trial": E. W. Leschek et al., "Effect of Growth Hormone Treatment on

Adult Height in Peripubertal Children with Idiopathic Short Stature. A Randomized, Double-Blind, Placebo-Controlled Trial," *Journal of Clinical Endocrinology and Metabolism* 89 (2004): 3140–48.

trial in Europe: J. M. Wit et al., "Growth Hormone (GH) Treatment to Final Height in Children with Idiopathic Short Stature: Evidence for a Dose Effect," *Journal of Pediatrics* 146 (2005): 45–53. A meta-analysis of thirty-eight clinical trials of hGH put the average gain in adult height at 4 to 6 centimeters (roughly 1½ to 2½ inches) (B. S. Finkelstein et al., "Effect of Growth Hormone Therapy on Height in Children with Idiopathic Short Stature," *Archives of Pediatric & Adolescent Medicine* 156 [Mar. 2002]: 230–40). Finkelstein et al. concluded, "Given current treatment costs, this corresponds to more than $35,000 per inch (2.54 cm) gained in adult height in idiopathic short stature." By 2006 the estimated cost per inch had risen to more than $50,000 (see J. M. Lee et al., "Estimated Cost-Effectiveness of Growth Hormone Therapy for Idiopathic Short Stature," *Archives of Pediatric & Adolescent Medicine* 160 [2006]: 263–69).

To put these measurements (and the efficacy of human growth hormone treatment) in perspective, the "gain" in height reported in all these studies was an estimate of drug-assisted growth versus what doctors predicted would naturally occur, so it is by definition an indirect quantification. If a child with ISS grows eight inches while on growth hormone, for example, doctors cannot tell what percentage of the growth was due to the drug and what percentage was due to the child's natural growth process. Furthermore, the predictions of adult height were based partially on measurements of growth velocity over a "screening period" of six months ("Briefing Document," p. 34). In the view of some growth experts, six months is inadequate to distinguish a growth problem from normal variations in growth rate. When I asked James Tanner about this, he suggested that tracking growth velocity over only six months was "absolutely inadequate, and that for several reasons, all fatal" (James M. Tanner, personal communication, April 3, 2005).

the drug was safe: "Briefing Document," p. 19, and the remarks of Chairman Quigley, in FDA transcript, pp. 54–55. For additional safety data, see FDA transcript, pp. 54–69, and "Briefing Document," pp. 81–127. According to subsequently published data, an estimated 200,000 patients had been treated with growth hormone; rare adverse effects included benign intracranial hypertension (high blood pressure in the brain) and slipped capital femoral epiphysis (slippage in the hip joint). See C. A. Quigley et al., "Safety of Growth Hormone Treatment in Pediatric Patients with Idiopathic Short Stature," *Journal of Clinical Endocrinology and Metabolism* 90 (Sept. 2005): 5188–96.

244 *"short children may be subject":* "Briefing Document," p. 27.

"provided evidence of potential": Ibid., p. 79. The additional irony here is that Lilly cited, without elaboration or qualification, the work of two growth experts (Sandburg and Voss) whose main findings have repeatedly suggested that short stature in children is *not* psychologically disabling.

If you read the transcript: For the sentiments of committee members on the "clinical meaningfulness" of growth hormone in idiopathic short stature (ISS) children, see the remarks of D. Grady (p. 257), G. Braunstein (pp. 258–59), D. Schade (p. 263), P. Woolf (p. 264), M. Gelato (p. 265), N. Watts (p. 266), and N. Worcester (p. 267), in FDA transcript. Chairman Braunstein, for example, noted at one point, "One of the major problems is that there's no quality of life data that is sufficient for us to judge whether the clinical benefit of the height augmentation is really clinically significant . . . And, in regards to whether it is a clinically meaningful response, three members of the panel felt the answer was 'yes,' and five had a very large question mark, and one felt that the definition of 'clinically meaningful' really must be defined by the patient and the family" (pp. 323–24). The author's follow-up interviews included Glenn Braunstein, M.D., Department of Medicine, Cedars-Sinai Medical Center, Los Angeles, telephone interview, July 8, 2005; Paul Woolf, M.D., Department of Medicine, Crozer-Chester Medical Center, Upland, Pa., telephone interview, Apr. 18, 2005; Deborah Grady, M.D., Department of Epidemiology, University of California, San Francisco, telephone interview, Mar. 25, 2005; Harvey Guyda, M.D., Montreal Children's Hospital and McGill University, telephone interview, Mar. 18, 2005; Ron Rosenfeld, M.D., Department of Pediatrics, Oregon Health and Sciences University, Portland, telephone interview, June 23, 2005; Allen Root, M.D., All Children's Hospital, St. Petersburg, Fla., telephone interview, Apr. 11, 2005; and Charmian Quigley, M.D., Eli Lilly and Company, Indianapolis, telephone interview, July 12, 2005.

"I think the FDA": Joel Frader, telephone interview, July 7, 2004.

245   *"With all sorts":* This and all other quotes are from Alan D. Rogol, telephone interview, June 15, 2005.

sales of growth hormone: See 2004 annual reports for Pfizer, Eli Lilly, Genentech, Novo Nordisk, and Serono.

a child at the twenty-fifth percentile: CBS News, "Kids' Hormones: A Growth Industry," Sept. 8, 2004, cbsnews.com/stories/2003/11/18/60II/printable584265.shtml (accessed July 12, 2005).

"My conclusion about": Glenn Braunstein, quoted in FDA transcript, p. 259.

"cosmetic endocrinology": Braunstein, interview.

246   *"Oh, my gosh":* Camille Weichlein, telephone interview, June 22, 2005. This interview was conducted in connection with my 2005 *New York Times Magazine* article (Hall, "The Short of It").

"On my knees": This and all other quotes are from Deno Andrews, in FDA transcript, pp. 193–203.

247   *"You can look at someone":* Steven D. Chernausek, telephone interview, Apr. 14, 2005.

In 1956 Robert M. Blizzard: For the early history of growth hormone, see Robert M. Blizzard, "Growth Hormone as a Therapeutic Agent," *Growth, Genetics and Hormones* 21 (Dec. 2005): 49–54, and S. M. Rothman and D. J. Rothman, *The Pursuit of Perfection: The Promise and Perils of Medical Enhancement* (New York: Pantheon, 2003), pp. 168–207. Additional background is from Robert M. Blizzard, M.D., chair emeritus, Department of Pediatrics, University of Virginia School of Medicine, Charlottesville, telephone interview, June 8, 2005; Leslie Plotnick, M.D., Department of Pediatrics, Johns Hopkins University School of Medicine, Baltimore, telephone interview, Apr. 19, 2005; and Selna Kaplan, M.D., Department of Pediatrics, University of California, San Francisco, telephone interview, Mar. 22, 2005.

248   *In 1963 Blizzard predicted:* Robert M. Blizzard, "The Past, Present, and Future of Pituitary Growth Hormone," *American Journal of Diseases of Children* 106 (1963): 439–40.

Then tragedy struck: See C. Norman, "Virus Scare Halts Hormone Research," *Science* 228 (June 7, 1985): 1176–77; Fradkin et al., "Creutzfeldt-Jakob Disease"; and J. L. Mills et al., "Long-Term Mortality in the United States Cohort of Pituitary-Derived Growth Hormone Recipients," *Journal of Pediatrics* 144 (Apr. 2004): 430–36. This last article put the total number of CJD cases at twenty-six.

"Bob and I were": James M. Tanner, personal interview, Sept. 29, 2004, Dunkeswell, Eng.

One of the first: On the cloning of the growth hormone gene, see Stephen S. Hall, *Invisible Frontiers: The Race to Synthesize a Human Gene* (New York: Atlantic Monthly Press, 1987).

a bit murky: See M. Barinaga, "Genentech, UC Settle Suit for $200 Million," *Science* 286 (1999): 1655, and R. Dalton and Q. Schermeier, "Genentech Pays $200 M. over Growth Hormone 'Theft,'" *Nature* 402 (1999): 335.

The company sent: William F. Crowley Jr., telephone interview, May 5, 2005.

250 *"horrible":* Braunstein, interview.

"do not support the use": Judith L. Ross et al., "Psychological Adaptation in Children with Idiopathic Short Stature Treated with Growth Hormone or Placebo," *Journal of Clinical Endocrinology and Metabolism* 89 (Oct. 2004): 4873–78. For "inconclusive" Lilly data on the psychological benefits of hGH treatment in ISS children, see the remarks of Judith Ross, in FDA transcript, pp. 102–8.

romantic partner: L. T. Rekers-Momburg et al., "Quality of Life of Young Adults with Idiopathic Short Stature: Effect of Growth Hormone Treatment," *Acta Paediatrica* 87 (1998): 865–70.

In 2004 researchers: F. Ulph et al., "Personality Functioning: The Influence of Stature," *Archives of Disease in Childhood* 89 (2004): 17–21.

He even admitted: See the remarks of Deno Andrews, in FDA transcript, pp. 198–99.

251 *"Is this . . . a placebo":* David Sandberg, personal interview, June 6, 2005, Buffalo.

"We're really having": This and all other quotes are from David B. Allen, personal interview, Oct. 7, 2004, Madison, Wisc. The Allen and Fost position was first outlined in David B. Allen and Norman C. Fost, "Growth Hormone Therapy for Short Stature: Panacea or Pandora's Box?" *Journal of Pediatrics* 117 (1990): 16–21. For an updated appraisal, see Allen and Fost, "hGH for Short Stature: Ethical Issues Raised by Expanded Access," *Journal of Pediatrics* 144 (May 2004): 648–52.

252 *the argument that Eli Lilly:* See the remarks of Gordon Cutler (p. 31) and Charmian Quigley (pp. 82–83), in FDA transcript.

253 *"expansive biotechnology":* Allen Buchanan, "Growth Hormone: A Paradigm of Expansive Biotechnologies," *Endocrinologist* 11 (2001): 78S–82S.

255 *I've looked into:* See Stephen S. Hall, "Short Like Me," *Health,* Jan./Feb. 1996, pp. 98–106. For a more recent perspective on the familial dilemma about hGH therapy, see J. Everett, "My Little Brother on Drugs," *Popular Science,* Apr. 2004, pp. 78–84, 110. This article describes the initiation of growth hormone therapy for the author's nine-year-old brother, Alex Everett, who ranked in the third percentile in height. William Tamborlane, a member of the FDA advisory committee who voted to approve hGH at the 2003 meeting, is asked by the author, "If Alex were your son, would you put him on hGH?" Tamborlane, a pediatric endocrinologist at

Yale University School of Medicine, replied, "Given the uncertainties, probably not."

Even ten years ago: For the percentage of hGH use that was "off-label," see L. Cuttler et al., "Short Stature and Growth Hormone Therapy: A National Study of Physician Recommendation Patterns," *Journal of the American Medical Association* 276 (Aug. 21, 1996): 531–37.

256   *Those charts have been supplanted:* Tanner, interview.

"This may be the only": Michael Freemark, "Growth Hormone Treatment of 'Idiopathic Short Stature': Not So Fast," editorial, *Journal of Clinical Endocrinology and Metabolism* 89 (July 2004): 3138–39. A more recent editorial in the same journal concluded that the high cost and uncertain psychological benefits of growth hormone for ISS "may well dampen enthusiasm" (L. Cuttler, "Safety and Efficacy of Growth Hormone Treatment for Idiopathic Short Stature," editorial, *Journal of Clinical Endocrinology and Metabolism* 90 [Sept. 2005]: 5502–4).

258   *the possible role:* See Adda Grimberg, "Cancer," in *The Growth Hormone/Insulin-Like Growth Factor Axis During Development,* ed. I. Varela-Nieto and J. A. Chowen (*Advances in Experimental Medicine and Biology* 567, 2005): 305–39.

"When you look": Adda Grimberg, telephone interview, June 14, 2005; and personal interview, July 11, 2005, Philadelphia. Additional background is from Pinchas Cohen, M.D., Department of Pediatrics, University of California, Los Angeles, telephone interview, June 13, 2005.

13. College *and Beyond: The End of Physical Growth*

263   *"The secret of getting":* This and all other quotes are from *College,* James Horne, director, 1927.

265   *For adult males:* For comparisons of male and female adult heights throughout the world, see "Human Height" in the on-line encyclopedia Wikipedia, http://en.wikipedia.org/wiki/Human_height.

other physical changes: Stephen Shalet, "Stepping into Adulthood: The Transition Period," *Hormone Research* 62, Suppl. 4 (2004): 15–22.

266   *As growth expert:* Barry Bogin, *The Growth of Humanity* (New York: Wiley-Liss, 2001), pp. 93–95.

"few boys successfully": Ibid., p. 95.

"My war with my skin": John Updike, *Self-Consciousness* (New York: Knopf, 1986), p. 72.

267   *"What do you tell":* This and all other quotes, unless otherwise noted, are from David Sandberg, personal interview, Oct. 22, 2004, New York.

268   *"I found that these kids":* Partial results were published as David E. Sandberg et al., "Short Stature: a Psychosocial Burden Requiring Growth Hormone Therapy?" *Pediatrics* 94 (1994): 832–40.

269   *"minimal detectable impact":* D. E. Sandberg, W. H. Bukowski, C. M. Fung, and R. B. Noll, "Height and Social Adjustment: Are Extremes a Cause for Concern and Action?" *Pediatrics* 114 (Sept. 2004): 744–50. See also "Shortness Is No Stigma," *New York Times,* Sept. 14, 2004, p. F-6.

270 *Wessex Growth Study:* See A. B. Downie et al., "Are Short Normal Children at a Disadvantage? The Wessex Growth Study," *British Journal of Medicine* 314 (1997): 97–100, and Linda D. Voss, "Short Normal Stature and Psychosocial Disadvantage: A Critical Review of the Evidence," *Journal of Pediatric Endocrinology and Metabolism* 14 (2001): 701–11.

"no significant differences": F. Ulph et al., "Personality Functioning: The Influence of Stature," *Archives of Disease in Childhood* 89 (2004): 17–21.

parents of short kids: For parental statements of concern, see Food and Drug Administration, Center for Drug Evaluation and Research (CDER), Endocrinologic and Metabolic Drugs Advisory Committee Meeting, June 10, 2003 (transcript), www.fda.gov/ohrms/dockets/ac/03/transcripts/3957T1.htm. For additional perspectives, see Human Growth Foundation, www.hgfound.org, and Magic Foundation, www.magicfoundation.org.

271 *When Eli Lilly:* See Lilly Research Laboratories, "Briefing Document: Endocrinologic and Metabolic Drugs Advisory Committee, June 10, 2003: Humatrope (somatropin [rDNA origin] for injection) for Non–Growth Hormone Deficient Short Stature," pp. 102–8, www.fda.gov/ohrms/dockets/ac/03/briefing/3957B1_01_Lilly-Humatrope.pdf.

"The data do not support": Judith L. Ross et al., "Psychological Adaptation in Children with Idiopathic Short Stature Treated with Growth Hormone or Placebo," *Journal of Clinical Endocrinology and Metabolism* 89 (Oct. 2004): 4873–78. David Sandberg was one of the authors of this article. In addition to Ross et al., an earlier European study reached a similar conclusion about growth hormone: "The assumption that growth hormone treatment improves [health-related quality of life] in children with ISS could not be supported in this study" (N.C.M. Theunissen et al., "Quality of Life and Self-Esteem in Children Treated for Idiopathic Short Stature," *Journal of Pediatrics* 140 [May 2002]: 507–15).

Pinchas Cohen, a pediatric: See www.biocritique.com/viewref.cfm?messageid=bf8a5ffe5-32d4-4f7d-b43b-5da5591250b2 (accessed Feb. 20, 2006).

"toilet paper": Pinchas Cohen, telephone interview, Apr. 22, 2005.

got in a dig: Charmian Quigley, telephone interview, July 12, 2005.

272 *"I would think":* Jerry Avorn, telephone interview, July 14, 2005.

"David Sandberg's data": Alan D. Rogol, telephone interview, June 15, 2005.

"I have great respect": Robert M. Blizzard, telephone interview, June 8, 2005.

273 *If you are performing:* For an assessment of "referral bias," see J. H. Kranzler et al., "Is Short Stature a Handicap? A Comparison of the Psychosocial Functioning of Referred and Nonreferred Children with Normal Short Stature and Children with Normal Stature," *Journal of Pediatrics* 136 (Jan. 2000): 96–102.

more likely to be a boy: See A. Grimberg, J. K. Kutikov, and A. J. Cucchiara, "Sex Differences in Patients Referred for Evaluation of Poor Growth," *Journal of Pediatrics* 146 (Feb. 2005): 212–16.

274 *many health insurers:* Rogol, interview; Henry Anhalt, M.D., Division of Pediatric Endocrinology and Diabetes, St. Barnabas Medical Center, Livingston, N.J., telephone interview, Mar. 15, 2005; and Stephen S. Hall, "The Short of It."

researchers have shown: For a version of this treatment algorithm, see D. E. Sandberg and M. Colsman, "Assessment of Psychosocial Aspects of Short Stature," *Growth, Genetics and Hormones* 21 (June 2005): 17–25.

276 *"focusing illusion"*: D. A. Schkade and D. Kahneman, "Does Living in California Make People Happy? A Focusing Illusion in Judgments of Life Satisfaction," *Psychological Science* 9 (1998): 340–46.
during a conversation: Selna Kaplan, telephone interview, Mar. 22, 2005.

278 *"It seems that the problems"*: Jan J. V. Busschbach et al., "Some Patients with Idiopathic Short Stature See Their Short Stature as a Problem but Others Do Not: Why This Difference?" in *Growth, Stature, and Psychosocial Well-Being,* ed. U. Eiholzer, F. Haverkamp, and L. D. Voss (Bern: Hogrefe and Huber, 1999), p. 34.

279 *So what would I:* A good guide to some of these issues is P. Reiser and H.F.L. Meyer-Bahlburg, *Short and Okay: A Guide for Parents of Short Children* (Falls Church, Va.: Human Growth Foundation, 1997). See also E. Parens, "Introduction," in *Surgically Shaping Children: Technology, Ethics, and the Pursuit of Normality,* E. Parens, ed. (Baltimore: Johns Hopkins University Press, 2006).

14. The Tallest People on Earth: Historical Anthropometry and the Standard of Living

283 *"White men like to dig"*: Sitting Bull, "The Life My People Want Is a Life of Freedom," in *Great Speeches by Native Americans,* ed. Bob Blaisdell (Mineola, N.Y.: Dover, 2000), p. 169.
The scene depicted: Standing Bear, *Battle of Little Big Horn,* circa 1885, exhibited at the George Gustav Heye Center, National Museum of the American Indian, Smithsonian Institution, New York.

284 *"excellent dental health"*: This and all other quotes, unless otherwise noted, are from Richard H. Steckel, personal interview, June 28, 2004, New York; and personal interview, July 31, 2004, Columbus, Ohio.
height data from the muster: Richard Steckel, personal communication, Feb. 19, 2006.

285 *"How did apparently"*: Richard H. Steckel and Joseph M. Prince, "Tallest in the World: Native Americans in the Great Plains in the Nineteenth Century," *American Economic Review* 91 (2001): 287–94. The paper was originally presented at the meeting of the International Commission on Historical Demography, Oslo, 1999.
biological form of economic history: For an excellent review of the use of anthropometry as an economic indicator, see Richard H. Steckel, "Stature and the Standard of Living," *Journal of Economic Literature* 33 (Dec. 1995): 1903–40. For a thorough explanation of how height surveys can reveal socioeconomic factors, with many examples specific to different parts of the world, see Phyllis B. Eveleth and James M. Tanner, *Worldwide Variation in Human Growth,* 2nd ed. (New York: Cambridge University Press, 1990).

286 *"secular trend" in Japanese men:* See Eveleth and Tanner, *Worldwide Variations,* pp. 103–4, 206.
Researchers in the Netherlands: Ibid., p. 206.
average height of Americans: Richard H. Steckel, personal communication, Feb. 5, 2006.
The word "anthropometry": Tanner traces the word back to Johann Elsholtz, a German physician who published a thesis in 1654 titled *Anthropometria* (James M.

Tanner, *A History of the Study of Human Growth* [Cambridge: Cambridge University Press, 1981], 45).

"Misery produces": Julien-Joseph Virey, quoted in J. Komlos, M. Hau, and N. Bourguinat, "The Anthropometric History of Early-Modern France" (working paper, University of Munich, 2001).

A latter-day French scholar: For a recent survey of the history of the field, see T. Cuff, *EH.Net Encyclopedia*, 2004, s.v. "Historical Anthropometrics," www.eh.net/encyclopedia/article/cuff.anthropometric (accessed Jan. 23, 2006).

287 *a hugely controversial book*: Robert W. Fogel and Stanley L. Engerman, *Time on the Cross: The Economics of American Negro Slavery* (New York: Little, Brown, 1974). Writing on the transformative impact of anthropometric data in an afterword to the paperback edition (New York: Norton, 1989), Fogel and Engerman note, "The new data not only made it possible to resolve points that were at issue in 1974–76, but have revealed aspects of slave nutritional status and health that were not even contemplated during these debates" (p. 270).

288 *"age of slaves at menarche"*: For early slave height studies and the relationship between female height and menarche, see James Trussell and Richard Steckel, "The Age of Slaves at Menarche and Their First Birth," *Journal of Interdisciplinary History* 8 (1978): 477–505, and Richard Steckel, "Slave Height Profiles from Coastwise Manifests," *Explorations in Economic History* 16 (1979): 363–80.

289 *"Well," Tanner replied*: Steckel, interview.

290 *statistical tricks necessary*: For background on the interaction between Tanner's group and American economists and demographers, I relied on Robert W. Fogel, telephone interview, Dec. 7, 2004; James Trussell, telephone interview, Dec. 23, 2004; and James M. Tanner, telephone interview, July 20, 2004.

291 *stunted childhood growth*: For differences in nutritional treatment between slave children and adults, see Richard Steckel, "A Peculiar Population: The Nutrition, Health, and Mortality of American Slaves from Childhood to Maturity," *Journal of Economic History* 46 (1986): 721–41.

this spectacular catch-up: For male slave heights and nutrition, see R. Margo and R. Steckel, "The Height of American Slaves: New Evidence on Slave Nutrition and Health," *Social Science History* 6 (1982): 516–38.

292 *average height of nineteenth-century Americans*: See R. A. Margo and R. H. Steckel, "Heights of Native-Born Whites During the Antebellum Period," *Journal of Economic History* 43, no. 1 (Mar. 1983): 167–74.

"I got up": Tanner, interview.

By analyzing skeletons: For the derivation of anthropometric data from skeletal remains, see Richard H. Steckel, "Health and Nutrition in Pre-Columbian America: The Skeletal Evidence," *Journal of Interdisciplinary History* 36 (Summer 2005): 1–32.

293 *"The records went"*: Richard L. Jantz, telephone interview, July 14, 2004.

"unregenerate idealist": Franz Boas, quoted in Claudia Roth Pierpont, "The Measure of America," *The New Yorker,* Mar. 8, 2004, pp. 48–63.

"an astonishingly ambitious": R. L. Jantz, D. R. Hunt, A. B. Falsetti, and P. J. Key, "Variation Among North Amerindians: Analysis of Boas's Anthropometric Data," *Human Biology* 64 (June 1992): 435–61. This article contains a detailed discussion of Boas's Native American measurements.

294 *"arguably the most important"*: Ibid.

"*some of the highest quality*": Richard L. Jantz, "The Anthropometric Legacy of Franz Boas," *Economics and Human Biology* 1 (2003): 277–84.

But aside from producing: According to Jantz, Boas's lone publication on the Native American data was Franz Boas, "Zür Anthropologie der nordamerikanischen Indianer," *Zeitschrift für Ethnologie* 27 (1895): 366–411.

Jantz and a colleague have challenged: C. S. Sparks and R. L. Jantz, "A Reassessment of Human Cranial Plasticity: Boas Revisited," *Proceedings of the National Academy of Sciences* 99 (2002): 14,636–39.

295   "*the tallest in the world*": Steckel and Prince, "Tallest in the World," p. 287.

"*scarcely a man*": George Catlin, quoted ibid., p. 290.

"*The Tall Indian*": Laura Ingalls Wilder, *Little House on the Prairie* (New York: Harper & Row, 1953).

"*net nutrition*": See Amartya Sen, *The Standard of Living* (Cambridge: Cambridge University Press, 1987). Steckel writes, "Sen rejects the notion that the standard of living can be portrayed in terms of opulence or commodities alone, though it is influenced by them, in favor of the idea that one must consider the balance between functionings (the various living conditions that one can or cannot achieve) and capabilities (the ability to achieve various living conditions)," in Richard H. Steckel, "Stature and the Standard of Living," pp. 1905–6.

296   *patent medicines:* See Tanner, *History of the Study,* pp. 158–59.

297   "*they would disband*": The idea of dispersal as a strategy to minimize smallpox epidemics is controversial. Steckel (personal communication) cites M. A. Trimble, "The 1832 Inoculation Program on the Missouri River," in *Disease and Demography in the Americas,* ed. J. W. Verano and D. H. Ubelaker (Washington, D.C.: Smithsonian Institution, 1992). Trimble writes, "When an epidemic struck a tribe or even a band, the group dissolved into small family units to escape the disease. The strategy could not prevent an epidemic, but it often diminished its impact" (p. 260).

"*The general operating*": Jantz, interview.

298   "*psychosocial stunting*": Robert M. Blizzard, "Psychosocial Short Stature," in *Pediatric Endocrinology,* ed. F. Lifschutz (New York: Marcel Dekker, 1990), pp. 87–107.

"*modest sample*": Richard H. Steckel, "New Light on the 'Dark Ages': The Remarkably Tall Stature of Northern European Men During the Medieval Era," *Social Science History* 28 (2004): 211–29.

299   *This stagnation in growth:* Richard H. Steckel, "Alternative Indicators of Health and the Quality of Life," in *Unconventional Wisdom: Alternative Perspectives on the New Economy,* ed. Jeff Modrick (New York: Twentieth Century, 2000), pp. 189–206. The state of stagnation is not universally accepted. Tanner, for example, warned of the difficulty of assessing growth trends in a large, diverse population where even the second generation of immigrants can have a large historical impact on demographic trends. "It's very complicated, because you've got a lot of Hispanics coming in, and they're genetically shorter and environmentally shorter, so you have to be careful," he said. "If you take Holland, okay, they've had some immigrants, but they can do a very good survey. To do a good survey in the States is almost impossible" (Tanner, interview).

"*the Dutch, Swedes*": John Komlos and Marieluise Baur, "From the Tallest to (One of) the Fattest: The Enigmatic Fate of the American Population in the 20th Century," *Economics and Human Biology* 2 (Mar. 2004): 57–74.

15. Final Height: Heightism Deconstructed

301   *"No shoes!":* This and all other quotes, unless otherwise noted, are from Adda Grimberg and Terri H. Lipman, personal interview, July 11, 2005.

"Final height": Paul Saenger, M.D., Montefiore Medical Center, Bronx, N.Y., grand rounds, May 21, 2004, Jacobi Medical Center, Bronx, N.Y.

Some people add: See Barry Bogin, *The Growth of Humanity* (New York: Wiley-Liss, 2001), pp. 93–95.

302   *several years ago:* Terri H. Lipman et al., "A Multicentre Randomised Controlled Trial of an Intervention to Improve the Accuracy of Linear Growth Measurement," *Archives of Disease in Childhood* 89 (2004): 342–46.

boys were referred: On gender differences in referrals to pediatric endocrinology clinics, see A. Grimberg, J. K. Kutikov, and A. J. Cucchiara, "Sex Differences in Patients Referred for Evaluation of Poor Growth," *Archives of Disease in Childhood* 146 (Feb. 2005): 212–16.

Mismeasurement also introduces: See Lipman et al., "Multicentre Randomised Controlled Trial," and J. O'Neill, "Evaluation: Measuring the Squirming Baby," *New York Times,* May 11, 2004, p. F-6.

303   *In 1995 the Economist:* "Short Guys Finish Last," *Economist,* Dec. 23, 1995, pp. 19–22. All quotes are from this source. (The article was unsigned, although it is sometimes attributed to Jonathan Rauch.)

304   *a 1984 experiment:* N. Eisenberg et al., "Sex Differences in the Relationship of Height to Children's Actual and Attributed Social and Cognitive Competencies," *Sex Roles* 11 (1984): 719–34.

305   *a survey of several hundred:* Leslie F. Martel and Henry B. Biller, *Stature and Stigma: The Biopsychosocial Development of Short Males* (Lexington, Mass.: Lexington Books, 1987), pp. 41–77.

"Well, all those students": David E. Sandberg, personal interview, Oct. 22, 2004, New York. The students were from three New England universities and were largely Caucasian and from middle-socioeconomic backgrounds.

In animal research: See, for example, P. W. Taylor and R. W. Elwood, "The Mismeasure of Animal Contests," *Animal Behavior* 65 (2003): 1195–2005.

306   *the divorce rate:* See D. Hurley, "Divorce Rate: It's Not as High as You Think," *New York Times,* April 19, 2005.

307   *made a preliminary pass:* James D. Sargent and David G. Blanchflower, "Obesity and Stature in Adolescence and Earnings in Young Adulthood: Analysis of a British Birth Cohort," *Archives of Pediatric and Adolescent Medicine* 148 (July 1994): 681–87. The primary focus of the study was obesity.

Postlewaite and colleagues' 2004 study: Nicola Persico, Andrew Postlewaite, and Dan Silverman, "The Effects of Adolescent Experience on Labor Market Outcomes: The Case of Height," *Journal of Political Economy* 112 (2004): 1019–53.

308   *experts on puberty:* Julia Graber, Department of Psychology, University of Florida, telephone interview, Jan. 20, 2006; Richard Steckel, Ohio State University, tele-

phone interview, Apr. 18, 2006; and James Tanner, personal communication, April 19, 2006.

adolescent psychology, not height: See Linda D. Voss, "Short Normal Stature and Psychosocial Disadvantage: A Critical Review of the Evidence," *Journal of Pediatric Endocrinology and Metabolism* 14 (2001): 701–11; D. E. Sandberg et al., "Height and Social Adjustment: Are Extremes a Cause for Concern and Action?" *Pediatrics* 114 (Sept. 2004): 744–50; and A. B. Downie et al., "Are Short Normal Children at a Disadvantage? The Wessex Growth Study," *British Medical Journal* 314 (1997): 97–100. This last paper, derived from the extensive longitudinal, community-based Wessex study, concluded, "Social class seems to have more influence than height on children's psychological development" (p. 97).

A group in Finland: See David J. Barker et al., "Infant Growth and Income 50 Years Later," *Archives of Disease in Childhood* 90 (Mar. 2005): 272–3.

"Ultimately, I think": Dan Silverman, telephone interview, Jan. 19, 2006.

309 *Cope's rule:* See Edward D. Cope, *The Origin of the Fittest* (New York: Appleton, 1887), and D. K. McLain, "Cope's Rules, Sexual Selection, and the Loss of Ecological Plasticity," *Oikos* 68 (1993): 490–500. For a popular account of the evolutionary importance of size, see C. Zimmer, "'Bigger Is Better' View of Evolution Gains Credence," *New York Times*, Dec. 28, 2004, p. F-4.

"research biases": Wolf U. Blanckenhorn, "The Evolution of Body Size: What Keeps Organisms Small?" *Quarterly Review of Biology* 75 (Dec. 2000): 385–407.

"In regard to bodily": Charles Darwin, *The Descent of Man* (1879; New York: Penguin, 2004), p. 84.

310 *pygmy chimpanzee:* See Frans de Waal, *Our Inner Ape: A Leading Primatologist Explains Why We Are Who We Are* (New York: Riverhead, 2005), pp. 7–9. As de Waal explains, the original name is a bit of a misnomer since bonobos are only slightly smaller than chimpanzees and their social organization and behavior is markedly different (see p. 29, for example).

"very insightful": This and all other quotes, unless otherwise noted, are from Frans de Waal, telephone interview, Jan. 30, 2006.

311 *"selfish gene":* Frans de Waal, *Our Inner Ape*, pp. 19–25.

cooperation is hard-wired: J. K. Rilling et al., "A Neural Basis for Social Cooperation," *Neuron* 35 (July 18, 2002): 395–405. See also Natalie Angier, "Why We're So Nice: We're Wired to Cooperate," *New York Times*, July 23, 2002, p. F-1.

312 *the biology of altruism:* See Matt Ridley, *The Origins of Virtue: Human Instincts and the Evolution of Cooperation* (New York: Viking, 1997), and Robert Wright, *The Moral Animal: Why We Are the Way We Are: The New Science of Evolutionary Psychology* (New York: Pantheon, 1994).

at best modest evidence: Paul Henry Mussen and Mary Cover Jones, "Self-Conceptions, Motivations, and Interpersonal Attitudes of Late- and Early-Maturing Boys," *Child Development* 28 (June 1957): 243–256.

315 *women seeking sperm donors:* Jennifer Egan, "Wanted: A Few Good Sperm," *New York Times Magazine*, March 19, 2006, p. 48.

"quick thinking": Alison Jolly, *The Evolution of Primate Behavior* (New York: Macmillan, 1985), p. 289.

316 *a new and fascinating wrinkle:* See W. M. Brown et al., "Dance Reveals Symmetry Especially in Young Men," *Nature* 438 (Dec. 22, 2005): 1148–50.

"mental agility buffers": Ibid.

317 *"Oh, Stan"*: *Revenge of the Nerds,* Jeff Kanew, director, 1984.

318 *"nothing you focus"*: D. A. Schkade and D. Kahneman, "Does Living in California Make People Happy? A Focusing Illusion in Judgments of Life Satisfaction," *Psychological Science* 9 (1998).

Epilogue: "If They Get a Good Nipple . . ."

321 *"Amazing"*: This and all other quotes are from John Crispino, personal interview, Apr. 20, 2005, Saugerties, N.Y. I am especially grateful to John for allowing me to visit his newborn piglets on the farm.

322 *"Tell me about it"*: This and all other quotes are from Albert Destramps, telephone interview, Feb. 7, 2005.

325 *Frederick II of Sicily:* L. I. Gardner, "Deprivational Dwarfism," *Scientific American,* July 1972, pp. 76–82.
"It's amazing what we're learning": Richard Tremblay, telephone interview, Mar. 4, 2004.
he mentioned the work: See I.C.G. Weaver et al., "Epigenetic Programming by Maternal Behavior," *Nature Neuroscience* 7 (2004): 847–54.

327 *Bigger people place:* See Wolf Blanckenhorn, "The Evolution of Body Size: What Keeps Organisms Small?" *Quarterly Review of Biology* 75 (Dec. 2000): 385–407.
"It is not certain": James M. Tanner, *A History of the Study of Human Growth* (Cambridge: Cambridge University Press, 1981), p. 399.

Acknowledgments

Allow me, first off, to thank the many people — from the primatologist Frans de Waal to my parents — who at one point or another asked, "Do you know that Randy Newman song?" Yes, I do, but not by heart. Let's just say it's not an accident that I didn't mention "Short People" anywhere in the text, as befits a song that begins with the suggestion that those of us well south of the fiftieth percentile have no reason to exist. But, like the scene from *A Hard Day's Night* in which Paul McCartney's grandfather effortlessly provokes a squabble between the band's two handlers by pointing out that one of them is "always being taller" than the other, the song is a useful reminder that it's easy to start an argument when you get people to think about what it means to be big or small in a very size-conscious world.

When I started work on *Size Matters*, the book's "argument" was based primarily on my childhood experience of being short. Then I discovered Frederick William I of Prussia, James Tanner, the biology of growth, the importance of pubertal timing, and a host of related issues. As is so often the case, many of those discoveries began in libraries, so I want to thank librarians at some favored outposts of discovery: Arlene Shaner and Christopher Warren at the New York Academy of Medicine Library; Jacqueline Gold at the New York Public Library's Science, Industry, and Business Library; and Stephen Greenberg at the National Library of Medicine at the National Institutes of Health in Bethesda, Maryland, among other sites. Others who facilitated research were Linda Corcoran of the Wildlife Conservation Society; Robin Lloyd at the American Museum of Natural History; Ann Marie Sekeres at the National Museum of the American Indian in New York; Donald Heisel at the Center for Migration Studies in Staten Island; Deirdre Lawrence, Laura Peimer, Angie Park, Beth Kushner, and Karen Hinkle at the Brooklyn Museum; Gregory Clarke of Eli Lilly and Company in Indianapolis; Salvatore LaGumina; Mary Brown; and Jim Collins of the Bloomfield Hills Middle School in Michigan. A special thanks to Edward Bleiberg of the Brooklyn Museum.

A person's size and shape are a work in progress from infancy to adulthood, and it seems as if I've been thinking about it for almost that long. When those thoughts began to coalesce as prose, I was aided, abetted, and (editorially) cut down to size by a number of helpful journalistic colleagues. I wish to thank Susan West and Lisa Davis at *Health* magazine; Laura Chang and James Gorman of the Science Times section of the *New York Times*; and Katherine Bouton, Vera Titunik, Chuck Wilson, and Adam

Moss at the *New York Times Magazine*, all of whom challenged me to shape my thoughts on the subject at various times.

One of the most savory pleasures of book writing is that when friends learn what you're up to, they come bearing gifts, often in random acts of conversational kindness or epistolary generosity. It's especially gratifying to thank Jessica Nicoll and Barry Oreck, for *College*; Victor McElheny, for the usual breathtaking range of his random thoughts; Tom O'Neill, for remembrances of his early retirement from Little League; Nelson Smith, for tidbits ranging from Hollywood film angles to the myth of Procrustes; Ellen Rudolph, for the height of Wilt Chamberlain's father; A. O. Scott, for Rabbitiana; David Shenk, for recollections of adolescence; Steve Burnett, for an altocratic perspective on sibling pecking orders; Susan Weseen, for many useful observations about bullying, peacemaking, and *Wringer*; Clarissa Bullitt, for Adleriana; Charles Mann, for thoughts on Native American epidemiology; Ryan Blitstein, for telling me about the Chinese limb lengtheners; Pam and Andy Hamingson, for reportorial help; David White, for observations about size and dance; Gary Taubes, for critical thinking about fetal origins; Jan Witkowski, for Huxleyana; Thomas Halaczinsky, for *Olympia*; Mark Ptashne, for scientific citations and personal perspectives; Vicky Olson, for "My Inner Shrimp"; Christopher Smith, for the importance of height to political kingmakers; Marguerite Holloway and Sean Elder, for allowing me to inflict a little auxology on their classes at Columbia University and the New School, respectively; Peter Sherwood, for allowing the same at Cold Spring Harbor Laboratory; Richard Klug and Kate Stearns for teenage sociology; Joe McElroy, for his long-standing support; and farmer Ray Bradley, for putting me in touch with some very cute pigs.

Several people spent a lot of time helping me understand aspects of growth and its ramifications. I'm greatly indebted to David Allen, M.D.; David J. P. Barker, M.D.; Robert M. Blizzard, M.D.; Barry Bogin; Noel Cameron; William F. Crowley Jr., M.D.; Julia Graber; Adda Grimberg, M.D.; Andrew Postlewaite; Alan D. Rogol, M.D.; David E. Sandberg; Richard Steckel; and Richard E. Tremblay. I also want to thank my old school chums, friend and foe alike, for sharing their experiences and thoughts about long-ago events: Albert Destramps, James Finkelstein, Stephen Aronoff, Scott Novotny, George Knue, Ken Monti, and Tom Andersen.

As usual, a miscellany of experts worked behind the scenes, propping up the author and lending strength, structure, and authority to the final product. In that vein, for helpful conversations and published thoughts, I'd like to thank Thomas Murray and Erik Parens of the Hastings Center in Garrison, New York; Dan Kindlon at Harvard Medical School; Steve Warner and Steve Cohen at the Allen-Stevenson School in Manhattan; Joseph LeDoux of New York University; Colleen McCann at the Wildlife Conservation Society; Sean Carroll of the University of Wisconsin; Daniel Kahneman of Princeton University; John Crispino; John Alroy; Mercedes de Onis of the World Health Organization; Robert Fogel and Derrell Bock, both of the University of Chicago; Michael Schwartzmann of Manhattan; Mary Hediger at the National Institute of Child Health and Human Development; Mary Overpeck of the New Mexico State Department of Health; J. Richard Udry of the University of North Carolina; Jeffrey Hogue of Charles Atlas, Ltd.; Ellen Frankel; and Michael Zanussi.

To the extent that the biomedical and historical matters discussed in *Size Matters* are scientifically accurate, I have a stable of expert readers to thank, including Alan Rogol, M.D.; Noel Cameron; Phil Lichtenstein, M.D.; Adda Grimberg, M.D.; David

Sandberg; Robert Elwood; Susan Alberts; David Scher, M.D.; William F. Crowley, Jr., M.D.; Roberto Olivardia; Daniel Nagin; Reginald Puckett, M.D.; Robert Sapolsky; Richard Steckel; and Stephen Spear. To the extent that the text is readable and lay-friendly despite its aspirations to scientific accuracy, I have an equally essential stable of general readers to thank: Nelson Smith, Tom O'Neill, Justine Henning, Susan Weseen, and, through multiple drafts, my wife, Mindy. Any errors that may remain are of course my responsibility.

The research, wisdom, and elegant prose of James Tanner animate almost every page of this text. It has been a pleasure to meet him, first on the page and then in person, in the course of this project. More to the point, the work he and his colleagues did at the Institute of Child Health in London, and the research it inspired among other scientists, has probably done as much for the health and welfare of growing children throughout the world as any research done at any institution in the past century; the fact that he is not more widely recognized as one of the great scientists of the twentieth century says much more about the imperfect way contemporary society recognizes scientific excellence than it does about his prodigious contribution to human well-being.

As in two previous projects, I have been the very grateful beneficiary of a grant from the Alfred P. Sloan Foundation. Like Arthur Singer before him, Doron Weber has been not only a generous supporter but an enthusiastic and discerning sounding board for ideas (dare I say?) large and small.

My colleagues at Houghton Mifflin have consistently exhibited a level of professionalism and collegiality that would be (and indeed is, when described to writing friends) the envy of many an author. Eamon Dolan, despite his unflagging generosity and politeness, is gleefully ruthless about interrogating a text to maximize its clarity and impact; every question he raised inevitably provoked better prose and clearer thought. I also want to thank Barb Jatkola, for her copy editing; Peg Anderson (again), for her terrific editorial oversight; Susannah Ryan, for proofreading; Christina Smith, for her marketing input; Holly Bemiss, Michael Webb, and the much appreciated Whitney Peeling for their publicity efforts; Denny Renshaw for the photographs; and the always patient Anne Seiwerath for her gentle mastery in prodding the author into action. As always, my agent, Melanie Jackson, has been as fierce and loyal an advocate as any writer could hope to have.

Always last, never least, ever the most important: family. To my in-laws, Gerry and Hindley Mendelsohn and Susan and Jedd Levine, gratitude for their exemplary support. To my parents, Delores and Robert Hall, I offer thanks, not only for their unconditional love and guidance but, in the context of growth, for my genes and nurture and for giving me every chance to reach my full human potential, regardless of the size of the container. To my brother Eric and his family, similar thanks for their support and, given my bullying and occasionally intemperate childhood, forgiveness — and to my nephew Nathan, who began to tower over me by the time he turned fourteen: wipe that smile off your face! To my wife, Mindy, thanks for the enduring love, the endless succor, and the enriching daily reminder that stature and grace have to do only incidentally with feet and inches; none of this would have been possible without her support. And to my still growing and always astonishing children, Alessandro and Micaela, thanks for the daily reminder that muses come in all sizes, and that nurture is a two-way street.

Index